Small business enterprise

Small business enterprise
An economic analysis

Gavin C. Reid

London and New York

First published 1993
by Routledge
11 New Fetter Lane, London EC4P 4EE

Simultaneously published in the USA and Canada
by Routledge
29 West 35th Street, New York, NY 10001

© 1993 Gavin C. Reid

Typeset in 10/12pt Plantin by
Mathematical Composition Setters Ltd, Salisbury, Wiltshire
Printed and bound in Great Britain by
Mackays of Chatham plc, Chatham, Kent

British Library Cataloguing-in-Publication Data

*A catalogue record for this book is available from the British
Library.*

ISBN 0–415–05681–0

Library of Congress Cataloging in Publication Data

Reid, Gavin C.
    Small business enterprise : an economic analysis / Gavin C. Reid.
        p. cm.
    Includes bibliographical references and index.
    ISBN 0-415-05681-0
    1. Small business—Scotland. I. Title.
HD2346.G72S387 1993
338.6′42′09411—dc20   92-37256
                                                          CIP

To Eilidh Ferguson Reid

Sweet näiveté of feature,
Simple, wild, enchanting elf,
Not to thee, but thanks to Nature,
Thou art acting but thyself.

'On seeing Miss Fontanelle in a favourite character',
Robert Burns *(1793)*

Contents

Figures

Tables

Preface

This book could not have been written without assistance from various sources. I gratefully acknowledge financial support from the following bodies: University of Edinburgh Travel and Research Grant Fund, Scottish Economic Society, Nuffield Foundation, David Hume Institute and Leverhulme Trust.

I have enjoyed working with many people on the projects upon which this book is based. I should particularly mention my appreciation for Lowell R. Jacobsen's involvement at the inception of the earliest project. He assisted with the field work and the database construction, and collaborated in the earliest published work, Reid and Jacobsen (1988). Cliff Pratten was an important source of encouragement at the stage of building on this early work. Julian Read and Sandra Rice advised on the design of the database. Many people have advised me on the statistical front, of whom I should mention, with thanks, John Duffy, the late David Williams, Gordon Hughes, Brian Main, Steve Satchell, and Michael Prentice. Sandra Rice and Karen Chan undertook the necessary computer programming and Shane Voss and Julian Crowe have given me helpful advice on local computing arrangements.

Anne-Theresa Lawrie assisted in the reinterview fieldwork, as did Jacqueline Campbell, who also provided invaluable help in auditing the database and ensuring it was as complete and accurate as human frailty permits. Christopher Corrie acted as my statistical assistant during my holding of a Leverhulme Trust Research Fellowship. I should also acknowledge fruitful collaborations with V. Bhaskar, S. Machin and A. Snell. Where joint work is involved, this is indicated in the text.

I enjoyed corresponding with R.D.S. Jack, Professor of Scottish and Mediaeval Literature, University of Edinburgh, concerning the appropriate dating of the quote from Burns' 'On seeing Miss Fontanelle in a favourite character' which I use on the dedication page. †

To the many people in the business community who so willingly gave me assistance, and to the academic community in industrial economics which has

---

† See: James Kinsley (ed.) *The Poems and Songs of Robert Burns* (1968), Oxford, Clarendon Press.

been such a healthy collective critic of my ideas for many years, I express my thanks. I have drawn freely on my recent published work in industrial economics, and related fields, in drafting this book. I have used material from *The Economic Journal*, *The Scottish Journal of Political Economy*, *The Journal of Industrial Economics*, *The Journal of Economic Surveys*, *Business Ethics*, *The International Journal of Industrial Organization*, *The International Journal of Social Economics*, and *Small Business Economics*, with the permission of Basil Blackwell, North Holland, MCB University Press and Kluwer Academic Publishers.*

Finally, a daily source of inspiration for preparing a manuscript on the birth, growth, and survival of the small firm has been the birth, growth and survival (nay, robust flourishing!) of the small person, in the form of my young daughter, Eilidh, to whom this book is dedicated.

St Andrews
GCR

---

* See: Reid (1990a, 1992a, 1991a, 1990b, 1992b, 1991b, 1987, 1992c respectively), in references.

Part I
Introduction

1 Analysing the small business enterprise

1.1 INTRODUCTION

This book is concerned with one of the major economic issues of the 1980s: the role of the small business enterprise (SBE) in a mature, mixed market economy. My focus is on how SBEs start up, and on how they subsequently survive the competitive pressures of the market-place in their first few years of existence. My method is empirical (though I have sought to make it informed by economic theory) and aims to be well grounded in the realities of small business enterprise. It is based on a unique and extensive database of small businesses, containing over 40,000 data points, gathered by myself and several co-workers in the 1980s using field work methods. This database is relational,[1] and combines qualitative (interview based) and quantitative (administered questionnaire based) data which can be cross-accessed and codified in sophisticated ways.

The basic structure of this work is: statistical analysis of the small firms database (covering employment, products, markets, pricing, costs, sales, competition, and finance); cross-site analytical case studies based on Porter's competitive advantage framework[2] (covering firm profiles, competitive and defensive strategies); econometrics of small business enterprise (covering determinants of survival, pricing behaviour, and growth); and the political economy of small business (emphasising the ethics of competition amongst small firms and their perceptions of enterprise). The full instrumentation used in this work, which is crucial both to an understanding of it and to an evaluation of its conclusions, is provided as an appendix at the end of the book, and also in more accessible summary form at the end of chapter 2 (page 43).

As a native Scot, working in Scotland, it is natural that I have used business contacts cultivated over many years as the initial source of introduction to the rich patterns of small business enterprise. My object of inquiry is therefore the small business enterprise in Scotland. As primary-source data formed the basis of the empirical work, with a very detailed characterization of each firm being obtained by going into the field, proximity to my object of analysis was crucial to the inquiry. However, the methods of field work, data construction, computing, statistics, econometrics, and economic analysis used are not strictly contingent on this context. Had I been located in Hong Kong, in Ontario, or in Colorado, the basis on which I would have proceeded would have been very similar.

It must be confessed, however, that having Scotland as my workshop or laboratory has been a happy circumstance. As Graham Ross, for many years Director of Scottish Business in the Community (Scot BIC), remarked when stung by critical comments about Scottish entrepreneurs by former-Chancellor Nigel Lawson, 'After all, who invented the enterprise culture?'[3] It has been a pleasure working in the milieu from which 'The Enterprising Scot'[4] emerged historically, and from which 'Enterprise Scotland'[5] has recently emerged. Further, it has been the source of a great sense of intellectual continuity to be inquiring into small business enterprise from a standpoint that derives from the framework for the systematic study of economics created by Adam Smith and David Hume over two hundred years ago. An important further influence has been the founder of modern industrial organization, Alfred Marshall, a man who was fond of saying, 'it is all in Adam Smith' before we got used to saying, 'it is all in Marshall'. I have, for example, found it useful to develop (in chapter 3) a statistical characterization of the typical SBE which has been influenced by the Marshallian 'representative firm', though it is not an identical concept.

1.2   QUALITATIVE AND QUANTITATIVE ANALYSIS

Despite my reference above to intellectual influences, economic science, like all science, is not governed by personalities: it is a concrete and dispassionate method. It is, provided one attaches oneself to a powerful research agenda, a progressive method. What I have aimed to achieve in this book is not in large part an aspect of political economy, which I do not consider until part V in a small business context, but rather of positive economics. I have viewed the formulation and testing of hypotheses in a broader way than is traditional in positive economics, for I consistently use both qualitative and quantitative methods of analysis. Qualitative evidence emphasises relationships rather than numbers. It is concerned, for example, with causality (as in, 'does advertising cause industrial concentration, or vice versa, or both?') and with appropriate categories (as in 'profit': does it mean the net revenue which is reported, that which is discretionary, that which is post-tax or what?'). In expressing these relationships, one may have reference to numbers, but that is not essential.

Quantitative evidence is expressed in terms of numbers, which may include binary variables (for example one, two, three standing for sole proprietorship, partnership, limited company) as well as real numbers. This evidence may be assembled for predictive purposes (for example, how would the proportion of small firms surviving after three years be affected if gearing ratios were decreased by 10 per cent?).

Qualitative analysis has often been regarded as 'soft' by economists, to be contrasted unfavourably with 'hard' quantitative analysis, especially of the econometric variety. As even casual perusal of the following pages will have indicated, I have not eschewed 'hard' analysis in the above sense. However, it will rapidly become apparent that I do not accept this distinction between 'hard' and 'soft' analysis. My intention has been to make the qualitative analysis of small business enterprise just as intellectually keen a cutting edge as quantitative. Here I am in agreement with Kirk and Miller (1985: 17) that 'qualitative research has always retained the proper ideals of hypothesis-testing research, sound reasoning and the empirical risking of theory'. This enhancement of the status of qualitative methods has been assisted in three ways. First by recent advances in econometric methods which draw together the qualitative and quantitative approaches. Thus what one might regard as essentially qualitative, like rankings of actions, can be expressed in a quantitative framework suitable for statistical inference.[6] Second, enhancement has been assisted by the use of modern relational database methods, combining the analysis of qualitative data of the textual variety, based on observations and comments generated by semi-structured interviews, with quantitative data of a variety of forms (the balance sheet, market conditions etc.) generated by administered questionnaires. Third, it has been assisted by the realization that it is closely allied to familiar methods, employed as everyday practice in fields like law. When the lawyer uses qualitative data, his method is best described as 'triangulation', and involves sifting the evidence, viewing it from different angles or perspectives. For example, the method of triangulation applied to the workings of the SBE might involve viewing the firm as a balance sheet, as a hirer of factor services, or as a seller of products. More generally, triangulation involves, as Fielding and Fielding (1986: 24) put it, 'a situation in which a hypothesis can survive the confrontation of a series of complementary methods of testing'. An aspect of triangulation is the combined use of qualitative and quantitative methods. Thus 'qualitative work can assist quantitative work in providing a theoretical framework, validating survey data, interpreting statistical relationships and deciphering puzzling responses, selecting survey items to construct indices, and offering case study illustrations' (Fielding and Fielding 1986: 27).

It is my hope that the systematic combination of qualitative and quantitative evidence, of which the next section provides a simple example, is one of the significant contributions of this study of small business enterprise. This is an aspect of methodology. Chapter 3, on the representative small firm, provides an introduction to the use of this methodology. More important, I also present for the evaluation of my peers, and hopefully for the edification of both this group and a wider audience within economics, business administration, industrial organization, and small business enterprise, a detailed and systematic empirical analysis of factors influencing small firm inception, competition, and survival in recent years. My method is positivist in that it involves the formulation and testing of hypotheses, using new empirical evidence, on the small business enterprise. Let me turn first to empirical evidence, and look at the workaday task of gathering it in the field.

1.3 GATHERING EVIDENCE ON SMALL BUSINESS ENTERPRISE

There are many accepted ways in which the economist may look at the small business enterprise, each of which involves a different blend of theory and empirical evidence. Unfortunately, one gets the impression that most microeconomists have no direct contact with firms: their experience of the very object on which they lavish such intricate mathematical analysis is entirely second-hand. Happily such isolation from the proper object of analysis, the firm, is by no means typical of the history of economic analysis. Adam Smith, the founder of modern economics, was well acquainted with the business community of Glasgow. He was on good terms with the leading merchants of the day including, most notably, Provost Andrew Cochrane who assisted Smith in the acquisition of statistical and institutional information later to be used in *The Wealth of Nations* (Smith 1776). Alfred Marshall also had a serious concern for the realities of business activity. In 1875 he made an extended visit to the United States which took him into many factories and provided the basis for his 1875 paper 'Some features of American industry'.[7] Even ten years later, 'his zeal for fieldwork remained unimpaired', and the months of August and September 1885 saw Marshall undertaking extensive tours of English mines and factories.[8] One hundred years later, one sadly notes too little enthusiasm on the part of economists to put time aside for fieldwork of this sort, that would take them into the business enterprise.[9] A welcome sign of the possibility that this parlous state of affairs would be modified was contained in an article by Lawson (1985), where it was argued that 'more resources should be allocated, and attention paid, to the results of forms of case-study, to personal histories, and to the study of primary sources. At the very least a re-evaluation of research priorities and methods may be in order' (Lawson 1985: 927). Such an attitude is in sympathy with the line of argument pursued in this section. I accept and applaud the case made by Carlsson (1987: 145) for gathering primary-source data appropriate to the research questions being asked, despite the effort and costs involved.

Investigating the factors fostering the survival and growth of SBEs, starting from the viewpoint of economic theory, involves a consideration of balance sheet, product, and factor market variables as well as age. The approach is what Carlsson would call 'industrial dynamics'. It cannot be pursued seriously on the basis of inappropriate official statistics. One is therefore involved in gathering primary source data on things like assets, gearing, market share, price flexibility, scale economies, and capacity utilization. If accuracy is important and the data required are extensive, an administered, as opposed to postal, questionnaire is the indicated research tool. There are also other ways to do industrial dynamics. Like Carlsson (1987: 144), I would identify

Porter (1980, 1985) as being an important contemporary member of the school of industrial dynamics, through his analysis of how firms create, and then defend, market niches. Here, a semi-structured interview is the indicated research tool. In each case, primary-source data must be gathered by field research. After doing field work on the link between technological innovation and growth in the international semiconductor industry, Flaherty (1984), herself possessed of a considerable reputation as a theorist in industrial economics, concluded that field research could be stimulating and useful to economic theorists and econometricians alike. It helped them to focus on groups of assumptions which were empirically significant. It saved them from struggling with a large and bewildering variety of possible assumptions, some mutually inconsistent, which only might (but then again, just might not) have a bearing on problems of dynamics, uncertainty and rivalry.

The use of field research methods to gather data, suggest categories and hypotheses, and, under certain circumstances, to test hypotheses, has now become very much the preserve of sociology, ethnography, social anthropology, social administration, and social psychology. In the various disciplines, different types of field research have been chosen, depending on the object under examination, the purpose of the investigation and the methodological stance of the investigator. A fairly full catalogue of field research methods would include: direct observation; participant observation; structured, semi-structured, and unstructured interviews; and document collection.[10]

The purpose of this section is to advance arguments for applying field research methods to the analysis of the small business enterprise. Two field research methods will be singled out from the above catalogue as being of special relevance to the economist: the structured and the semi-structured interview. Methodological issues which arise in the application of field research methods in a general sense will be briefly discussed, and then the context will be made more specific by reference to the empirical application of these methods to small, new, owner-managed business enterprises. I take as starting points the notions of a field and a site.

The field is any clearly delineated area which may be the subject of social research. The area might in certain circumstances be interpreted in a spatial sense (for example, a New Town housing development, a football stadium prone to 'fan' violence, a street connected with drug dealing), but more commonly the term has analytical rather than physical connotations (for example, families subject to bereavement, firms set up through Enterprise Trusts). The characteristic of field research which separates it from most other research methods is that it eschews the 'arm's length' approach practised frequently by economists and social statisticians, who often use secondary sources which were gathered for non-academic reasons (for example to appraise income or corporation tax liability). The field researcher, by contrast, specializes in the collection and analysis of whatever social world is to be defined as the field. Knowledge of the field is obtained by collecting data at a set of sites. A site is frequently defined by the context of the investigation, and obvious examples include a household, a church, a hospital, and a firm. More formally, one could regard the set of sites as constituting a partitioning of the field.

Typically, one is unable to explore all sites, so sampling is involved. Access may be limited, and field work is highly labour intensive and therefore very costly, so the exhaustive examination of all sites is usually not possible, given limitations on time and funding. To gain access to a site one usually operates through one or more 'gatekeeper'.[11] If the site were a school the gatekeeper would be the headmaster or mistress; if a prison, the governor; and if a small business enterprise, the owner-manager. Getting agreement from the gatekeeper is essential to the sampling process, and a certain measure of persuasiveness may be required before consent is obtained. In this study, gatekeepers were introduced to me and my co-worker by field contacts who were 'high communicators' in the information network described in Reid and Jacobsen (1985: chapter 5). Undoubtedly this greatly enhanced access to firms, as sites. Of course, one cannot ethically investigate a site without the consent of the individual(s) and/or institution(s) concerned.

An important feature of field work is that it enables the empirical investigation to be well grounded in reality, in a way that using official secondary source statistics does not. 'Grounded theory' in the sense of Glaser and Strauss (1967) may be generated and validated by the field work itself. The industrial economist who is taking Glaser and Strauss as his methodological inspiration should approach his empirical investigation free from theoretical preconception, and should avoid exact prior instrumentation; by 'instrument' I mean a device for gathering or codifying data like an event-diary or a questionnaire. Miles and Huberman (1984) provide a sensible balancing of the case for and against prior instrumentation, and come down slightly in favour of at least some early instrumentation, even if only to acknowledge that no investigator could ever in practice start with a *tabula rasa* before going into the field. If one goes into the field in a sequence of investigations then one has the opportunity to let field experience influence what instrumentation might be used in subsequent rounds of the investigations, so there is a case for making early instrumentation minimal.

The data analysed in this book were all gathered by field work methods, and with an eye to an appropriate field work methodology of the sort introduced above. Between December 1983 and December 1988 the author and a series of co-workers were engaged in a field work study of small, newly-formed, owner-managed enterprises in Scotland. The project began with my first co-worker, Lowell R. Jacobsen,[12] becoming a participant observer at the Ardrossan, Saltcoats, and Stevenston Enterprise Trust Ltd (ASSET) from 21 May to 27 July 1984. Details of this experience were recorded by Jacobsen (1986). This early unstructured field work led to the design of two instruments of investigation: an administered questionnaire and a semi-structured interview. The shorthand expressions for these two instruments which I use in the rest of the book are AQ 1985 and SSI 1985. The data obtained from these instruments from April 1985 through to October 1985, which were both quantitative (numerical) and qualitative (textual), were then mounted on a database. This constituted the first phase of the research. The second phase involved a re-interview of all participants traceable from the 1985 interviews, over the period 1 July to 31 September 1988. The instrument used was a new administered questionnaire which I describe as the RIQ 1988 in further discussion. The schema given in table 1.1 outlines the essential components of the project.

There was no overlap between the sample of firms examined in the participant observation stage and the sample of those firms examined using the various instruments, though the population was the same. The semi-structured interviews (SSI 1985) were applied to firms that had previously participated in completion of the administered questionnaire (AQ 1985). The re-interview administered questionnaire (RIQ 1988) was applied three years later to all traceable firms that had participated in the 1985 administered questionnaire (AQ 1985).

It will be observed that in this study a substantial degree of prior instrumentation was favoured once the qualitative field work had been

Table 1.1 Stages of the field work

Stage		Dates	Method	No. in pilot study	No. in study proper
P H A S E	1	Participant observation: Dec. 1983–July 1984	Qualitative unstructured field work	–	–
	2	Administered questionnaire: Apr.–Oct. 1985	Field structured interview	13	73
O N E	3	Semi-structured interview: July–Oct. 1985	Field interview agenda	7	17
	4	Establishing of database			
P H A S E	5	Administered questionnaire: July–Sept. 1988	Field structured interview	10	47
	6	Updating of database			
T W O					

completed, having suggested appropriate ways of 'grounding' the theory. Opinions vary as to the wisdom of proceeding in this way. No doubt in many areas of anthropological research it would be unwise to have any preconceptions about instrumentation. In the case of the economic study being discussed here, it was felt that fairly precise prior instrumentation was appropriate, provided the instruments were carefully tested in pilot work. The advantages of this approach have been well documented by Miles and Huberman (1884), and include both avoiding superfluous information and data overload, and facilitating comparability across studies.

As regards the conduct of the field work, general methodological guides were available, as developed above, and these could be augmented by the specific advice on industrial field work analysis contained in Porter (1980: appendix B), an authority who very much influenced the design of the semi-structured interview agenda. Recommendations of Porter that were specifically followed include:

1 Starting the administered questionnaire (AQ 1985) schedules with the SIC codes.
2 Getting into the field as early as possible, even before completion of library search and instrument design.
3 Using the telephone as a follow-up to an introductory preletter.
4 Offering respondents a quid pro quo (in this case in terms of a structured examination of their enterprise).
5 Lowering the possible level of threat in an interview by starting with benign general questions, and subsequently only asking for rough estimates of magnitudes in potentially sensitive areas (for example, market share, turnover).

The above guidelines were relevant to the design of both the 1985 and 1988 administered questionnaires and the semi-structured interview agenda, although Porter's concepts of competitive advantage and competitive strategy are only relevant to the latter instrument.

The ethical standard adopted, widely regarded as an international norm, was that respondents should give 'informed consent' to the study. At every stage of the field work, the fullest information was made available to respondents, and the application of instruments only proceeded after clear agreement had been reached. I have referred previously to field contacts in general, and to 'gatekeepers' in particular. The pivotal field contact in this study was usually the director of a development corporation or Enterprise Trust. He was initially approached through standard institutional channels in the early stages but subsequently, once field activity had commenced, further contacts were made available by referral and introduction. The director was asked if he was willing to supply a list of firms which were representative of those with whom he had dealings The extent to which the samples offered were indeed 'representative' over the many dimensions on which this concept could be defined is, of course, a matter of contention. In retrospect, now that the field work has been accomplished, it seems that each director usually attempted to provide a sample which conveyed the variety and diversity of the firms which he encountered. In section 1.4 I give a more detailed account of the sample and its composition.

On the basis of the lists provided, a standard preletter was sent out to all potential respondents (see appendix page 249, which covers instrumentation). Frey (1983: 91) provides evidence to the effect that preletters lower refusal rates, improve the quality of data and increase the cooperativeness of the respondent.[13] Other advantages include permitting the respondent to undertake a considered evaluation of the prospects of his participation, and signalling the authenticity of the investigation. The letter was couched in very general terms, naming the individuals involved in the interviewing and emphasising the benefits that respondents could obtain from taking time to look at their business in a structured, and probably novel, fashion. In this, as in other areas of field work, it is important to offer a quid pro quo for participation. This 'transaction' should not in itself have altered the general conduct of the individuals concerned, in that it neither sought to persuade nor to train respondents.

One week after sending out the preletter, the enterprise was contacted by telephone in order to arrange an interview date for the administered questionnaire. Frey argues that 'constructing an introductory message should command the same (or even more) attention as question design and arrangement...the respondent may not even "hear" the bulk of the introductory message because he or she is so busy concentrating on whether or not to participate' (Frey 1983: 91). Guidelines which were followed in the introductory telephone message included the following suggestions of Frey (1983: chapter 4): identifying the caller; explaining why the call is being made; explaining the sort of information that is being sought; explaining the conditions (especially terms of confidentiality) under which interviews will be conducted; and explaining the benefits of participation. Additionally, the field contact's name was mentioned (typically, the director of an Enterprise Trust), and it was explained that the respondent had a free choice on the place and time of interview. Typically only one person was involved in the day-to-day running of the business, so it was not usually difficult to identify the appropriate respondent. In this second stage of the field research an administered questionnaire (AQ 1985) was used, more detail of which is provided in chapter 2. Typically, it took about an hour to work through the schedule, although it could be completed in a brisk 40 minutes, and in some cases, given frequent digression, two or more hours were required. Most respondents chose to be interviewed at their own workshop or office, which in some cases amounted to a home interview. The general rule was that the investigator went to the respondent rather than the other way around. Usually interruptions were not a major problem, although almost invariably some break in the flow of conversation did occur. This did not have any apparent effect on the flow or quality of data. At some stage in the proceedings, the possibility of a further interview (the semi-structured interview, SSI 1985) was raised with the respondent. Most proved reasonably willing to participate further, though few wanted to do so in the immediate future.

The particular form of administered questionnaire used in the case of AQ 1985 involved a large number of questions. The design was intended to meet the criticism of economists such as Johnson (1986) that many small-firm studies use very short questionnaires, and thereby only generate very 'sparse' data. It its final form, the questionnaire ran to over thirty pages, with five show cards and thirteen lists. In view of the complexity of this instrument it was felt that a postal questionnaire would result in a low response rate and, furthermore, a poor quality of return. It was decided, therefore, that the questionnaire should be administered in person, hence the sequence described above of preletter, telephone call, then interview. This meant that in practice the investigator was conducting a structured interview. As a consequence, a very high response rate was obtained,[14] with all returns being completed to a high level of accuracy and detail. After preliminary remarks, intended to convey the essence of the information mentioned under (c) of the 'Guide to Interviewer' (reproduced page 250), the interview proceeded. The general structure of the schedule permitted the interviewer to control the pace of the proceedings and to maintain an authoritative (rather than authoritarian) position by feeding the respondent as required the relevant lists and show cards, if necessary with further explanation. The level of expertise required by the interviewer was high, and in this case was facilitated by the direct involvement of each investigator in the construction of the questionnaire. It was also a deliberate part of the approach that the respondent be allowed to digress in areas of potential interest to the second stage of the investigation, the semi-structured interview. However, a clear attempt was also made to expedite the interview and to screen out irrelevances.

At the same time as administering the questionnaire, respondents were asked whether they would be willing to participate in what was generally described as a 'follow-up' interview. The 'follow-up' was strictly speaking concerned with a quite distinct instrument of measurement, the semi-structured interview SSI 1985. This instrument would be described in the classical terminology of Lofland (1971) as 'an intensive interview with an interview guide'. This instrument consisted of an agenda inspired by the writings of Porter (1980, 1985), with each agenda item having a number of probes attached to it. Interview time for this instrument averaged one-and-a-half hours. The criteria used for selection for the semi-structured interview were judgemental. Representativeness was aimed at, especially as the subsample was considerably smaller than the initial sample. If in the initial interview the respondent displayed a reluctance to be interviewed again, the matter was dropped. This is not to suggest any hostility or negativity of respondents to the investigation: this did not occur in any instance. However, some businesses felt too hard-pressed to grant a further interview. Others, frankly, felt that they could not offer much of use in a less structured framework.

The first phase of the study concluded with constructing a database for storing and codifying the data gathered using the instruments AQ 1985 and SSI 1985, with a view to enhancing my capabilities for processing the data, including using it for econometric analysis (described in part IV below) and for cross-site analytical case studies (described in part III below). A database was set up with the assistance and advice of two members of what was then the Centre for Applications Software and Technology at the University of Edinburgh, using the SIR/DBMS software developed at the University of Wisconsin. This database contains two record types. For firms there is (i) one record containing primarily numerical and categorical data; and (ii) a set of records containing the text of notes obtained from the semi-structured interviews. The first record type contains over 200 variables corresponding to the answers represented in the questionnaires. In the study proper there are 73 such records. Each text record (one for each probe item on the agenda) contains 15 to 20 lines of data and the text of the probes used in the semi-structured interviews are also loaded in the database. There are 17 such sets of text data in the database. Chapter 2 provides further detail on this database.

The second phase of the study involved the administration of a further questionnaire in 1988 (which I call RIQ 1988) to the same sample of small business enterprises first interviewed in 1985. Experience gained in devising the previous two instruments and in extensive field work were useful in devising this new instrument. Simply seeking an interview provided an initial basis for discovering whether the SBE was still in business. As with the AQ 1985, the initial approach was by a preletter, followed by a telephone call to arrange an interview. Data obtained from the RIQ 1988 were used to extend the database described in the previous paragraph. Administration of the questionnaire involved tracing the relevant firms and owner-managers and then organizing and effecting an interview to complete the questionnaire, typically at the place of work. The instrument was less elaborate than that used in 1985 and interviews took about twenty-five minutes on average, although some extended to an hour or more. Of the 73 firms first interviewed in 1985, 56 firms were found to be still trading, or their owner-managers were still in business but with a different firm. Just 17 firms had ceased trading. There were 8 firms that could not be traced and 3 were unwilling to take part in this reinterview study. A total of 47 interviews were obtained using RIQ 1988, of which 2 were incomplete. Retrospective data for 1985 on net profit and net profitability, which were considered to be too sensitive to be gathered at the time of the AQ 1985, were obtained for two-thirds of the original sample. This, together with data on survival rates, was the principal research objective. Extra data were also gathered on subsidiary issues like competitiveness, innovation, cost structure, skill shortages, the emergence of an enterprise culture, etc. The final part of the second phase of the research involved upgrading the database using the same SIR software. This was done by inserting a new record type containing the data on new variables. Textual comments on the enterprise culture were also stored.

1.4   THE SAMPLE AND ITS COMPOSITION

Some comments on the sample design are in order. The starting point for the work, the AQ 1985, which depended crucially on field contacts, was not of a calculated probabilistic form. The geographical areas from which firms were drawn, Lothian, Fife, and Strathclyde, were selected out of considerations of accessibility and budgetary economy. However, it would be true to say that these regions contain much of the significant economic activity of Scotland. They are also contiguous. Field contacts were established in the Edinburgh Venture Enterprises Trust Ltd (EVENT), the Leith Enterprise Trust Ltd (LET), the Glenrothes Enterprise Trust Ltd (GET), the Irvine Development Corporation (IDC), and the Scottish Development Agency (SDA). Typically the field contact was the chief executive of the relevant organization (for example, the director of an Enterprise Trust). Given earlier qualitative field work of Jacobsen (1986: chapter 4) at the Ardrossan, Saltcoats, and Stevenston Enterprise Trust (ASSET), I have no reason to suspect systematic bias arising from the use of these field contacts and of the ports of entry gained thereby to SBE. The sample of field contacts used could have been one which arose from simple random sampling of Enterprise Trusts and development corporations, and in this sense may be termed quasi-random.

This is also true of the samples of firms chosen on our behalf by our field contacts. They were asked to provide samples which were typical of their case loads. I have no reason to believe that these samples were provided in bad faith, quite the contrary, nor that they knowingly involved bias. Field contacts were not specifically directed to use simple random sampling from their client lists, though one cannot exclude that this in fact, or in effect, is what was done in selecting their typical samples. Again I have no evidence of systematic bias over crucial dimensions like age, products, size, and structure, so the sum of these samples provided by field contacts has an appearance which could be described as quasi-random. That is to say, it presents itself to the empirical investigator as though it could have been obtained from a random process. The dispersion of field contacts over the three regions used, and the manifest independence which characterized their selection of samples, are further factors militating against systematic bias. Thus I feel it is appropriate at various points in the rest of this volume to use statistical techniques like regression analysis which treat the sample as a random drawing from a population of small firms. Current work, described in Reid and Anderson (1992), on small firms in Scotland, using more strict sampling methods, provides further independent support for this argument. The essential characteristics of the population can be regarded as governed by the institutions which provided the field contacts. Thus the relevant population is of very small firms within a few years of financial inception who have approached institutions concerned with fostering new small business enterprises. It is broadly speaking the sort of population that is *not* investigated by the Business Statistics Office, which only collects census data for business establishments employing twenty or more persons. The great bulk of firms examined (85 per cent) employed 20 persons or less, so the sample offers empirical insight in an area where data are particularly scarce.

Field work methods which involve intensive interviews with respondents offer the potential for very accurate and complete data, and very high response rates. They also eliminate category confusions over the firm and the business establishment. However, they have the drawback of introducing a subjective element into the sampling. On the other hand, given that postal questionnaires typically have very high non-response rates, and that the nature of the bias engendered by the non-respondents is difficult to judge, the main methodological alternative seems to have substantial drawbacks as well. Telephone surveys also have drawbacks in terms of non-response, inaccurate responses, and paucity of information: in short, little and low-grade data. In the research reports which accompanied the Bolton Committee report (1971) on small firms, the response rates obtained were 30 per cent, 40 per cent, and 50 per cent. These are not untypical figures for studies of this sort. It seemed to me at the time when I was determining the research design of the project that response rates as low as this were unacceptable. In my chosen design the non-response rate for the AQ 1985 was 17 per cent, essentially because the field contact used was a trusted and well regarded figure from the viewpoint of the owner-managers of the SBEs. I would not suggest that the sampling procedure I have used is ideal from the standpoint of statistical theory, though I think the sample obtained might plausibly be regarded as quasi-random. However, I do think it stands up well compared to its alternative, which is calculated to encourage a false sense of security about the sample design, and the relation of the sample obtained, typically with a poor response rate, to the population of firms. Given my interest in issues like survival rates of SBEs, it seems to me highly likely that the non-responses in my alternative, and rejected, research design would have contained a systematic and substantial bias toward ailing and vulnerable firms.

On balance, therefore, the research design adopted appeared to offer the best solution to one of the perennial problems of sampling. My procedure did not knowingly incorporate a bias in selection, and given the safeguard of independence in the sub-samples presented by field contacts, I think the argument for regarding the sample as quasi-random has considerable merit. It is on the basis of this position that the econometric modelling of this volume proceeds.

The composition of the sample of firms used for the AQ 1985 is as in table 1.2 The basic composition is made up of manufactures and construction (SICs 16 to 50), and services and transport (SICs 61 to 97). Broadly speaking, in this book I shall refer to this division as the manufactures/services dichotomy, for the construction (8 per cent) and transport (7 per cent) components of each are relatively small. The split between manufacturing and services so defined is 63 per cent and 37 per cent. That is to say, we have a strong representation of small manufacturing enterprises. Indeed, in

Table 1.2 Composition of sample of small business enterprises for the 1985 administered questionnaire

	SIC	Classification*	Raw numbers of SBEs
M	16	Production and distribution of electricity, gas and other forms of energy	1
A			
N	22	Metal manufacturing	1
U	31	Manufacture of other metal goods	2
F	32	Mechanical engineering	4
A	34	Electrical and electronic engineering	7
C	35	Manufacture of motor vehicles and parts	1
T	37	Instrument engineering	1
U	41/42	Food, drink and tobacco manufacturing	3
R	43	Textile industry	3
I	45	Footwear and clothing industries	2
N	46	Timber and wooden furniture industries	4
G	47	Manufacture of paper and paper products, printing and publishing	4
	48	Processing of rubber and plastics	1
	49	Other manufacturing industries	8
	50	Construction	4
S	61	Wholesale distribution	3
E	63	Commission agents	1
R	64/65	Retail distribution	3
V	66	Hotels and catering	1
I	67	Repair of consumer goods and vehicles	1
C	72	Other inland transport	1
E	75	Air transport	1
S	76	Supporting services to transport	2
	83	Business services	5
	84	Renting of movables	1
	85	Owning and dealing in real estate	1
	95	Medical and other health services	1
	96	Other services provided to the general public	4
	97	Recreational services and other cultural services	2
		Total	73

*Taken from 1980 Standard Industrial Classification (SIC)
Note: 'Manufacturing' means 'manufacturing and construction'; and 'services' means 'transport and services'

chapter 2, I regard the typical SBE as being a manufacturing enterprise. This distribution of representation is something which was typical of the case loads of ETs at the time that field work was being carried out in 1985.

Precise knowledge of the small firm population, particularly at the very bottom of the statistical size distribution, does not exist. The average firm size for my sample in terms of full-time employment (eight, in this study) puts it into a category (0–19 employed) which accounted for 5 per cent of total gross output and 7 per cent of total employment in Scotland in 1986.

As far as manufacturing business is concerned, the sample proportion of firms by SICs is compared in table 1.3, with actual proportions for firms employing between one to nine persons, which is the size class within which the average firm of the 1985 sample lies. The relevant figures for Scotland are displayed next to those for the United Kingdom as a whole for comparative purposes.

In a sample of 73 firms drawn from a somewhat different universe, one does not expect anything like an exact correspondence in proportions. Particularly noteworthy are the high representation in the sample of firms in SIC code 34 (which is 'electrical and electronic engineering') and code 49 (which is 'other manufacturing'). The latter high representation is probably partly explained

Table 1.3 Small business enterprises in manufacturing

Classification	SIC code	Percentages		
		Sample	Scotland	UK
Extraction of metal ore and metal manufacturing	21/22	2.43(1)	1.24	0.91
Extraction of and manufacture from non-metallic minerals	23/24	–	6.68	4.56
Chemical industry/man-made fibres	25/26	–	2.38	2.21
Manufacture of other metal goods	31	4.88(2)	8.72	9.31
Mechanical engineering	32	9.76(4)	16.00	16.44
Manufacture of office machinery and data processing equipment	33	–	0.74	0.79
Electrical and electronic engineering	34	17.07(7)	5.23	6.42
Manufacture of motor vehicles and parts	35	2.43(1)	1.29	1.13
Manufacture of other transport equipment	36	–	2.40	1.48
Instrument engineering	37	2.43(1)	1.87	1.57
Food drink and tobacco manufacturing	41/42	7.32(3)	11.45	6.64
Textile industry	43	7.32(3)	4.18	2.66
Manufacture of leather and leather goods	44	–	0.59	0.96
Footwear and clothing industries	45	4.88(2)	4.92	8.24
Timber and wooden furniture industries	46	9.76(4)	10.92	10.46
Manufacture of paper and paper products, printing and publishing	47	9.76(4)	13.02	16.53
Processing of rubber and plastics	48	2.43(1)	2.40	2.92
Other manufacturing industries	49	19.51(8)	0.93	6.68

Note: Percentage representation of SBEs in manufacturing in firms with 1 to 9 employees by SICs in 1985. Total of 41 firms in sample were in manufactures, raw numbers are given in brackets under the column headed sample.
Source: Employment Gazette (1986).

by owner-managers self-selecting their SIC code at the beginning of the 1985 administered questionnaire, rather than being assigned to an SIC as in the gathering of official statistics. If the owner-manager were in doubt, he might nominate the 'other' category. However, the similarity between percentages in the sample and in the populations of firms in both Scotland and the UK is comforting.[15]

Unfortunately, our knowledge of the small business sector for SBEs in services is very slight for the size range of relevance to this study. In general, services are the most important contributor to value of output and employment in Scotland. In 1986, 67 per cent of Scottish employees were in services (cf. 67 per cent also in services in the UK) and 60.2 per cent of Scottish GDP was created in services (cf. 61.9 per cent in the UK). Figures for Scotland and the UK as a whole are very much in line. Regionally within Scotland, proportions employed in services are fairly stable around the two-thirds mark, falling to about a half in the Borders and in Fife, and rising to as high as three-quarters in Orkney. This suggests that the case loads of Enterprise Trusts and development corporations, from which our sample was drawn in 1985, were oriented towards manufactures rather than services, for just 37 per cent of the sample was in services. However, one should not jump to the conclusion that what is true of total employment across sectors is also true of small firm employment across sectors. In particular one notes the important role of the public sector in service sector employment. In 1984, 48 per cent of service sector employment was in 'other services', which is heavily dominated by public sector employment in the areas of public administration, defence, medical and other health services, education, etc. One notes also the large and increasing role of banking, finance, and insurance in Scottish service sector employment. It accounted for 12 per cent of service sector employment in 1984. It is dominated by very large employers; for example, in banking the major institutions based in Scotland are the Royal Bank of Scotland, the Bank of Scotland, the Clydesdale Bank, the Trustee Savings Bank, and the National Savings Bank, which are all substantial enterprises.

Self-employment figures give some indication of the relative importance of small firm employment in services. In 1987, the self-employed made up just 9 per cent of civilian employment. There are no detailed figures currently available for the exact time period relevant to my sample of SBEs, but in 1981 about two-thirds of the self-employed were in services, the rest being predominantly in agriculture, forestry and fishing (21 per cent) with small numbers in construction (11 per cent) and manufacturing (6 per cent).

Perhaps the closest one can get to any kind of comparative figures for SBEs in services is the set displayed in table 1.4. The figures relate to 1981 and refer to census units rather than firms. I have taken the size band 1 to 10 employees in view of the size of the representative firm in 1985. There is the strong possibility that large firms are again over-represented, for we are told 'where more than one kind of activity is conducted at a single address, especially if it is large, each activity may form a separate census unit'

Table 1.4 Small business enterprises in services

	Population SIC codes	Sample SIC codes	Percentage employment	
			Sample	Scotland
Industrial classification:				
Wholesale distribution repairs	61–63, 67	61–63, 67	18.52	11.61
Hotels and catering	66	66	3.70	14.53
Retail distribution	64–65	64–65	11.11	39.5
Transport	71–77	72–75, 76	14.81	4.99
Banking, finance and insurance	81–85	83–84, 85	25.93	14.77
Health and veterinary services	95	95	3.70	3.97
Other services	94, 96–98	96, 97	22.22	12.66

Source: Scottish Abstract of Statistics (1985).
Notes: (a) SIC classification groupings are as published in the Scottish Abstract of Statistics, and do not correspond exactly with sample SICs. Sample SICs are indicated where they lie within the bands of published SICs. (b) Percentages are expressed as percentages of sums of sample numbers and population numbers in SICs indicated. (c) Percentages are based on number of employees in size band 1–10 employees for 'census units' (i.e. paypoint or establishment, whichever is smaller). (d) Figures relate to the 1981 census in Scotland.

(Scottish Office 1985: 103). For the SIC codes used in table 1.4, 90 per cent of employment for firm size 1 to 10 employees in transport and services in 1981 is captured. In the sub-population of transport and services, retail distribution is the predominant employer, followed by banking, finance, and insurance, then hotels and catering. In my sub-sample of transport and services, it is banking, finance, and insurance which is the predominant employer, followed by transport and other services. The relationship between this sub-population and this sub-sample, as displayed in table 1.4, is not outlandish, but neither is it very close. Given differences in date, definitions of firm or establishment, and indeed of population itself, this is scarcely surprising. However, the composition of the sub-sample itself is of interest, and these comparative figures may be of use in interpreting results in relation to the more general body of small business enterprises in Scotland. The importance of the sample is precisely that it provides further highly detailed information in an area in which we are currently extremely ignorant.

By firm type, the sample was made up of private companies (50 per cent), partnerships (20 per cent), and sole proprietorships (30 per cent). There are marked and systematic increases in employment and sales as one moves up through the categories of one-man business, partnership, and private company. Sales for a sole proprietorship are £20,000, for a partnership £100,000, and for a private company £225,000 on average (all at 1985 prices) with employment for these same firm types being on average three, five, and thirteen persons. The number of products produced was about thirty for all firm types and in each case the degree of product differentiation was perceived to be slight. The main market for the principal product was perceived to be the particular region for sole proprietorships and partnerships, and Scotland as a whole for private companies. Market shares differed little and were estimated to be less than 10 per cent for all small firm types. Presumably firms re-define their perceived market extent as they grow – how else can one explain the fact that the smallest firm types had owner-managers who believed they had the largest market shares (8 per cent as against 3 per cent for partnerships and 7 per cent for private companies). It is likely that for the very smallest firms competition was perceived to be extremely localized, and looked at in terms of a few well-known local rivals.

1.5   THE SMALL BUSINESS SECTOR

Regarding Scotland as a regional economy, its small business characteristics are slightly different from those of the UK as a whole. For manufacturing in 1986, for example, Scottish SBEs with less than twenty employees accounted for 5 per cent of gross output (compared to 8 per cent in the rest of the UK) and 8% of employment (compared to 10 per cent in the rest of the UK), indicating a larger small business manufacturing sector in the rest of the UK. This is true across the range of sizes which are regarded as 'small'. For example, in 1986 small businesses employing less than 200 in manufacturing had an employment share of 26 per cent in Scotland compared with 30 per cent in the rest of the UK. For share of total manufacturing output the corresponding figures were 20 per cent in Scotland compared to 23 per cent in the rest of the UK. Most significant for this study is that the greatest difference between the Scottish and the rest of the UK characteristics of small firms occurred in the 'very small'-size class (less than twenty people) which is the focus of this work.

Whilst the small firm sector is smaller in Scotland than in her generally more prosperous partner, there was nevertheless a marked increase in small business activity in the 1980s. Between 1976 and 1986 the numbers in self-employment rose from 151,000 to 205,000: about 10 per cent of the civilian work force. Companies registered rose from 31,000 to 49,000 over the same period, with the number of new companies registering per year rising nearly threefold (from about 2,000 to about 6,000). Registrations for value added tax (VAT) purposes[16] through from end-1979 to end-1986 were as in table 1.5. They indicate a 10 per cent rise in VAT registrations over the period. For both company and VAT registrations, the great majority of firms concerned would be small.

During the 1980s a variety of Government schemes were created to encourage small business enterprise, including the Loan Guarantee Scheme, the Business Expansion Scheme, and the Enterprise Allowance Scheme. Corporation tax was also reduced. The Scottish Development Agency (SDA)

Table 1.5 SBE registrations for VAT purposes

	Period	Numbers
Stock	end–1979	99,000
Registrations	1980–86	78,900
Deregistrations	1980–86	67,600
Net change	1980–86	11,300
Stock	end–1986	110,300

Source: Scottish Office (1988) *Scotland: An Economic Perspective*, Edinburgh: HMSO (p. 61)

assumed an active role in enterprise stimulation through its Small Business Division. Of particular note were its involvement with the Enterprise Trust (ET) movement, jointly funded by the private and public sectors, providing a wide range of business services on a 'one door' basis at the local level. During the 1980s the ETs grew in number from zero to over forty. They are an important focus of attention in this study.

1.6 CONCLUSION

This chapter has been wide-ranging, and attempted to introduce the reader to the full set of issues addressed elsewhere in this book: working in the field; using qualitative and quantitative evidence; estimating models for the representative firm; and extracting evidence from a relational database. Whilst the issues are diverse, one hopes that these preliminary treatments will provide a useful underpinning to the more detailed arguments of the rest of this volume.

2 The small firms relational database

2.1 INTRODUCTION

Using field work methods of the sort described in chapter 1 to gather information on small business enterprises (SBEs) generates a great deal of information. The concern of this chapter is with how these data are generated (instrumentation), how they may be stored and retrieved (database design), and how they may be manipulated (relational database analysis).

Initially all the data gathered were directly recorded during interviews, using the schedules designed for the administered questionnaires of 1985 (AQ 1985), the semi-structured interviews of 1985 (SSI 1985) and the re-interview administered questionnaires of 1988 (RIQ 1988). The first instrument (AQ 1985) investigated general characteristics, pricing, costs, sales and competition, and finance. The second instrument (SSI 1985) investigated competitive forces, competitive strategy, and defensive strategy. The third instrument (RIQ 1988) investigated survival rates, innovation, scale economies, skills shortages, and financial structure.

Initially the data gathered were recorded on upward of 170 physical schedules, which occupied some twenty large box files. In order to answer even the simplest questions about average values of employment, sales and profits, etc. one is involved in much labour, with a fair likelihood of confusion and error arising. Considerably more complicated questions are often contemplated, beyond enquiring into averages, standard deviations etc. One might ask what is the strategic segment favoured by those firms which, in following a focus strategy, emphasise low cost and product differentiation.[1] Alternatively, one might ask how market share, as a dependent variable, can be explained by independent variables like advertising, price flexibility, competitiveness, and degree of product differentiation. For such questions, the performance of data analysis using physical files rapidly becomes unmanageable.

This is true of both qualitative and quantitative data analysis. The time-honoured technique of qualitative analysts, which involves laying out on the floor or carpet pieces of paper with certain written evidence on them, and re-arranging them to display sets and relationships between them, will not work as the number of sites becomes at all large, say more than ten. Also, the compact data files traditionally used by econometricians in quantitative work, very often on a single floppy disc, provide poor service. When one is dealing with hundreds of variables, which themselves might be combined and modified or transformed to define many hundreds more, the number of files one might wish to manipulate, and to perform calculations upon using statistical and econometric software, rapidly runs into many thousands. What one needs in order to use this abundance of data efficiently, accurately and economically, and in a way which facilitates scientific discovery, is a database management system. This is a device for centralizing and automating the storing and handling of large amounts of data. In this current age, automation involves computerization. The design and structure of a database to facilitate work on the small firms data discussed earlier must clearly take into account both the sorts of tasks to be performed (for example, cross-site qualitative analysis of interview probes, cross-section regression analysis), and the way in which data were originally gathered (for example, using the three instruments AQ 1985, SSI 1985, and RIQ 1988).

With a computerised database in place, gathering together the data from the field work on SBEs in a way which facilitates easy access, issues of the manipulation of the database, using its management system, become significant. A variety of general principles govern the design of databases, of which the most important for the small firms work presented in this volume is that of the flat file.[2] As this term suggests, the principle is rather similar to that used by field workers who have few sites and display their properties by laying sheets of paper on the floor, with each representing a two-dimensional table. Introducing this principle to database design implies that qualitative (and specifically textual) as well as quantitative data can go onto each flat file; and that there is no limit of floor space, metaphorically speaking, restricting to very few the number of files that may be arranged in this way. Databases organized along these lines are said to be relational[3] (as opposed, for example, to hierarchical),[4] as the flat files impose very little structure on the data. Thus the investigator is left to explore and discover structures for himself, by manipulating flat files in an organized way (for example, by an algebra, a logical calculus, or a language).

2.2 INSTRUMENTATION (AQ 1985, SSI 1985, RIQ 1988)

The organizing frameworks for data collection were the instruments used for the field work in 1985 (two instruments) and in 1988 (one instrument). I turn now to a more detailed consideration of the three instruments of measurement: the administered questionnaire; the semi-structured interview; and the administered reinterview questionnaire.

The administered questionnaire (AQ 1985)

Formally, the administered questionnaire was divided up into five sections:

- general
- pricing
- costs
- sales and competition
- finance

A reproduction of this questionnaire, with an indication of colour coding. and complete with lists and show cards, is given at the back of the book. For the convenience of the reader, a much shorter summary of the principal features of the instrument AQ 1985 is given in the appendix to this chapter.

In keeping with the literature, it was felt to be important to use previously successful question designs as the point of departure. In the first four sections, the work of Wied-Nebbeling (1975) and Nowotny and Walther (1978), which strictly speaking is relevant to postal questionnaire design, provided the ground base. The fifth section on finance was developed by Jacobsen (1986) using the same sort of question construction and question-naire design as was adopted in the first four sections of the administered questionnaire. Distinctive features of this administered (as opposed to postal) questionnaire included colour coding, filtering, interviewer prompts, show cards and a 'guide to interviewer'.

The general section (part 1) of the questionnaire aimed to identify the basic characteristics of the firm and the environment within which it functioned. It involved discovering the SIC classification, the legal nature of the business, the turnover, the number of employees, and the market environment. The last-named was particularly important and had several dimensions. Firms were asked to distinguish between product groups and products *per se*, to identify their principal market, to distinguish between major and minor com-petitors, to characterize the degree of product differentiation, and to provide a ranking of customer attributes over a scale ranging from ignorant to expertly informed.

The pricing section, in keeping with the original intention of Wied-Nebbeling, provided information which could help resolve the marginal-ist/full cost pricing controversy, but much more besides. Of particular importance were questions which contrasted buyers' and sellers' market behaviour. What the administered questionnaire enables one to do is to identify sequences of decisions in a contingent set of circumstances. Traditional methods of analysis are woefully deficient in this regard: causality has to be imputed, based on a priori reasoning, and the appropriate lag struc-ture has to be determined by a 'data mining' approach. As an example of the approach adopted in the administered questionnaire, consider the question set out in figure 2.1 (based on question 2.5 and list 2.5 of the administered questionnaire AQ 1985).

2.5 What action do you take when a boom in demand occurs and this demand cannot be met from stocks? On this list, pleast tick any that apply.

[Hand over list 2.5. Pause to permit its completion.]

2.5.1

Now please indicate where possible on this list, the order in which you do things by ringing the number on the right-hand side, where ringing a '1' for an option would indicate that this is what you would do first.

[Pause to permit completion. Retrieve list 2.5.]

List 2.5
What action do you take when a boom in demand occurs and this demand cannot be met from stocks?

Please tick any that apply:

(a) Increase overtime or shift work   ( ) 1 2 3 4 5 6 7
(b) Increase capacity (this could include the recruitment ( ) 1 2 3 4 5 6 7
     of more personnel)
(c) Engage subcontractors   ( ) 1 2 3 4 5 6 7
(d) Buy up rival firms   ( ) 1 2 3 4 5 6 7
(e) Lengthen your order books   ( ) 1 2 3 4 5 6 7
(f) Raise price   ( ) 1 2 3 4 5 6 7
(g) Other   ( ) 1 2 3 4 5 6 7

If (g) please specify, if possible.

Indicate where possible the order in which you do things by ringing the numbers on the right-hand side, where ringing a '1' for any option would imply that this is what you would do first.

Figure 2.1 A question displaying possible sequences of actions in the face of a boom in demand

The contingent circumstance here is that of a boom in demand which cannot be met from stocks (a further question relates to the case of a recession). Given this circumstance, certain actions may be taken (for example, raise price, increase overtime, lengthen order books). Once a sub-set of actions is nominated, the respondent is asked to place them in a ranking which reflects temporal ordering. Causality is clear, for it is a 'stimulus' (excess demand) which gives rise to a 'response' (for example, increased price). Furthermore, information on lag structure is forthcoming and enables one to reach conclusions like 'The increased overtime lag is shorter than the price raising lag.' An even more detailed approach, which was regarded as being too burdensome on the respondent, would have asked for the real time frames within which these actions would be taken. Table 2.1 indicates, based on the thirteen-firm pilot for the AQ 1985, what the responses to this

Table 2.1 Summary of responses to question 2.5 of the administered questionnaire (AQ 1985): actions nominated by firms in the pilot study

Firm number	Actions
01	b a e
02	a b
03	a b c d f
04	b
05	a e
06	a e b
07	a
08	a f
09	b c
10	a b
11	a
12	a c b
13	a c b f

Count of actions: $a = 11$, $b = 9$, $c = 4$, $e = 3$, $f = 3$, $d = 1$, $g = 0$

question were like. The question design was unchanged in the main study. It is to be noted that raising price, action (f), which is the sort of response that would be given most attention using traditional neoclassical reasoning, was nominated as a possible action by only three firms, and in each case it was ranked as the last action taken. Action (a), increasing overtime or shift work, was the most frequently nominated action overall and, furthermore, the most frequently nominated first action.

Data of this sort raise interesting issues of statistical methodology, of the sort that econometricians rarely encounter using traditional cross-sectional or time-series data. I provide a detailed discussion of these issues in chapter 5, so here my treatment is brief and informal. If every respondent ranked all alternatives, with no alternative having tied ranks, then the method of m rankings due to Friedman (1937) would apply. For the data of table 2.1 the Friedman test statistic, computed by imputing tied ranks to unranked options, is 30.28. For significance level $\alpha = 0.05$ the critical value for the relevant variate is 12.59, suggesting rejection of the null hypothesis of random rankings. If ties occur then a correction can be applied, but if some alternatives are simply not ranked (for example if they are irrelevant to a particular respondent) then difficulties arise. One procedure would be to treat unchecked alternatives as tied ranks, and then to apply the appropriate correction to the Friedman statistic. More satisfactory, but then more complex, is to use the generalization of the method of m rankings due to Benard and Van Elteren (1953) in its original form, which permits unchecked items. A further, and more efficient, variant has more recently been devised by Prentice (1979): it involves scaling the reduced ranks[5] of a respondent in proportion to the total number of items ordered.

What these techniques enable one to do to define a 'modal sequence'. Such a sequence is not one which most firms will follow, as not all firms will undertake all actions in the face of an increase in demand. Further, it is not implied that items which occur later in the sequence must inevitably follow those which occur sooner. Rather what it does show is that if, of the set of all possible actions, a firm actually undertakes say, a, b, d and e in the face of a rise in demand, these will tend to occur in the order indicated by the modal sequence. If the modal sequence were c, b, a, d, g, f, e then it indicates that the firm would tend to take these actions chosen in the order b, a, d, e. The administered questionnaire uses such devices frequently, and the manipulation and interpretation of such sequences is an important characteristic of this sort of approach to industrial organization. The technique is also applied to such issues as actions to be taken in a recession and actions to be taken when demand falls for a particular product in the main product group.

Part 3 of the administered questionnaire, on costs, was brief and was principally concerned with getting an idea of how costs varied with output, using 'show cards'. The device of the show card has already been used in postal questionnaires, but field work experience suggested that it frequently required explanation for the businessmen interviewed. The cards were as shown in chapter 4 and the appendix to this book (page 269). Figure 2.2 gives a description of the total cost curve on each card. In figure 2.3 the way in which these show cards were deployed is illustrated. The most favoured response (55 per cent) was for an everywhere concave total cost curve. A questionnaire 'check question' was incorporated into the instrument design which ran as follows: 'Do you have a level of output which you regard as the capacity or maximum possible output?' Then, for affirmative responses, an estimate was required of the percentage of this output at which firms normally operated. If (a) rather than (e) (as described in figure 2.2) were ticked as being representative of the firm's costs, but the above question was answered in the affirmative, the validity of the respondent's choice might be

(a) Total cost increases in line with amount supplied, i.e. for each extra unit supplied, your cost rises by the same amount. (11%)
(b) Total cost does not increase as fast as amount supplied, i.e. the extra cost of supplying each additional unit falls as more is supplied. (55%)
(c) Total cost increases faster than supply, i.e. each extra unit supplied adds more to the cost than the last unit supplied. (0%)
(d) At first cost does not increase as fast as supply but then it increases faster than supply. (15%)
(e) Total cost increases in line with supply until the maximum supply possible (full capacity) is reached. After this point, the extra cost of supplying another unit rises sharply. (14%)

Note: Reponse rates are indicated in brackets

Figure 2.2 Descriptions of cost curves on show cards

3.4 This next question aims to get an idea of the way your costs vary as you increase your output up to the maximum level possible. Could you examine the cost pictures of these sheets and hand to me any which approximate to your cost pattern?

[Hand respondent show cards 3.4(a) to 3.4(e).]

Underneath each picture you will find an explanation in words which you may prefer to use in making your choices. Please ask me if the pictures are not entirely clear.

[Pause for selecting to take place. Retrieve selected sheets, and note below the selections made.]

(a) ( )   (b) ( )   (c) ( )   (d) ( )   (e) ( )

[Retrieve remaining sheets.]

Figure 2.3 Rubric used with show cards on cost curves

called into question, or possibly the clarity of the interviewer's exposition might be called into doubt.

Part 4, on sales and competition, tried particularly to illuminate the demand side of the firm. Controlled questions on price elasticities, of the sort discussed by Reid (1981) were used. The questions were controlled in the following manner. First, the state of business conditions was specified. Second, price cuts and price increases were treated in a way which did not assume symmetry. Third, the pattern of reaction of competitors was specified. Fourth, different magnitudes of possible price changes were assigned. The latter point was of significance to a further set of questions relating to price inflexibility, and to the possibility of a certain measure of elbow-room in pricing, within which a price change by a firm brought about no reaction from competitors. Finally, price discrimination, bulk discounting, and non-price competition were investigated.

The last section in the administered questionnaire, on finance, was devised by L. R. Jacobsen in consultation with the author, using design techniques employed in the earlier four parts of the questionnaire. Full details may be found in Jacobsen (1986). Briefly, this section looked at the availability of funding, and at the actual as well as prospective behaviour of the gearing of firms (here defined as the ratio of borrowing to owners' injection of finance).

The semi-structured interview agenda (SSI 1985)

The second instrument used in this study of owner-managed firms was a semi-structured interview. In keeping with the philosophy that a fair degree of prior instrumentation is an efficient approach to work in the field, a specific framework was adopted. This revolved around Michael Porter's books

Competitive Strategy (1980) and *Competitive Advantage* (1985). The relational diagrams and matrix representations of Porter fit particularly well into the qualitative data analysis paradigm (for example, his 'five forces of competition' diagram, and his value chain matrix).

Under *competitive forces*, the SSI 1985 looked at rivalry, customers (including both bargaining leverage and price sensitivity), suppliers, potential entrants, and substitutes. Under *competitive strategy* it looked at cost leadership, differentiation, and focus. Finally, under *defensive strategy* it looked at increasing barriers to entry, increasing retaliation which challengers can expect, lowering the inducement for attack, deterrence, and responding to attack.

Interviews involved working through an agenda with the respondent whilst taking notes. Lofland (1971) proposed as a principle of global design for agenda construction that no more than ten main topics should be covered, with eight being the normal limit. In the semi-structured interview agenda being examined here only three main topics were introduced, although the framework suggested by Porter would have implied many more. A total of three was found to be a sensible practical limit given the attention spans of interviewer and respondent alike, and (not unrelated) the need to keep the interview length within reasonable bounds (no more than two hours at a maximum). More detailed structure is obtained by using a nested or hierarchical arrangement. This was accomplished by using a 'probe' structure. For example, under competitive forces, one can probe further about potential entrants; under potential entrants the sub-category on absolute cost advantages can be probed further in terms of considerations like location, subsidies and learning by doing.

It is generally recommended that interviews be taped.[6] However, there are advantages and disadvantages in this procedure. The advantages are well documented, hence the widespread application of the technique, but the disadvantages have been less carefully considered.

The first disadvantage is the difficulty in obtaining 'informed consent': the respondent may not be willing to talk if the interview is to be recorded. Covert recording can be dismissed as being unethical. The second disadvantage is that the respondent may consent, but might then behave in a more guarded way, if s/he felt that a very complete record of the interchange was to be kept with the possibility that it could subsequently be selectively used without a proper regard for context. In short, a transfer of power from respondent to investigator takes place. A third disadvantage is that tape recording is too passive. It leads to the possibility that the interviewee's remarks may not be listened to carefully because the investigator is aware that everything is going down on tape. The structure of the interview can therefore suffer and the quality of data gathered is thereby reduced. A fourth disadvantage is that the process of tape-recording and subsequent transcription is enormously expensive in a strict economic sense, which includes taking a proper account of the investigator's opportunity cost. A fifth disadvantage lies in the lack of economy with which data are accumulated by this method, for much of it involves irrelevant and over-determining information (i.e. data redundancy). Thus some data are simply not needed, but acquisition cannot be interrupted for fear of destroying the flow of the interview. Further, specific information may be given to the interviewer more than once, though the respondent may not necessarily be aware that he is simply conveying the same information in a variety of different ways. Natural conversation is frequently markedly over-determined in this way. Finally, there is the disadvantage of the sheer volume of information obtained from interview transcriptions, which makes the development of generalizations and the detection of relationships perplexingly difficult.

It was decided, therefore, to eschew the use of the tape recorder, and to

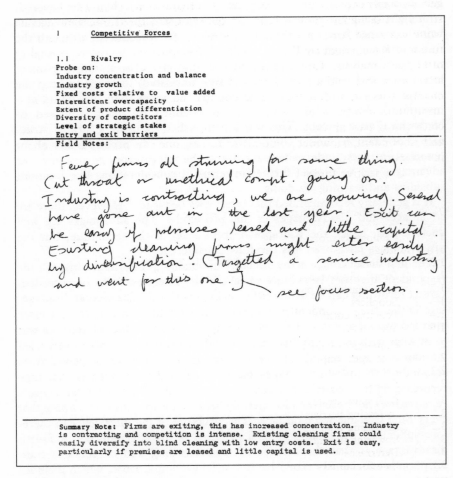

Figure 2.4 Facsimile of a page from SSI 1985

depend on field notes and debriefing. Schatzman and Strauss (1973) have pointed out that memory of field events improves markedly with practice. They suggest having a model for recording notes. For the semi-structured interview, the model was as follows. Rough field notes were jotted down, in a special area allotted for each agenda item. Then summary notes of greater detail and precision were constructed from field notes and memory in a debriefing session. These summary notes were subsequently entered on the database. Figure 2.4 is a facsimile of a typical page from the SSI 1985, used to explore rivalry. The field notes are augmented, modified and edited in the summary note. Other pages of this instrument were designed in a similar fashion.

I now turn to the design of the semi-structured interview agenda, SSI 1985. The inspiration for the agenda was Porter (1980, 1985), but his analysis is generally prescriptive for it aims, first, to tell firms how to devise an effective strategy, and second, how to carry it out. By contrast, the concern in the field work was to use Porter's categories as a means of investigating industry structure and firms' conduct. Part III of this book provides detailed applications of Porter's analysis. Table 2.2 provides a summary of the agenda devised to accomplish this, and a more detailed listing is given in the appendix to this chapter (page 43). If the respondent were willing to read a prescriptive implication into the proceedings of the interview, that could be regarded as constituting part of the quid pro quo of the transaction between interviewer and respondent. However, prescription was not a deliberate purpose of the investigator.

The competitive forces of the first section of the agenda relate to what are

Table 2.2 Outline of semi-structured interview agenda (SSI 1985)

1	**Competitive forces**
1.1	Rivalry
1.2	Customers
1.2.1	Bargaining leverage of customers
1.2.2	Price sensitivity of customers
1.3	Suppliers
1.4	Potential entrants
1.5	Substitutes
2	**Competitive strategy**
2.1	Cost leadership
2.2	Differentiation
2.3	Focus
3	**Defensive strategy**
3.1	Increasing barriers to entry
3.2	Increasing retaliation which challengers can expect
3.3	Lowering the inducement for attack
3.4	Deterrence
3.5	Responding to attack

described as 'forces driving industry competition' in Porter's *Competitive Strategy* (1980) and 'elements of industry structure' in Porter's *Competitive Advantage* (1985). The simple idea is that four principal forces impinge on the rivalrous structure of competitors in an industry: the threat of new entrants; the threat of substitute products or services; the bargaining power of suppliers; and the bargaining power of customers (described as 'buyers' by Porter). The fifth component of industry competition is rivalry amongst existing firms. This so-called 'five forces of competition' framework is illustrated by Porter's scheme in figure 2.5. Traditionally, industrial economists have emphasised rivalry amongst existing firms. The advantage of Porter's approach, as represented by the above schema, is that it enlarges the framework for competitive analysis to what has sometimes been called 'extended rivalry'. The competitive position of a firm is influenced not only by the actions of incumbent firms, but also by potential entrants and substitute goods and services. Further, unlike the situation under traditional competitive analysis, customers and suppliers may have some measure of leverage or

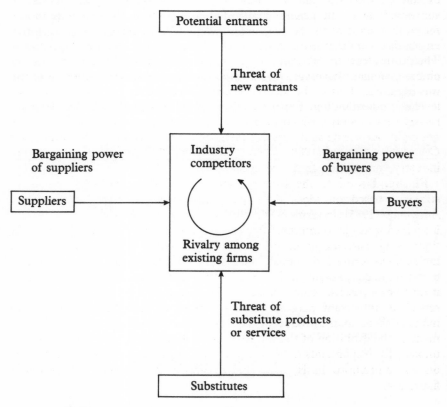

Figure 2.5 Forces driving industry competition
Source: Porter (1980)

bargaining power in goods and factor markets, especially if numbers are small. Very often, customers as well as suppliers will be firms. Typically such firms operate by using established trade connections.

Several specific features of the probes are worth remarking upon. Switching costs of customers as compared with suppliers are investigated. Switching costs are essentially the adjustment costs incurred in changing your supplier if you are a customer or your customer if you are a supplier. They are not solely psychic and include search, experience, inventory, production, and human capital costs. The notion 'value/price', a probe under the substitutes heading, is also important and is essentially an attempt to get at the idea of a 'quality adjusted' or 'hedonic' price. Under competitive strategy the three so-called generic strategies of Porter (1980: 39; 1985: 12) are introduced. The basic idea is that competitive strategy may have as its principal targets either the industry or a segment of the industry; and that strategic advantage may be gained either through product differentiation or cost leadership. Logically this should lead to four, rather than three, generic strategies, but it is argued that the two strategies which can be deployed to exploit a market segment (as distinct from the market as a whole) should be subsumed under the general heading of a focus strategy. It was generally found that firms of the type investigated deployed a focus strategy with an emphasis on differentiation, particularly in the direction of quality of service. The probe structure attached to each agenda item enabled the interviewer to obtain systematic coverage and, in certain instances when the probe structure was hierarchical (as in the section on potential entrants), to achieve a deeper level of understanding. Experience in the field was that the probe items on rivalry very quickly enabled the interviewer to exhaust this category. This is not really surprising as the rivalry category constitutes the 'node' in Porter's *Competitive Strategy* (1980) scheme into which the four influences driving industry competition feed (see figure 2.5).

Finally, I come to the section of the agenda concerned with defensive strategy, based on ideas developed exclusively in Porter's *Competitive Advantage* (1985). In terms of standard terminology in industrial organization it seemed sensible to interpret Porter's phrase 'raising structural barriers' as 'increasing barriers to entry'. Increasing retaliation in its initial form included lowering inducement for attack, but this latter category seemed better treated separately, as indicated in the agenda, the reasoning being that it involves a passive rather than an active response to attack. Under 'deterrence' an important part of Porter's scheme of thought, the idea of an industry scenario, is introduced, it being a qualitative and quantitative assessment of the evolution of the industry over a limited time period. It was not unusual for respondents to be able to construct their own industry scenarios, on an impromptu basis, as is hinted at by the responses recorded in figure 2.4.

The reinterview administered questionnaire (RIQ 1988)

In 1988 a reinterview study in the field was undertaken, the primary goal being to discover what had happened to firms and owner-managers since the 1985 field study. Again the instrument used was a questionnaire administered directly by an interviewer. A full version of the RIQ 1988 is given at the end of the book (page 288), and a fairly comprehensive summary in the appendix to this chapter (page 47). In outline, the RIQ 1988 had the form indicated in Table 2.3.

The same method of approach to respondents as I have described earlier was used, involving preletter, telephone call, and then interview. Part 1 of the instrument aimed to make possible the construction of an exhaustive account of what had happened to all firms and owner-managers contacted in 1985. It enquired into: whether the 1985 firm was still trading; whether it was trading under the same owner-manager; what happened to the firm if it were no longer run by the same owner-manager (e.g. in terms of being wound up, bought up, or bought out); and what happened to the owner-manager if s/he were no longer running the firm analysed in 1985 (for example, in terms of running a new business, taking up wages or salaried employment, becoming unemployed, retiring, going to college, etc.). On the basis of this a quite complex flow diagram was constructed, giving a complete account of the subsequent history of events for the 1985 sample. This diagram is presented in chapter 9.

Part 2 of the RIQ 1988 was concerned with profitability, innovation, output, size, skills, finance, and enterprise. In order to undertake econometric work on a number of important propositions in industrial economics, one required data on profits and profitability. Unfortunately, this is a very sensitive piece of information. For this reason, it was not requested in the course of the field work of 1985. It was felt that by 1988 sufficient time had elapsed to make this a rather neutral piece of information, and indeed this generally proved to be the case. It was possible to construct profitability

Table 2.3 Outline of reinterview questionnaire (RIQ 1988)

Part 1
Trading status

Part 2
Profitability
Innovation
Size
Output
Skills
Financial structure
Enterprise culture

---

figures for 1985 using the AQ 1985 asset figures and the RIQ 1988 profit figures. Further, in the RIQ 1988, respondents were asked for direct estimates of profitability. In general, the estimates of profitability by the first method were much lower than the estimates by the second method, the mean value of the former being 5 per cent and of the latter 29 per cent. The lower figure nets out directors' remunerations whereas the higher does not. The two variables were negatively but not highly correlated, and generally the first lower measure was preferred, it being both more accurate[7] and also more in keeping with the concept of entrepreneurial profit as a residual. In a number of cases it was necessary to contact the firm after the reinterview to obtain profit figures. In a small number of cases even this did not prove possible.

The rest of the RIQ 1988 did not require access to figures from 1985. Innovation and competitiveness, and the identity of the innovator in the market were the next concerns. Five possible current size indicators were sought in terms of sales, employment by several employee types, and total assets. These could be of use for a number of structural models of individual organization (for example, market share equations) and can also be used in models of the growth of the SBE (cf. chapter 11). Scale economies were first examined using show cards in the AQ 1985; the RIQ 1988 approached this same problem in a different way, using detailed questions on output changes and corresponding unit cost changes. New issues examined on the output side included changes in the main product line; and in the product mix in terms of both value and volume. This enables one to examine market re-positioning by the firm. This is part of the SBE's spectrum of alternatives to harvesting a small niche and winding up the business. Such a firm may subsequently re-start in a new niche in proximity to the earlier one, with a substantial transfer of physical, human, financial and reputational capital. Re-positioning is a half-way house to voluntarily liquidating and then re-starting.

As the 1980s witnessed a reassertion of the importance of decentralized economic activity at the level of economic policy, so the small-firm sector has expanded, as indicated briefly in chapter 1. Along with this expansion one might expect shortages of certain types of specialized inputs to appear fairly rapidly, particularly so in the case of relatively immobile factors of production like skilled labour. Another way of recognizing shortages in a relatively price-sensitive factor market is in terms of rapidly rising factor prices. However, labour services are not bought and sold on a spot market, and contracts to hire labour can be complex, so this simple price (i.e. wage) flexibility argument may not be relevant. To address issues such as this, questions were devised to look at shortages of skilled labour. Three questions in the RIQ 1988 were concerned with the possibility of a 'skills gap', the consequences it might have (for growth in particular), and the form in which its effects were felt (e.g. in terms of the need to re-skill personnel, to pay premium rates to labour possessed of scarce skills, and to assess the relative skill advantage or disadvantage of rivals). The existence or not of skills shortages has a bearing both on technical issues of economic analysis like the SBE's probability of survival (cf. chapter 9), and on prescriptive issues of economic policy like the role to be played by institutions for stimulating enterprise in providing skills training.

The financial structure section of the RIQ 1988 returned to an important issue of the first administered questionnaire, the AQ 1985. It concerned the trajectory of the equity gearing ratio. In 1985 owner-managers were asked to forecast whether they thought gearing ratios would rise, fall, or stay at the same level over each year of a three-year time horizon. In 1988, respondents were asked what had actually happened to gearing ratios over this same three-year period, without being reminded that they had been asked the preceding question earlier in 1985. This enables one to answer questions about the rationality of the financial structure of the small business enterprise. At the same time, a figure for the current gearing ratio in 1988 was obtained.

Finally, the RIQ 1988 concluded more qualitatively with questions on the 'enterprise culture'. Respondents were asked whether they had sensed the emergence of such a culture since 1985, and were allowed to elaborate if they so wished. These responses have a bearing on the political economy of enterprise, as discussed in part IV of this book. Quantitative and qualitative data from the RIQ 1988 were then entered into the small firms database. The form of this database is the concern of the next section.

2.3 DESIGN AND STRUCTURE OF DATABASE

In the introduction to this chapter, it was stated that relational databases adopt what some[8] call a 'flat file' approach,[9] in which no, or as few as possible, relationships are imposed (for example, by hierarchical organization), but data are simply a set of two-dimensional tables. It is particularly fitting to store data in this way for this study of SBEs, because data were gathered by field work methods and a basic tenet of this technique is that as little structure should be imposed upon the data as possible. This allows for an interplay between data analysis and theorizing. In this way, one hopes to develop theories which are well 'grounded' in business reality. Figure 2.6 illustrates this 'flat file' approach.

An important aspect of the relational database is that it breaks down the distinction between entities and attributes. The firm is an organizational form (an entity) which has certain characteristics like sales, assets, and market share (all attributes). A set of attributes may nominally be attached to an entity, but that is not necessarily important for manipulation of the database. In cross-site analytical case studies, for example, one might be interested in the way in which cost leadership and differentiation combine to form a focus strategy (see part III below). The relationships between the relative costs of competitors and their sources, and customers' purchasing criteria are then instances of the way in which one would want to explore relationships

	Numerical and categorical data	Textual data
Administered questionnaire and semi-structured interview of 1985	*Type 1 Record* AQ 1985, numerical and categorical data	*Type 2 Record* SSI 1985, textual data
Reinterview questionnaire of 1988	*Type 3 Record* RIQ 1988, numerical and categorical data	*Type 4 Record* RIQ 1988, textual data

Note: Regarding each firm as a 'case', every 'case' may have four record types.

Figure 2.6 Flat file structure of small firms database

between attributes without any necessary reference to specific entities (here, SBEs).

Although many varieties of sophisticated software are available for database construction, they impose very little restriction on their implemented form. Indeed, it would fly in the face of database philosophy to impose the form of implementation, for this would not encourage features like responsiveness to new requests and 'evolvability'.[10] Thus each operational database is unique, even if the software used in constructing it is an industry standard. A piece of advice one gets from software manuals is to develop two mental pictures of one's unique database. The first picture is of the contents of the database and the way it is organized; and the second picture is of what can be done with the contents. Briefly, in the case of the small firms database, the contents were the qualitative and quantitative data obtained with the three instruments AQ 1985, SSI 1985, and RIQ 1988; and the way in which they were handled was governed by a language made available with the software used, known as SQL (Structural Query Language).[11] In this section I shall confine comment to the contents of the database; to how it was designed and structured. In the next section I shall look at how the contents of the database are manipulated.

The database was initially created in 1985 and then extended in 1988, and had the form indicated in figure 2.7.[12] In 1985 the numerical and categorical data collected for each SBE using the AQ 1985 were stored in one record type (type 1 record) and corresponded to the replies recorded in the questionnaire completed with each owner-manager. Every SBE had one of these records, although information on all items for each firm was not always available. Such data were assigned a missing value. For some of the SBEs there were

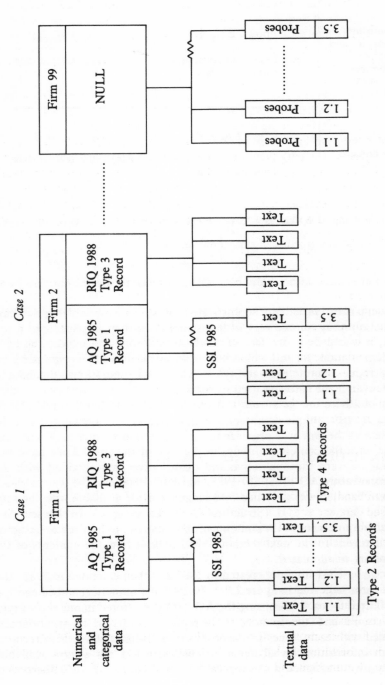

Figure 2.7 The structure of the small firms database

in addition a set of agenda records which contained the textual information of the summary notes constructed after the SSI 1985. An example of the sort of summary note stored in each record of this type (type 2 records) is given at the bottom of figure 2.4 above. Each firm was uniquely identified as a 'case' (cf. 'entity' above) in the database. An additional dummy firm, number 99, was used as a technical device to link the agenda records containing the probes of the SSI 1985.

In 1988 two further levels (i.e. records types) were added to the database, one containing numerical and categorical data from the RIQ 1988 (type 3 record) and the other containing textual data from the RIQ 1988 (type 4 records). Thus the final form of the database involved seventy-three firms treated as cases, with four record types attached to each firm (or case), two record types containing numerical and categorical data and two record types containing textual data. For convenience, I refer to the database as having four levels, each level referring to a type of record. This is illustrated in figure 2.6. At the time of updating and extending the database in 1988, the opportunity was taken to undertake a full audit of the data mounted in 1985 by reference to the original physical interview schedules. In the autumn of 1989 a further full audit was undertaken of the data added in 1988, again by reference to the original schedules. Some design modifications were also implemented in autumn 1989 to enhance the compatibility of records. As a consequence one hopes that the data, whilst not perfect, are of about as high a quality as the usual human and computing resources will permit.

Once fully installed, the database contained 29,200 data items in the AQ 1985; 2,635 data items in the SSI 1985; and 3,519 data items in the RIQ 1988 making 35,354 data items in all. Allowing a mean value of 4 characters per data item the total disk space used was 141.416 k bytes.

So much, then, for the contents of the database. I turn now to the uses to which it may be put.

2.4 MANIPULATION OF THE DATABASE

I mentioned above the way in which a flat file approach to database construction minimized, by design, the extent to which structure was imposed on the data. The data are simply a set of tables. These tables may be manipulated by an algebra or a logical calculus. However, on the grounds of simplicity, a language which is as similar to English as possible is to be preferred. The best known of such languages is SQL (Structured Query Language) first developed by IBM for internal purposes, but now used much more widely. It is this language that was used for database manipulations in the present study. The full 'vocabulary' is rich and extensive, but here I wish to do no more than illustrate the use of a very limited part of it, motivating discussion by small firms examples which have a bearing on other parts of this book.

The basic building block of the SQL language is the 'select' command. For example, if numerical and categorical data on firms in 1985 are gathered in the type 1 record of the database relating to the AQ 1985, and denoted as level 1, a select statement might take the form:

select firm sic employ trainno from 1 where employ le 2

One is interested here in firms at the very lower end of the size distribution, for which employment is less than or equal to (i.e. 'le') 2 persons. For such firms, one wants to know whether they take on trainees, and if so, how many. Further, one wants to know which industrial classification (SIC code) each of these SBEs lies within. This sort of information might be relevant to an analysis of training functions in an enterprise culture. I can report, having implemented the above instruction, that twenty-six firms (35 per cent) employed two or less full-time workers. The database also provides all the requested SICs and full information on trainees, but they are too lengthy to report upon in detail in this illustration. Briefly, just four of these firms with less than three employees also employ trainees. That is just 5 per cent of the total and only 15 per cent of this sub-sample of very small firms. Two of these SBEs were in manufactures and construction, and two were in transport and services. By contrast, 47 per cent of firms employing more than two persons did also employ trainees, the great bulk (82 per cent) of these being in manufactures and construction. Here, the average number of trainees was two. Broadly, the training function in this sample tends to be most fostered in the larger SBEs in manufactures. To pick out those specific firms which employed two or less full-timers and had trainees (irrespective of numbers), one would write the instruction,

select firm from 1 where employ le 2 and train eq 1

Here, train = 1 is the value of the binary variable when the firm does employ trainees. Such binary variables are a common feature of the database.

Other refinements are possible. As suggested above, one could look at the distribution of the SBEs across industrial classifications. SICs of 60 or over relate to transport and services. Thus the instruction:

select firm sic from 1 where employ le 2 and sic ge 60

gives us the number of SBEs in transport and services that employ less than three people. There were twelve of these (46 per cent of the sub-sample for which employment $\leqslant 2$). Further, one can focus on more qualitative issues. Referring now to the RIQ 1988, one might ask whether the owner-managers of such firms sensed the emergence of an enterprise culture in Scotland since 1985.[13] To be even more specific, what was the reaction of an SBE in, say, wholesale distribution (SIC = 61) and an SBE in, say, recreational services (SIC = 97)? Level 1 of the database informs us that two firms were in the relevant size range and operating in wholesale distribution in 1985. Level 4 of the database informs us that one of these owner-managers thought that the government had 'led the way' and that more people would 'have a go on their own'. This owner-manager observed that older SBEs had better subsequent survival rates than younger SBEs.

According to level 3 of the database the other owner-manager in wholesale distribution (whose SBE distributed cane- and basketware) had ceased trading by 1988 and could not be traced. There were also two firms in the sub-sample operating in recreational services in 1985. One owner-manager, a tour operator, thought the successful setting up of many small firms selling tours in recent years was indicative of an emerging enterprise culture. The other SBE in recreational services had ceased trading by 1988, though a different owner-manager was running a different business from the same premises in 1988. All the above qualitative information was extracted from level 4 (the type 4 records) in the database which held text from the RIQ 1988 (see figure 2.6).

Pursuing qualitative evidence further, one could extract text from the type 2 records (i.e. level 2 of the database) which related to the probes of the SSI 1985.[14] For example, for the firm in wholesale distribution that survived, a detailed account was given of the nature of rivalry. The SBE was a wholesale wine business. The owner-manager felt the increased pressure of competition mounting 'day by day'. A particular pressure was felt from brewers who had diversified into wine sales because wine had become fashionable and beer sales were on the wane. It was felt that profit margins of SBEs in wine distribution were being squeezed by these new big players in the market. Balanced against this, in 1985 wine sales were growing at 24 per cent per annum in the UK and were expected to continue at this rate for two further years, with market saturation being reached after five years. It was felt that cheap continental holidays had given customers favourable consumption experience of wine, which had subsequently encouraged the boom in the UK market. Brewers who had diversified into wine had high strategic stakes and were here to stay.

For the firm in recreational services that survived, the tour operator, a similarly full account of rivalry was given. The fact that many SBEs operated in the business was explained by low fixed costs and opportunities for specialization. The number of firms was continuing to rise because of perceived growth potential in Scotland. The location was felt to be well suited to touring both because of Scotland's natural beauty and because an extensive infrastructure, which tour operators could readily utilize, was already in place. It was observed that there was as much specialization amongst tour operators as there were kinds of holidays. Seasonality meant that there was intermittent overcapacity, but at the time of interview in 1985 the owner-manager was experiencing excess demand for his firm's services and was sub-contracting. He felt that the industry was robust, and markets were so highly fragmented that SBEs could always find niches that did not overlap with other firms' markets. This clustering of products in tours can be explained by the information externality analysed by Pepall (1990). Firms can observe information about demand by looking at the market for similar products produced by rivals. At low cost they can market new goods in those parts of characteristics space which are 'spanned' by the qualities of existing products (over characteristics like transport, meals, accommodation, and entertainment).

Both the examples on rivalry are of firms that survived to 1988 and which operated in buoyant markets. One could go on to enquire why these two firms survived but their partner firms in the same SIC classifications did not. The failed firm in wholesale distribution did not complete the SSI 1985, but the failed firm in recreational services did. The owner-manager in the latter case ran an SBE which provided 'kit' aeroplanes for aerobatics. In 1985, looking at the agenda item on rivalry, one notes the owner-manager expressing doubts about his product and the market. It depended on the existence of a special type of customer who had 'flying in his blood' and was 'very self-indulgent'. Investment was over a long period of time and during that time there was no return; only four kits could be constructed a year; and government regulations on components and construction were very strict. Clearly, survival for this firm was not going to be easy. One can probe further, using two good predictors of survival, as revealed in chapter 9, the gearing ratio and cash flow. Higher gearing lowers the probability of survival, as does the existence of cash flow problems. Accessing level 1 of the database, using select commands similar to those above, one discovers that of the two firms in recreational services both had experienced cash flow difficulties, but the one which failed (the kit aircraft firm) was much higher geared (250 per cent compared to 75 per cent) and arguably, therefore, more exposed to risk. Looking at the two firms in wholesale distribution, the one that survived (the wine distributor) had not experienced cash flow problems, whereas the one that failed (the cane- and basketware distributor) had. Further, the one that survived had a zero gearing (i.e. no debt at all), whereas the one that failed had a 400 per cent gearing ratio. One could go on and make the investigations increasingly complex, looking at advertising form, advertising strategy, assets, and so on, but perhaps enough has been done to demonstrate the methodology.

The sorts of data I have referred to above are very diverse, and have been presented in terms of tightly defined variables (for example, employment) or well-defined agenda items (for example, rivalry). They are intended to be illustrative, and were also chosen for intrinsic interest and to introduce ideas to be used later in the book. The significant point to realize is that all the above data, numerical, categorical, and textual, were obtained without departing from a computer terminal. All retrievals were obtained using the SIR software. In a more complicated context, the characterization of the 'representative SBE' in the previous chapter was achieved using similar, but obviously much more extensive, database manipulations.

2.5 CONCLUSION

This chapter has largely been concerned with research design: with instrumentation; and with the systematic organization of the data obtained from the instruments in a relational database. Many examples have been given, but they were all illustrative. My purpose now is to move on from mere illustration to more serious and systematic analysis.

APPENDIX TO CHAPTER 2

Summary of administered questionnaire (AQ 1985)

1 *General*
- SIC code
- starting date
- employee details
- legal form of business
- turnover
- product groups and products
- principal market
- market share
- major and minor competitors
- extent of product differentiation
- customer characteristics

2 *Pricing*
- price/volume decision
- price level determination
- competitor interdependence in pricing
- pricing over the business cycle

3 *Costs*
- division into fixed and variable costs
- marginal cost
- capacity constraint
- total cost schedule

4 *Sales and competition*
- market research methods
- price elasticity: controlled by magnitude of price change, competitors reactions, and phase of business cycle
- extent of elbow-room in pricing
- pricing strategy by market segment
- price discrimination and bulk discounting
- price controls
- transaction v. list price
- forms of advertising
- advertising over the business cycle
- forms of competition, including dominant form

5 *Finance*
- start-up advice
- initial and current assets
- start-up finance: availability, types, security
- trajectory of gearing ratio over next three years
- usefulness of special financial schemes (e.g. EAS)
- cash-flow difficulties
- external finance
- expected growth

Semi-structured interview agenda (SSI 1985)

1 *Competitive forces*

1.1 Rivalry
Probe on:
industry concentration and balance
industry growth
fixed costs relative to value added

intermittent overcapacity
extent of product differentiation
diversity of competitors
level of strategic stakes
entry and exit barriers

1.2 Customers

   1.2.1 Bargaining leverage of customers
         Probe on:
            customers' concentration
            seller dependence
            relative buyer volume
            customers' switching costs
            ability to backward integrate
            extent of customers' information

   1.2.2 Price sensitivity of customers
         Probe on:
            significance of costs in relation to total costs of customers
            extent of differentiation of products purchased
            profitability
            bearing of your product on customers' product quality
            motivation of customer

1.3 Suppliers
    Probe on:
       extent of suppliers' concentration
       suppliers' in relation to customers' concentration
       availability of substitutes
       significance of suppliers' product as a customer's input
       extent of differentiation of supplier group's products
       switching costs of customers as compared with suppliers
       ability to forward integrate

1.4 Potential entrants
    Probe on:
       economies of scale
       product differentiation
       capital requirements
       switching costs
       access to distribution channels
       absolute cost advantage including:
          • product know-how or design characteristics
          • favourable access to inputs
          • favourable location
          • government subsidies
          • learning or experience curve
       government policy (regulation, pollution control, etc.)
       expected retaliation
       entry deterring price

1.5 Substitutes
    Probe on:
       products that perform the same function as industry's
       relative value/price of substitutes

substitutes produced by high profit industries
collective industry response to substitutes
customers' propensity to substitute

2 Competitive strategy

2.1 Cost leadership
Probe on:
value chain and assignment of costs and assets
cost drivers and their interaction
competitor's value chain
relative costs of competitors and their sources
strategies to lower relative costs including:
- control of cost drivers
- reconfiguration of value chain
- reconfiguration of downstream value

trade-off between differentiation and cost reduction
sustainability of cost reduction strategy

2.2 Differentiation
Probe on:
identification of real customer
identification of customer's value chain
customer's purchasing criteria
existing and potential sources of uniqueness in firm's value chain
identification of existing and potential sources of differentiation
value activities that create the most valuable differentiation for customers
(relative to costs of differentiation)
sustainability of differentiation strategy
cost reduction in activities that do not affect differentiation

2.3 Focus
Probe on:
whether strategy is towards cost or differentiation focus or both strategically
relevant segments including:
- product variety
- customer type
- channel (i.e. immediate buyer)
- customer location

significance of chosen segment(s) for competitive advance
interrelations among segments

sustainability of focus against:
- broadly targeted competitors
- imitators
- segment substitution

3 Defensive strategy

3.1 Increasing barriers to entry
Probe on:
filling product gaps
blocking channel access
raising customers' switching costs
raising costs of product trial
defensively increasing scale economies

defensively increasing capital requirements
foreclosing alternative technologies
tying up suppliers
raising costs of competitors' inputs
defensively pursuing interrelationships with other firms
encouraging government or agency policies that raise barriers
forming coalitions to raise barriers
forming coalitions to co-opt challengers

3.2 Increasing retaliation which challengers can expect
Probe on:
signalling commitment to defend
signalling erection of barriers
establishing blocking positions
matching guarantees
raising own penalty of exit or of loss of market share
accumulating retaliatory resources
encouraging 'good' competitors
setting examples
establishing defensive coalitions

3.3 Lowering the inducement for attack
Probe on:
reducing profit targets
managing competitors' assumptions

3.4 Deterrence
Probe on:
choosing defensive tactics to block likely attacks
managing the firm's image as a tough defender
setting realistic profit expectations
using industry scenarios to examine deterrence possibilities
knowledge of specific sources of barriers
anticipation of likely challengers (especially dissatisfied competitors)
forecasting likely avenues of attack

3.5 Responding to attack
Probe on:
putting priority on early response
investing in early discovery of moves by:
● contact with suppliers
● contact with advertising media
● monitoring of attendance at trade shows
● contact with most adventurous customers in industry
● monitoring of technical conferences, college courses, etc.
basing response on reasons for attack
deflecting challengers
taking challengers seriously
viewing response as a way to gain position
disrupting test or introductory markets
leap-frogging with new product or process
litigation (e.g. patent, anti-trust suits)

Re-interview administered questionnaire (RIQ 1988)

Part 1

Identity of firms and owner-manager:

● Whether still trading, and if not what became of firm and owner-manager

Part 2

Characteristics of SBEs first examined in 1985:

● retrospective questions on data too sensitive to request in 1985: net profit; profitability
● innovation and competitiveness
● size in 1988 of SBE examined in 1985: turnover, employment, assets
● output changes: scale; returns to scale; output mix; main product line
● skill shortages: extent of; effect on growth; how filled (e.g. training, paying premium rates)
● financial structure: gearing in 1988; trajectory of gearing 1986, 1987, and 1988
● perception of enterprise culture

Part II
Statistical analysis

3 The typical small business enterprise

3.1 INTRODUCTION

Before becoming immersed in abstract argument and econometric details, a more concrete approach may assist the reader in understanding the nature of the typical small business enterprise (SBE) with which I shall be dealing. In his influential study of *The Economics of Small Firms* (1981), Graham Bannock opened his book with a riveting description of a small business and its owner-manager in a way which would have done credit to a novelist. In a sense, he created a picture. I would not want to copy that memorable device here, but the illuminating impression it made does suggest to me that some kind of picture of the central object of analysis in this volume, the small business enterprise, would be helpful as a reference point.

Rather than proceed as Bannock did, I want to attempt something more prosaic, expanding on an example used in the preface to Reid and Jacobsen (1988). It is to provide a characterization of a typical or average small business enterprise. The concept does not refer to any specific firm in a population of firms but rather to an idealized firm, which is best described as possessing average attributes in relation to the distribution of attributes of firms.[1] By considering this fictional, but typical, firm and in some measure also the attributes of its rivals, I hope to give the reader a good intuitive feel for the population of firms that is analysed in this book. As well as being a good way of getting an immediate simple grasp of what are in reality tens of thousands of data points, the reader will be prepared for the idea of a typical or representative firm about which one can make predictions using econometric methods.[2]

3.2 CHARACTERISTICS OF THE TYPICAL SBE

The typical firm of this study is a new firm (nearly three years old) which has been set up after seeking advice from an Enterprise Trust in Scotland. It employed eight full-time workers in 1985 and fifteen in 1988. Thus the typical firm is a growing firm. This applies to several measures of growth, including assets. For example, between 1985 and 1988 sales turnover (excluding VAT) grew about threefold, as did total assets (in book value, net of depreciation). The main growth in employment created by the representative small firm (see table 3.1) was for full-time workers, with part-time workers and trainees enjoying far less of an increase in employment opportunities.

In institutional form (for example, sole proprietorship, partnership etc.) the typical firm is a private company. It sells over eighty products, which can be classified into three product groups. The number of products may seem large, but it is a consequence partly of advanced market fragmentation and partly of minor variations in size, colour, odour and other dimensions which are very flexible attributes of product specification. Thus, though plastic pipes are clearly a product group, or part of a product group, the product 'a three-inch diameter white plastic pipe with a smooth finish' is different from the product 'a two-inch diameter black plastic pipe with crackle finish', over several dimensions. Looked at in this way, product proliferation is inevitable.

The typical firm, small though it is, does not operate solely in a local or regional market but regards Scotland as a whole as its principal market. It is surrounded by some rivals with regional markets (25 per cent) and others with no more than local markets (20 per cent). A few (2 per cent) operate internationally. The typical firm is very small in relation to its principal market, and has less than a one per cent share of market sales. It can readily distinguish major from minor competitors and has about three of each. Its principal product is a mildly differentiated commodity which it would characterize as 'similar' to that of its rivals. Its customers vary in the extent to which they are well-informed. The typical customer *is* well-informed, and has a least some familiarity with the technical features of the products, and some experience, directly or indirectly, of consuming them.

Table 3.1 Growth of the typical firm

Size measure	Year	
	1985	*1988*
Full-time employees	8	15
Part-time employees	3	3
Trainees	1	2
Assets (book value, net of depreciation)	£76,360 (1985 prices)	£210,327 (1988 prices) £186,130 (1985 prices)
Sales (excluding VAT)	£175,000 (1985 prices)	£680,608 (1988 prices) £602,308 (1985 prices)

Note: C.P.I. price index = 100 in 1985 and 113 in 188

In setting price, the typical firm takes account of the volume it expects to sell of the product. Price is set as a flexible percentage mark-up on unit direct cost, with flexibility being used to improve gross profitability. Profitability, measured as the ratio of gross profit less taxes to the book value of assets, is 29 per cent. Net profit (after taxes and directors' remunerations), is £6,500 at 1985 prices. This gives a net profitability of 8.5 per cent in 1985, after taxes and directors' fee.

Though price might be held down to beat competitors, the typical firm does not necessarily behave conjecturally with respect to rivals' prices. If a boom in demand cannot be met from stocks, it typically responds by increasing overtime or shift-work. It will then most likely increase capacity by means which could include recruiting more personnel, followed by lengthening of the order book, engaging sub-contractors. raising prices, and finally by buying up rival firms.[3]

During a slump in demand caused by a recession, the typical firm is likely to respond first by increasing sales effort, followed by reducing overtime. Then capacity is reduced, which may include laying off personnel, followed by efforts to improve productivity or efficiency. Next price is cut, indicating, as in the boom case, that price is by no means the prime strategic instrument of small firms. Finally, average stockholdings are reduced and short-time working may be introduced.

The typical firm can distinguish between fixed and variable costs and finds this distinction useful. It can compute marginal cost should it propose an output increase, and can estimate its maximum (or capacity) output. However, it typically works well below capacity output: perhaps at 75 per cent of capacity. This firm is aware of bearing a positive fixed cost at zero output and expects unit and marginal cost to fall as output rises.

The typical small firm does not engage in formal market research methods, though it does advertise. Its usual form of advertising is competitive, as opposed to generic, aiming to promote its own product over that of its rivals. Usually no attempt is made to vary advertising with business conditions: certainly it is unlikely to be cut in a boom, and will probably not be increased in a recession. It perceives competition to be generally strong (perhaps over quality and service) but weak in some respects (perhaps over price).

At inception, the typical firm sought advice and found the bank manager, the accountant and the Enterprise Trust (ET) of roughly similar importance. Less important were the Scottish Development Agency[4] and family or friends, with the local authority being of least importance. The size of the typical firm in terms of the book value of total assets at inception, was £15,300 at nominal prices (about £17,790 at 1985 prices) nearly three years earlier (i.e. in 1982).

The typical small firm started up in business using only personal finance, and in this limited sense did not find it difficult to obtain finance to start the business. It operates with an equity gearing ratio of about 0.7 which is above the minimum of 0.4 and below the maximum of 1.7 attained since inception.

At inception, equity gearing was just over one in value. It expects its gearing to fall over a three-year time horizon, year by year, but finds it can be over-optimistic about actually achieving this.[5]

Special financial schemes were not found to be particularly helpful for financial inception. The typical firm has encountered cash-flow difficulties in its almost three years of existence, caused by a complex of forces, of which an insufficient overdraft facility and delinquent debtors are the most important, followed by over-investment (e.g. in stocks or capital goods), an inadequate credit policy with suppliers or buyers, and delinquent buyers. It has experienced the need to use external finance since inception, mainly because of purchasing new plant and equipment. This external funding has been in the form of debt finance. Also important in creating cash-flow difficulties were: acquiring new or expanded premises; and increasing the average levels of stocks (i.e. inventories). The hiring of new employees was another, but minor, reason.

Because of innovation, the typical firm's competitive position changed between 1985 and 1988. There was roughly a 150 per cent increase in the physical output of the main product line, with a very slight (about 1 per cent) associated reduction in unit costs of production. This was also associated with a change in the output mix in favour of the main product line, amounting to a shift of about 10 per cent in terms of the proportion of value of total sales. This re-positioning in the market is commonplace amongst rivals as well.

The typical small firm has not itself experienced any shortage of labour over the period 1985 to 1988, though a significant proportion (almost one-third) of its rivals have experienced labour shortages. For those rivals who were skill-constrained, none thought this had caused a contraction of their operations. In trying to deal with skills gaps, the rivals of the typical firm faced diverse problems. Of those which can be categorized, meeting the costs of training was the main problem, followed by assessing how rivals were themselves coping in terms of their competitive 'edge'. Less important, but non-trivial, were (in declining order of importance) problems like releasing personnel for training, paying premium rates for scarce labour skills, and finally identifying the skills required to fill the perceived gap.

The typical firm of this study is confident that an enterprise culture is emerging in Scotland. Rivals of the typical firm who in 1988 no longer ran the same business as three years earlier (about a quarter) were often still in business, usually running a new, but similar, business and less probably running a new, and different, business. Few went into waged or salaried employment. A few quite naturally ended up drawing a pension and/or retirement benefit, or living off private income. It is also uncommon for the owner-managers of firms rivalrous to the typical firm to end up drawing unemployment benefit or social security: once an entrepreneur, always an entrepreneur.

The typical firm operates in markets in which industrial concentration is not high. It regards competition as intense, mainly because there are low entry and exit barriers. Capital requirements are low, scale economies are not paramount, and advertising is not intense or sophisticated. It tries to maintain a competitive edge over rivals by the quality of service, emphasising reliability, courtesy, quick delivery, and efficient service, as well as by the more obvious commercial methods of competitive pricing and vigorous selling. Establishing a stable, contented – and hence loyal – client list of customers is an important objective of the typical SBE. It is constantly under pressure to absorb the fluctuations in fortunes that impinge on larger rivals (for example, by taking up excess orders in good times, but being deprived of referrals in bad times) and resists this by trying to stabilize its customer base.

The typical firm purchases factors of production in markets where there are many suppliers. Apart from skilled labour, many of its factor inputs are relatively homogeneous and the price dispersion between suppliers is small. Costs of switching between suppliers are therefore low. The typical firm has the somewhat arrogant belief that substitute products supplied by rivals are inferior. Confidence in the existence of a sound market is boosted by the fact that others are willing to operate in it as well.

In terms of Porter's terminology, the typical firm adopts a focus strategy which emphasises low cost and product differentiation. Its principal strategic segment is location: either in physical space, or characteristics space. Over time, its market positioning can vary markedly. This is not to be confused with failure, but is rather an aspect of flexibility or adaptation. The firm is aware that, of its available strategic instruments (e.g. quality), sales effort has the major effect on revenue. Therefore it devotes considerable resources to it, in an informal sense. Drumming up business through trade contacts is more important than refined market research and exploitation techniques. Its principal determinant of cost variations is capacity utilization. Limiting the extent of excess capacity (which may frequently be as high as 25 per cent) is a major operational goal

Defensive strategy is rudimentary, mainly because, being relatively young, the typical firm is more concerned with discovering or creating market niches rather than with defending them. Furthermore, it attempts to foster 'good' rivals who will refer business to it on a reciprocal basis. Its planning horizon is short, certainly no more than three years, mainly because small size and uncertainty preclude any deterministic view of the firm's future progress. Information about markets and innovations is obtained through channels like trade shows, suppliers, customers, and trade journals, but they are largely anodynes in a complex, changeable economic world in which adapting to unseen contingencies is a better survival strategy than trying to plan the unplannable.

3.3 SIMPLE STATISTICAL ANALYSIS OF THE TYPICAL SBE

To conclude my discussion of the typical SBE, I should explain a statistical device that arises from it. I talked of the typical firm as a kind of statistical average over a set (or vector) of attributes, like employment, assets, profits, gearing, etc. In doing so, my use of this version of the typical SBE was descriptive. Going beyond this, an important use of it is to make qualitative or, even better, quantitative predictions about the reaction of the typical SBE to a change in external (or exogenous) conditions. For example, a qualitative prediction might be that the entry of new firms in an industry would decrease the sales and lower the profitability of the typical firm. A quantitative prediction for the same example would be of the form: x per cent of new entry (for example in sales) would cause a y per cent reduction in sales and a z per cent reduction in profitability of the typical SBE. Theory alone might suffice for the first prediction, though it would certainly help if the theorizing were informed by familiarity with the empirical universe to which it related. The combined use of theory and evidence is intrinsic to the second type of prediction, and is facilitated by the use of econometric methods.

Suppose we had, say, a systematic relationship between profitability and the debt/equity (i.e. gearing) ratio of the SBE. In its simplest form it might be expressed:

$$\pi = \alpha + \beta G + \varepsilon \tag{3.1}$$

where π is profitability, G is (equity) gearing, α and β are constant coefficients and ε is a random variable. I use this simple linear example for illustrative purposes only. In general, such a relationship would be implied by the theoretical work of De Meza and Webb (1987, 1988). It suggests that firms with a high fraction of self-finance (i.e. low gearing) will be more profitable on average than those with a low fraction. This is, β is thought to be negative. One can identify the particular realization of this relationship for the typical SBE by evaluating the fitted average relationship (for example, fitted by least squares, using cross-section inter-industry data, to determine estimates $\hat{\alpha}$, $\hat{\beta}$ of the parameters) at the point of means $(\bar{\pi}, \bar{G})$ (or at the mode, or median, or whatever average one wants to regard as 'typical'). Thus the relationship, for the typical SBE is:

$$\bar{\pi} = \hat{\alpha} + \hat{\beta}\bar{G} \tag{3.2}$$

Now the qualitative prediction that lower gearing will be associated with higher profitability can be made a quantitative one, by reference, for example, to the estimated elasticity of profitability with respect to gearing:

$$k = \frac{\partial \pi}{\partial G} \cdot \frac{G}{\pi} \bigg|_{\substack{G=\bar{G} \\ \pi=\bar{\pi}}} = \frac{\hat{\beta}\bar{G} < 0}{\bar{\pi}} \tag{3.3}$$

where k is a precise numerical prediction of the responsiveness of profitability to gearing. This is, of course, all simple regression analysis, but the important point to note is that the relationship one is working with is derived from a distribution of attributes across firms. Here, one is interested in what is implied for the typical (average) small business enterprise, which is to be thought of as being governed by this typical or average response.

Bearing in mind that this example is used for illustrative purposes only, an idea of practical procedures can be conveyed by estimating (3.1) above by ordinary least squares. The data I use for this example are a sub-set of the data obtained by field work methods for SBEs using methods described in chapter 1 (page 8). Profitability (π) was measured as the ratio of net profit in 1985 (as reported in 1988) to total assets (book value) in 1985, in percentage terms. Gearing (G) was measured as the ratio of borrowing (typically from a bank) to the owner-manager's injection of finance at financial inception, as reported in 1985, in percentage terms. Variants on the estimation method reported, including the introduction of further variables, non-linearities and transformations of the error term can be undertaken, but detract from the uncluttered presentation which is my aim here, without adding much further light.

Ordinary least squares estimation of (3.1) on a sub-sample of forty-eight observations on (π_i, G_i) gave:

$$\hat{\pi} = 31.225 \quad - \quad 0.24128 \ G$$
$$\quad\quad (1.6751) \quad (-3.1137)$$
$$R^2 = \ 0.1741 \quad F(1,46) \quad = 9.695 \tag{3.4}$$

where t-ratios are given in brackets under the regression coefficients. The t-ratio on the coefficient of G is highly statistically significant (prob value less than 0.0025) as is the F-statistic (prob value less than 0.01).[6] The gearing elasticity of profitability, as given by k in expression (3.3) above, is evaluated at the point of means ($\bar{\pi} = 4.9508$, $\bar{G} = 108.90$) giving:

$$k = \frac{\hat{\beta}\bar{G}}{\pi} = \frac{-0.24128(108.909)}{4.9508} = -5.3075 \tag{3.5}$$

which suggests a high degree of negative responsiveness of profitability to variations in the gearing ratio. Thus a 10 per cent reduction in gearing should lead the typical SBE to experience a 50 per cent increase in profitability. More important than the model and this specific result is that (3.4) and (3.5) provide very simple illustrations of how the typical SBE can be used in not only qualitative, but also quantitative, predictions.

3.4 CONCLUSION

To set the scene, and to illustrate the motivation of this study, I have introduced early the concept of the typical small business enterprise (SBE). I have indicated what its main characteristics are, and how one can make predictions about it. However, the developments in this chapter have all been by way of illustration. I move now to more substantive analysis.

4 Cost curves and scale economies

4.1 INTRODUCTION

In this chapter I report on subjective cost curve estimates obtained by field work methods using the 1985 administered questionnaire and show cards. They indicate the prevalence of static, short-run increasing returns up to maximal physical output for a wide range of products in manufactures, services, construction, and transport. The dynamic scale effect, measured over a three-year time period using data from the 1988 re-interview questionnaire, is less clear and suggests a slight average tendency to dynamic increasing returns. Long-run equilibrium, as identified by unconstrained cross-section production function estimates, appears to be characterized by decreasing returns to scale. Finally, I report on more qualitative evidence on scale economies and costs, using semi-structured interview evidence.

4.2 BACKGROUND AND METHODS

In a much-debated study, Eiteman and Guthrie (1952) were bold enough to suggest that one way of finding out about the cost curves of businesses was simply to ask businessmen. They used a postal questionnaire sent to 1,000 manufacturing enterprises in the USA, and got responses from 366 (i.e. 36.6 per cent) of them. The enterprises employed between 500 and 5,000 employees and typically, it was claimed, a senior executive officer (for example, president, vice-president, treasurer or secretary) replied, rather than an accountant or production manager. Pictures of eight possible unit cost curves were sent, with a single sentence of explanation attached to each. By far the most commonly cited cost curve (61 per cent) was one in which unit cost fell until capacity output was achieved. It was described as follows: 'If you choose this curve you believe that unit costs are high at minimum output, and that they decline gradually to capacity at which point they are lowest'. Also popular (35 per cent) was the notion that unit costs fell until capacity was almost reached, at which point they rose slightly. No other response got more than 4 per cent confirmation.

One can dispute the validity of this method. Perhaps the chief executive was not the best person to ask (though whether he completed the form, rather than his accountant, is a moot point), and possibly the notion of capacity that many had in mind was optimum (i.e. unit cost minimizing) capacity rather than physically maximal capacity. However, with some changes of design these sorts of questions have been used again quite successfully, by Nowotny and Walther (1978) for a sample of firms in Austria and by Wied-Nebbeling (1975) for a sample of firms in the former state of West Germany. Again, large enterprises were the focus of interest, and the postal questionnaire method was used.

This chapter aims to extend the scope of this method to the case of small business enterprises (SBEs), and to improve its efficacy by using field work methods rather than a postal questionnaire. As the SBEs of the sample are very small, with an average of eight full-time employees and six product ranges, agency-type problems were unlikely to be a significant impediment to the investigation.[1] That is, unlike in the case of the corporate enterprises which were the subjects of the previously mentioned studies, one has no problem of divorce of ownership and control to contend with, and little likelihood of ignorance of cost conditions on the part of owner-managers, nor a desire to misrepresent them. This chapter also augments evidence from show cards with other forms of evidence. Here, I investigate the properties of cost curves of small entrepreneurial firms using all three instruments: the relatively elaborate administered questionnaire of 1985 (AQ 1985); the semi-structured interview of 1985 (SSI 1985); and the shorter reinterview questionnaire applied to the survivors of the same set of SBEs who were still in business in 1988 (RIQ 1988). For comparative purposes, four forms of evidence from the same sample of SBEs are brought to bear on this issue of scale economies. First, short-run unit cost curves are looked at using show cards from the AQ 1985. Second, dynamic scale effects are looked at over a three-year time period, using data generated by appropriate questions in the RIQ 1988. Third, static returns to scale are also investigated using cross-section econometric estimates of production functions, unrestricted by degree of homogeneity, fitted to data generated by the AQ 1985. Fourth, more qualitative case-study evidence from the SSI 1985 is used. The results obtained by these four methods are important, for example, in terms of what one can expect SBEs to achieve in an extended EC market after 1992.

4.3 SUBJECTIVE EVIDENCE FROM SHOW CARDS

In the 1985 administered questionnaire (AQ 1985), the author and a co-worker interviewed owner-managers about the forms of their cost curves for their main product line.[1] The curves presented for examination, and the explanations attached, are as in figure 4.1, which has already been discussed from a methodological standpoint in chapter 2.

The respondent was told by the interviewer that the question aimed to get an idea of how costs varied as output was increased up to the maximum possible. They were asked to examine 'cost pictures' on sheets of paper (known as 'show cards' in the questionnaire design literature) and asked to return to the interviewer the sheets which displayed costs that approximated to their own firm's pattern. The sheets were handed over for perusal and then the respondent (typically the owner-manager him or herself) was told, further, that underneath each picture was an explanation in words which could be used in making choices. The respondent was asked to request an explanation if the meaning of any picture was not clear. The choice having been made, the sheets were returned.

I turn attention now to the results obtained from the use of show cards. The percentages of the total responses allocated to each picture (cost curve) are indicated in brackets next to each picture and its associated explanation in figure 4.1. The clear favourite (55 per cent) as a description of costs for the main product line was picture (b), depicting falling average variable and falling average total costs at all output levels. Also regarded as plausible were picture (a) the linear total cost curve (11 per cent), (d) the falling reversed-S (roughly, cubic) cost curve (15 per cent), and (e) the linear cost curve, with tight capacity (14 per cent). The paradigm neoclassical case, giving rise to U-shaped average variable, average total, and marginal costs, with marginal cost cutting each average cost curve at its minimum, is of course pictured in (d) (15 per cent response).

Most owner-managers (93 per cent) recognized the distinction between fixed and variable costs (or synonyms for this, like overhead and prime costs) and most (94%) found this useful. In this sense, owner-managers were conceiving these cost pictures to be relevant to the short run. A capacity (also described in the interview as a 'maximum possible') output was recognized by 70 per cent of firms. For this majority who recognized a capacity output, the distribution of normal output was bi-modal, with 30 per cent of SBEs putting it at below 50 per cent, and 30 per cent putting it at 71 to 80 per cent. However, the norm appeared to be to work at reasonably high levels of capacity utilization, with 54 per cent of SBEs working at 71 per cent or more of capacity.

An accuracy check on the responses of owner-managers can be made from the cost curve in picture (e) which depicts a cost curve with a clear capacity point, beyond which costs shoot up. The other pictures do not rule out the existence of a capacity output, but picture (e) definitely rules it *in*. Of those owner-managers who had nominated picture (e), 70 per cent had recognized, by a response to an earlier question, that they had a capacity output, which suggests a reasonable level of response validity.

The findings of this part of the study, as they relate to the use of show cards, appear to confirm those of Eiteman and Guthrie (1952), and are consonant with many other forms of empirical evidence: statistical cost analysis, econometric estimates of cost curves, interviews, and survey data.[2] The sample excluded the agricultural, fishing, mining and quarrying sectors, thus ruling out the archetypal increasing cost industries. The SBEs of the sample

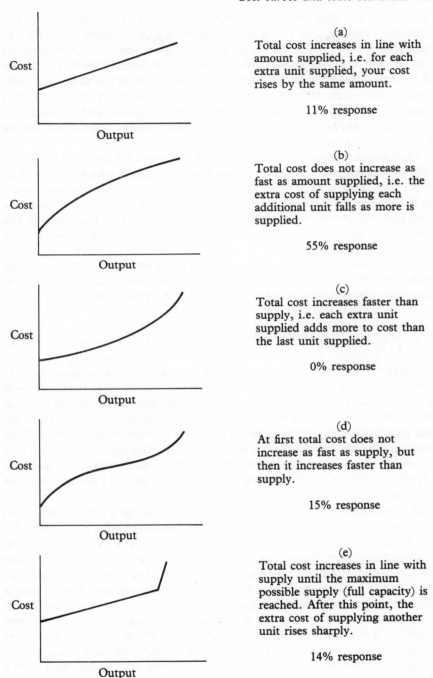

(a)
Total cost increases in line with amount supplied, i.e. for each extra unit supplied, your cost rises by the same amount.

11% response

(b)
Total cost does not increase as fast as amount supplied, i.e. the extra cost of supplying each additional unit falls as more is supplied.

55% response

(c)
Total cost increases faster than supply, i.e. each extra unit supplied adds more to cost than the last unit supplied.

0% response

(d)
At first total cost does not increase as fast as supply, but then it increases faster than supply.

15% response

(e)
Total cost increases in line with supply until the maximum possible supply (full capacity) is reached. After this point, the extra cost of supplying another unit rises sharply.

14% response

Figure 4.1 Cost curves and descriptions from show cards

were from manufacturing and construction (64 per cent), and services and transport (36 per cent), with manufacturing and services being the predominant firm groupings. In terms of SIC categories, all types of firms are represented under the most favoured pattern of costs (i.e. picture (b) in figure 4.1), with manufacturing (59 per cent) best represented but with a considerable representation also (25 per cent) from services. Groupings by cost curve type (a, b, c, d or e) are given in the appendix to this chapter (page 67), which indicates also the SIC code, the owner-manager's description of the main product group, and capacity utilization.

One would not wish to make too much of these category differences, for it is important to know not just the relevant sectors in which firms operate but also, in extremely precise terms, what product within their product range is being referred to when costs are described as continuously falling in unit and marginal terms. What seems clear is that the evidence in the short run for falling unit costs is overwhelming, and for falling marginal costs is substantial.

This bodes well for firms contemplating forays into larger European markets after 1992, but again one should interpret evidence cautiously. The cost patterns indicated were for experiences of limited output ranges.

4.4 QUESTIONNAIRE EVIDENCE ON DYNAMIC SCALE ECONOMIES

Outside the limited output ranges relevant to the short-run approach of the previous section a whole new picture emerges, especially if essentially new plant is installed to facilitate expansion. In 1988 all firms which had survived from 1985 (75 per cent) were investigated by myself and two co-workers, and the great bulk were reinterviewed. For those SBEs which had stayed in business, growth had generally been substantial. The average growth of physical output for the main product line between 1985 and 1988 was 150 per cent. Average growth in full-time employees was 88 per cent, in real assets was 144 per cent, and in real sales was 244 per cent. Thus growth over three years was substantial by any measure. An attempt was made to get at the notion of dynamic scale economies in a reinterview study in 1988, three years after the owner-manager had first been approached. In an interview the owner-manager was asked whether the output of his main product line had increased 'substantially' (meaning more than 20 per cent) since 1985. Subsidiary questions asked for an approximate figure, or range, for the percentage increase or decrease in output, and for the corresponding percentage change in unit variable cost. The latter is the crucial question from the viewpoint of this chapter. It was made clear that my interest was in cost per unit of the good or service, and that the relevant cost was variable, which shifts with output, as distinct from fixed or overhead, which does not. The questions from the RIQ 1988 revealed that between 1985 and 1988, the majority of small firms (55 per cent) had experienced output shifts of more than 20 per cent for their main product line. I noted above that the percentage output change on average for the sample was high, being + 150 per cent. On average, the corresponding change in unit variable cost was low, being − 1 per cent. Thus the evidence for dynamic scale economies overall is not great. When growth is rapid, unit costs may actually be pushed up, but this is justified if market opportunities must be snatched before they are exploited by eager rivals. The dispersion of patterns of dynamic scale economies and diseconomies was great for the sample, and it would be hard to make a reliable generalization.

4.5 ECONOMETRIC EVIDENCE FROM PRODUCTION FUNCTION ESTIMATES

As a summary, or descriptive device, to use the justification advanced by Schmalensee (1989), I also fitted a number of production functions to cross-section data from the AQ 1985. In a strict sense one talks of returns to scale proper by reference to a production function $y = f(x)$, with y output and x a vector of inputs, arguing that f(.) has homogeneity of degree k when $\mu^k y = f(\mu x)$ for $\mu > 0$. Then increasing or decreasing returns to scale prevail according to whether $k > 1$ or $k < 1$, with constant returns when $k = 1$. Returns to scale proper, in this sense, are a static, long-run concept. They can therefore be best approached using cross-section data at a given point in time. I ran estimates of two-factor production functions on data for all firms and for various subsets of firms using the AQ 1985, with the returns to scale parameter (i.e. degree of homogeneity of the functional form) unrestricted. The dependent variable was sales (excluding VAT, at 1985 prices) and the two independent variables (proxying the factors of production labour and capital) were number of full-time employees (*Employ*), and the book value of assets net of depreciation (*Passet*) reported in 1985 at nominal prices. Two types of production function were estimated, the Cobb-Douglas and the constant elasticity of substitution (CES). The Cobb-Douglas production function was first expressed in log-linear form and then estimated by ordinary least squares. The CES production function, after being subjected to a log-transformation, was estimated by non-linear least squares using the Davidon–Fletcher–Powell algorithm. Various tests of specification and robustness were applied to these estimates. Results for the production function estimates are given in Table 4.1.

The Cobb-Douglas specification, estimated by White's heteroskedastic consistent covariance estimators, suggests a greater elasticity of output with respect to employment (0.29) as compared to assets (0.17) and this is a feature of estimates with various sub-sets of data, and different definitions of the labour and capital variables. The sum of the exponents on the variables *Employ* and *Passet* was 0.46679 which is considerably less than unity. The t-value for testing the null hypothesis of constant returns to scale (i.e. $\alpha + \beta = 1$) was −9.428, which is highly statistically significant, and clearly suggests decreasing returns to scale. The generalized CES production

Table 4.1 Production function estimates

Cobb-Douglas:
log (PQ) = log A + α log(Passet) + β log(Employ)

Coefficient	Estimate	t-ratio
β	0.29139	3.7878
α	0.1744	2.2021
log A	−1.2129	−1.5641

$\bar{R}^2 = 0.4708$	$F(2,70) = 33.031$
$\overline{(\log PQ)} = 1.0469$	
SEE = 0.5342	n = 73

Test of Ho: $\alpha + \beta = 1$
gives $t(70) = -9.428$
$F(1,70) = 88.896$

CES: $\log(PQ) = \log \gamma - (\nu/\rho)\log[\delta(\text{Passet})^{-\rho} + (1 - \delta)(\text{Employ})^{-\rho}]$

Coefficient	Estimate	t-ratio
ν (degree of homogeneity)	0.43610	7.5050
γ	1.4418	7.7095
ρ	3.6226	5.6701
δ	0.30642	0.88259

n = 73

Legend: $PQ \equiv$ sales (excluding VAT) at 1985 prices; Passet $\equiv$ book value of assets (net of depreciation) at 1985 prices; Employ = number of full-time employees.

function estimates suggest similar properties of the data. In Table 4.1, the δ coefficient is the only one estimated with low precision. It is of the order of 0.3 for the variable *Passet*, with $(1 - \delta)$ being about 0.7 for the variable *Employ*. The ρ estimate suggests a low value for the elasticity of substitution (0.216 approximately, using $1/(1 + \rho)$), though low estimates of this parameter are commonly found in cross-section studies. It does cast some doubt on the wisdom of imposing the value of unity on this parameter. The degree of homogeneity parameter ν was highly statistically significant ($t = 7.5050$). Its magnitude of 0.43610 is consistent with the degree of homogeneity of 0.46679 displayed in the Cobb-Douglas case, and of course implies decreasing returns to scale.

The general findings are of a low elasticity of output with respect to the financial capital variable (*Passet*), a high elasticity of output with respect to the labour variable (*Employ*), and decreasing returns to scale. These conclusions are unaffected by using variants of the asset and employment variables. If labour is treated simply in terms of full-time employees, as in the examples in table 4.1, or in terms of more refined formulae for the workforce, estimates do not vary greatly. For example, one formula which was used for equivalent full-time employees, without enhancing the production function estimates, was: (full-time employees) + 0.5 (part-time employees) + 0.25 (trainees). Similarly, the capital (asset) variable can be tried in various forms. For example, it may be weighted by percentage capacity utilization. None of these adjustments altered the general picture for a variety of estimation procedures.

For a variety of sub-sets of the data, estimates were also well behaved. If one considers, for example, only the manufacturing enterprises (SIC codes from 22 to 49) for which one might perhaps most expect evidence of scale economies, Cobb-Douglas estimation on the 42 manufacturing observations yields coefficients of 0.33069 ($t = 2.2554$) on employment and 0.10527 ($t = 1.2317$) on assets. This gives a sum of exponents ($\alpha + \beta$) of 0.43596 which is much as for the full sample. The t-value for a test of the null hypothesis of constant returns to scale ($\alpha + \beta = 1$) was -6.2533. This firmly rejects constant returns and provides strong evidence for long-run, static decreasing returns to scale. Estimates of the coefficients also remained stable when sub-sets of data were employed using the robust estimation method of trimmed least squares.[3] For example, under 5 per cent trimming ten observations were required to be dropped. The coefficient on *Employ* was 0.2857 ($t = 3.4851$) and on *Passet* was 0.20142 ($t = 2.9147$) when estimated by trimmed least squares, both of which are close to the untrimmed estimates. The t-statistic for testing the null hypothesis of constant returns was -9.428 under trimmed least squares, again suggesting decreasing returns to scale.

Estimates in the CES case were robust under alternative choices of initial parameter values. For the estimates reported in table 4.1, I started off with $\nu = 0.3$, $\rho = 0.5$, $\gamma = 3.6$, and $\delta = 0.7$. When the different initializing values of $\nu = 0.4$, $\rho = 0.3$, $\gamma = 2.6$, and $\delta = 2.5$ were used, coefficient estimates were much the same. In this latter case the homogeneity parameter was estimated to be identical as $\hat{\nu} = 0.43610$ and the t-value was slightly larger (7.5425). This suggests robustness of the parameter estimates. It is further evidence for decreasing returns in the static, long-run sense.

4.6 CONCLUSION

To conclude, new evidence has been presented on scale economies in SBEs. In a static framework, the evidence for short-run scale economies, right up to capacity (in the sense of physically maximal) output is strong, over a diverse range of firms in manufactures and services. Further, my interview evidence is that in terms of batch production, a common practice in small firms, the outputs achieved whilst exploiting these economies can be large in relation to the firm's market niche. For example, a firm specializing in plastic injection mouldings was substantially the largest supplier of product lines like plastic shower rings in the UK. As another example, a firm supplying specialized rubber and cotton laminated blankets was the sole producer of this product line in Europe. Both firms engaged in very high volume production. In this sense, it is possible even for small firms to be 'large' in terms of their ability to exercise market power and to use scale as a potential barrier to entry. However, when small firms attempt to grow rapidly, cost controls may suffer: this can be a calculated risk, if handsome rewards seem likely from a rapid invasion of new market niches. It may be that this explains the less clear picture in the case of evidence on dynamic scale economies. Finally, for the case of static long-run returns to scale, using cross-sectionally estimated production functions, the evidence favours decreasing returns to scale. Further, this effect seems to be quite strong. This suggests that there is some merit in the argument that the ultimate scarce resource in the small entrepreneurial firm is the entrepreneur himself.[4] He is the fixed factor that cannot be made variable, even in the long run, and it is this which ultimately gives rise to decreasing returns. These decreasing returns may be viewed as arising from increasing agency costs as the firm grows larger. Owner-managed firms effectively bypass agency costs when they are small, but as they grow such costs arise inexorably. Faced with this, the small entrepreneurial firm must either stay small and run the risk of decline predicted by life cycle theories of the firm, or attempt to grow bigger, but with a modified organizational form which aims to minimize agency costs. Typically this involves some form of hierarchy, with associated control and monitoring devices, and often some change in capital structure, almost certainly involving outside equity and perhaps a form of market flotation.

The advantages of the show card evidence presented are as follows. First, it permits subjective cost evaluations by the respondents, in keeping with the so-called LSE subjective cost doctrine. Second, it uses responses from owner-managers, who are likely to be relatively skilful monitors and unlikely to be subject to 'agency effects' like misrepresentation. Third, in terms of investigative efficiency it has advantages of high or perfect response rates (mitigating the non-response bias of postal questionnaires) and considerable accuracy (given the presence of an informed interviewer familiar with the instrumentation). Finally it avoids the regression effect of statistical cost analysis based on a cross-section of firms, which tends to favour the 'discovery' of falling unit costs if lucky firms produce more, and unlucky firms produce less, than expected when contracts determining the costs of expected output were being concluded. The evidence presented suggests that short-run falling unit variable costs are other than a pure regression effect. Balanced against this short-run evidence is dynamic and long-run evidence. The dynamic evidence suggests almost constant returns, but may confound a number of disequilibrium effects. Certainly this average tendency to constant returns stands in contrast to the widely varying experience of individual firms with respect to dynamic increasing or decreasing returns to scale. The static, long-run evidence clearly points to decreasing returns to scale. These seem likely to be caused by the uniqueness, and therefore the indivisibility and fixity, of the entrepreneur himself in relation to his own small firm. To achieve larger size without paying the penalty of decreasing returns, small firms will have to change their organizational forms. From being firms where agency costs are zero, because no incentive and monitoring problems arise when they are small, they must become firms which tackle these problems as they grow larger, by an organizational design which attempts to minimize agency costs.

APPENDIX TO CHAPTER 4

Products and capacity for each type of cost curve

A 'Total cost increases in line with amount supplied, i.e. for each extra unit supplied, your cost rises by the same amount.'

% Nominating this type of cost curve = 11%

SIC code	Description of main product group	Capacity	% Capacity
46	Double-deck fun beds	Yes	95
35	Panelwork	No	★
47	Lamination	Yes	65
96	Travel services	Yes	95
49	Picture framing	Yes	55
67	Auto servicing	Yes	85
50	Quantity surveying	Yes	75
50	Housing services	Yes	75

B 'Total cost does not increase as fast as amount supplied, i.e. the extra cost of supplying each additional unit falls as more is supplied.'

% Nominating this type of cost curve = 55%

SIC code	Description of main product group	Capacity	% Capacity
96	Blind cleaning	Yes	> 50
49	Security printers blankets	Yes	65
43	Cardigans	Yes	55
32	Steel plate cylinders	Yes	75
84	Vending machines	No	★
16	Flue stack economizers	No	★
61	Cleaning chemicals	No	★
41	Pies	No	★
49	Frame tents	Yes	75
97	Holiday tours	No	★
49	Wall murals	Yes	> 50
41	Popcorn production	Yes	> 50
34	Prototype electronic components	Yes	85
34	Cassette tape manufacturing	Yes	95
96	Aircraft engineering	Yes	75
46	Furniture restoring	No	★
34	Electronic test equipment	Yes	75
34	Mobile radio communications	Yes	> 50
97	Light aircraft construction kits	Yes	> 50
43	Textile packaging bulk bags	Yes	> 50
47	Self-adhesive labels	Yes	55
49	Glassware	Yes	85
95	Hospital pharmaceutical supplies	Yes	> 50

22	Sheet metal manufacturing	Yes	55
34	Electrical contracting	No	★
50	Window manufacturing	No	★
32	Sheet metal working	Yes	85
41	Single portion meals	Yes	55
76	Hot foil blocking printing	No	★
48	Plastic insulation	Yes	75
46	Wooden fencing	Yes	85
50	Chimney repairs	Yes	85
85	Property dealing	Yes	65
47	Printing	No	★
61	Basket- and caneware	No	★
32	Hi-fi pick-up arms	Yes	55
64	Steel forging	No	★
66	Food products	Yes	75
96	Dry cleaning	Yes	> 50
31	Electro-plating	Yes	75

C 'Total cost increases faster than supply, i.e. each extra unit supplied adds more to cost than the last unit supplied.'

% Nominating this type of cost curve = None

D 'At first total cost does not increase as fast as supply, but then it increases faster than supply.'

% Nominating this type of cost curve = 15%

SIC code	Description of main product group	Capacity	% Capacity
46	Garden tubs	Yes	65
64	Natural hair and skin products	No	★
34	Software development	No	★
61	Wine distributor	Yes	> 50
45	Dressmaking	No	★
72	Parcel delivery service	Yes	55
96	Re-lining chimneys	Yes	95
37	Industrial measuring instruments	Yes	95
31	Fuels manufacturers	No	★
83	Placing of advertising	Yes	95
83	Business consultancy services	No	★

E 'Total cost increases in line with supply until the maximum possible (full capacity) is reached. After this point, the extra cost of supplying another unit rises sharply.'

% Nominating this picture = 14%.

SIC code	Description of main product group	Capacity	% Capacity
49	Manufacture of pool tables	Yes	> 50
83	Business package design	No	★
43	Knitted outer-wear	Yes	85
83	Training courses for public sector	Yes	85
34	Printed circuit boards manufacture	Yes	> 50
45	Bedcovers	No	★

47	Manufacture of office stationery	Yes	75
32	Electronics	No	⋆
83	Accountancy business services	Yes	85
49	Theatrical props manufacturing	Yes	55

Legend: The percentage capacity variable is given as the mid-point for ranges indicated in the questionnaire.

5 Rankings data on financial inception

5.1 INTRODUCTION

This chapter is concerned with the analysis of rankings data on financial inception of the small business enterprise (SBE). It will be shown that orderings of actions or options which were relevant to the key financial aspects of the SBE were not disorganized but had strong systematic patterns. Thus, it is possible to conceive of a typical or modal ranking for actions or options generated by the sample, and to attach a probability level to the tendency for owner-managers to rank them in this way, rather than in a disorganized fashion. For example, there was a systematic tendency to rank delinquent debtors as being more important than an inadequate credit policy in contributing to the cash-flow difficulties which were experienced by a large proportion $(50/73 = 68$ per cent) of the SBEs in the sample.

5.2 THE RANKINGS DATA

Much of the data gathered from the first administered questionnaire (AQ 1985) was in the form of rankings. Typically, the owner-manager of an SBE was asked what action s/he would take in a contingent circumstance. In Reid (1990a) I have examined a range of such circumstances, but here I shall confine myself to the financial inception of the SBE. An example of rankings data of relevance to this chapter would be that arising from questions put to owner-managers about sources of advice used at the point of financial inception. These would include family or friends, the bank manager, and the local Enterprise Trust. If the owner-manager were asked to say whom s/he would consult first (for example, his or her family) and whom next (perhaps his or her accountant) and so on, s/he would be providing a type of ranking, which in this case would be a temporal ordering. Alternatively, s/he might be asked to rank the sources of advice used at financial inception according to their importance to him/her. Thus, the accountant might be ranked as most important, family and friends next most important, and so on.[1] Here, the owner-manager is again providing a type of ranking, this time based on utility, or intensity of preference. From a statistical viewpoint, one makes no distinction between rankings generated by either of these methods (or indeed by any others), and a range of statistical procedures is available for analysing such rankings. A brief account of some of the more formal aspects of these techniques, as they can be applied to economic data, is given in the appendix to this chapter (page 78).

Proceeding less formally here, the rankings of potential actions by owner-managers may be displayed in a ranking matrix or array. The rows of this matrix relate to owner-managers, or their firms (denoted F_i for $i = 1, 2, ..., m$) and the columns of this matrix relate to the actions the owner-managers might take (denoted A_j for $j = 1, 2, ..., n$). Thus the ranking matrix has the form given in (5.1) below:

$$
\begin{array}{c}
\\
\\
\text{Firms}
\end{array}
\quad
\begin{array}{c}
\text{Actions} \\
\begin{array}{ccccc}
A_1 & A_2 & \cdots & & A_n \\
\hline
F_1 & r_{11} & r_{12} & \cdots & r_{1n} \\
F_2 & r_{21} & r_{22} & \cdots & r_{2n} \\
\cdots & & & \cdots r_{ij} \cdots & \\
F_m & r_{m1} & r_{m2} & \cdots & r_{mn} \\
\hline
& R_1 & R_2 & & R_n
\end{array}
\end{array}
\qquad (5.1)
$$

Column rank-sums are denoted by:

$$
R_j = \sum_{i=1}^{m} r_{ij} \qquad (j = 1, 2, ..., n) \tag{5.2}
$$

The first problem being posed in this chapter is whether owner-managers of firms agree in their opinions about the ranking of actions.

The questions on financial inception which generated the rankings of interest are given in detail in the appendix to this book (p. 260).[2] Briefly, owner-managers were asked:

1 Who did you contact for advice on how to get your business started? (ADVICE)
2 What were the obstacles in obtaining financial support? (OBST)
3 What sources of finance, apart from personal finance, did you use in setting up your business? (EXTFIN)
4 What factors contributed to your cash-flow difficulties? (CFP)

ADVICE, OBST, EXTFIN, and CFP are the names given to the data sets corresponding to questions (1), (2), (3), and (4) above.

Before using any statistical refinement, it is useful to look at these rankings responses to (1), (2), (3), and (4) in a descriptive sense, as in Reid and Jacobsen (1988: chapter 3).

5.2.1 ADVICE

Owner-managers of SBEs were first asked which sources of advice they drew on when they were getting their businesses started, and second, which of these sources of advice were most important. Six categories of advice were emphasised: family and friends, the bank manager, the accountant, the Enterprise Trust, the Scottish Development Agency (SDA), and local government, although a few further minor categories were identified in actual interviews including industrialists, franchisors, and the Manpower Services Commission. Nearly one-third of the sample did not seek advice as such. This does not mean that the standard commercial services (such as banks and accountants) were not consulted, but rather that the owner-managers in this subsample had made up their own minds about how to set up in business without feeling the need to be guided by advice. However, over two-thirds (51/73 = 70 per cent) of owner-managers *did* seek advice about starting up in business. For these owner-managers, the most frequently nominated source of advice, setting aside issues of importance, was the Enterprise Trust (23 per cent), which is clearly influenced by sampling methods. In descending order of frequency of mention, other sources of advice were: accountants (17 per cent), family or friends (15 per cent), banks (15 per cent), the Scottish Development Agency (SDA) (12 per cent), and local government (6 per cent). On average, owner-managers consulted three sources of advice.

Turning now to the relative importance of these sources, and ordering by the rank-sum of choices of advice, using expression (5.2) above, the first four in order of importance were: the accountant, the Enterprise Trust, the bank manager, and the Scottish Development Agency (SDA). If advice categories are grouped into triads of 'third, second or first' in order of importance, which one notes creates categories which are not mutually exclusive, one finds that accountants are judged to be the most important source of advice (57 per cent) followed by banks (54 per cent), Enterprise Trusts (52 per cent), family or friends (37 per cent), the SDA (29 per cent), and local government (13 per cent). Thus different ways of handling rankings give somewhat different pictures, but the general one that emerges is that when the owner-manager took advice on starting up in business, the most important sources were the conventional ones of banks and accountants, with Enterprise Trusts (understandably for this sample) also figuring prominently. Whilst friends and family were certainly frequently consulted, this source was generally found to be less important than professional sources.

5.2.2 OBST

For this variable, owner-managers of SBEs were asked what obstacles they had experienced in obtaining financial support for starting their businesses. Only 42 per cent (31/73) of the sample had experienced such difficulties. Those who had were asked to identify obstacles to obtaining finance from a list which included lack of personal financial injections, difficulty in convincing backers that a market existed for the product, lack of success in previous ventures, difficulty in preparing a business plan, and inappropriate employment experience. In interviews, leasing arrangements and lack of a previous track record in obtaining finance were identified as further obstacles.[3] Lack of personal financial injections (35 per cent) and difficulty in identifying the market (35 per cent) were the most frequently nominated reasons for difficulties in obtaining finance. Using the rank-sum statistic (5.2) above, the most important obstacle to obtaining financial support was convincing backers of the market, followed by lack of personal finance, a poor business plan, inappropriate previous employment and lack of previous business success. The most important point that emerges is that history was *not* the most important factor in determining whether an outside backer (almost invariably a bank) would be willing to provide financial support. The competence and wealth of the owner-manager were the more important.[4] That is, capital, either human (e.g. skill in market research or business plan preparation), or non-human (e.g. finance capital available for personal financial injections into the business), was the key determinant of ability to raise outside funds for financial inception of the SBE.

5.2.3 EXTFIN

This variable was constructed by asking owner-managers what sources of finance, apart from personal finance, they had used in setting up in business. They were then asked to rank the sources of finance they had identified, according to their importance in financial inception. Typically, an SBE was started by using only personal finance. This was true of nearly one-half (45 per cent = 33/73) of the sample. The types of non-personal (i.e. external) finance which owner-managers were asked to identify as relevant to financial inception were: borrowing from friends, relatives or acquaintances; borrowing from banks; hire-purchase; leasing; and outside equity. In interviews, a further two categories were identified – business colleagues and the ICFC (later 3i's) – and, under a residual category, further sources like local and regional government, the Scottish Development Agency, Enterprise Trusts, development corporations, and the Industry Department (Scotland). Just 18 per cent of owner-managers used sources of external finance which lay within this residual category. The banks emerged as the dominant form of external finance. If one looks at the 'first, second or third' rank of importance, the banks were nominated by 82 per cent of owner-managers. By this same criterion, but displaying much lower frequencies, family and friends came next (27 per cent), followed by hire-purchase (21 per cent), leasing (18 per cent), and equity finance (15 per cent). By this same criterion of 'top three ranks', local and regional governments were regarded as the most important (12 per cent) within the residual category.

Using the column rank-sum criterion of (5.2) above, across the sample the most important source of external finance was borrowing from banks, followed by borrowing from friends, hire-purchase, others (the residual category), leasing, and equity finance. This ranking agrees well with those produced in the previous paragraph by the 'top three ranks' criterion, and further emphasises the importance of banks as providers of external finance. For the same set of SBEs it was possible to get evidence on the sort of security which had to be provided when outside funding was sought. Personal guarantees (implying a liability to repay loans) and so-called 'floating charges' (in other words, securities on plant, equipment, stocks, etc.), were the two most frequently mentioned forms of security or collateral followed by life policies, guarantors, so-called 'heritable securities' (for example, home, property, promises, land), and finally, and much less important, stock exchange securities. No other categories of security were mentioned by owner-managers.

5.2.4 CFP

I now come to the variable defined by asking owner-managers whether they had ever had cash-flow difficulties. For over two-thirds of them (71 per cent) this had indeed been the case. They were asked to identify the factors contributing to this, and were then asked to rank them in order of importance. The factors to be considered, then ranked, were: delinquent debtors; delinquent suppliers; over-investment; inadequate credit policy with buyers; inadequate credit policy with suppliers; and insufficient overdraft facilities. Other possible factors contributing to cash-flow problems were admitted through an open category. In interviews, this included the factor of growth.

Insufficient overdraft facilities were the most frequently cited (62 per cent) factor leading to cash-flow difficulties, followed by delinquent debtors (56 per cent) and over-investment (42 per cent). Using the criterion of the 'top three ranks', the most important factor was an insufficient overdraft facility, followed by delinquent debtors and over-investment. Thus for this variable, prevalence of a factor is also reflected in the importance of that factor.

To complete the picture on the cash-flow problems variable, I refer to the column rank-sum criterion of (5.2) above. Using this, factors contributing to cash-flow difficulties are, in descending order of importance, insufficient overdraft facilities, delinquent debtors, over-investment, inadequate credit policy with suppliers, inadequate credit policy with buyers, and delinquent suppliers. Thus, viewed from many stand-points one finds overdrafts, debtors and investment at the core of the cash-flow management decision, with over-extension in any of these areas likely to lead to difficulties. External finance had commonly (60 per cent) been used by owner-managers since starting up the business.[5] For nearly a third (30 per cent) of them who used it, this was in response to cash-flow problems.

5.3 STATISTICAL INFERENCE ON RANKINGS DATA

In the previous section I have confined myself to descriptive statistics. Whilst useful in their own right, because they highlight key features of the small firms database, they assume much greater force, and certainly have an enhanced scientific validity, if backed up by formal methods of statistical inference. The data under scrutiny all conform to the general pattern of the rankings array (or matrix) in (5.1) above. Any row of this matrix represents a single owner-manager's ranking of options. In this section, I want to reinforce the conclusions of the previous section by showing first that the rankings discussed are indeed statistically significant, and second, that it is legitimate to construct and discuss typical or what might be called modal rankings. Aside from the scientific value of this, it enables one to present policy makers with some useful guidelines on policy priorities (for example, when considering methods of enterprise stimulation). [6]

In earlier work on these rankings, in Reid and Jacobsen (1988: chapter 3), I adopted a simple and obvious inferential procedure. Actions which were *not* assigned by owner-managers were assumed to be assignable in principle, but simply much less important than other actions. Suppose, for example, that an owner-manager had to rank seven factors which contributed to cash-flow difficulties, but only ranked two (such as over-investment and delinquent debtors). One would then assume that other factors, like overdraft facilities, would indeed have a bearing on cash-flow difficulties, but were much less important, and hence not worth ranking explicitly. To account for such an effect, all unranked actions or options were given imputed 'mid-ranks'. For example, if only three factors out of the potential seven contributing to cash-flow difficulties were explicitly ranked, the remaining factors would all be given the tied rank of $(4 + 5 + 6 + 7)/4 = 22/4 = 5.5$. Then the Friedman formula (5.4) given in the appendix to this chapter (page 78) was used. To recapitulate on the previous section, the questions used to generate rankings data are given in summary form in table 5.1. As before, they relate to the variables ADVICE, OBST, EXTFIN, and CFP.

The number of owner-managers or firms (m) and the number of options or actions (n) involved in the rankings analysis were as follows: ADVICE ($m = 51$, $m' = 49$, $n = 9$); CFP ($m = 50$, $m' = 35$, $n = 7$); EXTFIN ($m = 33$, $m' = 21$, $n = 7$); and OBST ($m = 31$, $m' = 13$, $n = 6$) where m' denotes numbers of firms, excluding those that ranked only one action. [7] The basic Friedman statistic [8] (F) and the Friedman statistic corrected for ties (F') [9] are displayed in the first two columns of table 5.2. All the statistics are statistically significant at the conventional $\alpha = 0.05$ level, and indeed the probability levels are often much smaller than 0.05. That is, one concludes that there are indeed systematic patterns to the rankings data, for one clearly rejects the null hypothesis of rankings being chosen randomly, from permutations of the numbers 1 to n, and independently, by owner-managers. On the contrary, there appears to be a marked degree of concordance amongst owner-managers

Table 5.1 Questions used to generate rankings data

ADVICE

Who did you contact for advice on how to get your business started?

(a) family and/or friends, (b) bank manager, (c) accountant, (d) enterprise trust, (e) Scottish Development Agency, (f) local government authority, (g) franchisor, (h) Manpower Services Commission, (i) industrialists

OBST

What were the obstacles in obtaining financial support?

(a) lack of personal financial injections, (b) establishing the idea that a market existed for your product, (c) lack of success in previous business ventures, (d) difficulty in producing satisfactory financial statements of proposed business, (e) previous employment experience, (f) other

EXTFIN

What sources of finance, apart from personal finance, did you use in setting up your business?

(a) borrowing from friends, relatives, or acquaintances, (b) borrowing from banks, (c) hire-purchase, (d) leasing, (e) equity finance, (f) business colleagues, (g) the ICFC

CFP

What factors contributed to your cash-flow difficulties?

(a) delinquent debtors, (b) delinquent suppliers, (c) over-investment, (d) inadequate credit policy with buyers, (e) inadequate policy with suppliers, (f) insufficient overdraft facilities, (g) growth

---

Table 5.2 Test statistics and probability levels

Data set	Friedman	Friedman corrected	Benard-Van Elteren	Prentice
ADVICE	77.7137*	109.3885*	17.6336*	16.3921*
	(<0.0005)	(<0.0005)	(<0.025)	(<0.05)
OBST	20.6959*	35.9280*	6.7703	6.1617
	(<0.001)	(<0.0005)	(<0.3)	(<0.4)
EXTFIN	28.3409*	47.4402*	11.7746	12.8042*
	(<0.0005)	(<0.0005)	(<0.075)	(<0.05)
CFP	49.4079*	79.4156*	7.9678	5.7610
	(<0.0005)	(<0.0005)	(<0.3)	(<0.5)

Note: *denotes significant at the $\alpha = 0.05$ level. Probability levels are given in parentheses

on (i) the most important sources of advice for getting started in business, (ii) the factors most important in creating cash-flow difficulties, (iii) the most important obstacles to obtaining financial support, and (iv) the most important sources of external funds for setting up in business.

The previous section referred to the key results on rankings, and often used the orderings by column rank-sums to get an idea of the typical, modal, or average ranking across owner-managers. There are a number of alternative methods of computing rankings, as mentioned in the appendix to this chapter. However, as the detailed treatment of this issue in Reid (1988) indicates, these alternative methods are unreliable and should be rejected. The best simple guide to modal rankings is to use column rank-sums, and this gives results which are very close to those of the most sophisticated method available, which is, however, enormously computationally burdensome.[10]

I therefore report, in table 5.3, on the modal rankings for the options or actions indicated in table 5.1 using rank-sums (R_j) as the criterion. These rankings can be regarded as typical for the sample, and as supported by the results of statistical inference. Thus one finds, for example, accountants being the chief source of advice, and bank loans being the chief source of external finance at inception of an SBE. An insufficient overdraft facility is the main reason for cash-flow difficulties, and difficulty in convincing others that the SBE would have a market niche is the main obstacle to obtaining financial support. One can use these ranks of table 5.3 with some confidence in making further comparisons, given the reported statistics of table 5.2. For example, delinquent suppliers are much less important than delinquent debtors in creating cash-flow problems for the SBE. Or, to take another example, lack of success in previous business ventures is much less important than establishing that a market exists, when it comes to obtaining financial support for the SBE. Neither of these conclusions is by any means trivial, and it would have been difficult to anticipate on a priori grounds what these comparisons would yield in practice. This perhaps best illustrates the value of using these rankings methods.

Having said this, some caveats should be recorded. A basic tenet has been that rankings are, in principle, complete. If this is not so, then my conclusions are somewhat weakened. As the appendix to this chapter explains, the Prentice and the Benard-Van Elteren tests provide alternative tests, which may be applied to incomplete ranks. Of the two tests, the Prentice one is preferable in the way that it scales ranks (see page 79). Referring to table 5.2, one finds that under the Benard-Van Elteren test only the ADVICE rankings are significant, and under the Prentice test, only the ADVICE and

Table 5.3 Orderings by Rank-Sum (R_j) of options in table 5.1

Data set				Modal orderings					
ADVICE	c	d	b	e	a	f	g	i	h
OBST	b	a	d	e	c	f	g		
EXTFIN	b	a	c	f	d	e	g		
CFP	f	a	c	e	d	b	g		

the EXTFIN rankings are significant, choosing the $\alpha = 0.05$ level in each case. However, I would tend to reject these methods as being unreliable for the data used. It seems unreasonable to argue for any of the variables being discussed that a unique cause lay behind any experience of owner-managers, be it lack of funding, cash-flow problems, or whatever. This would apply, even if a prime cause were identified in the interview (AQ 1985). Therefore, by the principle of insufficient reason, one argues that other alternatives to the prime causes should have equal rank. In such cases, the Benard-Van Elteren and Prentice tests remain silent. Unfortunately, this reduces the effective sample size, and lowers the power of these tests to reject the null hypothesis.[11] Arguably, the data that one deletes in order to perform these alternative tests are the most informative of all about owner-managers preferences for actions or options.

5.4 CONCLUSION

One concludes the case, therefore, in favour of the rankings by rank-sum indicated in table 5.3 and in favour of the Friedman significance test statistics in the first two columns of table 5.2. By more formal methods, one thereby buttresses the arguments previously put forward, without the benefit of inferential methods, in Section 5.2.

APPENDIX TO CHAPTER 5

The statistical analysis of rankings

We have m judges or observers, which in our case are *firms*, with the i'th being $F_i(i = 1, 2, ..., m)$. They are confronted with the problem of ranking n objects, which here will be treated as actions which a firm may take, with the j'th action denoted $A_j(j = 1, 2, ..., n)$. The rankings of these potential actions may be displayed in a *ranking matrix*, $R \equiv (r_{ij})$ with column sums R_j. The problem being posed is whether firms (or, more strictly, owner-managers) agree in their opinions about the ranking of actions.

If there are no ties, the null hypothesis H_0 appropriate to a problem of this sort is that the rankings r_{ij} are chosen at random from the collection of all permutations of the numbers 1 to n and that they are mutually completely independent. One approach to a problem of this sort is to use the method of m-rankings due to Friedman (1937). The appropriate statistic (F) when there are no tied ranks depends upon S where

$$S = \sum_j [R_j - 0.5m(n + 1)]^2. \tag{5.3}$$

Then we have $F = 12S/[mn(n + 1)]$ (5.4)

For m large, H_0 true, and no tied ranks, F has an asymptotic χ^2 distribution with $(n - 1)$ degrees of freedom. For m and n small, the exact probability distribution of S is available in Friedman's paper. Brunden and Mohberg (1976) advise that the χ^2 approximation is considered acceptable when $m \geqslant 12$, $n \geqslant 3$, $m/n \geqslant 4$ and $(3/2 mn) < \alpha < (1/2)$, where α is the level of significance.

When tied ranks are allowed, the Friedman statistic must be modified. This case is important in economics because, as we shall show below, if some actions are simply not checked by some firms, which in our experience is commonplace, one has to devise ways of imputing ranks to the unchecked alternatives. One obvious procedure, the 'mid-rank' method, would impute tied ranks to the unchecked alternatives. Benard and Van Elteren (1953: 366) have derived the modified χ^2 statistic (F') for the method of m rankings corrected for ties.

The reason for the appearance of ties in applying the Friedman test to economic data is that they may have to be artificially introduced to make rankings complete. This is necessary, as the test is only applicable to the complete rankings case. However, a generalization of the test due to Benard and Van Elteren (1953) admits of the possibilities both that rankings may be incomplete and that ties appear in the data. In our case, the generalization to incomplete rankings is all that is required, for in such cases no tied ranks are possible for our data. Under the assumption then of no tied ranks, and that each firm ranks each action only once, the relevant Benard and Van Elteren statistic (B) is given by

$$B = u'V^{-1}u \tag{5.5}$$

In (5.5), u is an $(n-1)$ column vector with j'th element

$$u_j = \sum_{i \in S_j} [r_{ij} - \tfrac{1}{2}(k_i + 1)] \tag{5.6}$$

In (5.6), S_j refers to the set of firms who ranked action j, $[j = 1, 2, ..., (n-1)]$ and k_i is the number of actions ranked by the i'th firm. Then $(k_i + 1)/2$ is the arithmetic mean of the ranks assigned by the i'th firm, and within the square brackets in (5.6) appear the so-called 'reduced ranks' for each of this firm's ranks of actions. Clearly, $\Sigma_j u_j = 0$, implying linear dependence among the full set of u_j. Therefore to ensure the existence of a positive–definite variance–covariance matrix V of the u_j, an arbitrary u_j must be dropped, which in this case was chosen to be u_n. The variance–covariance matrix is given in Prentice (1979).

One method of ordering suggested by the work of Benard and van Elteren (1953) is to scale the reduced ranks by the corresponding standard deviations, and then to order by the magnitudes of $u_j/\sqrt{v_{jj}}$.

When the k_i are not all equal, a suggestion due to Prentice (1979) is to scale the reduced ranks for each firm in proportion to the number of actions nominated. Thus in place of the reduced rank of (5.6) we might use this expression divided by $(k_i + 1)$, that is, what might be called 'standardized reduced ranks'. As Prentice puts it, 'to take an extreme case, it does not seem sensible that an object ranked first out of four objects should have the same reduced ranks as an object ranked 49th out of 100 objects' (Prentice 1979: 168). The appropriate text statistic is then given by the quadratic form $P = y'W^{-1}y$ where y_j are standardized reduced ranks. The elements of the variance–covariance matrix W are given in Prentice (1979). Again an arbitrary single y_j is omitted, which we choose to be y_n. Under certain regularity conditions on u and y, both B and P have asymptotic distributions, if H_0 is true, which are χ^2 with $(n-1)$ degrees of freedom (Prentice 1979: 168). A more complete account of ranking methods, as applied to economic data, is given in Reid (1988).

Part III
Case studies

6 Enterprise profiles

6.1 INTRODUCING SEVEN SMALL BUSINESS ENTERPRISES

In earlier chapters I have given numerous characterizations of parts of the small firms database upon which the results in this book depend. However, only occasionally, as in Chapter 1.3, Chapter 2.4, and Chapter 3 have I allowed the reader so much as a glimpse of what firms in the database actually look like. The purpose of this section (Chapters 6, 7 and 8) is the quite prosaic one of conveying what an SBE looks like, through a series of enterprise profiles, which are a special form of cross-instrument case study. I do so partly because my potential readership demands it. No amount of econometric and statistical analysis can convey the sense of what makes a small firm tick. If one has not been out into the field, as is so often the case with even the most able of economists, one can have virtually no grasp of business reality. This leads to the construction of economic theory which is misleading, or worse, plain nonsense. Even if it is not logically absurd, it may well be practically irrelevant. A powerful corrective to this form of self-delusion is the workaday task of laying bare the bones of small business practice. For these purposes of communication I have done this below using the language of economists, though for the less serious purpose of enlivening the material I have spiced discussion with the argot of the business world, expressed as direct quotes from interviews. I have called these pictures of SBEs 'enterprise profiles', as they do not fit the mould of conventional case studies.

I have set myself quite limited goals here. In this chapter, I examine a set of seven enterprise profiles of SBEs in a cross-instrument fashion. The instruments in question are the 1985 administered questionnaire (AQ 1985), the 1985 semi-structured interview (SSI 1985), and the 1988 reinterview questionnaire (RIQ 1988). The seven firms looked at were carefully examined before the main study, yet provide a picture which is entirely consistent with it. By their separate status, yet their congruence with the main study (for example, in the sense of their relatedness with the 'typical firm' characterization of chapter 3), these profiles provide another angle or slant on our object of enquiry, the SBE. In the next two chapters (7 and 8) I engage in the task

Table 6.1 Age, size, and products for seven profiles

Profile	Age (years)	SIC	Product	Employment*	Assets +
A	1	83	Business services	2	£5th
B	25	48	Plastic injection moulding	24	£100th
C	2	96	Window, carpet and building cleaning	2	£5.5th
D	2	34	Manufacture and design of printed circuit boards	17	£85th
E	6	83	Commercial and industrial microfilming	3	£30th
F	11	47	Camera-ready artwork	17	£200th
G	8	47	Bespoke cardboard packaging	10	£300th

Notes:
Medians: Age 6 years; employment 10; assets £85th.
*Here, no distinction is made between worker type. Details are given in the individual case studies.
+ Where the figure was given as a range, I report upon the average value, at 1985 prices.

of a cross-site analysis of these same seven SBEs. This involves a grouping of evidence by analytical categories, like cost leadership and differentiation, and something of the flavour of the individual SBE is lost. I start, therefore, with a case-by-case approach.

Profiles are denoted A, B, ... through to G, and table 6.1 presents some summary statistics, on age, size, products and industrial group. Immediately following the table are the seven cross-instrument profiles, considered seriatim. The analytical framework for these enterprise profiles is contained in chapter 2.2. For the purposes of orientation the reader may find it useful to refer first to the analysis of chapter 3, which provides a typical enterprise profile. Here, I go from the typical to the specific.

6.2   PROFILE A: FURNISHED OFFICES, TELEPHONE AND MAIL SERVICES

Firm A had been established for just seven months at the time of initial interview and mainly supplied the business service of furnished offices for rent, though ancillary services going along with this were also available (for example, secretarial support, word processing, *poste restante* mail service, international telephone service, car rental, etc.). It operated in a local market, and enjoyed about a quarter of the market share. Firm A found contacts difficult to establish in the initial stages. There was a steep learning curve in understanding what services the customer wanted. Building up customer loyalty was found to be important, and the owner-manager's intention was to establish a stable client list. A typical customer was a large business needing a satellite office in the city. Only one month's notice was required on the lease. Another type of customer used the address for business, but worked from home, delivering and collecting paperwork to and from firm A, or getting home deliveries if a favoured customer. The total number of competitors did not exceed ten, and major and minor competitors were approximately evenly matched. The product was differentiated, and customers were reasonably well informed about its technical features. Customer requirements were diverse and essentially unique, and though they were knowledgeable about what they wanted ('our customers are rather fussy'), they were frequently less well informed about what rival firms might have to offer. It was found that once customers had become satisfied with the quality of service they received, they were highly unlikely to switch to competitors. Essentially, exit or switching costs of customers were raised by giving good long-term customers privileged treatment (such as home delivery of mail). Only if 'awful mistakes' were made or the growth of the customer's trade were too rapid to be accommodated would customers leave the client list.

Price was an important decision variable. For new products it would not be set independently of anticipated volume, and firms were in significant interdependence regarding their pricing policies. Indeed, firm A was willing to hold down price to beat its competitors. In a buoyant market, price would be relatively rigid in the short run, with increases in overtime and shift work being the first response, followed by enlarging longer term capacity by methods like recruiting extra personnel and, beyond that, by engaging subcontractors. Price was not expected to be reduced in a recession either. Rather, capacity would be reduced and sales effort increased. In this situation, selling business services and renting out offices was perceived to be as much a problem of marketing as over-pricing.

Regarding product mix, if demand fell for a specific product line, the expected first response was to switch to a new product with the anticipation that this would lead to the possibility of short-time working. Next, sales effort might be increased, followed by an enhancement of quality. Last of all, price might be cut. Note this relates to the case of just one product in a range which ran up to ten, and is not in contradiction of the policy of holding price steady in the face of an overall recession. Here what is being distinguished is that of general business activity from specific narrow product demand.

There was no conscious distinction made between overhead and prime costs, though marginal cost was calculated when output increases were contemplated. A capacity output was recognized, though production was generally well below it (less than 70 per cent). Though overcapacity existed in terms of unrented office space and under-utilized business services, it was felt profit expectations were reasonable at this level of operations. An elongated, falling-forward 'reflection of an S' was the description of the total cost curve, implying a U-shaped unit cost curve. Presumably capacity was identified with something like minimum unit cost. The owner-manager was a self-conscious cost minimizer. A particularly cynical view was expressed of certain forms of marketing and sales activity. For example, mail shots were thought to be 'a complete waste of time and money'. Marketing was thought to be best developed through the cultivation of personal contacts, rather than through the expensive media exercises more commonly undertaken by large enterprises. The entrepreneur who ran the firm thought that the most significant cost savings had been achieved in the early stages of running the business when 'learning by doing' was marked.

No market research methods were used, though competitive advertising was used, with expenditure on it being counter-cyclical. Estimates of local (5 per cent) partial demand elasticities indicated a unit response to price increases and an elastic response to price cuts. Global or arc (10 per cent) elasticities appeared to be different, being inelastic for cuts and elastic for increases (this corresponding to the conventional kinked demand curve case). In all, the picture is of a doubly-kinked demand curve. See Reid (1981: chapter 4) for variants.

The reactions expected from price cuts and price increases across the trade cycle were as follows. Only in a recession was it expected that a price cut might be followed by the strongest rival, and only in a boom was it expected that a price rise would be followed. These correspond to buyers' and sellers' markets respectively. The owner-manager thought she had 'elbow-room' in pricing of about 8 per cent. This is higher than the 5 per cent average. One important factor determining the price sensitivity of customers was the significance of their purchase costs in relation to their total costs. In the case of firm A's customers, costs of the business services purchased were certainly low in relation to alternatives involving the long-term leasing of buildings and the hiring of permanent staff, and arguably low in relation to total costs, much of which, in the business services area, were accounted for by the payroll. This would tend to reduce the price sensitivity of customers. Firm A tried to present itself as offering the opportunity of high quality business services at a fraction of the cost of in-house provision, and with far greater flexibility. To the extent that the customer accepted this view, his price sensitivity was reduced. Selling price was likely to change when costs changed, when demand changed generically or when demand shifted, and also when competitors changed their prices. Price discrimination was practised between home and foreign markets, but no price rebates were offered. Within the domestic market all customers were charged the same prices for the same services, though as noted above the quality of service could be enhanced for established customers. There was no externally controlled price and no use of the device of a recommended price.

Advertising was exclusively aimed at promoting the firm's product over that of its rivals, rather than generally expanding industry demand. Much of the business acquired was through referral. Traditional advertising techniques like 'mail shots' and buying space in local newspapers were not found to be cost-effective. Competition was perceived as generally strong, but weak in some aspects, and included foreign competition.

The business had been started with advice from a broad range of sources, including family and friends, the bank manager, accountant, an Enterprise Trust, the Scottish Development Agency and the district council. The Enterprise Trust and family advisors were rated as being of first and second order of importance. As the property was rented, the assets of the business were small, being £2,500 initially and £5,000 at the time of interview (in 1985 prices). No financial difficulty had been experienced in starting the business. Apart from personal finance, leasing and borrowing were used at the stage of financial inception of the business. Extensive security was required when funds were sought, including guarantees, equipment, and property. The ease of financial inception suggested low entry barriers. However, exit barriers were more substantial. In order to get a good site for providing offices for rent, close to the commercial centre of the city in which firm A operated, it had been necessary to take on a relatively long-term lease. At the time of interview in 1985 the gearing ratio was one-and-a-half and was expected to fall over the following three years. In 1988, it was found that this goal had been realized. Indeed, the end point of this strategy of steadily reducing gearing was pursued in the face of negative profits. Of the special financial schemes available to this business in 1985, the Enterprise Allowance Scheme was found to be helpful, but most other forms of support were not applicable. The firm had not experienced cash-flow difficulties and had not required additional funding.

Three years after the initial interview the firm was still in business and run by the same owner-manager, an entrepreneur with a variety of skills including interior design, which had been put to good use in the presentation of the business. The scale of operation had doubled in terms of turnover, though it was at the time of reinterview a loss-making concern. Employment had gone up from one to three for full-time employees and from one to three for part-time employees. Fourteen offices were available for rent – a doubling of capacity. Competitiveness had changed because of innovation, with this being initiated by larger rivals, and then imitated by smaller firms such as this one. Suppliers played an important role in keeping firm A up to date about the latest in office equipment and services. For firm A, suppliers were not concentrated and therefore exercised little leverage. They provided a useful informal source of intelligence about firm A's rivals. The practices of American business centres were regarded as worthy of emulation and provided suggestions, along with rivals' practices, of product gaps. The product mix had changed substantially, shifting by expansion toward the office rental side of the business. Unit variable costs were perceived as constant in the face of this growth. A shortage of skilled labour was perceived to have impeded the growth of the firm, and the owner-manager had herself attempted to bridge the 'skills gap' by undertaking a computer course.

The owner-manager felt her firm was too busy trying to establish a competitive niche to be concerned with defensive strategy. Like many firms in the early stage of the life cycle, it was felt that the best form of defence was attack. This might involve lowering the price of services in the short run to establish a market position. Signalling commitment to its market niche was achieved through its marketing brochure. Not all rivals were regarded as bad. 'Good' rivals, in other cities for example, may be prepared to adopt a mutual referral system. This also applied to rivals who produced a different but complementary range of services. Keeping informed about rivals could be done partly through customers and suppliers. Despite this rather symbiotic view of competition, it was felt by the owner-manager that the niche her firm occupied was best defended by keeping the rental rates of her offices and her charges for the telephone answering service sharply competitive. Beyond this, being innovative, 'people oriented', and working to nurture loyalty, were felt to be the sources of competitive advantage.

It was claimed by the owner-manager that, since the original interview, she had sensed the emergence of an enterprise culture. More people, especially the young and/or the redundant, were perceived to be setting up their own firms. The local Enterprise Trust was thought to be a particularly suitable source of advice for these new entrepreneurs.

6.3 PROFILE B: PROCESSING OF RUBBER AND PLASTICS

The firm was a well-established business which had been in operation twenty-five years. It was run by two brothers. It had started as an offshoot of their father's small plumbing business. In 1985 it employed 24 people full time, 3 part-timers, and 2 trainees. This employment had increased to 36 full-time workers by 1988, with 5 part-timers and 1 trainee. Sales turnover had risen dramatically from £480,000 in 1985 to £1.2 million in 1988 (at 1985 and 1988 prices respectively). On reinterview in 1988, a substantial adaptation of plant was apparent. Many new machines had been installed, and also a new computer control system, and the factory floorspace had been extended for both production and storage purposes. The firm was a private company and plastic injection moulding was its main activity. The principal product group was shower and curtain rings. Entry barriers were low for the more basic type of product. A comment made in interview was that 'air machines are cheaply bought and could be operated in a garage'. There was a thriving second-hand market for such machines. However, newer machines were a much more expensive proposition, and high capital requirements were a barrier to entry. Firm B consciously tried to maintain a technological advantage over rivals in terms of machines and equipment. It also aimed to concentrate on very high volume orders.

Because of the ease with which the product specification could be changed (by colour, by finish of plastic etc.) the total product range was large (over eighty). However, by grouping products into similar types, the effective range based on these groups was perhaps three or four. The principal market was the UK, but the company had substantial overseas sales, and for some narrow product ranges was the principal world producer. Nevertheless, firm

B regarded itself as 'operating at the small end of the market'. Customers in the local economy were important, even though transport costs were low.

A general business ethic was: 'Don't intrude on rivals' markets.' The owner-managers could distinguish between major and minor competitors and thought there were no more than five in each group. Though some buyers in the trade were highly expert, technical differences between the firm's products and those of its rivals were thought to be too small for the customers to distinguish. Some customers were not well informed, and in such cases firm B provided design help. Pricing, design, advertising, and packaging all determined the customers' attitudes. Colour, for example, could be important. Product differentiation achieved in this way, though quite effective, was virtually costless. There were some 5,000 colours to choose from. For bathroom equipment, fashions in colour came and went and having a colour which was 'in season' was important to sales. Another cheap, or even cost-saving, form of product differentiation was by the finish on the plastic. For example a crackle finish on an electrical component might be cheaper, and more desired, than a smooth finish. In terms of product differentiation the firm's goods were thought to be similar, but not identical to those of rivals. Customer concentration was low. Firm B tried to avoid being dependent on too few customers. Many customers were well established. Firm B also aimed to avoid seller dependence. There were about eight major national suppliers of the main raw material, polypropelene. This product was homogeneous, and firm B tended to rely on one supplier, though using sub-agents for the occasional supply of small lots. Given the homogeneity of the good supplied it was felt there was little danger of seller dependence. The source of supply could be changed if necessary. Suppliers were somewhat differentiated by the extent of the technical back-up they could provide and it was the quality of this which sustained the trading relationship.

Pricing policy was fairly refined, with the firm perceiving itself to interact with rivals' prices, and being willing to hold down prices to beat competitors. Although price was set as a mark-up on unit variable cost, this mark-up was not inflexible and price would not have been set independently of volume. In boom conditions, the main strategy to meet a demand which could not be supplied from stock was to increase capacity, which could include the recruitment of more personnel. In a recession, of the available courses of action, the last thing that would have been done was to reduce price. The first action would have been to increase sales effort, followed by increasing stockholdings and improving production methods. In a market squeeze, firm B tried to emphasise speed of response (for example, on design, and especially on delivery). Faced with a fall in demand for a specific product, as distinct from a general downturn in business conditions, the first reaction would be to increase sales effort, followed by improving quality. Cutting price would then be the next action, followed by switching to a new product.

Clearly, price adjustment was undertaken, but price was not the only, nor necessarily the most important, instrument of competition. Italian producers of kitchen utensils had made a successful attempt to capture more of market demand in a specific product group. A collective industry response to this was thought to be possible, but difficult. This type of fall in demand for a specific product was interpreted as a successful attack on market share, but given the great range of products, it was very hard to anticipate where rivals might strike and to organize an appropriate policy of deterrence. The owner-managers felt it was more sensible to spread risks of this happening by producing a diversity of products and said 'If some fail, others can be emphasised, or new ones developed.' Some slumps in specific markets were uncontrollable. For example, the French government had at one point inhibited imports of foreign substitutes.

The firm's owner-managers did distinguish between fixed and variable costs, and found this distinction useful. Sometimes customers were asked to pay fixed costs. Given the bespoke nature of many orders, this typically involved paying for a new die for a plastic injection moulding machine. Variable costs were used as the base for firm B's mark-up. However, marginal cost was not computed. This does not rule out marginal cost pricing, but considered in conjunction with the previous paragraph and the emphasis on non-price competition and relative price stability, it makes it less likely. The notion of capacity operations was well understood, and an average figure of below 70 per cent of capacity operations was given, largely because batch production was so common as a method of production. Batch production involves high intensity production for limited periods of time, after which the plant may be put aside for a while while other machinery is used intensively. The owner-managers were also aware that by carrying excess capacity which could very readily be intensively employed, they were deterring entry. It was thought that falling unit and marginal costs typified the production process. In 1988, when production was 150 per cent greater than in 1985, unit variable cost was 20 per cent lower. Though the owner-managers did not seek cost leadership, they were highly cost conscious; all items produced were put through a rigorous costing system. The principal cost drivers were homogeneous raw materials, and their prices, because bargaining leverage was low, were effectively given. At the time of reinterview in 1988, a new system had been organized to retrieve and re-use plastic cuttings from moulded objects, providing a good example of the reconfiguration of costs. The value chain was set monthly so that costs were covered, and a good profit margin provided.

Firm B did not use systematic market research methods, although informal channels for gathering market information were important. These channels needed to be cultivated, which took time. Word-of-mouth was important for trade intelligence.

For local shifts (5 per cent) in price up and down, given no reaction by competitors and normal business conditions, the amount purchased of the main product (curtain and shower rings) was felt to be price insensitive. That is, the elasticity of demand with respect to price was zero. Customers whose goods were of high quality were observed to be less price sensitive than customers whose goods were of low quality. Often this quality image was enhanced by a form of packaging which was not only functional but could also improve the appearance of the customer's product. Such packaging could be produced by firm B. For larger price changes, of the order of 10 per cent, demand was thought to be price elastic for cuts and price inelastic for increases ('most customers don't reject price increases out of hand'). This mimics the reversed kinked demand curve thought to characterize buoyant business conditions (i.e. sellers' markets). Rivals were thought likely to match price reductions or price increases in normal, boom, and recession conditions. This might explain why price was not usually used as an instrument of strategy: unilateral price action seemed impossible under all circumstances. Though the owner-managers thought there was a band (i.e. 'elbow-room') within which price could be moved without bringing forth a response from competitors, this was thought to be narrow (no more than 3 per cent). Price, we see, was not very flexible. Reasons for changing it were changes in costs (which is consistent with mark-up pricing), the conclusion of a wage round (an aspect of costs), and the starting of a new business year (when demand factors would also be considered). Bulk discounting was practised, but not the offering of price rebates, a practice which one owner-manager viewed with incredulity ('Why should I work to pay my customers?'). If under competitive pressure by rivals, firm B was willing to increase discounts. No goods were sold at controlled or recommended prices.

Competitive advertising was used to promote firm B's products over those of its rivals, but the level of advertising was not set at different amounts depending on whether demand was high or low. Thus firm B's advertising expenditure could be regarded as a fixed cost. Competition was perceived to be strong in quality but weak in price. Foreign competition was significant.

As a business which had been in existence for some time, firm B had needed to survive long-run competitive pressures. The owner-managers claimed to seek success through innovation, cost reduction, etc. rather than by increasing barriers to entry or blocking channel access for rivals. They recognized the idea of 'good' competitors, and some measure of referral took place. Knocking rivals was thought to be bad form, though 'avoiding praising them' was acceptable. The closest to retaliation that the owner-managers might get would be to feed dummy information to sales representatives who might be used as channels of information by rivals. The general view taken of competition was that it was symbiotic.

Firm B had been started without specific advice, using assets of just £50 in 1960. By 1985 assets were £100,000 and this had jumped to £254,000 by 1988, reflecting substantial investment in new plant and computer control systems, as well as expansion of the premises. No difficulty had been experienced by the founder member (the owner-managers' father) in starting the firm. At financial inception itself only personal finance had been used. In the early stages the most important other source of finance had been bank borrowing, with hire-purchase playing a secondary role. Life policies and heritable securities (like home, property, premises, and land) had been used. At the time of interview in 1985 the gearing ratio was zero, though this was expected to rise over a two- to three-year time horizon. In the event, this did not happen, according to the reinterview evidence of 1988, implying that the substantial investments which had still been undertaken were financed entirely from retained profits. The owner-managers could not cite any special financial scheme as having been of benefit in the early stages of the business. Debt finance had been used in the past, though the general financial aim of the owner-managers appeared to be a gearing ratio of zero. When debt finance had been used it was not to solve cash-flow problems, which the owner-managers claimed not to have experienced, but to promote growth of the business through new or expanded premises, the purchase of plant or equipment, increased stock or inventory, or the hiring of new employees.

The owner-managers claimed a net profit in 1985 of £4,500 and a net profitability of 40 per cent. These figures are sensitive, and subject to a variety of interpretations. They are presumably net of directors' remunerations. Innovation had occurred in their market, first undertaken by the largest firm and then by firm B itself. The owner-managers regarded themselves as technologically progressive. They did not feel particularly vulnerable to attack, but continued to diversify products to spread risk, and tried to stay one step ahead technologically. They did not particularly fear entrants who came in using older types of plant, for which second-hand prices were relatively low, because the quality of output was poorer. New materials were becoming available, but were not yet commercially viable. By 1988, the main product line had substantially increased in importance (by volume) since 1985. The growth of the firm had been impeded by a shortage of specific types of skilled labour, and the response to this 'skill gap' had been to undertake training within the firm.

Over the three years between interview and reinterview the owner-managers had perceived a development of the enterprise culture. In their own area of plastics more firms were starting up. Rewards were perceived to be 'high for people who worked hard to succeed as their own masters'.

6.4   PROFILE C: CLEANING SERVICES

Firm C was an example of the legendary window cleaner, much loved as an illustration of small firm inception and growth, but rarely analysed in practice. This firm was two years old at the time of interview in 1985 and largely engaged in domestic, shop, and office window cleaning. Cleaning fluids were also occasionally supplied as a side-line. The typical customer of firm C was disenchanted with undertaking its own cleaning, but keenly aware that cleaning services were essential to a professional presentation of the business. The use of cleaning services was perceived by the customer as an aspect of quality enhancement, who sought reliability, accessibility, and efficiency. Firm C was essentially a one-man business, though at the time of interview, two people were working for the owner-manager, one of whom was a trainee. Sales turnover was estimated at £18,000 in 1984, which was to say, around the VAT limit at the time. The services sold could be put into about four product groups, and the total number of products was no more than ten. In 1988 the same firm was in business, run by the same owner-manager, an articulate and lively entrepreneur with a keen general interest in small business enterprise. Output was reported as having doubled, with turnover estimated at £30,000 (in 1988 prices) and four people working regularly for the firm.

The main market for firm C's cleaning services was the local community. Unless a job was very large, firm C would be unlikely to do business outside of its immediate locality. Because transport costs were a major cost driver in the business, high customer density ('a lot of business in one place') was an imperative. Market share was very small (less than 1 per cent) in a trade with a large number of rivals. The owner-manager could identify up to thirty major competitors and more than fifty minor competitors. Many, but by no means all, were also very small businesses, employing between one and three persons. Customers varied widely in terms of their knowledge of the products, though none was regarded as uninformed. Some customers were found to be adventurous, capable of dissimulation, and eager to play off one firm against another. Customers were both domestic and commercial, and the owner-manager's intentions were to target commercial business as the area of expansion. Commercial customers included large companies. The main product was regarded as similar to, but not identical with, nor different from, that of rivals.

If a new product were brought on to the market the owner-manager would not set its price independently of expected sales. Prices set were in an established relationship to unit variable cost, but the mark-up was flexible. The price could be set at what the market could bear. It was felt that the customer may need to be convinced that a price was right for a job, and this required experience. This 'pricing knowledge' was felt to be a barrier to new entry. The behaviour of competitors was important to firm C's pricing policy and price might be held down to beat rivals. Matching prices was common amongst firms competing for new customers, though 'poaching' established customers by this or any other means was frowned upon. The first response to an increase in demand which was too great to be met from existing resources was to increase overtime or shift work and then to increase capacity, which in this case would involve recruiting more personnel. 'Good' competitors would be encouraged by sub-contracting work to them which could not immediately be handled. Such privileges could be withdrawn if a 'good' competitor turned 'bad' and started trying to 'poach' customers. There was a tendency for referrals from 'good' competitors to rise as business conditions became buoyant, no doubt partly reflecting widespread capacity limitations as well as sympathetic rivalry. In good times, rivals would sometimes work as coalitions to handle big jobs, usually by sub-contracting devices. This form of collusion was seen as a kind of barrier to entry. 'Good' competitors were likely candidates for collusion, as they were willing to discuss how custom could be extended. In a recession, the first reaction would be to increase sales effort, then price would be cut, and finally short-time working would be introduced. For a fall in demand which was specific to just one product the same actions would be taken, but the order of the last two items would be reversed (i.e. last of all, price would be cut). In fact the firm had experienced considerable buoyancy in demand for its products and had enjoyed a substantial growth (of about 100 per cent) in its main product line between 1985 and 1988, and had responded by recruiting more personnel (up from two to four).

Costs were divided into fixed and variable, and this distinction was found useful. Further, marginal cost was computed. The owner-manager identified a capacity output and claimed to operate normally at 71 to 80 per cent of capacity. An important aim was to utilize plant as heavily as possible, given the spatial distribution of customers. A considerable effort was devoted to job scheduling so that transport costs were minimized and active cleaning work was maximized. Transport costs were a principal cost driver, and control in this area was tight. The owner-manager aimed at 'getting a lot of jobs together in the same vicinity'. Jobs in housing and industrial estates were favoured for the economies they offered in this respect. No general pattern of cost schedule was identified: both increasing and falling unit costs, with some fixed cost element being present, were thought possible. In the face of the large increase in output between 1985 and 1988, unit variable costs were thought to have remained constant.

The owner-manager claimed to use market research methods for a number of purposes, to find out: how interested buyers were in his products; the reaction of competitors; and how the market was likely to develop in the future. One gathers the methods used were informal.

Firm C was thought to enjoy some 'elbow-room' in pricing with a range of variation of up to 10 to 15 per cent being thought unlikely to provoke rivals' reactions. This elbow-room, or price insensitivity, was encouraged by the fact that clean business premises were considered a necessity by customers, yet cleaning costs were only a small proportion of their total costs. For both local (5 per cent) and global (10 per cent) price variations, demand was thought to be totally inelastic for price cuts and relatively inelastic for price increases. The pictures are consistent for local and global price variations, and are one limiting case of a kinked demand curve. Presumably price variations downwards of more than 15 per cent (the limit of elbow-room) would eventually lead to an elastic response. No matter what the business conditions, it was felt that a reduction of price would not be followed by rivals. However, an increase in price would be followed in a boom and in a recession, though not in normal conditions. Presumably other firms would conjecture, like firm C, that a price cut was not worth pursuing, and hence none would be willing to follow a price-cutting initiative. In abnormal business conditions, however, price increases would be followed, which makes sense in terms of the presumed price inelasticity of demand with respect to increases. The upshot of the owner-manager's responses seems to be that there is a kind of focal or bootstrap equilibrium which keeps prices where they are except in abnormal conditions. Reasons for changing price were both institutional (a new tax year, conclusion of wage round) and market-driven (substantial demand shift), though clearly the use of an institutionalized point at which to revise price does not rule out that revision was being dictated by a wider set of economic conditions, including costs, rivals' behaviour, and innovation. Suppliers appeared to have no leverage on firms in this line of business. Costs of switching suppliers were thought to be minimal, and suppliers were thought to be passive, even complacent, in their trading activities. Suppliers were thought to be 'worthless', for example, in providing leads to new customers, though this was not typical of the sample.

Price discrimination was practised between different market areas and by different customers. Price rebates were offered, but at a flat, rather than variable (increasing) rate. No prices were controlled, nor was there any recommended price.

No formal advertising methods were used, though promotional effort of an informal sort (largely word-of-mouth, presumably) was stepped up when demand was low, and scaled down when demand was high. Competition was thought to be generally strong, but weak in some respects, with quality being its most important dimension. Firms were very protective of clients, once acquired, though any new customer was fair game for all. It was said that 'stealing customers was like taking a bone away from a dog'. For this reason most firms focused competition on acquiring new business. Great importance was attached to being the first to approach a new potential customer. Then an aspect of defensive strategy was to put rivals off the idea of poaching such customers. Customers, once acquired, tended to remain with a firm. The market did not facilitate switching. Firms resisted poaching by moral suasion ('those who poach existing firms' customers can expect a "stiff talking to" in the first instance'), and the customer would tend to find that the only option to not buying the service from his established cleaning firm would be to take it 'in-house'. Such attempts at 'in-house' productions of cleaning services were discouraged by the trade. It was accepted that you must 'shame the customer into accepting you' by pointing out the 'nuisance value' (high cost, low quality, and inconvenience) of in-house cleaning. Experience with customers suggested that once having purchased cleaning services, this perceived nuisance value would discourage a return to in-house production, unless the quality of such services deteriorated ('generally only bad service will lose customers'). Maintaining or enhancing the quality of cleaning services was perceived as a way of enhancing customer loyalty and increasing customer switching costs. Keeping a high level of service and looking and acting professionally was perceived as a way of setting an example to rivals about commitment to the market. 'Looking professional' meant things like 'dressing appropriately and having a smartly painted van'.

The owner-manager had initially taken advice at financial inception from someone already operating in the business. Subsequently, the bank manager, accountant, and local Enterprise Trust were contacted, in that order. At inception in 1983 assets were approximately £500. By 1985 they had grown to £5,500. There had been no difficulty in obtaining financial support at the time of inception. At start-up, only personal finance was used. By 1985, debt of £4000 had been acquired which, given equity of £1500, implied a gearing ratio of 2.7. Apparently, an extra van and a computer had been acquired. It was expected that gearing would rise in 1986 and then fall in both 1987 and 1988. In fact, the 1988 reinterview indicated that gearing had fallen throughout the three-year period. As was common in the study as a whole, the aim was to reduce gearing as rapidly as possible. By 1988 firm C's gearing had been reduced to zero. To the extent that cash-flow problems had been experienced, they were caused by the purchase of plant or equipment. The cash-flow problems had been dealt with by raising temporary debt-finance, and at the time (1985) the owner-manager regarded this as over-investment.

Between 1985 and 1988 no shortage of any type of skilled labour had been experienced, though in the case of firm C, labour skills could be rapidly acquired on the job and arguably desirable attributes of employees were intrinsic rather than cultivated. In cases of labour shortage, the owner-manager had sub-contracted, or else temporarily filled the gap by increasing his own hours. The owner-manager was highly individualistic and claimed no help from any special schemes in running his business. He was optimistic about the future and, because he had not experienced losing customers to competitors, was more concerned with acquiring new business than with the tactics of deterrence. He regarded his market as subject to innovation, and expansion, particularly in the area of commercial premises, and felt he was participating in these changes. He had witnessed new firms being set up, and felt that a new atmosphere was emerging in which 'more people are willing to have a go themselves'.

6.5   PROFILE D: MANUFACTURE AND DESIGN OF PRINTED CIRCUIT BOARDS

This was quite a new business at the time of first interview, having been started two years earlier by an owner-manager with strong previous corporate experience in microelectronics. Firm D was located in an area well known for its small electronics companies working in the high quality/high technology end of the market. The firm employed seventeen people, of whom seven were part-time and three were trainees. It was set up as a private company manufacturing and designing printed circuit boards (PCBs) and had a sales turnover at 1985 prices of £130,000. It produced a limited range of products (no more than ten) which could be put into about four product groups. The main product in 1985 was high-volume produced printed circuit boards, though a certain amount of prototype work was also done. By 1988 firm D was characterized as engaging in prototype, pre-production, and low-to medium-volume production. Scotland was the main market, and, within it, market share was very small (less than 1 per cent). The owner-manager felt his firm had no market power. He could distinguish between major and minor competitors. There were no more than five of each. The owner-manager thought in terms of there being six to eight competitors and of these, 'we compete head-on with four'. These competitors had known strengths and weaknesses.

The main product was mildly differentiated. Differentiation was by service, particularly on delivery, quality, and know-how. On purely technical specification, the main product was weakly differentiated. Customers were generally best characterized as expert, and capable of judging the technical quality of the product, though some were less well-informed. The latter sometimes required guidance on factual matters, and used specialist publications or trade journals to inform themselves. There were about seventy customers, of which thirty were regular and about eight were main customers. None accounted for more than 15 per cent of business, and the owner-manager was aware of trying to avoid dependence on a limited number of customers. There were significant customer switching costs, primarily in the form of tooling costs. The owner-manager was aware of the potential for customers to engage in backward integration. Larger customers already had their own prototype capability and could readily vary the scale of their prototype workshop. Though that could imply using technical leverage on firm D, this had not been experienced.

Price and volume decisions were not made independently for new products. Price was determined as a mark-up on average variable cost, but the mark-up was flexibly varied to increase profit. Pricing was influenced by competitors, but the owner-manager would not hold down price to beat competitors. This suggests a price followership role, and this is consistent with firm D's small market share. It is also consistent with the evidence presented below of mark-up pricing and cost followership. To meet a boom in demand which could not be met from stocks, firm D was most likely to increase overtime or shiftwork first of all. After this, subcontractors would be engaged, then capacity would be increased, possibly by taking on temporary labour and, last of all, price would be raised. In a recession, firm D would first reduce overtime and then increase sales effort. After this would come reducing capacity by measures which included laying off personnel. Here, the temporary workers would be laid off first. Then price would be cut and, last of all, the permanent staff might be put on short-time work. Given the competitive nature of the product market, the first and main reaction to an autonomous fall in demand for a product would be to switch to producing something else.

On the factor market side, supplies were fairly concentrated, with around four to six for each factor supply. Suppliers were much more numerous for the supply of generic chemical compounds than for the supply of proprietory goods. This suggested little bargaining leverage on the supply side. No suppliers had shown an interest in forward integration.

Costs were split into fixed and variable costs and this was found to be useful in the running of the firm. Unit variable cost, we have observed, was the base for the profit mark-up. Associated with a 100 per cent increase in production between 1985 and 1988 had been an 11 per cent decrease in unit variable cost. The firm did not aim at cost leadership. The owner-manager felt that larger rivals with £5–20m turnovers could, and often did, aim at cost leadership. However, this required very high volume production, much higher than firm D could ever achieve. Firm D did not aim to be the cheapest, but rather emphasised quality and service. Some re-configuration of the value chain had led to cost reductions by changes to processes and reorganization. Marginal cost was calculated, though not used directly to fix the mark-up. An output of around 85 per cent of capacity was regarded as normal. The total cost curve was regarded as roughly linear. The owner-manager was technically competent in quantitative techniques, so this might be taken as firm evidence of constant marginal costs for normal ranges of output.

The owner-manager used market research methods to get an idea of further developments in the market, with a view to determining his own market position. This was particularly true of new market opportunities when the firm was effectively in a start-up position. The owner-manager claimed to have used 'price experiments' and in this way to have learned about elasticity of demand. For local price variations, point demand elasticity estimates were zero. Global demand elasticity estimates were zero for a 10 per cent price cut, and less than one for a 10 per cent price increase. These estimates were based on the assumption of no rivals' reaction. They emphasise the importance of non-price competition. Speed of delivery was a key factor in clinching an order and, provided this was managed, price sensitivity was not felt to be marked. Some companies which were customers at the high-quality end of the market, especially military and medical, were especially quality conscious and, by the same token, less price conscious. The owner-manager felt that his firm had an 'elbow-room' in pricing of possibly up to 15 per cent. In normal and boom conditions, it was not thought that rivals would follow a price cut, though they might in a recession. It was assumed that competitors would not follow a price increase in any business conditions. Cost and demand changes were factors which could lead to a new price being set, and so also was the conclusion of a round of wage bargaining at the firm or industry level.

Price discrimination was practised for different customers, though price rebates were not offered. Controlled and recommended prices were not recognized. No advertising was undertaken, after a trial effort had proved ineffective. The owner-manager felt personal contacts were the best way to promote trade. He had worked on image building to enhance his firm's market position. He attended trade shows and tried to get local and trade press coverage. For example, an eminent Scottish politician had opened his factory, which had brought good press reports. The owner-manager found this more successful than formal advertising. He tried to manage the image of the firm as being tough in the sense of highly professional. As part of this image he emphasised the time spent on process control and business planning. He tried to cultivate channels, in the sense of specific key personnel, but did not use business gifts or perks. He was the sole supplier to a number of customers and claimed: 'I like to look at problems from the customer's angle'. In his experience, new customers were often dissatisfied with rivals' products.

Competition was described as generally strong, but weak in some aspects. The nature of rivalry was symbiotic. Rivals exchanged materials, information, and even manufactures. The owner-manager was quietly confident in his firm's capabilities and seemed to welcome competition. He said: 'We do not fear rivals. We have helped support rival firms with information and know-how. By helping, we can get custom.' There were low entry barriers. For example, people with craft ability could get in at the bottom end of the market ('bucket shops and home garages'), using skills acquired in established firms. However, they lacked managerial skills and found survival difficult. The owner-manager knew of recent entrants of this sort in the PCB market, one of which had failed within months. But generally, for legitimate traders, business was plentiful. Firm D regularly turned business away. The owner-manager claimed he might even help a new start-up, who might subsequently become a 'good' competitor. Though the owner-manager tried to discover competitors' weaknesses, he would not overtly 'knock' rivals but rather would try to emphasise his own firm's relative merits. He tried to set an example in terms of reputation. This would include the defensive strategy of matching guarantees offered by rivals to obtain custom. Rivals could become upset and nervous and had been known to complain to the SDA. The owner-manager tried to manage his competitors' assumptions through information given to his supply channels. Supply and customer channels were crucial and 'had to be established by patient effort over the first six months'. He thought reputation was established in about a year. Given this, he did not think an overtly defensive strategy was necessary.

The owner-manager had turned to four sources of advice at the time he was starting his business. Most important were the Scottish Development Agency (SDA), followed by the ICFC, and then professional sources: the bank manager, and finally the accountant. In 1983 the firm started with assets of £50,000. These had grown to £85,000 in 1985 at the time of first interview, and further to £98,000 by the reinterview in 1988. The net profit in 1985 was £13,000 with an estimated net profitability of 72 per cent. Sales turnover had increased markedly by 1988 to a figure of £500,000 (compared to £130,000 in 1985). All this had occurred with little growth in number of employees (up from seventeen to twenty-three from 1985 to 1988) and relatively little growth in assets.

General market growth was estimated at 20 per cent per annum, in which firm D was expected to get at least its share. The owner-manager foresaw problems of growth bringing his firm to the point of being 'stuck in the middle' between a medium and large size. Large firms were hard to get on terms with by self-financed expansion, as capital requirements were so great. He said, 'I have seen other firms come to grief at this stage.'

The competitive position had changed in the principal market from 1985 to 1988 because of innovation. There had been a worldwide shift to new techniques. There were a number of new trends of which surface-mounted components was the most significant. The owner-manager felt this development could be accommodated readily by firm D. Leaders in the field were pressing on with new products and designs. Though copying went on by weaker rivals, this was ignored. The owner-manager said that his response was 'to change faster'.

The owner-manager had not found it difficult to start firm D, in a financial sense, but had been disappointed that it was impossible to find risk capital. Only personal finance had been used to start the firm. Twelve months after financial inception a bank overdraft had been made available for working capital. In 1985 the gearing ratio was zero, and had never risen above one-third. The owner-manager intended to keep it at zero over the next three years. The 1988 reinterview confirmed that this objective had been achieved. Generally speaking no special financial schemes had been important at financial inception, barring the offer of a small loan from the local government authority because of the employment potential of the firm.

There had been cash-flow difficulties at points, caused mainly by growth, but delinquent debtors had also been a problem. One defaulting company had been taken to court. Because of slow settlement of some accounts, firm D now used the services of a credit control company, and had credit checks carried out on potential customers. When debt had been incurred it was to enable new employees to be hired, or stocks to be increased.

Despite fast growth, firm D had not experienced a shortage of any type of skilled labour. The owner-manager had not been too convinced of signs of an emerging enterprise culture. He saw 'pockets of it, but not over a broad range'. He was critical of traditional Scottish thinking which he felt militated against risk-taking. He referred, for example, to the stigma that attaches to business failure. His complaint about non-existent risk capital in 1985 was echoed in 1988 when he thought it was still difficult for an entrepreneur to get venture capital backing in Scotland.

6.6   PROFILE E: MICROFILM SERVICES

Firm E was a very small business. It was four years old at the time of initial interview (1985) and employed three persons. Three years later it employed two persons and two trainees. It was initially a two-person partnership. It had stopped trading in 1985 because of the death of an earlier partner, and was sold to a rival. In early 1986 a similar firm, trading in a similar market, was launched under a similar name. Firm E provided a microfilm service to industry and commerce. It produced two to five product groups and one to ten products, which is rather a narrow product range. Scotland was the main market for Firm E's services, and its market share was estimated to be very small (less than 1 per cent). The industry was thought to be of a reasonably balanced structure in that all the firms occupied comfortable (i.e. stable) niches. Major and minor competitors could be distinguished. There were thought to be three large companies and six small ones in the microfilm industry in Scotland. Sales turnover was £16,000 in the previous tax year (at 1985 prices). This had increased to £35,000 (approx.) in 1988, a real increase of 94 per cent.

The services provided by competitors were thought to be similar, that is to say mildly differentiated. Product differentiation mainly manifested itself through quality of service. It was felt that 'all firms can provide a good service, but most do not.' Because of this limited product differentiation, firms in the industry tended to be 'chasing the same customers'. For most of these firms, a microfilm service was their only line of business, so quality of service and trade contacts were important. Special trading relations established in this way tended to discourage the price wars that might otherwise ensue. On the spectrum of knowledgeability, the customers of firm E were thought to be moderately well-informed. Even if they were not technically inclined, they knew certain technical features should be present in the service. Some were better informed on technical features and were guided by their knowledge. The spectrum of customer types was wide, ranging from sole proprietorships at one end to large companies like Scottish Gas at the other. Local authorities were major and desirable customers in that they had the ability to pay and a great need for microfilm services. Once the customers became committed to microfilm services, they tended to stick with them. Microfilming itself was cheap, though the machines used were dear (around £2,000), so backward integration was unlikely. Switching costs were thought to be naturally low, so keeping customers attached by the special trading relationship was a way of raising switching costs. Demand was buoyant, so it was thought unlikely that customers could exert undue bargaining power: 'there will always be another customer'. It was thought that because costs of microfilming represented such a small proportion of customers' total costs, they were less likely to bargain on price. Customer motivation was high, in the sense that 'everyone has a paper problem'. Microfilming was an obvious solution to this problem, but customers had to be weaned away from regarding paper as the basic medium for data storage and retrieval.

The partner interviewed did not think his firm capable of bringing a new product on to the market in a manufacturing sense, though it could introduce a new type of service. For example, he thought that expansion into secretarial services was feasible. By 1988 innovations had sharpened up competitors in firm E's principal market, notably by advances in computer retrieval systems and electronic offices. However, at that time capital costs for such developments were high (by a factor of ten compared to microfilm technology), and also required considerable computer expertise. The view taken was that 'something this advanced will not take place overnight, given human nature'. It was admitted that the industry was in a period of flux. A large rival had undertaken innovations to benefit from these developments. It was felt that a new service, rather than a new innovation (which was felt to be beyond the firm's capability), would be priced independently of its expected sales volume. Price was set as a flexible mark-up on unit direct cost, with flexibility being used to improve profits. Under certain circumstances, profit targets might be reduced to lower the inducement for rivals to attack firm E's market niche. In general, it was not felt that the pricing of competitors was crucial to firm E's pricing, though the partner interviewed claimed that if knowledge of a rival's operations was sufficiently good, some account would be taken of their pricing. Initially price was pitched at the lowest level possible, to get business. However, it was felt that the quality of microfilm service offered was more important than price in attracting customers. It was felt that even if a competitor offered what was described as a 'crunching' lower price, business would not be lost provided service was good.

When asked what action he would take when a boom in demand occurred which could not be met from stocks, the partner first said it depended on circumstances. If it was important to take action, then first of all overtime or shift work would be increased, and subsequently capacity would be increased, which might involve recruiting more personnel. In a recession, the first action would be to reduce capacity, perhaps by laying off personnel, followed by introducing short-time working, cutting price, and finally increasing sales effort. If the demand for one of the services of the firm fell, without there necessarily being a general recession, the first reaction would be to cut price, after which sales effort would be increased.

The partner of firm E agreed that it was theoretically possible to distinguish between fixed and variable costs, but doubted its practical importance. He did not currently find these cost divisions were useful in running the firm, but thought in time they might prove useful. He did not calculate the additional cost of increasing output (i.e. marginalism was not consciously adopted). No strict capacity output was recognized, though variation in capacity utilization was a well-understood term. The wage bill was a major cost driver, and it was felt that with greater capacity utilization and monitoring of employees, labour costs would be better controlled. Materials costs were less important cost drivers and could not be controlled better by switching suppliers as all suppliers tended to offer similar products at similar prices and terms. This was thought to arise because of the awareness that all firms in the industry had of supplier operations. There was considerable market concentration of suppliers, with four or five being particularly important. These tended to be large companies like 3M, Kodak, and Bell and Howell. Costs of switching suppliers were low, and suppliers were perceived as constituting 'a stable and consistent force' in the market. The partner interviewed was unconvinced by the cost curve show cards and regarded them as 'pure speculation'. He claimed not to think of costs in these terms.

Firm E did not use any kind of market research methods. However, trade contacts and the trade press provided market intelligence. It was admitted that the pressure of dealing with day-to-day operations could lead to a neglect of market opportunities. The partner of firm E felt that there would be no increase in the sales of its main service given a 5 per cent cut in its price, in a situation where their competitors did not react to this price cut and given normal business conditions. Under the same conditions, the partner thought that for a price increase of 5 per cent the sales would not fall at all. That is, for small price variations demand was totally inelastic. Again under these conditions it was felt that a price cut of 10 per cent would lead to no increase in sales and that a price increase of 10 per cent would not lead to a fall in sales. This marked inelasticity for even quite large price variations up and down was attributed to strong customer loyalty. The low cost of the service, in relation to customers' total costs, was also a factor, as was the specialist (or bespoke) microfilm set-up required for particular customers. Under boom or recession conditions, the partner did not think that a reduction in the price of firm E's main service would cause its strongest competitors to react by reducing their prices. It was also believed that competitors would not raise their prices if firm E were to increase the price of its main product in any business conditions – boom, normal, or recession. It was believed that firm E had a certain amount of 'elbow-room' in pricing, within which a price change by it did not bring about a reaction from its competitors. The amount of elbow-room was estimated to be at least 10 per cent. Events which might lead to the firm altering selling price were deemed to be when cost changes occurred or when demand shifted substantially. Some goods with identical costs and qualities were sold at different prices to different customers. No price rebates were offered, and no goods were sold at controlled prices. Of the firm's services sold at recommended prices the percentage of customers who ended up paying this price was less than 30 per cent.

The form that firm E's advertising took was individual advertising; that is, advertising aimed at promoting its own product over that of its rivals. Advertising was not increased (decreased) when business demand was low (buoyant). The firm's advertising was described as 'random'. Presumably the idea being conveyed was that it did not have a systematic form. Mail shots had been tried, but typically advertising was restricted to the *Yellow Pages* telephone directory. Much sales promotion occurred through contacts obtained in a partner's merchant banking activities. Competition was described as generally weak, but strong in some aspects. Firms mainly competed by vying for customer loyalty. Switching costs were by nature low, but by design high, implying customers once captured, if treated well, would remain loyal. Firm E had been started in its first incarnation without outside advice and with practically no assets. At the time of interview in 1985, which was six years from initial inception, assets were approximately £30,000. The owner-manager was unwilling to give asset figures in 1988, so soon after a trade sale and subsequent re-start. The partner had found no difficulty in getting financial support for starting up. Only personal finance had been used. Thus the original equity gearing ratio was zero. In 1985 it was one, and had risen as high as high as one-and-a-half. The partner's reaction to being asked what would happen to his gearing ratio over the next three years from the interview was 'I don't know.' He guessed it might stay the same throughout. In the event, the business was sold later that year to a rival when a partner died. The re-born similar firm had a zero gearing ratio in 1988 (two years after the re-start), though gearing had previously been higher. Firm E had not needed to defend its market position vigorously. The aim was to convince rivals that the firm was satisfied with its particular niche and was not concerned with 'pinching' rivals' business. In this way, the partner thought that he was managing firm E's image as a good competitor. An attempt was also made to encourage rivals to be good competitors, by offering rewards or inducements through sub-contracting orders to favoured rivals. It was felt that behaving professionally and being recognized for providing a good service were fundamental to gaining the respect of rivals, and this in itself was a good defensive strategy. It was felt that managing firm E's image as a tough defender was not necessary, though you needed to 'watch your back'. Barriers to entry were also an impediment to rivalry and it was felt that the high cost of capital and an initial lack of trade contacts could constitute significant barriers. Because demand was much more sensitive to service (i.e. quality) variations than price variation, know-how, with its attendant quality-enhancing consequences, conferred absolute cost advantages to incumbent firms over potential rivals. Experience was important, for example, in being able to design a bespoke microfilm set-up for a specific customer. As well as entry barriers there were also exit barriers, primarily caused by high equipment costs which were not fully recoverable on exit. The partner interviewed did not think there was an emergent enterprise culture in Scotland. He was amazed that in 1988 one could employ people for as little as £2 an hour, when he thought these employees were bound to do better by working on their own account. He said: 'I think the education system has something to do with it.'

6.7 PROFILE F: PHOTOTYPESETTING

Firm F was one of the longest lived of the sample and had been in operation for eleven years at the time of interview in 1985. It provided artwork and phototypesetting services and the owner-manager regarded himself as operating in printing and publishing. Firms in his industry produced a vast array of services and products, with each firm concentrating on a particular niche (for example, photocopying, typesetting). There were seventeen full-time employees in the firm, no part-timers, and one youth trainee on an MSC scheme. In legal form, the business was a partnership, and had a sales turnover (excluding VAT) of approximately £$\frac{1}{4}$ m in the previous tax year at 1985 prices. Three years after the initial interview, the firm had a similar turnover and workforce, though the volume of business had grown by 20 per cent. It was felt there had been a shortage of skilled labour which had impeded the growth of the firm. To some extent this 'skill gap' had been filled by the partner's own action: he installed equipment that economized on the labour input.

Firm F produced two to five product groups, and one to ten products in total. The main market for the services of the firm was perceived to be the local community. Within it, the partner thought he had from one-third to a half of the market share. He perceived his firm as being the market leader, and would defend this position to maintain reputation. The filling of product gaps was one way of achieving this. It was a necessity but also with practice 'came naturally'. He thought this rapid niche invasion 'critical to running the business'. It was a way of signalling a commitment to defend his market leadership reputation and, the partner also thought, it set an example to rivals in terms of demonstrated professionalism. He could distinguish between major and minor competitors and thought there were between one and five in the former category and between six and ten in the latter. Articles produced by firm F were thought to be significantly differentiated from those produced by rivals. Differentiation was thought to be sustained 'by personal touch and venue' (i.e. location). Customers were typically experts and able to judge for themselves the technical quality of the service provided. Here, the kind of customer the partner had in mind was a large company or a government agency. There was also the occasional 'man off the street'. Publishers in particular had extensive knowledge of the industry, and were the main expert customers. Aside from them, other customers were less well informed. Switching costs were low and customer loyalty was perceived as the main reason for not switching. Seller (i.e. supplier) dependence was perceived to be low; backward integration was easy ('we could do it our-selves') and it was always possible to 'choose another firm' because there were a great number of suppliers to choose from and access was easy. It was found difficult to characterize the typical customer: 'wanting something done that the firm could do' sufficed. The character of the business activity itself was thought to be 'amorphous'. The most desirable customers were those that gave 'carte blanche' to the firms. Key purchasing criteria of customers were: efficiency, availability, price, and quality.

The partner felt that price would not be determined independently of the volume of services sold, were a new service being launched. Price was set in a way which aimed to extract the maximum it could from each individual consumer. In setting price, a crucial consideration was the pricing policy of rivals, and price was held down, if necessary, to beat competitors. At the stage of reputation-building the partner thought new firms had been willing to price in a way which reduced their profit targets. If a boom in demand occurred which could not be met from stocks, the main action taken would be to increase overtime or shiftwork. In a recession price would be held steady, though not increased, an attempt would be made to increase productivity or efficiency, then capacity may be reduced (which might include laying off personnel), and finally an attempt would be made to increase sales effort. If demand fell for a particular service, it would be dropped from the range temporarily, saving some cost at present, and not ruling out the possibility of demand reviving in the future.

The partner claimed that costs were split up into fixed and variable, with the great bulk falling into the fixed cost category. These cost distinctions were not felt to be particularly useful in the running of firm F. Incremental cost (marginal cost) was calculated when an expansion of services was contemplated. No capacity output was recognized. The idea of cost curves was felt to be rather too academic by the partner, but he was willing to identify a linear cost curve with no capacity constraint as typifying his operations. Between 1985 and 1988 unit production costs were thought to have remained about the same in the face of a 20 per cent increase in business by volume. An attempt was made to reduce costs by tightly monitoring input activities, but it was thought that the cost cutting achieved was marginal.

The partner said he did not use market research methods, narrowly conceived (for example, in terms of forecasts by trade associations). Given a 5 per cent (i.e. local) price change, other things being equal, and in normal business conditions, the partner felt demand would be totally inelastic for price cuts, and would not react predictably to a price increase of this magnitude (i.e. demand may fall, but may not). For a global change in price of 10 per cent, it was felt again that demand would be totally price inelastic for price cuts of this magnitude and about unit elastic for price increases. These sorts of questions were thought to be rather big-business oriented, and changes in prices of the sort mentioned were thought to be a 'sophisticated' strategy. Costs to customers of the phototypesetting services were a small portion of their total costs, which provides one explanation of price inelasticity. Customers' motivation was more for speed, convenience and quality than rock-bottom pricing. They recognized that a good phototypeset product enhanced the perceived product quality of their own goods and contributed to value added: hence a high quality elasticity, but a low price elasticity. When asked whether the strongest competitor would reduce price if firm F did, the partner thought it would in normal or recession conditions, but would not in a boom. In the case of a price increase by firm F, it was thought that the main rival would not follow the price rise in normal and recession conditions, but would follow it in a boom. The partner thought his firm had a certain amount of discretion or elbow-room in pricing which would not provoke a response from rivals. The magnitude of the elbow-room was put at more than 15 per cent. The partner perceived this as his customers being, in the face of marked product differentiation, 'quite price sensitive'.

The main reason for changing selling price was thought to be a change in demand. Sometimes services which were essentially the same were sold at different prices to different customers, with some customers being distinguished by marketing area. Price rebates were offered, sometimes in the form of bulk discounting. None of the services was sold at a controlled price and none at a 'recommended' price.

Advertising was practised, in the sense of what the partner wished to call 'sales promotion'. An entry in the *Yellow Pages* telephone directory was his example of a form of sales promotion. He thought firm F's advertising was directed at promoting its products over those of its rivals, and that it would be increased when demand was low and reduced when demand was high. He felt that what he called 'classy' advertising would frighten potential competitors and make them aware of what they were up against. Competition was described as generally strong, but weak in some aspects. Part of the reason for strong competition was perceived to be the existence of many similar small firms in the market. The partner did not worry about competition. His role as the owner-manager of the market leader was 'to let them worry about me'. To his mind this meant 'acting rather than reacting'. For example, leap-frogging with a new service could be a means of beating competitors. The partner was not in favour of greater co-operation between firms in his main market. Whilst there was foreign competition to be considered, the partner did not feel there was a case for the protection of British firms, though he expressed an uneasiness with passing judgement on issues of this sort, which he felt to be more political than economic.

At financial inception the partner had not sought advice from anyone on how to get the business started. Setting up firm F had been easy, and he thought it would also be easy for others in terms of suppliers, premises, employees, and capital. However, subsequent success required overcoming obstacles like creating trade contacts and establishing credibility. Track-record and contacts were thought to constitute significant barriers to entry, but exit barriers were relatively small. The book value of the total assets of firm F at inception was £1,500 in 1974 and estimated at between £150,000 and £250,000 in 1985 (book value, at nominal prices, net of depreciation). In 1988 assets were estimated to be £386,000 before depreciation and £200,000 after, at 1988 prices. It was thought that no difficulty would have been experienced in obtaining external finance when the business was being started, had this been required, but in practice only personal finance was used. The initial equity gearing ratio was zero; it stood at $\frac{1}{5}$ at the time of interview and had been as high as $\frac{3}{7}$. It was expected to stay at $\frac{1}{5}$ for three years ahead, but it was admitted that this was partially a way of recognizing uncertainty and ignorance. In practice, gearing rose and stood at $\frac{3}{4}$ by 1988 though the partner claimed it had fallen for each of the three intervening years. A regional development grant had been useful at the point of starting up the business. Firm F had not experienced any cash-flow difficulties since starting. Regarding debt, there had only been an occasional need to use an overdraft facility.

The partner was unwilling or unable in 1988 to give estimates of net profit and profitability in 1985. It was admitted that because of innovation there had been a change in competitiveness in firm F's principal market over the period 1985–88. This had not been brought about by any of the larger firms in the market, but by a smaller rival. One gets the impression that firm F had achieved a kind of equilibrium. Growth had been achieved, but sales had not particularly benefited, suggesting some market sagging, or collapse, possibly through an unexpected excess supply of phototypesetting services. Whilst new equipment had been installed and the labour force slightly pruned, there had been no attempt to initiate innovation: this had been done by a smaller rival. The industry was perceived to be dynamic, because of new technology: 'one must have a constant awareness of new products and services'. Whilst not innovating the partner regarded himself as 'staying on top of technology'. It was felt that this conferred reputational advantages on firm F and increased switching costs. Typically, firm F kept ahead of suppliers in discovering what was new and wanted. Trade shows were of great importance in suggesting what the latest technology had to offer.

The partner did not perceive the emergence of an enterprise culture in Scotland in recent years. It was felt that people were encouraged to go into business and this might make his market more competitive but 'may not improve it'. It was felt that inexperienced new entrants, funded by the Enterprise Allowance Scheme, were coming into his line of business as 'an easy option'. This was depressing the market, the symptom of which was an underpricing of products.

6.8   PROFILE G: BESPOKE CARDBOARD PACKAGING

This well-established firm had been in existence for eight years at the time of interview in 1985. Then it employed ten people, of whom five were part-time workers. By 1988, it employed twelve people, of whom just two were part-time workers. The owner-manager was a trained engineer with a post-graduate degree and previous corporate experience. In form, this SBE was a private company. It converted cardboard to bespoke packaging, very often for orders placed for small volumes. In the previous tax year (1984–85) sales turnover had been £180,000 (in 1985 prices), and by 1988 this had grown to £300,000 (in 1988 prices) excluding VAT in each case. This represents a real growth of 47 per cent in sales. This growth had been facilitated by ploughing back a lot of profit. Firm G had two to five product groups and eleven to twenty products. The main product line was rectangular slotted containers, for which the principal market was the local community. For this product, the market share of firm G was thought to be very small (less than 1 per cent). The owner-manager could distinguish between major and minor competitors, with both major and minor competitors numbering one to five in each case. Five big firms accounted for 80 per cent of the market, three medium sized firms for 15 per cent, and six to eight small firms for 5 per cent. Industrial concentration was high.

Firm G was at the small end of the market. The owner-manager was aware of his competitors, 'but I largely ignore them'. His customers were typically not expert about the product, but could range from being informed on, and guided by, technical factors to being influenced more by appearance in cases where a very standard product was being considered. The main customers were some thirty in number, and 15 per cent of them accounted for 75 per cent of the turnover. The owner-manager was not aware of an asymmetry in his bargaining relationship with customers. He himself had control over re-orders, through his stock position, but customers had counter-leverage. Backward integration by customers was uncommon and had not to his knowledge been successful. The product was effectively homogeneous, in the sense that other producers could exactly mimic whatever bespoke product firm B produced, but product differentiation existed to the extent that rivals filled different types of bespoke orders.

New products would not be priced independently of volume, and a product price was set, by intention, at the highest level the market would bear. The pricing policy of rivals was not thought to be crucial to firm G's pricing, and price would not be held down to beat competitors. When there was a boom in demand which could not be met from stocks, the first reaction would be to increase overtime or shift-work, the second, to lengthen the order books, and the third, to increase capacity (which in this case might include the recruitment of additional personnel). The first reaction to a recession would be to reduce capacity (including the laying off of personnel), followed by reducing overtime, and then by attempting to improve production methods. If demand fell for a particular product, the owner-manager would seek first to switch to a new product, followed by efforts to increase quality. The first action was a kind of safety-net response, and the second was more remedial.

The owner-manager distinguished between fixed and variable costs in his SBE and found this distinction useful. He was able to calculate marginal cost, and indeed demonstrated such a computation during the interview on his personal calculator. He showed quite a refined understanding of economic concepts here and elsewhere in the 1985 interview, and his comments are salted with a healthy degree of cynicism. He did not regard firm G as having a capacity output, and this was confirmed by his choice of cost curve. He nominated the concave total cost curve with no apparent capacity constraint, which was also the modal choice for the sample as a whole (55 per cent nominated this case). His main cost drivers were wages and raw materials. He thought they could possibly be more tightly controlled (e.g. by reducing the quality of cardboard) but thought there was very little leeway to do this. He knew he broke-even at low volumes of output. Three years after the 1985 interview, the 1988 reinterviews revealed that many products were produced at similar volumes to those of 1985, but diversification had occurred. There had been a 40 per cent growth in die-cutting jobs performed 'in-house' for example. Unit variable costs were estimated to have fallen modestly ($2\frac{1}{2}$ per cent) over the three years, despite a steady upward drift of some raw materials costs. Firm G obtained 95 per cent of its raw materials from one supplier, and enjoyed a good service from him. However, the supplier could be changed if necessary. There was little price competition between suppliers. What kept a firm with his supplier was quality of service. Only in this sense did suppliers provide a differentiated product. There was not much forward integration, it being regarded as 'bad form' in the trade, but it was regarded as more likely than backward integration.

The owner-manager did not use systematic market research methods and was not sympathetic to the idea: 'we do little selling or advertising'. Referrals were important. He depended very much on established trade connections. He admitted such channels were important, but stuck to business. He did not like over-familiarity and business lunches. Over the three years which had elapsed between interviews (1985–88) the owner-manager had noticed a trend to better graphics and to the improved structural design of containers. He regarded the market as 'dictating what is acceptable', and saw the 'customer coming to the firms' for ideas involving design innovations. As the owner-manager observed, 'we do not set out to do this, it just happens'. He had no marketing or market tactics, and was not aware of consciously seeking a market segment on which to focus. He was very relaxed about marketing, saying 'we don't pick customers – they pick us'. He admitted that some potential customers did not conclude a deal 'if they were not comfortable with us'. He regarded this as desirable – customers should be keen. He said, 'we do not respond to customer-snatching'. Even commenting on it might suggest vulnerability – he wished to project the image of being the best.

The owner-manager had heard of the notion of elasticity of demand but was unconvinced of its relevance. For price cuts or price increases, given no response by rivals under normal business conditions he felt demand would be totally inelastic for both small (5 per cent) and large (10 per cent) price variations. He did not think that his own price reductions or increases would be matched by his strongest business rival, irrespective of business conditions, normal, boom, or recession. Naturally, given these earlier responses he did recognize an 'elbow-room' in pricing, which he put at 10 to 15 per cent in magnitude. The owner-manager was willing to reflect upon this price insensitivity of customers. He argued that 'a £10,000 instrument can be in a box worth a few quid'. This reduced price sensitivity. Many of the products sold by firm G were probably 'over spec.', but the customer would rather be safe than sorry. The main fear of customers was probably of being out of stock of packaging, rather than being over-charged. Price might be changed when costs changed, which could be caused by the conclusion of a 'wage round' in the industry. A good might be sold at different prices, even if production costs did not vary. Such prices might apply to different customers, or to large and small traders. However, price rebates were never offered. None of the goods was sold at controlled or recommended prices. Advertising was not undertaken, so no advertising strategy was deployed.

Competition was perceived to be generally weak, but strong in some aspects. The dominant form which competition took was by quality of service. The owner-manager thought firm G had a niche by nature of a professional outlook and good service. His relationship with larger rivals was symbiotic: 'large firms welcome the existence of small firms; we do work for them'. He thought large and small firms were complementary, in this sense, as well as competitive. He also thought that increased growth in the market might increase rivalry. Foreign competition was insignificant in firm G's branch of the industry.

Firm G had been set up after seeking advice from a variety of sources. Most significant were family and friends, followed by the bank manager. Next in importance were the Scottish Development Agency (SDA) and local government. The firm had been started with assets of under £10,000 in 1977 (nominal prices) and total assets in 1985 (book value, net of depreciation at 1985 prices) were £300,000. The owner-manager thought that anyone could get going in his business for about £15,000. He regarded this as a low barrier to entry. However, in practice entry was low, even though obvious entry barriers did not exist. He conjectured, 'learning and experience are hard to quantify but must be important'. The owner-manager had experienced difficulty in obtaining financial support to start his business. He put this down to the lack of a track record in small business: he had previously been a corporate employee. He had used a bank loan, as well as personal finance, in setting up his business. In seeking external funds he had been required to offer a variety of forms of security including a personal guarantee (which implied a liability to repay the loan), life policies, named guarantors, and securities on plant, equipment, stocks etc.

The gearing ratio was unity at the time of interview in 1985 (i.e. equity exactly matched by debt), and it was expected to stay the same over the next three years. The reinterview evidence in 1988 was that this goal had been achieved. An investment grant and reduced rental on premises had both been helpful financial schemes at the starting up of the business. The firm had not experienced cash flow difficulties and had not required additional debt finance since inception.

The owner-manager claimed a net profitability in 1985 of 25 per cent, where this is expressed as net profit divided by the book value of assets. Using information from the reinterviews in 1988, net profit in 1985 was reported as £25,000 and the book value of assets that year as £175,000 which should make the figure 14 per cent for net profitability. Further, the book value of assets reported in 1985 was £300,000, almost twice the estimate given three years later. This would imply a net profitability of 8 per cent in 1985. Finally, it should be said that the first net profit figure proffered in the 1988 interview was £50,000 which would imply a profitability of 29 per cent using the 1988 estimate of assets in 1985 (namely £175,000) and a profitability of

17 per cent using the 1985 estimates of assets in 1985 itself (namely £300,000). Depending on the basis of computation, profitability was somewhere between 8 and 29 per cent. What this confirms is the extreme sensitivity of the profit figure. Owner-managers do not like to admit to a high profit. It might imply certain levels of tax liability, might suggest that their market is not being adequately contested by actual and potential rivals, and might suggest that surpluses could be channelled to raising the wage bill. However, they do like to report high profitability because this is a yardstick of efficiency, and owner-managers wish to look efficient. Profitability also has the advantage that it is not particularly revealing, because the net profit and asset base are not specified. From the above figures one would conclude that the two net profit figures in 1988 with respect to the position of firm G in 1985 were with, and without, director's remuneration. As the owner-manager was asked to report his assets net of depreciation, one suspects that the asset figures given in 1988 were relevant to that year and *not* to 1985, and reflect depreciation of plant and equipment over the intervening three years. This is reinforced by the comment made in the reinterview in 1988 that the machinery used was still the same as in 1985. The upshot of all of this is that an appropriate net profitability figure for 1985, netting out director's remunerations, was 8 per cent.

Whilst plant had not been changed over the three-year period 1985–88, the balance of production had shifted, with new activity (die-cutting within the firm) accounting for rapid growth of one product line. Changes in graphics and design were invariably customer driven. The largest firms in the market were not initiators of such innovations. Changes in materials used were a less likely source of innovation than graphics and design. Plastic corrugated material had been tried but had flopped. It was still too expensive compared to paper products, and very sensitive to changes in oil prices. Foam too was a potential technical substitute, but it tended to be used in a complementary way with corrugated paper in the area where it was most cost effective, namely as padding. As an ex-engineer, the owner-manager had an eye for possible future technologies and hoped to use them. He thought that computer-aided production and multiple component packing were trends that could help a firm defend its niche. He would not glorify this projection into an industry scenario. If required to defend, he would cultivate a 'tough image'. However, the owner-manager felt 'we don't have to be defensive'. He thought his existing plant was (implicitly) his best defence, as it was quite modern. He agreed he might 'match guarantees' as an aspect of retaliation. However, his aim was 'to set a standard of proper trading'. This would exclude blocking tactics. However, it was legitimate to manage a rival's assumptions. Showing a deep involvement in the business lowered inducement for attack. Firm G had grown, but had not experienced a shortage of any type of skilled labour. Indeed many of the factory floor tasks were semi-skilled or unskilled in nature, and some of these were undertaken by handicapped workers.

The owner-manager had not sensed the emergence of an enterprise culture between 1985 and 1988. He saw the buying or starting of a business as more of a safety net for managers and others who had been made redundant, rather than a manifestation of the entrepreneurial event. He felt that in Scotland individuals were not attuned to an enterprise culture and were generally unwilling to bear the risk of setting up their own firms; they preferred the safety and security of working for someone else. He felt that many genuinely enterprising individuals tended to leave Scotland for America, Canada, and other locations overseas.

6.9 CONCLUSION

What has been presented above is the evidence for the two chapters that follow. This evidence has been displayed in the novel form of 'enterprise profiles', which aim both to enliven the conventional case study approach, and to provide a common format of presentation. The latter has been devised to facilitate further analysis within a competitive strategy framework. It is to this analysis that the discussion now turns.

7 Competitive and defensive strategies

7.1 INTRODUCTION

In this chapter I intend to engage in a richer form of interfirm analysis than is possible by conventional quantitative methods. My purpose is to demonstrate how cross-site, *analytical* case studies can illuminate small business practice in a comparative sense, even when one is dealing with small numbers of cases. Here I use the same seven enterprise profiles or cases[1] that were analysed in a within-site (i.e. cross-instrument) fashion in the profiles of SBEs in chapter 6. They are: A (business services), B (plastic mouldings), C (window cleaning), D (PCB manufacture and design), E (microfilm services), F (phototypesetting)[2], and G (cardboard packaging).

I shall not attempt to mimic cross-section econometric work, which is the concern of the chapters of the next section (part IV). In these following chapters (9, 10 and 11) my purpose, valid in its own way, will be to estimate parsimonious econometric models which are satisfactory both from the viewpoint of goodness of fit and of conformity with modern economic theory. However, the unsatisfactory aspect of these models, which I have to remedy here, is that one gets no empirical insight into the range of small firm types. Satisfactory estimated models should fit the data well and accord with economic theory. However, any single such estimated econometric model may coincide to *no* known small firm type, representing as it does an average over many small firm types. An industrial economist going into the field for the first time with no more background than econometric evidence would assuredly be in a state of permanent surprise at the very individual, even idiosyncratic, combinations of characteristics displayed by firms in the real word of small business enterprise.

To convey a sense of this business reality, my purpose here, by contrast to the cross-section econometric analysis, is to provide a richer, more dense inter-firm analysis. Parsimony is subordinated to detail, goodness of fit to congruence with general constructs (for example the pursuit of a focus strategy) and theory to full (or 'thick') empirical description. My emphasis will be on the qualitative data gathered using the semi-structured interviews of 1985 (SSI 1985). They are organized around the framework of a small firms variant of the 'competitive advantage' approach.[3] I shall also use statistical evidence on these seven cases which was gathered by the other two instruments, and shall relate this, as appropriate, to general statistics for the full sample of seventy-three small firms.

The general framework of this chapter is as follows. First, I provide a new extension of the competitive advantage analysis to the small firms case. Then, for the sample of seven case studies chosen for further analysis, I look at market structure, conduct and fragmentation. This lays the theoretical and empirical basis for the analysis of competitive strategy and defensive strategy which is the centrepiece of this chapter. It also sets the scene for the detailed analysis of the forces of competition on the seven SBEs which is the concern of the following chapter 8.

7.2 THE COMPETITIVE ADVANTAGE FRAMEWORK

Porter, in explaining that the empirical underpinning of his competitive advantage approach lay in the case study has said: 'a considerable amount of on-site interviewing is required to ensure that the case study captures reality' (Porter 1983: ix). This is very much the methodological presumption of this chapter, and furthermore a Porter-influenced analytical framework is used as well. However, Porter was talking about large firms, typically major corporations, and most of his field work interviews were conducted with chief executive officers (CEOs). By contrast my concern is with small firms (indeed, with very small firms) and my interviews were typically with owner-managers.[4]

In *The Small Entrepreneurial Firm* (1988), which I co-authored with Lowell R. Jacobsen, a first published attempt to apply a modification of Porter's analysis to the small firms context was presented. The methods used there were successful, but provisional in form. This chapter and the one that follows (chapter 8) represent a more detailed and mature attempt to develop that method, using the vehicle of a new set of cases.

To be able to transfer comfortably from large to small firms using Porter's framework, one has to be aware of two necessary and crucial modifications. First, life-cycle effects play an important role. Small firms which are close to the 'entrepreneurial event' of financial inception are common in my sample. They display the behaviour of firms in early life-cycle activity. Most notably, much effort is devoted to establishing, by discovery or creation, a competitive niche, and little to defending or blocking. The latter tactics are more typical of firms in mature or late stages of the life-cycle. Corporations are much more often in a mature phase than small firms, and being in principle infinitely long-lived, are less prone to ultimate decline than small firms.[5] A keen concern with defensive strategy is thus more natural for the mature large firm, by contrast with which a concern for aggressive competitive strategy is more natural for the young small firm. The second necessary modifications to Porter's framework required in the present context is to take the market segment, rather than the market as a whole, as the small firm's natural domain. SBEs are simply too small to be active at a generic industry-wide level. Their strategic targets must necessarily be market segments, very often through small niche exploitation (cf. Bradburd and Ross 1989). When an owner-manager of an SBE talks of 'my market' he usually means a segment of a much larger generic market (for example, if the generic market or industry is furniture, the market segment might be cane household furniture).[6] The above two modifications alter the balance of emphasis of Porter's approach, but in most cases the adjustments required to accommodate small firms into the analysis are modest and intuitively appealing.

Porter's analysis of competitive strategy in fragmented industries provides much material that is useful in formulating a small firms variant of his competitive advantage analysis. Markets which are fragmented are made up of many firms, each with small market shares, and little influence on industry-wide outcomes. The case studies examined here fall naturally into the fragmented markets category,[7] though owner-managers exercise their skills, with varying degrees of success, to try to overcome the negative features that often accompany fragmentation. Some of these negative features include: low barriers to entry; limited scale economies, or limited scope for 'learning by doing'; volatile sales and hence relatively high inventory costs; limited bargaining leverage *vis à vis* customers and suppliers; scale diseconomies (caused, for example, by a short product life cycle); extreme customer diversity; strong product differentiation; high exit barriers (especially with respect to the managerial input); legal restrictions (for example, local licence or franchise arrangements); and immaturity of the industry. A few of these negative features can sustain fragmentation, and the ambitious owner-manager of a small firm who is trying to gain competitive advantage will attempt to circumvent them. He might, for example, through innovation try to increase scale economies and learning effects, or might, by low-cost, high-quality standardization reduce customer diversity. The guiding principle of course will be the profitability of overcoming market fragmentation. If there is fragmentation which is intransigent, then the owner-manager of the small firm has to cope with it as a datum, and must simply aim to do better than his rivals. Possible strategies here include: increasing value added by increasing product differentiation (for example by providing an advisory service with sale); specializing by product type, customer type, or order type; and adopting a so-called 'bare bones/no frills' approach with rigorously controlled costs (payroll, overheads, and materials) and a limited range of tightly specified products.

A full dress performance of Porter's approach would be too lengthy and derivative to be worth attempting here. To achieve brevity I shall concentrate attention on three aspects emphasised in the semi-structured interviews: the forces of competition; generic strategies; and the value chain. To inject novelty into the analysis, I shall develop it for the case of SBEs rather than, as convention would have it, for corporations.

7.3 COMPETITIVE FORCES

The traditional emphasis by industrial economists when analysing competition is on rivalry amongst existing firms in the industry. This form of rivalry is never unimportant, but it may not tell all the story of the competitive environment, and may even neglect important parts of it. True, small firms must be aware of the number of rivals, be able to distinguish large from small rivals, be aware of the extent of sales concentration across rivals, be able to estimate the degree of product differentiation and also rivals' responses to various pricing strategies, etc. However, rivalry between incumbent firms is only one of a larger set of forces of competition. In Porter's analysis there are four further forces of competition: potential entrants, suppliers, buyers (customers), and substitutes.

The threat of entry (i.e. potential rather than actual entry) has an effect on overt competition within the small firm's market or market segment. Certainly it will influence pricing behaviour, and will encourage some measure of entry-deterring pricing[8] by incumbent SBEs. Even if a market segment is not fully contested,[9] one would expect the drift of price above marginal cost to be more attenuated the greater the threat of entry. Further, one would expect the SBE to make a variety of investments aimed at balkanizing its favoured market segments. Most obviously, there will be an increased level of investment in the creation and fostering of goodwill with customers, undertaken beyond the point that would occur in the absence of an entry threat. Such expenditures will raise the switching costs of customers and confer the benefits on an SBE of strengthening the bonding of customers to itself *vis à vis* both active and potential rivals. Goodwill so defined creates a powerful barrier to entry in many small firms contexts. Other possible entry barriers which may be especially relevant to SBEs include a strong brand image, privileged access to channels at both the supply and distribution ends, acquired trade know-how, and protected status by local or central government statute (for example by exclusive franchise agreement). These investments to deter potential entrants through raising entry barriers may have their strategic aspects. For example, if an SBE has exclusive control of a niche, it may deliberately carry excess capacity as a strategic deterrent to potential rivals. If the SBE is challenged by several rivals in a market niche and price competition is strong, it may be that there will be strategic under-investment in capacity, forcing on the potential entrant the prospect of low volume, high cost operations. As a general principle, the more marked is the commitment to his market niche by an SBE, and the greater is his effectiveness in signalling this (for example by threatening fierce retaliation), the less is the likelihood of potential rivalry becoming actual rivalry.

Not only suppliers, but buyers[10] as well, will exert bargaining power over the SBE if there is imperfect competition in both factor and goods markets. Obvious indices of potential bargaining power in factor and goods markets are the extent of supplier and buyer concentration, respectively. Also of importance are the volume of business a supplier or customer has with the SBE, the degree of factor and product differentiation, the switching costs of suppliers and buyers respectively, and the ability to forward or backward integrate. [11] Price sensitivity will, amongst other things, depend on switching costs and on the significance of goods traded in terms of their costs relative to total costs. For example, if the cost of a theatrical costume supplied by an SBE is very small in relation to the costs of running even an hour's operation of a film crew on location the movie making company will tend not to be sensitive to price variations in costumes supplied, provided they are supplied on time, and to the right technical specification (for example, as regards historical accuracy). [12]

Finally, the potential appearance of substitute products constitutes a threat to incumbent SBEs. A difficulty in evaluating substitutes is that they may be technologically unfamiliar. To take an example which is relevant to firm G (the bespoke packaging firm) a technical substitute for corrugated cardboard is a similar physical product (i.e. parallel flat sheets sandwiching a wavy sheet) made in plastic. The extent to which the latter might be substituted for the former depends in some measure on the relative prices of wood pulp and oil, which are the raw materials governing production costs in each case. But further special technical considerations might emerge, which have a bearing on the marketability of the product. For example, if the corrugated material were used for non-decorative packaging, a relevant consideration, as packaging is quickly discarded, is whether the product is biodegradable. Here the cardboard product would have an advantage over the plastic. This could be relevant if the packaging were used for fast foods like takeaway pizzas. If, on the other hand, the corrugated material were used to produce bicycle panniers, the plastic-based product would have many advantages over the cardboard one, in terms of strength and durability. In each case, the potential usefulness of the substitute has to be evaluated by asking what is the relative cost of obtaining certain levels of product performance or quality. In the latter case, for example, even if the plastic corrugated material is more expensive than the cardboard alternative, the resultant product performance is so greatly enhanced by using plastic that substitution is a serious threat. Other matters which would need to be evaluated in considering the threat of substitutes to products of incumbent SBEs would include switching costs and the willingness of customers to embrace new products. In the latter case, customer conservatism can sometimes deny technical substitutes in a market. For example, rock musicians got used to the sound produced by valve amplifiers, and these products continued to be favoured for ten to fifteen years after the appearance of cheaper, more reliable, solid-state amplifiers. To overcome customer conservatism, the strategy adopted by amplifier manufacturers was to design a microchip that would synthesize the (distorted) wave form of a valve amplifier, to get customers convinced at least of the relative reliability of solid-state amplifiers, before convincing them of the advantages of a purer wave form.

7.3.1 Generic strategies

Porter's three generic strategies involve cost leadership, differentiation, and focus. [13] A differentiation strategy aims to emphasise the uniqueness of a product as perceived by the customer. The relevant strategic target is the industry. A cost leadership strategy aims to exploit scale, scope, and other economies (for example, in purchasing), producing a highly standardized, homogeneous product, using state of the art technology. Again, this strategy is aimed industry-wide. Neither of these strategies we have hinted at above is usually feasible for an SBE because it is aimed at the industry as a whole. Probably more appropriate is a focus strategy, combining elements of product differentiation and cost leadership, directed at a specific market segment in a unique way.

If a firm is undecided about its competitive strategy it may face the problem, so-called by Porter, [14] of being 'stuck in the middle'. Smaller firms, targeting market segments rather than the whole industry and using a cost focus or differentiation strategy, and larger firms, operating at the industry level and pursuing a cost leadership strategy, frequently enjoy better returns on investments than firms with middling market shares which are not clear on their strategies. The latter may be unsure whether it is best to target the whole industry or to go for niche exploitation, and may not be clearly committed to either a cost leadership or differentiation focus. As a consequence competitive strategy may be formulated in an inconsistent fashion. Firms guilty of this may let themselves 'get stuck in the middle', thereby losing competitive advantage, to the detriment of profitability and rate of return on investments.

As a specific firm type, the SBE would typically avoid some of the dangers of being 'stuck in the middle' because it usually does not have a significant market share. However, should it come to dominate its chosen market segment, which a successful fast-growing SBE can do early in its life cycle, then there is the danger of losing focus. Although dominant in its niche, and possibly in neighbouring niches, such SBEs will still not have a large market share at the industry-wide level. If early niche invasion has been possible because of strongly differentiated, novel product lines, an attempt to go for cost leadership would be dangerous. Firms with larger market shares have natural advantage of scale, scope, technology, learning and bargaining power over such SBEs. They give significant cost advantages to the larger firms as compared to smaller rivals.

A focus strategy, aimed at the particular market segment, therefore seems most likely to offer the SBE a competitive advantage. This is Porter's third 'generic strategy'. A focus strategy involves a judicious mix of differentiation and cost control at the level of a single market segment or, more usually, several highly interrelated market segments. Typically, there may be several feasible successful focus strategies in an industry, depending on the characteristics of each market segment. As a focus strategy involves both differentiation and cost control, the SBE needs to beware of inconsistency in strategy formulation because product differentiation may, in itself, be costly to pursue.

Therefore, the SBE will often seek low, or zero-cost forms of product differentiation, if available. Firm B (plastic mouldings) mentioned first in chapter 6, provided several rather good examples of this. It produced high volumes of extruded plastic mouldings, using modern plant. However, cost leadership was not a possible focus strategy because, whilst enjoying scale economies, it lacked the scope and pecuniary economies of large rivals who operated at the industry-wide level. Firm B skilfully introduced a variety of low-cost forms of product differentiation as part of its focus strategy. One example of this was a plastic box cover for enclosing electrical fittings. In standard trade form this box would be buffed to give it a smooth finish. However, when it emerged from the mould, it had a 'crackle' finish. The owner-managers discovered that some customers actually preferred the crackle finish and were willing to pay extra to get it. As it did not involve the extra process of buffing, it was actually cheaper to produce than the smoothly finished version.

7.3.2 The value chain

Porter's analysis of the important strategic goal of cost leadership (or cost reduction) directs attention at the structural determinants of costs or 'cost drivers'[15] and the margin attached to total costs in arriving at the final value of the good in the relevant market place. Here value is increased by the revenue the product will generate. The novel twist to Porter's analysis over standard cost analysis is that costs are attributed to activities. These activities are of two types: primary activities, involving inbound logistics, operations, outbound logistics,[16] marketing, sales, and service; and support activities, involving the firm's infrastructure, like human resource management, technological development, and procurement. Put another way, primary activities are directly concerned with making, selling and servicing the product, whilst support activities create the firm's capability to undertake primary activities, typically over a range which, in principle, could extend considerably beyond its current primary activities.

These categories are perhaps overly complex if one's goal is the analysis of the relatively simple organizational form of the SBE. In a sole proprietorship, as an example of an SBE, the owner-manager could in principle flatteringly be conceived of as 'an economic agent skilfully controlling a multi-task environment'.[17] In practice, the level of skill exercised is less than this image would suggest. In the case of the typical SBE there is no issue of human resource management, and probably no technological development or marketing. To possess a complex of primary and support activities, as analysed by Porter, the firm would have to be large: most probably a company quoted on the stock exchange. I shall, therefore, rarely have recourse to the full value chain analysis as developed for large firms. Here, the most relevant part of Porter's analysis is probably the notion of a cost driver. [18] SBEs are acutely cost conscious and therefore are keen to identify and control their principal cost drivers. Some of the cost drivers identified by Porter are: scale economies, learning effects, capacity utilization, linkages across activities, location, and discretionary policies. The last-named category is a rich 'catch-all' for policies which might affect product mix, product performance, delivery time, quality of raw materials used, and so on. In the analysis below I have not slavishly adhered to Porter's categories, but cost drivers are frequently mentioned, as appropriate for the SBE under discussion. Often the relevant cost-drivers fall within the catch-all term. For example, the so-called 'human resource policy' towards hiring is an important discretionary area for an SBE. If it is engaged in labour-intensive activities, as many small firms are, then an important cost driver is the payroll. By reconfiguring patterns of part-time versus full-time employment, and by controlling the proportions of time employees are hired to work at normal rates of remuneration compared to overtime rates, the owner-manager can achieve a subtle control of this principal cost driver.

7.4 STRUCTURE AND CONDUCT

Having set out the framework of the competitive strategy/competitive advantage approach, as modified to the case of SBEs, I turn now to empirical analysis, using data on firms A to G.

Porter's approach will first be related to structure and conduct and then in the next section to market fragmentation. Table 7.1 provides a summary treatment of the main characteristics of firms A to G in terms of the AQ 1985. All of these SBEs had small market shares (by sales) of about one-third or less, and most had very small market shares (less than one per cent). They are all therefore potential candidates for a market fragmentation analysis, as elaborated below for firms A to G. Their markets were generally local or regional. For firm A (business services) most business was delivered locally, though international customers were sometimes involved (for example through an international 24-hour telephone switchboard). Firm B (plastic injection mouldings) had an international market for some goods (such as plastic shower rings), but his main market was national. Despite considerable ranges of age (1 to 25 years) and size (2 to 24 employees, £5k to £300k assets), product ranges were very similar, all lying within the range of 2 to 5 product groups. Major competitors were usually thought to be few in number, except in the case of firm C (window cleaning), and minor competitors too were thought to be similar in numbers (again, excepting firm C), typically between one and five.

Product differentiation was typically mild. Firm F's perception that his camera-ready artwork made his products 'different from' (rather than 'similar to') rivals was probably mistaken. This confuses the uniqueness of

Table 7.1 Main characteristics of firms A to G

Attribute	Firm						
	Business services A	Plastic injection moulding B	Window cleaning C	PCB manufacture D	Industrial microfilming E	Phototypesetting F	Cardboard packaging G
Employment	1	24	2	17	3	17	10
Sales	–	£480k	£18k	£131k	£16k	£250k	£180k
Product groups	3	3	3	3	3	3	3
Main market	international	UK	local	Scotland	Scotland	local	local
Market share	25%	35%	<1%	<1%	<1%	35%	<1%
# Major competitors	3	3	20	3	3	3	3
# Minor competitors	3	3	>50	3	3	7	3
Degree of differentiation	similar	similar	similar	similar	similar	different	identical
Rivals' pricing	yes	yes	yes	yes	yes/no*	yes	no
Beating rivals	yes	yes	yes	no	yes	yes	no
Capacity utilization	<70%	<70%	75%	81–90%	no capacity	51–60%	no capacity
Cost structure	~	~	~	~	no meaning	~	~
Advertising form	independent	independent	none	none	none	independent	none
Competition	strong/weak	strong/weak	strong/weak	strong/weak	weak/strong	strong/weak	strong/weak
Personal finance	no	yes	yes	yes	yes	yes	no
Cash-flow problems	no	no	yes	yes	yes	no	no
Assets	£5k	£100k	£500	£85k	£30k	£200k	£300k
Initial gearing	1.5	0	0	0	0	0	1
New debt	no	yes	yes	yes	yes	yes	no
Age in years	1	25	2	2	6	11	8

Notes: Employment – number of full-time employees; rivals' pricing – are your rivals' pricing decisions crucial to your own?; beating rivals – do you hold down prices to beat competitors?; personal finance – was your business started using only personal finance?

Where ranges were given, mid-point values have been entered (e.g. for product groups, and # of competitors).

* Depends on customer knowledge.

the artwork in itself with the similarity in provision of artwork services. Similarly, firm G's perception that his cardboard packaging was 'identical' to rivals was probably also mistaken. It confused the physical identity of certain types of boxes with the packaging service provided. These frequently involved unique ('bespoke') qualities of the packages produced (for example, in terms of how and where slots were cut and folds were made or in terms of the labelling and artwork put on packages). Though differences in products, as compared to rivals', were therefore apparent in all cases, they were never very marked. As a consequence, it is logical that most of these SBEs regarded the pricing policies of rivals as crucial to their own pricing, and most were willing to hold down price to beat competitors, if need be. This is one aspect of a willingness to 'match' rivals' strategies. Firm G (bespoke cardboard packaging) stands out as reporting rather different behaviour. On the face of it, to say that one's product is 'identical' to that of one's few rival SBEs, and yet to claim that the pricing policy of these few rivals is not crucial to one's own pricing policy and that, further, price cuts by rivals would not be matched, is dubious reasoning. It would contradict a contestable markets model, for example. However, firm G was quite long-lived, had enjoyed rapid growth, was reasonably profitable and technically progressive. It was, in short, a successful firm. A possible interpretation of the evidence here is that this SBE had previously been deceived by false signalling, or signal jamming, and had decided to ignore signals as likely to be weak, false, or deceptive. At the same time firm G tried to signal its own quality clearly and without guile, as a company of good reputation, which had been in business for some time, and employed 'state of the art' equipment.

All these SBEs experienced substantial excess capacity or recognized no capacity limitation at all (which could be interpreted as unlimited excess or spare capacity). Non-decreasing returns to scale were typical for normal scales of operation in the short run. Competition was generally perceived to have been a mixture of strong and weak elements, with the strong predominating. Advertising, if undertaken at all, was rivalrous, rather than generic.

Regarding financial structure, these SBEs had typically been set up using only personal finance, and had sometimes experienced cash flow difficulties. Gearing was either zero at inception (which was consistent, in each relevant case, to exclusive use of personal financial injections) or else close to one, which is typical of more conservative bank lending policy, which would aim to make loans fully secured.

I conclude from the summary data in table 7.1 that these seven independent cases (firms A to G) bear a recognizable relationship to the general characteristics of the seventy-three SBEs which make up the main study database (as presented, for example, in chapter 3 above). This gives some independent corroboration of the stability (or lack of idiosyncrasy) of the main sample characteristics. It is also the case that certain attributes are especially concordant, and it may be these, rather than the more widely used measures like sales, employment, or age, which best characterize the small business enterprise. I would pick out small market shares, a plurality (but not multiplicity) of competitors, significant (but not extreme) product differentiation, significant price interdependence (non-zero conjectural variation in prices), mixed competitive pressures (with the strong predominating) significant surplus capacity, and financial conservatism (high inside equity, low gearing) as particularly significant characteristics, which also make sense in relation to economic theory. In chapter 10, for example, small numbers competition, non-zero price conjectures, strong competition and surplus capacity all play a part in the theoretical analysis that is subsequently tested by econometric methods.

7.5   MARKET FRAGMENTATION

I turn now to what Porter (1983) calls the 'generic industry environment'. Porter considers many types of environment, including the global, the declining, and the emerging. I would wish to argue that the cases considered here (firms A to G) are best treated as operating in what Porter terms fragmented industry environments. As noted above, such industries have low seller concentration and typically no stable industry leadership. According to Porter the essence of competition in fragmented markets is 'personal service, local contacts, close control of operations, ability to react to fluctuations or style changes, and so on' (Porter 1980: 211). Amongst the many US examples of fragmented markets given by Porter one notes their Scottish counterparts in several cases. For example, firm G's market (cardboard packaging) corresponds to 'folding paperboard boxes, corrugated and solid fibre boxes'. Firm B's market (plastic mouldings) 'plumbing fittings', and firm F's market (phototypesetting) corresponds to 'commercial printing'. Firm A (business services) provided a particularly good example of an SBE which was closely controlled, emphasised personal service, used local contacts heavily and was highly adaptive to fluctuations and variations in business style. It also had high transport costs in a particular sense mentioned by Porter (1980: 197). The customer had to deliver himself at his own expense to the firm to receive the service,[19] or alternatively the service had to be produced at the firm's premises.[20]

The full characterization of a fragmented industry is complex. It is also non-unique, in the sense that not all of the full set of potential characteristics need be present for a market to be regarded as fragmented. What I have done in table 7.2 is to prepare a check list for fragmented markets, listing eighteen important attributes. If an attribute is present for an SBE this is denoted by a tick, and if not, by a cross. It will be evident that only firm B (plastic injection mouldings) has less than a majority of attributes associated with fragmented markets. This SBE used quite expensive equipment to produce standardized plastic mouldings at very high volumes. In many product areas

Table 7.2 Checklist for fragmented markets

Attributes	Firm						
	Business services A	Plastic injection moulding B	Window cleaning C	PCB manufacture D	Industrial microfilming E	Phototypesetting F	Cardboard packaging G
1 Low entry barriers	✓	×	✓	×	×	×	×
2 No scale economies	✓	×	✓	×	✓	✓	×
3 High transport costs	✓	×	✓	×	×	×	×
4 Erratic sales	✓	×	✓	×	×	×	✓
5 No bargaining power	✓	×	✓	✓	✓	✓	✓
6 Specific diseconomies	✓	✓	✓	✓	✓	✓	✓
7 Low overheads	×	×	✓	×	✓	×	×
8 Diverse product lines	✓	✓	×	✓	✓	✓	✓
9 High creative content	✓	×	×	✓	×	✓	×
10 Close local control	✓	×	✓	✓	✓	✓	✓
11 Personal service	✓	×	✓	✓	✓	✓	✓
12 Local image and contacts	✓	✓	✓	✓	✓	✓	✓
13 Diverse market needs	✓	✓	×	✓	✓	✓	✓
14 Differentiation on image	✓	×	✓	✓	✓	✓	✓
15 Exit barriers	✓	×	×	×	×	×	×
16 Local regulation	×	✓	×	×	×	×	×
17 Government regulation	×	✓	×	×	×	×	×
18 New industry	✓		×	✓	✓	✓	×

Notes: Tick denotes presence of attribute; cross denotes absence of attribute.

(for example, plumbing, electrical fittings) there was close government control on technical specification. The former factors work against the fragmentation category and the latter for it, and one could extend this argument to say that there is a balance of factors both ways.[21] Probably the most important factor suggesting why this SBE is only marginally recognizable as operating in fragmented markets is its age (25 years), and the maturity of the industry. This SBE was a family business that had grown from a small local plumbing sole proprietorship. Initially, it would have had more fragmentation characteristics (for example, personal service, differentiation on image and close local control). However, the brothers in partnership, who had inherited this business from their father, had greatly increased the scale of operations and relied much more on technical specification and high volume sales to maintain their market position, than attributes emphasising more human dimensions (for example, service, image, creativity). The nationwide, and occasionally worldwide, trading of the firm also put some distance between them and their customers, increasing the anonymity of their trading relationships. Finally, as the operational side of the business had become more complex, with advanced automatic control systems being installed, and the active plant being run on a continuous 24 hour basis until high volume batch orders had been filled, the partners had ceased that earlier close local control of the business, which had involved being willing to 'put out fires' almost any time of the day or night on any day of the week. They adopted a much more 'hands-off' approach, with less frequent visits to the site, more delegation and more substitution of capital for labour. Their managerial style was best characterized as 'selective intervention', in the terminology of Williamson (1985), involving a willingness to get directly involved in various areas and levels of the business (for example marketing, sales, production, personnel) on a selective and temporary basis (for example to solve a labour relations crisis, to discuss the purchase of a new type of plant) without losing sight of the overall structure and mission of the business and drawing on a large personal 'knowledge base' (namely, a quarter of a century of successful business experience in the same trade).

As well as being the oldest, firm B (plastic injection mouldings) was by far the largest of these SBEs of table 7.2 in terms of sales turnover (£480,000) and employment (24). The figure given for assets (£100,000) was probably highly conservative, based on very low imputed values to the prospective second-hand sales prices of specialized machinery. It is probably reasonable to categorize this SBE as thoroughly into its mature phase, in terms of life cycle analysis of the firm, and operating in a stable and mature market for highly standardized products. As it develops, assuming continued good performance, one would anticipate a shift from a focus strategy to a cost leadership strategy.

An interesting contrast can be made between firm B and firm F (camera-ready artwork). Firm F had also been in business for some time (11 years), had a similar market share (35 per cent) and was quite large in terms of assets

(£200,000), sales (£250,000) and employment (17). It was also similar to firm B in many other ways (product range, number of rivals, intensity of competition, debt, gearing, etc.), as is evident from table 7.1 above. However, turning to table 7.2, firm F scores much higher than firm B on fragmentation characteristics. Image, personal service, creative content, erratic sales, lack of scale economies, and (despite this SBE's own maturity) operating in a relatively new market, all mark out firm F as pursuing competitive strategy in a fragmented market. It is a good example of what Porter (1980: 191) calls 'creative business'. This is especially true of firm A (business services) which scores highest on the fragmentation count in table 7.2. Firm A achieved its sales very much as a by-product of its image. The owner-manager was a well-presented and articulate entrepreneur with a previous career in interior design; and her business premises, which clients could use on a rental basis, reflected imaginative design skills. Other SBEs in table 7.2, like firms C, D, and E share average fragmentation market characteristics, despite their diverse product markets (window cleaning, design of printed circuit boards, and microfilming respectively).

Firm G (bespoke cardboard packaging) bears some comparison with firm B (plastic injection moulding) which perhaps least displayed fragmentation characteristics. Firm G had also been in existence for some time (8 years), and had substantial assets (£300,000). However, its market share (< 1 per cent) was by contrast very small and the bespoke nature of its orders was quite unlike the production style of firm B. Though the owner-manager of firm G had insisted his products were 'identical' to rivals (probably a misnomer, as the analysis above has earlier suggested), I was impressed during interviews by the extent to which he was involved in the design of packages. This was quite a creative act, involving the capacity to see how a two-dimensional sheet could be converted to a three-dimensional container, which not only required engineering properties like the strength to hold or protect their contents, but also aesthetic properties, like displaying goods in an attractive way.

Two examples come to mind of how the owner-manager of firm G ran what was in some measure a 'creative business'. Clients had come to him who produced Scottish 'home produce' jams. The value added of this enterprise hinged on being able to convince the customer of the exclusiveness of the product. The clients felt their firm's image had become dreary and needed re-vamping. The owner-manager of firm G came up with a triple-pack cardboard package in an attractive floral design which displayed three different pots of jam simultaneously to good effect. It had proved a significant marketing success for the client. The second example concerns the use of plastic, rather than cardboard, corrugated sheets. This material was found to be too expensive to substitute for cardboard packaging for conventional purposes (for example the transportation of bottles of wine in divided boxes). However, the owner-manager came up with the idea that it could be used for higher value-added products, and had developed a prototype for a bicycle pannier as mentioned briefly in section 7.3 above. The available trade substitute would be made in fibreglass or light metal and would have slight aerodynamic advantages. However, the plastic corrugated pannier would be cheaper, lighter, and of comparable strength. It presented a low-cost alternative to established rival products, and provides a good example of creative selling in fragmented markets.

7.6 COMPETITIVE STRATEGY

Discussion so far has had two aims. First, to set out an appropriate analytical framework for analysing small firms, involving an extension of the existing large firms framework (section 7.2). Second, to relate in a preliminary way the case study evidence on SBEs to the familiar categories of structure and conduct (section 7.4) and to justify the empirical presumption that a market fragmentation approach is appropriate (section 7.5). These theoretical and empirical preliminaries having been set aside, the way is now clear to get at the core concepts of competitive strategy and defensive strategy in the next two sections.

In section 7.3.1 I set out the elements of the competitive advantage/competitive strategy approach as applied to SBEs. The components of it were analysed under the headings of cost leadership, differentiation and focus. These same headings will be used here and empirical content injected into them from the cases of firms A to G.

7.6.1 Cost leadership

Given the competitive pressure under which all these SBEs operated, there was always a pressure to control costs.[22] Cost control was thought of in both organizational as well as engineering and accounting terms. There was an awareness that organizational design (for example, assignment of tasks, fostering of learning) was as important for cost control as attempts to exploit scale economies, or to get the best deal in terms of purchasing factors of production.

For given plant and equipment, firms A to G did not record decreasing returns in any case, though there was considerable variation in experience of scale economies. I shall distinguish between SBEs with potentially large-scale economies (firms B, D, and G) and those without (firms A, C, E, and F).

In principle, firm B (plastic injection moulding), firm D (PCB manufacture and design) and firm G (cardboard packaging) could all enjoy substantial scale economies. Yet of these three, probably only firm B exploited scale effects. Firm D specialized by preference in the design side of printed circuit boards (PCBs) rather than the volume production side. Firm G had a high volume production capability, but instead preferred to use its flexibility to fill bespoke, smaller batch orders. Firm B (plastic injection mouldings) has previously been shown to be less obviously operating in fragmented markets than the other six SBEs under consideration, making the use of a focus strategy less necessary, yet it had not been seeking to pursue a pure cost leadership strategy. Economies of scale for this firm were very significant, and cost control was very tight. Every product item was put through a detailed costing system, and it was known that raw materials were the principal cost driver. As a consequence, excess plastic was trimmed off at the extruding stage, and then subsequently chopped up, melted, and reused in manufacturing. The value chain was set at monthly intervals to cover costs and provide good profit margins. However, there was limited discretion in price setting, because prices were set by purchasing oligopsonists. Whilst better placed to pursue cost leadership than the other SBEs analysed, sufficient benefits from low-cost differentiation remained (see section 7.6.2 below) for a focus strategy to be pursued. Firm D (PCB manufacture and design) was much more explicit in denying a cost leadership strategy. Whilst capable of volume production, which certainly gave rise to significant scale economies, its capabilities in this direction fell far short of very much larger rivals who achieved massive production levels. Rather than play this game, which it was felt bound to lose, firm D concentrated on achieving cost reductions through changes to production processes and by reorganization. Firm G (cardboard packaging) could, and did on occasion, engage in high volume production. The owner-manager admitted to a low break-even point, suggesting the high profitability of volume production. The main cost drivers were identified as wages and raw materials, and a sufficiently tight costing system was run that it was thought there was little leeway for further cost control. However, its specialization in bespoke orders limited firm G's ability to exploit scale economies.

The main point that emerges from these cases is that a mere potential for high volume production does not imply it will be fully exploited. The flexibility to produce a wide variety of batch sizes (including the very large) according to agreed ('bespoke') specification is apparently the form of specialization conferring competitive advantage on SBEs in these cases.[23]

7.6.2 Differentiation

A differentiation strategy may go hand in hand with a cost leadership strategy if sales are targeted at a market segment, rather than aimed at the industry as a whole. Firms A to F all agreed that they pursued some form of differentiation strategy, and this strategy, whilst not admitted by firm G, was also characteristic of it under any sensible interpretation, as suggested by the earlier discussion of product differentiation in section 7.4 above. A common theme in all cases is the importance of personal services. Such services are often the source of efficiency advantages of small over large firms. They are, as Porter has observed, 'the key to the business' and emphasise the 'quality of personal service and the customer's perception that individualized, responsive service is being provided' (Porter 1980: 198). Thus firm A (business services) said that the main source of differentiation was 'the personal touch', firm E (industrial microfilming) thought its competitive advantage lay in the quality of its service over that of rivals, arguing that quality was an important though often neglected control parameter. Firm F (phototypesetting), like firm A, also explicitly mentioned 'the personal touch' and identified customers' purchasing criteria as efficiency, availability, price, and quality. Similarly, firm C (window cleaning) emphasised differentiation in terms of 'reliability and accessibility to customers'. Even where cost leadership provided a potential strategy emphasis, as with firm B (plastic mouldings) and firm D (PCB manufacture), the predominant emphasis was on differentiation. [24] In the case of firm B, as analysed earlier in section 7.3.1 above, it was found that some forms of physical product differentiation could even be unit cost reducing (for example, the use of 'crackle' rather than smooth finishes on components). More typically, however, expenditure is incurred to increase product differentiation and this raises the unit cost of production. The SBE may be regarded as undertaking a kind of investment in reputational stock for its product. Investments of this sort, if rationally undertaken, will be profit enhancing. They bring a return in terms of capturing additional customers, increasing customers' loyalty, and reducing customers' sensitivity to upward price adjustment (partly through raising customers' switching costs). The choice typically made by the seven cases considered was to seek relatively low cost forms of product differentiation, emphasising rapid response, quality of service and personal treatment of customers. In short, they capitalized on inputs of entrepreneurial and managerial effort, viewed as specialized factors of production.

7.6.3   Focus

A focus strategy aims to achieve for each individual SBE a unique mix of cost control and product differentiation. I would suggest from the evidence above that the focus strategy emphasised for the SBEs considered, was more on differentiation than cost leadership. Typically cost control was thought to be tight, and the confinement of operations to market segments (rather than the industry) provided limited potential for scale economies, where they might exist (for example, for firms B and G, operating in plastic mouldings and PCB manufacturing, respectively). Indeed, some SBEs supplied products for which scale economies were not important (for example, firms A and E, operating in business services and industrial microfilming, respectively).

Product modifications were often customer driven. Firm B (plastic mouldings) said that design improvements were often customer stimulated, and firm D (PCB manufacture and design) said that customers could suggest innovations. These customer inputs clearly might have cost leadership benefits as well, but were primarily governed by the willingness of the SBE to take the customer seriously. To illustrate, firm A (business services) aimed to be 'people oriented', firm D (PCB manufactures) said 'we look at problems from the customer's angle' and firm G (bespoke cardboard packaging) said 'we take things from the customer's end'.

Thus a preoccupation in the pursuit of a focus strategy by these SBEs was with the customer. He was well treated, listened to carefully, and in some measure allowed to participate in the activities of the SBE (for example by commenting on product design, and making suggestions for modifications). Supply and demand were therefore interdependent. When firm G (bespoke cardboard packing) said that 'differentiation appears in the personal touch' and 'we work to customer specification' it illustrated precisely this point. The demands of customers modified the form and extent of supply; and keeping channels open ('the personal touch') fostered this interdependence. The lack of such channels could lead to customer discontent and a diminution of loyalty. Firm D (PCB manufactures) found that a significant amount of trade came its way because new customers had been discontented with previous suppliers. In Hirschman's (1970) terminology, being denied a satisfactory voice option, they exited from the trading relationship. The customer desired a product which fitted his need, rather than one which was to the convenience of existing patterns of supply. Flexibility of the SBE in meeting these needs, and a fast response (for example on design and delivery) were important aspects of the focus strategy. To the extent that customers were localized, the SBE was better able to benefit from any interdependence between demand and supply of the sort I have analysed. These potential benefits from customer localization encouraged market fragmentation and, in turn, the pursuit of a focus strategy for competitive advantage.

7.7 DEFENSIVE STRATEGY

Defensive strategy is devised to deter or pre-empt potentially damaging moves by rivals. It is effective if rivals do not even attempt to damage the interests of an SBE. A clearly signalled commitment to sharp, accurately targeted retaliation against possibly hostile moves is an excellent way of deterring such moves. Communicating commitment can be done by having obvious asset advantages like cash reserves and excess productive capacity. Other ways of signalling commitment include a history of sticking to commitments, and the announcing of intentions through trade media (such as trade shows, journals) regarding desired market share, planned investment in open plant etc.

Bearing in mind that a defensive strategy has not necessarily failed if an SBE has never had to use retaliatory tactics, one observes that overt retaliation is rather uncommon in the cases considered (namely, firms A to G). Firm F (artwork and phototypesetting) tried to create a commitment to defend its market niche by projecting a highly professional image suggesting 'we are here to stay'. It was felt that high quality advertising would deter potential competitors by making them aware of the opposition they would have to overcome to get a toe-hold in the market. Firm A (business services), firm D (PCB manufacture), and firm E (microfilm services) also thought high professionalism signalled a commitment to the market. Firm G (cardboard packaging) felt that he tried to adhere to 'a standard for proper trading', which is another way of describing professionalism. This projection of a highly professional image was not only designed to discourage entry, and thus was an aspect of defensive strategy, but also, if it had substance, fostered that close control of a firm's operations which was necessary for success in fragmented markets.

The way in which professionalism would be used to defend a market position also sets bounds on legitimate forms of defence. 'Good' competitors were distinguished from 'bad' competitors, the hallmark of the former type of firm being that it adhered to proper standards in trading.[25] If it did so, certain benefits would arise. Rivals would gain respect, and would gain trade from referrals, and might even receive other forms of help (such as advice from well-established incumbents at the point of starting up). In other words, established firms would try to apportion such rewards as were within their discretion (for example excess orders, trade intelligence) to rivals who were behaving in ways which were beneficial to the group as a whole. The discrediting (more colloquially 'knocking') of rivals was not generally regarded as a proper practice, even though it had obvious use as a competitive strategy. As firm A (business services) pointed out, if the rival behaved he would not be 'knocked' though he might not be praised. Firm D (PCB manufacture and design) said a similar thing, claiming he would not 'knock' a 'good' competitor, but would rather emphasise what he called 'the relative merits' of his own products. A lapse from 'good' competitor status would change the reactions of rivals. If attacked, firm B (plastic injection mouldings) would feed misleading trade gossip ('dummy info') to sales representatives who were known to be gossipy and likely to carry tales to 'bad' competitors. Firm D (PCB manufacture and design) also claimed to put selective information through supply channels as a defence against attacks from 'bad' competitors. Thus whilst on occasion firms tried to provide good clear signals to make their market commitment unambiguous, they were also capable of selective use of 'signal jamming' for strategic purposes.

One of the serious lapses from being a 'good' competitor was thought to be the poaching of customers. Firm G (cardboard packaging), which was well established, disapproved of such behaviour, but took a lofty attitude, saying that there would be no response to the snatching of customers and 'no comment' was the best defence to this sort of attack. His experience had been that snatched customers often returned after a spell with a 'bad' competitor. Of course, the economic fortunes of a 'bad' competitor would not be helped by the withdrawal of group favours like the referal of excess orders. Firm C (window and industrial cleaning) said there was an industry understanding that firms would not poach customers. If poaching did occur, the 'bad' competitor could expect rivals to pay him a visit to condemn his action, in demotic terms. Firm E (microfilm services) also felt that it was important to avoid a reputation for poaching. If a firm got one, it would always need to watch its back.

A common form of defence involved the gathering of trade intelligence. Firm A (business services) found that suppliers could provide useful insight into rivals. It also used customers for gathering trade intelligence but thought it important to depend on loyal customers only for such information. Firm D (PCB manufacture and design) and firm E (microfilm services) found trade press coverage to be an important source of intelligence for defensive purposes.

Technical progressiveness was also perceived to be a good defensive strategy. Firm B (plastic mouldings) pointed out that it helped overcome the difficulty of anticipating the form of attacks by rivals. Being ahead of the pack, technically speaking, enabled the firm to take chances in terms of experimenting with new product lines. If this worked, then an advantage followed in terms of diversification. If it did not, then the new products (in this trade at least) could be rapidly withdrawn with little loss. This so-called 'shot-gun tactic' was thought to be a good way of pre-empting the invasion of potentially profitable niches by rivals. For this reason, technical intelligence was gathered and evaluated on new materials, even before their use for novel products seemed commercially viable. Firm G (cardboard packaging) thought that his use of modern plant was the best (passive) defence against rivals. Indeed, he felt that no active defensive strategy was necessary if the firm was technically progressive. For example, blocking tactics against rivals were thought to be unnecessary, and even improper. Effort was invested in keeping abreast of new technological changes in the industry, in recognition of the way in which new technology could deter attacks. For example, new developments in computer aided production and multiple packaging were being monitored. Firm F (phototypesetting) also worked in a market where technical progress was important. Like firm B, it constantly sought for new product lines. This had its defensive as well as offensive dimension. Filling product gaps was also a form of pre-emptive strategy, which aimed to defend a niche from invasion by rivals. It was thought to be critical to the running of this type of business. Firm E (microfilm services) monitored new technical developments through reports in trade journals, and kept a close watch on how developments toward the technological goal of a fully 'electronic office' would affect his trade. His technology was arguably as advanced as electronic alternatives, but possibly less convenient to use: hence being informed of emerging technical substitutes was an aspect of defensive strategy.

In military strategy it is sometimes said that the best form of defence is attack. This reminds one that a distinction is to be made between active and passive forms of defence. From the analysis of this section it is clear that the SBEs whose case histories are under scrutiny generally put less emphasis on a defensive strategy than on competitive strategy, and to the extent that they used defensive strategy generally did so in a passive rather than active form. By contrast to the strategies discussed in sections 7.3, 7.4 and 7.6, defensive strategies were less rich and pursued with less conviction, if at all. Firm D (PCB manufacture and design), for example, did not see a need for an overt defensive strategy. In this case, defensive strategy was more covert, and involved preparing in a lost-cost fashion for contingencies that might not ever arise (for example, collecting trade intelligence on potential rival products) or using low-cost propaganda (so-called 'cheap talk') to jam, or make more noisy signals through known trade channels. Firm C (window cleaning) was fairly typical in arguing that deterrence was not a large part of its concern because the firm was still establishing a market niche, and had not yet been confronted with a significant loss of customers. Only firm E (microfilm services) suggested it might lower profit margins to lower the inducement for attack by rivals, but this overt and active form of defensive strategy had not actually been used in practice by this SBE, and apparently had not been contemplated by the other SBEs.

7.8 CONCLUSION

This chapter has introduced a new variant of the competitive strategy/ competitive advantage approach, modified to be applicable to the case of the small business enterprise (SBE). First, the relevant analytical framework was developed. Second, empirical evidence bearing on this framework, from seven case studies, was introduced by way of an examination of structure and conduct, and of market fragmentation. Third, the centre piece of the chapter was developed, showing how this empirical evidence could be analysed in terms of competitive and defensive strategies. It was clear that whilst not neglecting defensive strategy, the typical SBE, especially if operating early in its life cycle, was more concerned with devising an aggressive competitive strategy. The next chapter (chapter 8) aims to extend the analysis of competitive strategy developed in this chapter, by looking in more detail at the forces of competition.

8 The forces of competition

8.1 INTRODUCTION

The natural starting point for an extended analysis of competitive forces, as applied to firms A to G, must be with intra-industry analysis of rivalry. The latter is the focus of attention in the well-known structure-conduct-performance (S/C/P) approach. Taking this as the starting point, Porter's 'competitive forces' approach enlarges the scope of (S/C/P) to embrace both extra-industry (for example, potential entrants, substitutes) and strategic considerations (for example, market pre-emption, signal jamming, the carrying of excess capacity). By reference to firms A to G this chapter takes a further step toward a full 'competitive advantage' analysis. I look at market fragmentation and the devising of a focus strategy, in terms of Porter's 'five forces of competition'.

Intra-industry rivalry will be considered under the headings of: industrial concentration and balance; industrial growth; fixed costs versus value added; intermittent overcapacity; product differentiation; competitor diversity; strategic stakes; and entry and exit barriers. These are the probes used under 'rivalry' in the semi-structured interviews (SSI 1985). The evidence used goes beyond this, to that generated by the other instruments as well (the AQ 1985 and the RIQ 1988).

Broadly speaking, the markets in which the SBEs operated were heterogeneous oligopolies. That is, firms produced differentiated products and were in significant interdependence with their (few) rivals. I have indicated earlier that major and minor rivals were readily distinguished, but this is in itself not necessarily a statement about industrial concentration and balance. Based on further evidence from semi-structured interviews, it is apparent that these seven SBEs operated in two types of industry, as indicated in table 8.1.

As a matter of general principle, in balanced industries firms are competing against rather similar sized rivals, whereas in unbalanced industries, whilst there may be a fringe of similar sized firms there are also much larger rivals. In the latter case, larger rivals are not necessarily regarded as major competitors: there is also a need to consider what niches the larger rivals attempt to occupy in implementing a focus strategy. As I shall argue, the main

Table 8.1 Industrial balance amongst firms A to G

Balanced industries	Unbalanced industries
Firm A, business services	Firm B, plastic mouldings
Firm C, window cleaning	Firm D, printed circuit board (PCB) manufacture
Firm E, microfilm services	Firm G, cardboard packaging
Firm F, phototypesetting	

implication of the evidence seems to be that it is proximity in niches that is regarded as the most significant competitive threat.

The occupation of niches is made easier if the industry is growing. Most SBEs of table 8.1 operated in high growth industries especially firms B (plastic mouldings), D (printed circuit board manufacture), and E (microfilm services). Growth was potentially high for firms A (business services) and F (phototypesetting) and 'steady' for G (cardboard packaging). Only firm C (window cleaning) operated in a low growth rate industry. It is noticeable that firm C regarded strategic stakes as being particularly high in new markets, undoubtedly because competition to occupy new niches was intense, given the relative infrequency with which such opportunities arose. Earlier discussion (section 7.7) above indicated that this also led to a more stringent defensive strategy on the part of firm C, aimed at discouraging the 'poaching' of customers.

Per contra, their general access to growing markets made most SBEs relatively non-hostile to rivals, provided they were not in neighbouring niches. There was the feeling amongst owner-managers that enough new market territory was available for all to get a share. For the unbalanced industries there was some evidence that large dominant firms facilitated better-organized markets.[1] For example, firm G operated in a market where five dominant firms had 80 per cent of the market in terms of sales, three medium-sized firms had 15 per cent and the remaining eight had 5 per cent. Firm G itself had less than 1 per cent of the market. Without fast growth (here growth was merely 'steady') there might have been the possibility that potential new entrants would upset market co-ordination, particularly given the low entry barriers in this case. However, the existence of dominant firms which in some measure dictated policy to fringe firms (for example firm G in the fringe took prices as 'given') had the consequence of improving co-ordination and reducing volatility in the market. Thus in firm G's market it was said that dominant firms were sufficiently confident of their position of power that they welcomed the entry of new small firms into the fringe. Given this well-established dominance, small new entrants would certainly not constitute a significant threat to the dominant group, and might even inadvertently confer benefits on it. For example, they could encourage retaliatory responses by incumbent small firms in the fringe, who might feel directly threatened by the prospect of entry by similar rivals. This would divert fringe firms from attempting to mount a challenge against the dominant group. Further, additional fringe members would multiply the sub-contracting possibilities for the dominant group and thus increase its bargaining power over the fringe.

None of the SBEs under discussion could be characterized as having high fixed costs, either absolutely or, more importantly, in relation to value added. Outside inputs did not account for a high proportion of costs, as is characteristic, for example, of certain extractive industries (for example the mining of valuable ores like gold, silver, copper, and aluminium). That sort of effect would tend to encourage high capacity utilization and price cutting, neither of which were characteristic of these SBEs. Further, none of the SBEs produced perishable products, or products that were difficult or costly to store. Only firm D (PCB manufacture) ran a particularly high level of capacity utilization (of the order of 90 per cent), most others running at 70 per cent or less of capacity, or even recognizing no capacity limit at all. Therefore one would not have expected downward pressure on profit margins or a tendency to price cutting wars, and indeed these were not observed. The limited evidence available on profit rates suggested good to adequate returns.[2] Price wars were not reported in any instance, and indeed the frequent reference to 'good' competitors suggested the reverse (namely, a tendency to tacit price agreements or to 'focal' price equilibria).[3]

Low product differentiation and/or low switching costs would tend to encourage market instability and intense price and service competition. For all the SBEs under discussion this was a potential danger; and they made great efforts to differentiate their products by service and delivery. In several cases the custom-designed aspect of orders was high, which would tend to raise switching costs.[4] Most SBEs perceived product differentiation to be significant, and where they did not (see section 7.4 above) this judgement was probably faulty or inaccurately communicated. Elbow-room in pricing was typically quite high (averaging 10 per cent), suggesting significant customer switching costs, even when product differentiation was perceived to be slight.[5]

Diversity of competitors may encourage disorganized markets and head-on collisions of rivals (for example destructive competition by two SBEs trying to occupy the same market niche). This arises because such rivals may be relatively poorly informed about one another, and may find it difficult to read meaning into one anothers' strategies. In short there may be a lack of what was previously referred to (section 7.7 above) as 'standards of proper trading'. For the SBEs considered here, diversity was low and a shared frame of reference was common. There appeared to be no vigorous attempts to mimic diversity through emphasising specific idioyncracies (for example of location or history) or through 'irrational' (for example non-pecuniary) owner-manager goals (for example emphasising control over profitability), though elements of both were present in some measure, in all cases. SBEs were well informed about close rivals which were typically few in number, say six) and invested effort through trade channels (for example travelling sales representatives) in trying to 'read' rivals strategic moves. Well-established 'standards of trading' were common and 'good' competitors were encouraged and rewarded. As a result, competition was typically symbiotic rather than cut-throat or destructive. A danger exists that small firms in a competitive fringe might limit the profitability of larger dominant firms,[6] for example through a willingness to trade off the utility of ownership against profitability. Diversity would encourage this effect. However, owner-managers in fringe firms and dominant firms alike generally seemed aware of the danger of letting the odd 'rogue' or idiosyncratic firm spoil the market. As analysed above (section 7.7) 'bad' competitors would be sanctioned for this perceived misbehaviour. SBEs in the fringe therefore tended to take the price of the dominant firm as given, and would, at least overtly, price up to it. No doubt some off-list price chiselling did occur occasionally, though fear of detection would limit this perceived trading misdemeanour.

High strategic stakes would normally imply volatility in rivalry, in a competitive strategy framework. Though all SBEs under consideration had owner-managers who claimed to have high strategic stakes, one wonders how this squares up with the known tendency of SBEs to reposition in the market quite substantially over time intervals like three years.[7] A high strategic stake appears to be a form of pre-commitment to a market niche. However, shifting to other niches is not necessarily very costly in most cases, and many niches vanish quite quickly because of a short 'time to harvest' of the product (i.e. a complete product life cycle). Thus signalling high strategic stakes at the time of occupancy of a niche is a good defensive strategy, and helps to bolster profitability. In the case of these SBEs, occupancy of a niche may be short-lived, and an ability to 'up stakes' and move to another niche is common and involves no apparent weakening of strategic credibility in defending the new niche.

Finally I turn to entry and exit barriers. The combination of low entry barriers with high exit barriers may have negative consequences: excess capacity; low or negative returns on investment; and the occasional resort to extreme tactics (for example dumping, pirating of designs) because of the vulnerability of SBEs in this situation. Typically, for the SBEs under consideration, both entry and exit barriers were low.[8] Of the two, there was a slight tendency for exit barriers to be perceived as higher than entry barriers. Low entry and exit barriers would partly explain the observed mobility of SBEs between adjacent niches.

High exit barriers are not typical, but when they do exist can undoubtedly lock-in the SBE to continued market activity in the face of poor returns. For example, firm A (business services) operated under conditions of low entry barriers and high exit barriers, the latter because of a commitment to a lease of several years on prestigious business premises. The rate of profit was not reported, but certainly for each year over the three-year period from inception this SBE had made losses though it had not gone out of business. It is true that early losses, for some time after financial inception, are typical of the life cycle characteristics of SBEs. However, in this case it may be that there were arguments for the exit of firm A which were not invoked sooner because of the existence of high exit barriers. [9]

Despite this case, low rather than high exit barriers appeared to be more typical. The implications of this are consistent with the analysis and observations above of market repositioning. Quite simply, one expects and observes, a willingness of SBEs to be flexible. They move to new niches as returns in the market dictate.

8.2 BARGAINING LEVERAGE OF CUSTOMERS

If customers are few in number, and are significant purchasers of an SBE's product, then they have some bargaining leverage. This can be used to enhance both the quality of the product supplied, and the terms on which it is supplied (including speed of delivery, guarantees, and after-sales service). More obviously, customers can also 'beat down' the transaction prices of products through the force of their threat to buy from an alternative supplier. For the SBEs considered here, customer concentration was generally low. Something like thirty regular customers appeared to be quite a common figure, with considerable customer diversity. Thus firm C (window cleaning) had customers ranging from households to large firms, firm E (microfilm services) had customers ranging from one-man businesses to a large public corporation, and firm F (phototypesetting) had customers ranging from 'the man off the street' to companies and government agencies. Customers were typically of two types: a core of regular customers; and a fringe often very much larger, of occasional or chance customers. [10] The longer the SBE had been in business, the more successfully could it handle a measure of customer concentration without a decline in profitability attributable to a disadvantage in bargaining. Firms A (business services) and G (cardboard packaging) illustrate this point well, from the perspectives of weak and strong bargaining power, respectively. Both firms had rather more concentration of customers than was typical. Firm G, for example, had some thirty main customers and said that 15 per cent of his customers accounted for 75 per cent of his sales. Nevertheless, firm G was relatively profitable. It had the significant advantage of being well established, and it enjoyed a lot of repeat custom. As a result of this, the owner-manager was very phlegmatic about the loss of any one customer. In his experience, customers often came back after the experience of buying rivals' products. By contrast, firm A was not well established and lacked a significant amount of repeat custom. It was still in the position of trying to establish a competitive niche. Firm A depended on the custom of a limited range of large companies and, to judge by its negative profitability in a market where value was very much subjectively (rather than 'cost-plus') determined was at a significant disadvantage in bargaining.

This study did not extend to investigating the customers of SBEs in as much detail as the SBEs themselves. It is therefore not possible to get a detailed picture of the extent to which customers felt, and actually were, dependent upon the SBE as a supplier. However, SBEs themselves are customers and one gets some idea of how seller dependence operates in the world of small firms from evidence on the factor markets of SBEs. I have therefore chosen to deal with seller dependence in section 8.4 below on suppliers.

In the same way as SBEs work to avoid seller dependence (see 8.4 below) they also try to avoid buyer (i.e. customer) dependence. An aspect of such dependence has already been discussed above under the general label of customer concentration. More narrowly, here I wish to look at the relative sales volumes generated by client buyers. Most of the SBEs being considered were subject to low relative buying volume, either in the nature of things or because of explicit policy, or both. Firm D (PCB manufacture and design) had a strict rule that there would be no more than 15 per cent of turnover accounted for by any one customer. Firm E (microfilm services) had a policy of avoiding over-dependence on customers who accounted for a significant fraction of sales, but found that a buoyant demand for microfilming services in general naturally attenuated this form of customer dependence. Firms B, C, F, and G were not too dependent on high volume and value customers. However again firm A (business services) stood out as being in an unfavourable situation. It was dependent on a few high purchase value customers.

Switching costs refer to costs incurred by customers on a one-shot basis when they change suppliers. They might involve retraining costs, redesign costs, and more generally psychic costs arising from the disutility of changed circumstances. To give an example, customers of firm B (plastic mouldings) frequently specified the characteristics of products in a way which required some in-house design activity on a new mould or die. It was at the discretion of firm B whether this fixed cost would be borne by itself or by its customer. For a favoured customer firm B would undertake the redesign gratis, in anticipation of further orders. Should that customer move to another supplier it would not be received as a favoured customer, and would therefore be liable to meet the fixed cost of a new mould or die. This fixed cost is part of his switching cost. There may of course, be additional switching costs in this case. Firm D (PCB design and manufacture) operated a similar system for tooling costs for a new printed circuit board (PCB).

Switching costs were generally evaluated as high, even in cases where they were perhaps not naturally so, in the sense of, for example, the practices of firms B and D with respect to redesign costs. Firm E (microfilm services) admitted that 'switching costs are not naturally high, but we attempt to raise them'. Because SBEs emphasise personal service so much in the delivery of their product, the discretion they can exercise in the supply of valuable personal services amounts to a switching cost. Thus, firm F (phototypesetting) claimed to raise switching costs in this way for valued customers: 'We would work to 5 a.m. to keep a good customer sweet'. Firm C (window cleaning) referred to the high 'nuisance value' imposed on switching customers. In conclusion, switching costs were typically high and their magnitudes were in some measure consciously controlled by the SBEs to 'lock-in' desirable customers.

Backward integration as a strategic threat might enhance a customer's bargaining position *vis à vis* the SBE. The credibility of this threat would in some measure rest on the perceived technological capability of the customer for carrying it through, which in turn would be made more valuable if there were several recent examples in the trade of successful backward integration. For the SBEs being considered here, backward integration was neither common not particularly threatening. The strategy was more likely to be contemplated, or even attempted, by larger customers.[11] A significant impediment to backward integration was the infrequency with which certain SBEs' products were required. Indeed, the externalization of some large firms' activities which has mostly accounted for the growth of small firms in the last decade, is driven precisely by the economics of disintegration rather than integration. Out-house provision may be more economic than in-house provision, with efficiency being promoted by the market (as opposed to the bureaucratic) mediation of transactions.[12] To illustrate, firm E (industrial microfilming) provided a service which was required only sporadically, even by very large enterprises. In general, it would not be economic to attempt to internalize this service by backward integration. In some cases, customers might attempt to employ the tactic of 'tapered integration' to enhance bargaining power.[13] This involves the customer installing a partial in-house capability for a certain good, procuring the rest externally. Firm D (PCB manufacture and design) was subject to the threat of backward integration in this way. Some of its customers (about eight out of seventy) were also rival firms, and they also had a prototype 'shop' for developing new printed circuit boards (PCBs). Backward integration could be 'tapered' by varying the scale of the prototype shop. Further, the credibility of full backward integration was greatly increased in this case because of the customers' manifest in-house technological capability. The classical way of countering a threat of backward integration would be to threaten forward integration into the customers' activities. Firm G (cardboard packaging) had consciously demonstrated an awareness of this strategy to customers who might contemplate backward integration. In the case of firm D, the 15 per cent limitation of turnover by value of any customer's trade was the device chosen to limit exposure to the risk of backward integration.

To the extent that the customer of an SBE is well informed, one would expect this to confer relative bargaining strength on him in his dealings with the owner-manager. The nature of the information in terms of detail (for example, technical specification) and extent (for example, from marketing to personnel) would govern the force of this bargaining power. Empirically speaking, a natural starting point is the fact that the supplier (as an SBE) and his customers are not equally well-informed about the product being produced and purchased. The SBE as a supplier has considerable in-house knowledge that is concealed from his customer and only imperfectly revealed by his behaviour (for example by his pricing strategy). On the other hand, the customer may on occasion have better knowledge than the supplier of aspects of demand conditions, and it is this which enables him to make suggestions to the supplier of desirable design modifications, as discussed in section 7.6.3 above. The typical picture for the cases being examined was that, for any given SBE, the customers varied widely in their knowledge-ability. At the polar extremes were firm D (PCB design and manufacture) who found customers were technically well informed and could be regarded as experts, and firm G (bespoke cardboard packaging) who considered his customers were not technically minded. [14] Firm E (microfilm services) found that customers were not technically minded, but might know of a few technical features of the products. This was similar to the experience of firm A (business services), whose customers were not knowledgeable but might be fussy about specific needs. If customers were not informed, that could be an impediment to sales. In such cases, it would be advantageous for the SBE to help the customer become better informed. Thus firm B (plastic mouldings) was willing to give uninformed customers some design assistance, as indicated above, this being paid for by new customers, but being provided free of charge to repeat customers. Trade customers, especially rivals, consti-tuted an important class of expert customers. For example, about a quarter of the customers of firm D (PCB manufacture and design) were in the same trade (and hence expert) and for firm F (phototypesetting) customers who were publishers were regarded as experts. Firms A, B, C, E, and F all had customer bases which varied from the expert to the uninformed. Other things being equal, one would expect customer knowledgeability to be negatively related to the elbow-room in pricing. For this small group of SBEs this effect did not generally show through. Thus firms D and G had, respectively, both expert and ignorant customers, yet the elbow-room in pricing of both types (10 to 15 per cent) was the same. Elbow-room in pricing was generally con-siderable (10 per cent or more). [15] For the only firm that deliberately aimed to reduce customer ignorance, firm B (plastic mouldings), the elbow-room in pricing (2 to 3 per cent) was considerably lower than the norm, confirming economic reasoning. For the other cases, it must be that further factors affecting elbow-room in pricing, like degree of product differentiation, had a more important influence than customer knowledgeability.

To conclude this section, it is apparent that, for the cases under consider-ation, the bargaining leverage of customers was not great. In general, customer concentration was not high and SBEs worked to keep it that way. Further, they worked to raise customers' switching costs, and were generally not vulnerable to threats of backward integration. Barring 'trade customers' most customers did not have an important informational advantage over their supplying SBEs to exploit. In short, the customer and the SBE (as his supplier) were evenly matched in bargaining power, and neither was powerful in an absolute sense.

8.3 PRICE SENSITIVITY OF CUSTOMERS

It has been indicated above that the price sensitivity of customers did not seem to be great, despite the substantial elbow-room in pricing which firms A to G (excepting firm B) enjoyed. In this sense from the viewpoint of the SBEs these customers may be regarded as what Porter calls 'good buyers'.[16] SBEs seek to create 'good buyers', and do not regard this characteristic as exogenous. For example, part of the advertising or marketing of an SBE, even if it is no more formal than verbal 'sales pitch', will aim to convince potential buyers that the quality of their own goods will be greatly enhanced if the products of their SBE are purchased.

If the cost of an SBE's product is low in relation to the total costs being incurred by the customer, it is to be expected that the price sensitivity of the customer will be reduced. For all the SBEs under consideration in this chapter (firms A to G), the relative cost of buying their products was low in relation to their customers' total costs. Running through some examples of the goods these SBEs produced, the empirical validity of this is evident by reference to table 8.2.

What I have done in this table is to indicate a typical product of an SBE (such as a printed circuit board) and next to it a typical product of a customer of this SBE (for example a heartbeat monitor). In the case of firm D (PCB manufacture), a printed circuit board purchased from it for several pounds might be used in hospital diagnostic equipment which sells for hundreds or even thousands of pounds. The owner-manager of firm G (bespoke cardboard packaging) put the matter very clearly when he said that a specialized microscope worth thousands of pounds might be put in a box worth just a few pounds. Customers, like their SBE suppliers, will try to identify and tightly

Table 8.2 SBEs' products and possible uses in customers' products

Firm	An example of a product	A possible customer's product
A (business services)	*Poste-restante* mail	Offshore oil consultancy
B (plastic mouldings)	Shower curtain rings	Fitted bathroom
C (window cleaning)	Clean windows	High street retailing
D (PCB manufacture)	Printed circuit board	Heartbeat monitor
E (industrial microfilming)	Microfilmed manual	Aircraft maintenance
F (phototypesetting)	Artwork poster	Musical review
G (cardboard packaging)	Slotted cardboard container	Box of vintage wine

control their principal cost drivers. Low-cost items will not attract such close attention, reducing price sensitivity. Further, intensive search for the lowest price per unit (i.e. cost) offered by the available SBE suppliers may not be justified, given search costs (i.e. the costs of 'shopping around'). For each of the two examples given (a printed circuit board and a cardboard box) the good is a low-cost item in relation to the cost of the customer's good within which it is embodied. Similar illustrations of this principle, suggesting low price sensitivity, can be constructed for all the other SBEs being considered. [17]

It may be added that most of the products of these firms, if not of the requisite quality, would impose high performance penalties on the customer's product quality, which in turn would impose high economic penalties on customers in terms of lost trade. Thus an erratically performing printed circuit board (unduly sensitive, perhaps, to temperature variation) would lead to unreliable diagnostic output from a heartbeat monitor. To avoid this unacceptably high penalty, the monitor manufacturer would be willing to pay premium prices for high quality PCBs: he would, in short, be relatively price insensitive. The other side of this coin is that if high product performance of the customer's good were facilitated by the high quality of the SBE's good the price sensitivity of the customer would be reduced. For some of these SBEs this was probably the case. For example, military and medical buyers of the products of firm D (PCB manufacture) were more quality conscious than other buyers because of their higher performance objectives, and they were therefore relatively less price sensitive. For some other SBEs the quality enhancement was less objective, and partly in the mind of the beholder. This was true, for example, of firm A (business services) and firm C (window cleaning). Such an SBE was particularly aware of the subjective basis of price insensitivity: it was known to be a matter of convincing the customer that quality was important and that quality could be enhanced by making purchases from it.

The motivation of customers can have an important bearing on their price sensitivity. If it is narrowly focused on cost cutting, price sensitivity will be high. If quality and image are more important, price sensitivity will be lower. For the sample of SBEs considered in this chapter, customer motivation was invariably high. In the case of firm A (business services) many customers were small and medium sized enterprises, and they relished the prospect of being able to emulate the image of a larger sized enterprise. For firm G (cardboard packaging) the worst fear of its customers was to be out of stock (i.e. having no packages in which to present their goods), because the image of customers would suffer if their goods were not presented in an appropriately packaged form.

Surprisingly, the more conventional economic forces which might be thought to have a bearing on price sensitivity (for example, product differentiation and profitability) provided little guidance on the causes of the observed relative price insensitivity of the SBEs being considered. I have indicated that customer types were diverse for each and every firm, and one cannot conclude therefore that either high or low customer profitability was typical of any one SBE. It would in any case be facile to argue that more profitable customers would tend to be less price sensitive, because profitability itself is governed, in some measure by the capability of SBEs to control costs. Turning to product differentiation, it was true, of course, that the goods produced by firms A to G were differentiated, as analysed in sections 7.4 and 7.6.2 above. However, this differentiation was mild rather than marked. More important, from the viewpoint of this discussion, the differentiation of an SBE's goods did not in itself appear to play a major role in the differentiation of its customers' goods, which would tend to reduce customers' price insensitivity. It was the customers themselves who combined factors in a novel way to create a product which their own customers, in turn, perceived as differentiated. The relatively small bearing that an SBE's differentiation had on a customer's differentiation was accentuated by the already noted tendency of SBEs to avoid customer concentration. Thus a customer might buy part of a product range from one SBE, and a different part of a similar product range from another SBE. In this way the differentiation characteristics of both SBEs are diluted, and of the customer are concentrated.

To conclude, price insensitivity was typical of the customers of firms A to G. The major factor behind this appeared to be the low cost of the SBEs' products in relation to customers' total costs. High customer motivation and product quality effects were also important. However, profitability and product differentiation, whilst potentially important influences on price sensitivity in traditional analysis, played a relatively minor role here.

The previous two sections, 8.2 and 8.3, examined the first category of extra-industry competitive forces, namely the buyers or customers. A much more detailed analysis of the demand side was undertaken than is usual in conventional industrial organization. For example, in a standard structure-conduct-performance framework, tastes, implying the patterns of customers' demands, are taken as given. They are not only exogenous, under this interpretation, but are also immutable. However, the above analysis has shown that the owner-managers of SBEs scarcely regard tastes as immutable and certainly not as exogenous. There are trends in tastes, governed by fashion for example. But, more important, customers' perceptions of a product can be modified by image management, and customer loyalty can be influenced through controlling switching costs. Thus the SBE takes tastes as endogenous, rather than exogenous, and an aspect of competition with rivals is the attempt to modify customers tastes towards the SBEs' own products and away from those of rivals. These insights are possible only if one breaks away from the narrow confines of intra-industry competitive analysis.

8.4   SUPPLIERS

In the same way as buyers can be the focus of detailed extra-industry analysis, so too can suppliers. Much of the conceptual groundwork for the analysis of suppliers has already been set out in the sense that analogous factors come into play when one considers the determinants of suppliers' bargaining power. Just as important as in the case of customers are, for suppliers: concentration; relative volume of trade; product differentiation; vertical integration; and so on.

The typical picture for firms A to G was of high supplier concentration, particularly when considered in relation to a single product of the SBE. Supplier concentration was typically higher than customer concentration. Around four or five key suppliers was fairly common, with firm G (cardboard packaging) being at one extreme, with 95 per cent of factors of production bought from one supplier, and firm C (window cleaning) at the other, with so many potential suppliers that 'suppliers don't count, they are simply there to be chosen'.

In terms of the value chain, principal cost drivers, if tightly controlled, enable the SBE to price competitively and to enjoy reasonable profitability. If the supply prices of important factors of production (for example polypropylene in the case of firm B) are negotiable, then an over-dependence on any one supplier can put upward pressure on the supply price, eroding an SBE's profitability and limiting its prospects of pricing its own good competitively. Being aware of this, SBEs try to avoid seller dependence. However, only one of those under consideration, firm F (phototypesetting), claimed there was no seller dependence: in this case because there were many suppliers, and factors of production were only mildly differentiated. Firm B (plastic mouldings) and firm D (PCB manufacture) took explicit steps to avoid seller dependence, the owner-manager of the former firm saying suppliers sometimes attempted 'to make the tail wag the dog'. The main stratagem for preventing this was to retain the right to change suppliers. This need not be frequently exercised to bestow bargaining advantages. Firm G admitted to potentially high seller dependence, but found it no problem in bargaining as long as other suppliers were around who were willing to bargain independently to attract an order. In this case, that was found to be true. There need not be many suppliers to achieve this diminution of suppliers' bargaining power. Firm E (microfilm services), for example, found it experienced little seller dependence. In this case, just five independent sellers were enough to provide strong competition: they produced similar factors at similar prices. The diversity of factor requirements by an SBE could also be a source of bargaining advantage over suppliers. Firm A (business services) found its diverse factor requirements made it appear less vulnerable to 'hold-up' strategies by any one supplier. For example, lack of acetone for the photocopier did not impede the operations of the *poste restante* mail service or the international switchboard facility.

None of the SBEs under consideration here felt that the nature or form of suppliers' products were crucial to the nature or form of their own products. Many of the products supplied were non-proprietory raw material, (e.g. paper and cardboard for firm G), and hence homogeneous. Chemicals inputs were important for firms B (plastic mouldings), C (window cleaning), D (PCB manufacture), E (microfilming), and F (phototypesetting). Suppliers of chemicals (for example, polypropylene for plastic injection mouldings) typically offered similar products at similar prices and terms. Suppliers' products would then only be differentiated by the service provided (e.g. in terms of technical advice and delivery). As a consequence suppliers were typically price conscious, and price differentials were small. This lack of significant differentiation of suppliers' products, barring the quality of service by which they were delivered to SBE customers, implied that switching costs had not been built up by suppliers for the cases under consideration. As suppliers were often SBEs in their own right, one would expect them to behave something like firms A to G did with respect to their own customers. In section 7.6.2 above I argued that SBEs typically sought low cost forms of product differentiation which emphasised rapid response, quality of service and the personalized treatment of customers. This appears to have been broadly true of the suppliers which provided factor inputs for firms A to G. The main difference was that suppliers had not been so successful in raising switching costs as had these SBEs with their own customers. This was partly a consequence of suppliers being further 'upstream' in the chain of production, with less scope for increasing their own product differentiation and thus raising switching costs.

Finally,[18] forward integration by suppliers appeared to be a virtually non-existent phenomenon for these seven cases. Only in the industry of firm G (cardboard packaging) had this occurred, but with little success. It was frowned upon and regarded as 'bad form'. An unwillingness to share trade knowledge with a new entrant arriving on the scene by forward integration would greatly diminish the entrant's prospects of success. The body of tacit knowledge necessary for successful commercial operations is often large, and, being uncodified, uncommunicable by conventional media like books. It is acquired by serving time in the trade, by observation within the trade, and by slowly being admitted into the company of the core of experienced traders. Thus one learns by demonstration how sound business judgements are made. Being excluded from this kind of 'trading fellowships' makes business operations difficult. It denies 'undesirable' entrants (namely entrants through forward integration) access to significant positive external economies which are enjoyed by incumbent SBEs.

8.5 POTENTIAL ENTRANTS

I have ended the last section by introducing some considerations which are relevant to a further competitive force – the threat of new entry. There, I particularly referred to experience as an entry barrier, and this is an important point to which I shall return below. It will, however, be embedded in a full analysis of potential entry. This starts with scale economies, product differentiation, capital requirements and switching costs, proceeds to look at absolute cost advantages under several headings (including know-how, learning, and experience) and concludes by looking at expected retaliation and entry deterrence.

The basic framework is simple, although more than a dozen items are referred to in the relevant agenda headings of the semi-structured interview (SSI 85). It argues that the extent to which potential entrants become actual entrants depends on entry barriers and expected retaliation. Earlier analysis in chapter 7 has downplayed the role of retaliation, based on the evidence from firms A to G, and this is reflected here as well. However, the treatment of entry barriers has not yet advanced beyond the enterprise profile remarks of chapter 6, and the brief introduction to the topic at the end of section 8.1 above. Therefore, the treatment here of entry barriers aims to be both more thorough and more complete.

Technical economies of scale, implying falling unit cost as production per unit period rises, provide one of the most obvious and closely analysed examples of a barrier to entry. The consequences of scale economies are most apparent if firms engage in massive production methods with very high outputs per unit of time. Though this might be thought most typical of large corporate enterprises, even the SBE can engage in massive production methods, producing batch sizes of many millions for particular components.[19] Scale economies as a barrier to entry should not, therefore be excluded from consideration just because firms A to G are small.

Scale economies constitute a barrier to potential entrants for one of the following two reasons. Either firms enter at a large scale and risk meeting retaliation from established incumbents, or they enter at a small scale, and operate at a unit cost disadvantage compared to incumbents. The large scale option may also have the drawback that a newcomer may lack bargaining power in the factor market, and may find his quest for technical scale economies thwarted. His goal of unit cost reduction may not be attained because of pecuniary diseconomies caused by higher factor price than those negotiable by incumbents.

In the last chapter, table 7.1 displayed some relevant information on scale economies. None of firms A to G experienced general scale diseconomies. Table 8.3 presents that earlier information in a new form and also displays further information on dynamic scale economies obtained from reinterview data (RIQ 1988). In either a static or dynamic sense, non-decreasing returns (or non-increasing unit costs) appear typical. When manufacturing or processing is involved (firms B, D, and G) scale economies are more apparent. When service activities are involved (firms A, C, and F) constant returns appear to be characteristic.

One would not conclude, even where clear scale economies existed, that

Table 8.3 Static and dynamic scale effects for firms A to G

Firm	Short-run average variable cost (AVC)	Dynamic average variable cost over three years
A Business services	U-shaped	Output up 100%, AVC constant
B Plastic mouldings	Falling	Output up 150%, AVC down 20%
C Window cleaning	Falling	Output up 100%, AVC constant
D Printed circuit board manufacture	Constant	Output up 100%, AVC down 11%
E Industrial microfilming	No meaning	Output up 400%, AVC down slightly
F Phototypesetting	Constant	Output up 20%, AVC constant
G Bespoke cardboard packaging	Falling	Output up 30%, AVC down

these constituted a significant barrier to entry. Only firm E (industrial microfilming) claimed high entry barriers, and these were a function of high finance-capital requirements and not marked scale economies.[20] In the cases of three SBEs, firm B (plastic mouldings), firm D (printed circuit boards), and firm G (cardboard packaging) the potential for production scale economies was great, but entry barriers were not thought to be high. The owner-managers of firms B and D admitted that high volume production by new entrants could be undertaken initially, and indeed sometimes was, at home or in a rented garage. In such cases, unit production costs might be above that of incumbent SBEs, and quality somewhat lower, but delivered unit cost could be lower and selling price lower as well. This illustrates the importance of looking at scale economies in terms of specific functional areas, of which production, which is traditionally emphasised, is but one. Quality control, packaging, and distribution costs per unit might well be lower in the case of the garage-based producer, for example.

The stronger is product differentiation, the greater is the cost that the potential entrant must bear in attempting to entice customers away from incumbent SBEs. If incumbents are long-established and have invested heavily in building up customer loyalty (for example, through advertising, after-sales service, and prompt delivery) potential entrants not only face high prospective entry costs but also bear the risk of an entire loss of value of reputational stock if the attempt to establish a new differentiated product, to rival existing products, is unsuccessful. Unlike investment in plant and equipment, a second-hand reputation has no re-sale value.

Previous analysis (section 7.6.2 above) has suggested that firms A to G all made serious efforts to differentiate their products from those of rivals. A new aspect to be considered is the extent to which this created competitive advantage over potential as well as actual rivals. As an entry deterring strategy, differentiation is passive rather than active, because the approach to differentiation to be adopted by potential entrants may often be unknown. Incumbent SBEs differentiated goods by quality, delivery, service, and what several owner-managers called 'the personal touch'. This was not contingent upon what a potential entrant might do. There is a limit to what can be achieved by the personalized approach to product differentiation, and the typical outcome was mild product differentiation with goods being perceived as 'similar' to those of rival SBEs. Such mild product differentiation would not constitute a serious disincentive to potential entrants. One aim of the personal touch and similar devices[21] was to raise switching costs of customers. This strategy was typically successful, though probably not completely entry deterring. Firms A (business services), D (printed circuit boards), E (microfilming), and F (phototypesetting) felt their customers were highly loyal and only firm C (window cleaning) thought loyalty, and switching costs, were low. In the latter case, to offset low switching costs, incumbent SBEs took a very hostile attitude to the 'poaching' of customers.

The younger SBEs (firms A, C, and D) provide some reliable evidence on what it was like to be a potential, and actual, entrant under reasonably similar conditions to those prevailing at the time of interview. They agreed that contacts were hard to establish early on, and that lack of 'channels' constituted a significant barrier to entry. The other SBEs, providing information based on older memories, also emphasised the initial difficulties of channel access. The 'networking' of trade connections has recently been emphasised in the small firms literature,[22] and clearly the richness of the network fosters small firm success. However, the network is partially or totally unknown to the potential entrant, and knowledge of it can only be acquired by actual trading. This in itself takes time, and the facility with which a new entrant can learn and exploit the network will be an important determinant of early success or failure. Firm D (PCB manufacture) found it had to put in patient effort on cultivating channels in the first six months after entry. It felt that a year or more was necessary to establish a reputation. Firm F (phototypesetting) thought that using the network to establish credibility was 'paramount' and had found it took three to four years to achieve this. Firm C (plastic mouldings) had found channels were important to business success, and that they took time to cultivate, mainly because they depended on 'word of mouth' communication. In short, channel access is important and lack of it constitutes a significant barrier to entry.

Knowledge of the network relates to the SBE's external environment, and it is particularly obvious that this knowledge is not initially in place when the SBE is new to the industry. Less obvious, partly so because it is neglected in much conventional economics theory, is that the new SBE has to learn about its internal environment: about what goes on within the office block, or behind the factory gates. Scale economies arise simply from the volume of production in a given unit of time, whereas experience or learning economies arise from the cumulative volume of production. Learning is not a very visible form of technical change and leads to unit cost reductions over time through, broadly speaking, a more effective division of labour.[23] Workers become more dexterous, tasks become better organized, machines are enhanced in efficiency by 'tweaking' controls and audits promote efficiency, and in this way unit cost falls as experience is gained. Strictly speaking, this effect should be attributed to specific functions in the firm, rather than to the firm as a whole.

Firms whose activities entail a high labour content, as is the case for many SBEs, are particularly subject to the benefits of experience and learning.[24] From the viewpoint of entry barriers, the existence of learning effects would discourage entry if they were entirely proprietory. Potential entrants, lacking production experience, would always be disadvantaged in terms of the cost of production achievable at entry, compared to incumbents. However, not all the consequences of experience are kept proprietory. There are trade journals, training programmes, mobile personnel, conferences and seminars, and so on, all of which promote a diffusion of knowledge. Many entrepreneurs starting SBEs have previous experience in the trade as employees, and carry much proprietory knowledge in their heads, to be put to use in their new firms.

Learning effects, because they are not entirely proprietory, may engender less powerful entry barriers than scale effects. Indeed they can, if observable, teach the potential entrants what pitfalls to avoid, and enable them to 'leap-frog' ahead of some incumbents at the time of entry. An advantage of the newly entered SBE may be its flexibility to adopt the latest technology, without being committed in any sense to the technological history of the industry it is entering.

Firms A to G all in some measure enjoyed cost advantages from learning, and felt these benefits were not fully appropriable by potential entrants. Thus to varying degrees learning constituted a barrier to entry. The words most commonly used by owner-managers to describe learning were 'experience' and 'know-how'. The learning curve was thought to be particularly steep for very young SBEs like firm A, and thought the learning effect was thought to be hard to quantify by some, none denied its importance. Most SBEs did not make a sharp distinction between the learning of the network mentioned earlier and the learning of in-house operations. They both amounted to 'experience' and a lack of it constituted one of the most significant entry barriers for potential entrants into incumbent SBE markets.

A further factor dissuading potential entrants from challenging incumbent SBEs is the form of retaliation expected and its intensity. The credibility of expected retaliation is important if it is to deter effectively. The carrying of excess capacity, the availability of an unused borrowing facility, and demonstrably high bargaining power, exercised through trade channels, would all make an SBE's capacity to retaliate a credible threat to potential entrants. To the extent that an SBE has in the past acted to repel actual entrants, for example by enhancing output to produce a higher quality product at a lower price than a new entrant can match, potential entrants will be aware of the retaliation they can expect, and will be deterred. The credibility of threatened retaliation is also enhanced if the SBE making the threat has a lot to lose should entry occur. This would be true if, for example, the incumbent SBE operated in an industry which was only growing slowly. Competition would take the form of a constant sum game, and a new entrant would unambiguously reduce the sales and profitability of incumbent SBEs. Firm C (window cleaning) provided the only example, of the SBEs considered, of an SBE in a slow growth industry. It is notable that this was also the only SBE which expressed a strong advocacy of retaliatory measures against new entrants. More generally, SBEs with a strong commitment to the industry would also tend to favour strong retaliation against attempted entry.

Such commitments have been analysed earlier in the discussion of rivalry (section 8.1 above), where they were described as 'strategic stakes'. These stakes would be perceived as higher by an SBE, the less liquid were the assets used in trading. Firms A to G all expressed the view that they were subject to high strategic stakes. Firm B (plastic mouldings), which was the most technically progressive, added the comment that strategic stakes were especially high in new markets. This firm had installed advanced plastic extrusion machines with modern computer control systems, which were highly liquid forms of capital investment. As predicted, this illiquidity sharpened the tendency to retaliation against entrants.

Firm B (plastic mouldings) was willing to carry excess capacity to deter rivals. It had increased discounts and lowered its profit rate (which it described as 'chiselling') to deter potential entrants. Firm A (business services), C (window cleaning), E (microfilming) and F (phototypesetting) also admitted to lowering price to deter entry. However, entry deterring pricing was not invariably adopted by the SBEs under consideration. Firm D (PCB manufacture) thought price chiselling ran the danger of being associated with a low quality operation. In the four months prior to initial interview, four new entrants had arrived in his market, and one had already failed. Some of them were described as 'home garage' operations. The owner-manager of firm D made it clear that he never asked a customer what his target price was, and certainly did not aim to be the cheapest operation in the business even if the rationale of this were deterrence. Firm F (photo-typesetting), whilst willing to use entry deterring pricing selectively, was aware of its potentially damaging effect on reputation. Price chiselling could be wrongly perceived as signalling a low quality operation. This SBE wished to establish a reputation for the speed, convenience, and quality of its service, and regarded these attributes as more important than price.

Several SBEs (firms B, F, and G) expressed the view that retaliation suggested a lost initiative. Thus firm B (plastic mouldings) aimed 'to anti-cipate attack, and keep one step ahead technologically speaking'. Firm F (phototypesetting) said it would 'try to act, rather than react', and firm G (cardboard packaging) said that retaliation 'may suggest vulnerability'. In other words a reputation for attack was preferred to a reputation for defence, thus strengthening the argument for aggressive over defensive strategies advanced already in chapter 7. Put another way, more experienced SBEs[25] wished to establish a reputation for leadership rather than followership in their markets.

To conclude this section, potential entrants to the SBEs' markets were not subject to high entry barriers, though entry was by no means free. Scale economies and product differentiation had some disincentive effects on potential entrants, and a limited use of entry deterring pricing was adopted. However, experience and learning, of both the intra- and extra-firm variety constituted the most significant barriers to entry. This, however, is all relative. As a collectivity, entry barriers, whilst not irrelevant, were of limited importance. They were generally perceived to be low. Whilst initially buffeted by the effects of lack of experience, of retaliation and the lack of a loyal customer base, robust new entrants eventually got a toe-hold in a market, or market niche, by using aggressive tactics.

8.6 SUBSTITUTES

Apart from the conventionally recognized competitive force of intra-industry rivalry, three further forces of competition have been analysed so far: customer bargaining power; supplier bargaining power, and potential entry. The fifth and final force of competition in this Porter-inspired framework for SBEs is the availability of substitute goods or services. The elasticity of the market or industry demand curve is a kind of index of the impact of substitutes upon the products produced by incumbent SBEs. Extreme substitutability with non-industry products would register its impact through a highly elastic market demand. This in turn sets close limits on the upward drift of prices within the industry. In this sense, the availability of substitutes imposes price discipline on SBEs in the industry and sets limits on their profitability.

I have already given some examples of the way in which substitute products can emerge from quite different industrial sectors. They have the capacity to create strong competitive pressure through being able to out-perform the functions of products produced within the target industry. In the case of firm G (bespoke cardboard packaging), plastic substitutes for cardboard packaging material had appeared. Firm G lay in SIC number 47; the rival product came from the adjacent SIC number 48. Firm E provided microfilm services to industry and commerce and lay in SIC number 83. An emerging substitute for its services, the electronic office, was a product which came from SIC number 33.[26] Whether technological substitutes will become economic substitutes, and hence exert competitive pressure on established products within the industry, depends partly on their relative price–performance attributes and partly on the profitability of the industries of origin of the substitutes. For the two examples given, the price–performance characteristics of substitutes were not sufficiently strong to favour their adoption. Partly because of relatively high plastic prices over the sample period, which in turn was related to relatively high oil prices over the same period, plastic corrugated packaging did not offer sufficient extra performance, given the extra price, to warrant adoption for many standard purposes (for example, the boxing of wine bottles) However, I have shown earlier (section 7.5 above) that for certain special uses (for example, bicycle panniers) performance characteristics were sufficiently superior to the cardboard materials alternative, that the plastic materials substitute was adopted. In this case, firm G had adapted flexibly to the emergence of a substitute product which was economic in some uses, and had pre-empted the creation of a new niche for this product by its rivals. It remained true that for many trade purposes, the price–performance characteristics of the substitute were inferior to the established product. In the second example, the electronic office, based on computer retrieval technology, presented a technological alternative to microfilming, the technology used by firm E, for which information retrieval was via a microfiche station. For some uses (for example police investigation work) the price–performance characteristics of the electronic office possibly surpassed those of microfilm. This presumes an environment in which high performance is elicited from the electronic substitute. However, in many commercial contexts such high performance is neither required nor achieved. [27] Given that the capital costs of the electronic office were ten times that of the microfilm system, and also the need for computer expertise in the former case, the price–performance characteristics of microfilm were superior for most commercial environments. However, given the tendency for the prices of new electronic systems to fall steadily after market launch, it will be the case in the future that the price–performance characteristics of the electronic office will increasingly dominate those of microfilm systems. Between 1985 and 1988, a noted trend amongst new firms in Scotland was to the adoption of computer based, rather than microfiche based, information retrieval systems. Firm E admitted to being willing to cut profit targets under competitive pressure, part of which could be attributed to this trend. From the data available, it was not possible to check whether the particular firms producing substitute products to those of firms G and E were highly profitable, but it is true that the industrial sectors out of which they operated (plastic processing, office machinery) were relatively profitable.

All the SBEs, from firm A through to firm G, showed an awareness of the competitive pressure that substitutes could create. The technically progressive SBEs kept track of new technologies, hoping to adapt flexibly if and when they became economically viable. Firm B (plastic mouldings) followed developments in materials technology closely, though few economic alternatives to plastics existed for most current uses. Firm D (PCB manufacture) saw innovation as a worldwide phenomenon, and was particularly attentive to new developments in surface-mounted components. It was felt that appropriate technological change could be readily accommodated. Firm G (cardboard packaging) had already adapted to using foam as a technological alternative, produced by a profitable industry. The response adopted had been to use foam materials in combination with traditional cardboard materials. It should not be assumed, however that technological advance will immediately, or even inevitably, provide superior price–performance characteristics to existing products. Personal service is important to the supply of many SBE products, as noted earlier in the analysis of market fragmentation (section 7.5). This was true for example, of firm A (business services). The use of a telephone answering machine is both an inadequate and ineffective alternative, from the customer's standpoint, to being able to share, even with many others, a telephone switchboard and reception facility. For many short-term business purposes, [28] the value/price of a substitute (for example setting up such facilities independently) is low compared to the value/price of purchasing office services. Neither the high technology alternative, nor the in-house alternative, provided superior value/price to firm A's package of business services. As this case illustrates so well, the personal service component of product delivery has the advantage, to the owner-manager of an SBE, of being difficult to supplant from a technological or organizational standpoint.

Finally, it may be noted that one time-honoured response to being subjected to competitive pressure from substitutes is to seek a form of group or institutional response aimed at banning substitutes. Though such tactics were rarely mentioned by firms A to G, firm B (plastic injection mouldings) did provide a good non-UK example. The French government imposed restrictions on the importing of Italian plastic kitchen utensils, which were proving very competitive substitutes to similar French (domestically produced) goods. A final resort, in the face of competitive pressure, as this example illustrates is always to restrict competition rather than to adapt to it by, for example, cost reduction, or technological change.

8.7 CONCLUSION

The last three chapters adopted a case study approach to the analysis of small business enterprise. I started with enterprise profiles, or case histories. Then I developed a small firms variant of competitive advantage/competitive strategy analysis. Competitive and defensive strategies were considered first, followed by the forces of competition. One is not attempting to generalize to hundreds of thousands of small firms from seven case studies, but rather one is using detailed evidence on seven small firms to undertake analytical exercises within the chosen framework. One wants to know whether the categories used in this framework make sense, empirically speaking. Detailed examples of a focus strategy or of market fragmentation endow these categories with meaning. Further, one wants to confirm that the logical coherence of the framework carries over to the real world. For example, which of the logically possible approaches to entry prevention are deployed by real SBEs and why?

This chapter completes the analysis of extended competition. The importance of additional forces of competition to the traditional and more visible intra-industry form has been amply demonstrated. There has been no difficulty in filling the relevant categories with empirical examples, and the actual choices made by SBEs of logically possible actions are coherent in terms of their circumstances. The bargaining power of customers, for example, has empirical meaning, and the logic of its operations carries over to real world actions. One can actually display the mechanisms by which this form of bargaining power works.

Chapters 6 and 7 already have their own summaries, so I shall end with conclusions on the detailed analysis of chapter 8. All five forces of competition have been identified and have meaning. None is sufficiently weak to be worth excluding on the grounds of simplicity or explanatory power. The major competitive force, as identified in earlier structure/conduct/performance approaches, namely the rivalry of incumbent firms, was confirmed as such for all the SBEs considered. In this sense, intra-industry rivalry remains a 'core' construct. Beyond this, potential competition is important, followed, in my judgement of the above evidence, by the bargaining power of customers, the bargaining power of suppliers, and the threat of substitutes. An important discovery, cutting across several of these categories of competitive forces, was of the role of experience. The SBE has a steep learning curve after inception. An understanding of how the full range of competitive forces works is enhanced by taking account of know-how, tacit knowledge, accepted standards of trading, networking, and all those other bodies of uncodified knowledge the possession of which amounts to good business experience. Such experience is readily translated into competitive advantage.

Part IV
Econometrics

9 Staying in business

9.1 INTRODUCTION

This chapter is concerned with a question that has been central to recent industrial policy (see Storey *et al.* 1987), namely what factors help a small business enterprise (SBE) to stay in business. The time scale for the survival analysis is three years (1985 to 1988). Whether a firm stays in business or exits is regarded as an aspect of rational choice. The work of Baden-Fuller (1989) on the exit of firms from the UK steel castings industry exemplified one approach, that of intra-industry analysis, inspired by the theoretical work of Ghemawat and Nalebuff (1985). This chapter, by contrast, uses an inter-industry approach. Jovanovic (1982) provides an appropriate formula for rational exit, which involves specifying a net profit variable $(\pi^\star)$, obtained by deducting exit costs, along with operational costs from gross profit. The requirement for staying in business for a period of years is $\pi^\star \geqslant 0$. Rational exit occurs when $\pi^\star < 0$.

Following the entrepreneurial model of Holmes and Schmitz (1990) an indicator function for staying in business (or not) is defined, with the probability of staying in business depending on the SEF's characteristics. It is constructed in three steps. First, net economic profit $\pi^\star$ is specified as an unobserved, or latent, variable. It is not the same thing as accounting profit, and owner-managers may be reluctant to provide estimates of net economic profit to an interviewer. This individual subjective estimate provides the basis for a business judgement about whether or not to stay in business. Second, business characteristics are conceived of in two broad groups, market and balance sheet. The latent variable $\pi^\star$ depends on these characteristics. Third, mapping from $\pi^\star$ to a binary variable S defines the appropriate indicator functions: $S = 1$ for staying in business and $S = 0$ for exiting from business.[1] This provides the basis for a binary probit model with market and financial explanatory variables. This is estimated[2] on primary source data for seventy-three SBEs sampled from the case loads of Enterprise Trust and development corporations in Scotland. The estimated probit model indicates that, for this sample, product range and gearing are the key market and financial variables, respectively. The greater the product range, and the lower the gearing, *ceteris paribus*, the better the chances of staying in business.

9.2   THE MODEL

The general hypothesis is that profit, net of exit costs, $(\pi^{\star})$, is a function of market variables (M), financial variables (F) and of other variables captured by the error term ε:

$$\pi^{\star} = f(M, F; \varepsilon) \tag{9.1}$$

According to McFadden (1978) this function f(.) may be linearized (see appendix to this chapter, page 170).

The decision problem of the individual entrepreneur involves comparing the value of net profit implied by his current market and financial variables with that value which justifies his staying in business, given his estimates of his opportunity costs. Provided these and other costs are appropriately netted out of profit, this decision problem can always be reduced to whether the condition $\pi^{\star} \geqslant 0$ is met, for the case of staying in business. The alternatives foregone which provide the basis for these opportunity cost estimates include starting up a new business, buying a new business, devoting more effort to other existing businesses, going into waged or salaried employment, and retiring on the proceeds of a business sale. According to Holmes and Schmitz (1990) the pursuit of these alternatives is an aspect of the advanced division of labour in an enterprise economy. Entrepreneurship, so conceived, consists in seeking new products to exploit unharvested economic niches. This process might involve changing the balance of product lines. This 'market repositioning' is common with SBEs and I report on it below. A point is reached when repositioning would take a firm into a new niche, in which case the old firm is wound up, and a new one started. This is identified as the exit of an SBE, and clearly it is simply an extension of market repositioning.

I indicated earlier how an indicator function was constructed for staying in business, (or not), defining the binary variable $S = 1$ for staying in business, and $S = 0$ for exiting from business. The way in which this leads to a binary probit using a linearization of $f(M, F; \varepsilon)$ is a standard technique which is explained in the appendix to this chapter (page 171).

Whether a firm stays in business or exits from business is an aspect of the theory of choice. The basic position taken in this chapter is that a decision whether a firm will function or not is made on rational grounds. This is in contrast to a more sociological view which might see the firm as subject to unknown and unknowable forces which make its continuance or demise a matter of caprice or convention rather than rational economic calculation. It is also in contrast to the view that sees the demise of a firm in a pejorative sense, as a business failure.[3] By contrast, the view taken is that the controlled founding and, by the same token, liquidating of firms is a sign of good health in an enterprise economy.

9.3 THE DATA

The data required for the empirical analysis should facilitate the identification of the factors that help a small business enterprise (SBE) to stay in business. In this case, the time period over which the SBE was examined to see if it did indeed stay in business was three years. The starting point is a new set of data gathered in 1988 from the same firms whose owner-managers were interviewed in 1985.

Many further issues were analysed, including scale economies, skills gaps and technological change, but of sole relevance to this chapter is the simple fact that seeking a reinterview provided the basis for finding out whether an SBE was still in business. For the 1988 reinterview study, which was financed by a grant from the Nuffield Foundation, the initial approach to SBEs was by a preletter sent to the address known from 1985, followed by a telephone call to arrange an interview. At the stage of telephoning, it was often possible to determine whether the firm had managed to stay in business or not. Most simply, if the response was to the same name of enterprise and the same owner-manager was put on the line, one had identified the same firm as in business. Of course, some cases were more troublesome than this, and a few required extensive enquiry to determine what had happened three years on.

A serious effort was made to provide an exhaustive categorization of outcomes. Again, field work methods were used to gather data, of which only one component is relevant to this chapter, namely whether the firm was still in business in 1988. The participation rate was high (over 80 per cent) and, after intensive efforts, untraced cases were few (11 per cent). Even for untraced cases, other evidence could be brought to bear (using comments of individuals in offices, shops, or factory sites adjacent to the original location of the firm in question) on whether a case should sensibly be categorized as in or out of business. Generally, there was no difficulty in categorizing the data.[4] The position taken was that staying in business, as a category, includes SBEs which have changed name, location, market positioning, or personnel, but have retained a substantially similar clientele (i.e. goodwill is intact), and are producing a substantially similar core range of products or services. Over three years the balance of this core range will probably have changed, and almost certainly the non-core range will have become substantially different, but this would not be regarded as exiting from the business.

Generally, two features of the data used are both their numerical accuracy, and their accuracy in the sense of congruence with the definitions and questions used in the 1985 and 1988 administered questionnaires (AQ 1985 and RIQ 1988). An audit was also conducted in 1988 on the data recorded on the physical schedules as compared to the data stored in the small firms database used for econometric estimation, so the quality of data should be high.

There were seventy-three firms in the sample, being representative of the case loads of the agencies concerned (namely Enterprise Trusts and development corporations). Details of the sample are given in part I (page 14), so the treatment here is abbreviated. Most SBEs in the sample were close to financial inception and few were over ten years old. The average age at the time of interview was 42 months. The average size was very small: eight full-time workers, two part-time workers and one trainee, in terms of employment; £76,000 in terms of book value of assets at 1985 prices; and £85,000 in terms of annual sales (excluding VAT), again at 1985 prices. Firm sizes ranged from one to ninety, in terms of labour force, from £1,000 to £600,000 in terms of assets, and from close to zero to over £1,000,000 (at 1985 prices) in terms of turnover. In terms of SIC codes, there was a wide dispersion of firms activities. Manufacturing (SICs 22 to 49) accounted for 56 per cent of the total. Timber, wooden furniture, paper products, printing and manufacturing (SICs 46, 47) were well represented (11 per cent), as were electrical and electronic engineering (SIC 34) (10 per cent) and food, drink, tobacco, and textiles (SICs 41 to 43) (8 per cent). Business services, banking finance, and insurance (SICs 81 to 83) (7 per cent) and wholesale and retail distribution (SICs 61 to 65) (10 per cent) were also well represented. Regarding firm type, 50 per cent were private companies, 20 per cent were partnerships and 30 per cent were sole proprietorships.

9.4   THE VARIABLES

Broadly speaking, the variables used to explain whether an SBE was in or out of business in 1988 were of the market (M) or financial (F) variety (cf. equation 9.1 above). That is, they were concerned with products, rivals, pricing, etc. or with aspects of the balance sheet like debt, equity, assets, and cash flow. A novelty of the approach used in this chapter is that it goes beyond an explanation of small firm survival (in terms of financial ratios and qualitative features of company accounts), as used in studies like Storey et al. (1987), to an explanation that may be more persuasive to industrial economists, in that it combines market with financial and other variables. Detailed definitions of these variables are given in table 9.1. Here I concentrate on their interpretation.

9.4.1   Market variables (*M*)

Two market variables, (*Pgroup*) and (*ProdDes*), are concerned with products. (*Pgroup*) defines the number of product groups. If the SBE sold different types of hats and also different types of gloves, 'hats' would be a product group, as would 'gloves'. Bowlers and boaters, on the other hand are products within the product group of hats; and similarly mittens and driving gloves are products within the product group of gloves. The average number of product groups and products produced by an SBE were six and fifty, respectively. Products themselves are easily multiplied in number, by colour and size variation for example, whereas product groups give a better idea of flexibility of production. An advantage of small firms is felt to be their

Table 9.1 Definitions of variables used in probit equations

Staying in business (*S*) (Determined by 1988 interviews) S = 1 for still in business in 1988; *S* = 0 for exiting from business between 1985 and 1988
Market variables (*M*) (Determined by 1985 interviews)
Adv = 1 if SEF advertises, = 0 if not
DesComp = 1 if competition in main market was intense, = 2 if strong, = 3 if generally weak, = 4 if weak
Employ Number of full-time employees
ProdDes = 1 if main product identical to rivals, = 2 if similar, = 3 if different
Pgroup Number of product groups
Financial variables (*F*) (Determined by 1985 interviews)
AddDebt = 1 if external finance had been used since starting the SEF, = 0 if not
Passet Book value of total assets in $'000s at 1985 prices at time of interview in 1985
PerFin = 1 if only personal finances used to set up the SEF, = 0 if not
Pgear Equity gearing ratio at time of interview in 1985, i.e. debt (borrowing) divided by owners' injection of finance (personal injections)

Other variables:
Age Age in months from financial inception to interview in 1985

---

flexibility (see Acs, Audretsch and Carlsson 1990), and a reflection of this is the size of their product range, as measured by the number of product groups. The larger the product group range, the more flexibly can the SBE reposition in the market in terms of niche exploitation. A more narrowly based SBE with fewer product group options is therefore less likely to stay in business. This interpretation of the consequences of the *Pgroup* variable for staying in business is reinforced by the argument of Ungern-Sternberg (1990) that diversification into several products is one of the ways SBEs try to adjust to fluctuating demands for their individual products. The reinterview data of 1988 indicated that market repositioning was common amongst the SBEs. A shift of 10 per cent in three years, on average, occurred for that proportion of value of total sales attributable to the main product line. Finally, one should mention the likely economies of scope arising in enlarged product ranges, which also foster staying in business.

ProdDes is a subjective variable that aims to gauge the degree of product differentiation. Owner-managers were asked to compare products in their main product groups with those of their rivals and to appraise (if they could) whether they were identical, similar, or different. The majority (53 per cent) felt that their products were 'similar', which could be interpreted as mild product differentiation. The variable is a self-appraised measure of product differentiation and represents an alternative to more tricky measures like cross-elasticity of demand. It was scaled to be greater, the greater the product heterogeneity. To the extent that product heterogeneity confers local monopolistic advantages on the SBE, the greater it is, the better the chances of staying in business.

A related variable, *DesComp*, is a self-appraised measure of intensity of competition. Owner-managers were asked how they would describe competition in the market for their main product group, and were given qualitative descriptions ranging from 'intense in every aspect', through 'generally strong, but weak in some aspects' to 'weak in all aspects'. The variable was coded such that low values denoted intense competition and high values denoted weak competition. Given that competitive intensity erodes profits, one might expect low values of *DesComp* to be associated with a diminished prospect of staying in business. However, there is a case for thinking in terms of what Porter (1985) calls 'good competitors'; that is, competitors who by engaging in sharp and challenging rivalry, actually promote the efficiency and innovativeness of incumbent firms and hence enhance their prospects of staying in business. The issue of advertising intensity as distinct from advertising *per se*, is, however, somewhat different, for increasing the range and quality of advertising messages is expensive; and a fine calculation (cf. Friedman 1983: chapter 6) must be undertaken of its costs *vis à vis* its likely effectiveness in terms of revenue enhancement. I found some evidence (Reid 1989) that SBEs were tempted to over-extend their advertising intensity, possibly by trying to mimic large firm behaviour in markets where advertising elasticities of demand were actually quite low. In some measure too, this increased advertising intensity is unrelated to output, and this assumes the nature of a fixed cost which depresses net revenue and reduces prospects for staying in business (cf. Simmons 1989).

Age is a variable which does not have a strict economic interpretation but is of relevance to theories of the growth of the firm. For example, in the work of Jovanovic (1982) and Frank (1988), SBEs are run by owner-managers who learn about their own ability over time. These models imply that the probability of surviving increases with age and with size. Such results have been verified empirically by Brock and Evans (1986: chapter 6) for a large US small business database. There, the size measure used was, perforce, employment rather than the more appealing assets measure. Here full-time employment (*Employ*) and sales turnover in 1985 (*Sales85*) were used as size measures from the list of market variables.

9.4.2 Financial variables (*F*)

The book value of assets in 1935 (*Passet*) was used as the size measure from the list of financial variables. The implications of Jovanovic's (1982) model are reinforced by Diamond's model of credit and the age of small firms, as reported in Rasmussen (1989: 288–90), in which young firms are more likely to default on debt than old firms. Essentially, it is a model of heterogeneous firm types ('risky', 'safe', and 'relatively safe'), and over time 'relatively safe' and 'risky' firms will be selected against, leaving more 'safe' types as survivors. The variable *Passet* has already been discussed in the context of a size measure, in the theory of the growth of the firm. Assets are also important as a balance sheet variable in games of economic survival (Shubik 1980: 24). They suggest an enhanced prospect of staying in business, the stronger the SBE's asset position. In the corporate failure literature, various financial ratios have been used for some time as predictors of exit. These include cash flow/assets, income/assets, debt/assets, etc. One of the contributions of Storey et al. (1987) was to modify these techniques for applications to SBEs, based on a new data set. However, the focus in that work was on prescriptive techniques for failure prediction, whereas here mine is on hypothesis testing. As a result, my financial variables were not derived in a way which directly tallies with financial ratio analysis, although the relationship between the approaches will be clear. In their univariate ratio analysis, Storey et al. (1987: chapter 6) particularly emphasised the importance of gearing and profitability for success or failure prediction. Gearing appeared to be a good short-term indicator of failure, having a tendency to rise as failure approaches. Profitability also appeared as a good predictor of failure, but by my argument low profitability is what requires to be explained: it is a dependent, rather than independent, variable. In multivariate ratio methods, liquidity appeared as the better success/failure discriminator. Financial variables used in my probits which can be related to those used in financial ratio analysis include equity gearing (*Pgear*), assets (*Passets*), debt (*AddDebt*), and cash flow (*Cfp*). A new variable is personal financial injections (*PerFin*), and the reason for its inclusion, in terms of economic theory, is indicated below. In financial ratio analysis, the approach is entirely pragmatic, and asks what makes a good predictor. Here, my purpose is also to make appeal to an appropriate body of economic theory.

Probably the most widely discussed ratio in the theory of finance is the gearing ratio. It has a variety of definitions. In this case the relevant variable (*Pgear*) was measured in 1985 at the time of interview with the administered questionnaire, and was defined as debt (i.e. borrowing) divided by the owner's injection of equity (i.e. personal financial injection). In a Leland and Pyle (1977) world, the value of the SBE rises with the equity stake of the entrepreneur, and the equilibrium equity position is declining in both the riskiness of the firm's activities and in the risk aversion of the entrepreneur. Essentially, in a world where entrepreneurs have private (concealed) information about the quality of projects being undertaken by the SBE, the extent of entrepreneurial ownership is a signal of worth. This suggests an inverse relationship between gearing and staying in business, in that firms with more worthy business operations have a better chance of surviving. This is reinforced by the argument of Blazenco (1987) that owner-managers who are risk averse have a preference for equity over debt. A distinction needs to be made between financial inception and points further down the line when the owner-manager may have established credibility by surviving. At inception, according to De Meza and Webb (1988), the owners of the SBEs with the highest quality projects will seek screened debt finance exclusively, those with projects of intermediate quality will seek to put all their wealth into the

SBE and top-up with the necessary unscreened outside debt finance, and those with low quality projects will remain unfunded. Because banks know that the best entrepreneurs can supply finance to themselves on better terms than the market, they will tend to require maximal self-finance. If an entrepreneur balked at this, he would signal a poor project and would be refused debt. One therefore concludes that if a firm were launched exclusively on personal finance, this would signal a poor project. Thus the binary variable (*PerFin*), constructed by asking the owner-manager whether he did (unity) or did not (zero) use exclusively personal finance in setting up his business, should be negatively associated with staying in business.

Even although gearing and survival should be negatively related, the ability to acquire debt is a signal of project quality. The additional debt variable (*AddDebt*) was constructed by asking owner-managers if they had used external finance (debt) since starting in business. Given that the affirmative was coded as unity, and that good projects should enhance survival, one would expect a positive association between the *AddDebt* variable and staying in business.

Finally, I come to the cash flow variable (*Cfp*). Storey et al. (1987) found that liquidity ratios were not the best predictors of failure in univariate analysis, although generally a decline in liquidity was symptomatic of a failing company and a rise in liquidity of a non-failing company. In the accounting literature a healthy cash-flow is regarded as an essential part of the picture of financial good health of an SBE. Owner-managers were asked if they had ever had cash-flow difficulties. A high proportion said 'yes' (73 per cent), and one would expect the binary variable so defined to be at least a weak predictor of exit. However, as Jovanovic's (1982) model suggests, exit may be caused by the chance drawings of a sequence of unfavourable shocks from Nature's urn, and even firms which do not exit may experience at least streaks of experience when adverse shocks precipitate cash flow crises. Thus, cash flow problems may be a necessary but not a sufficient condition for exit.

9.5 STAYING IN BUSINESS ESTIMATES

Of the seventy-three SBEs which had been interviewed in 1985, fifty-four were still in business in 1988. That is, roughly three-quarters of the firms managed to stay in business. A report produced in 1987 by Business in the Community (BIC) (Business in the Community 1987), relating to business survivors for SBEs which were part of the case loads of enterprise agencies in England, indicated 84 per cent staying in business over a three-year time scale. This compared with 66 per cent staying in business over the same time period for all new firms which appeared on the VAT register. Smallbone (1989) reports on a single enterprise agency case load sample of thirty-nine SBEs for an outer London borough and discovered 64 to 77 per cent staying in business (depending on how untraced SBEs were treated) after just one year. For Scotland's largest local economic development company, BASE

(Bathgate Area Support for Enterprise), Fass and Scothorne (1990) report 84 per cent of SBEs staying in business, for those started in 1984 to 1987, and assessed in 1989. Story and Johnson (1987) have established a widely quoted yardstick of small firm survival over a three year period, of 60 per cent. Thus my figure of 74 per cent of SBEs staying in business over three years for a sample drawn from case loads of diverse Enterprise Trusts in Scotland is not out of line with the range of figures suggested by the contemporary literature.

In order to get a statistical explanation of this survival probability, inter-industry probit models were estimated for the cross-section of seventy-three firms. Market and financial variables were used as the independent (or 'control') variables, and the dependent variable was $S = 1$ for staying in business until 1988, and $S = 0$ for exiting from business between 1985 and 1988. Inter-industry data were used, as described above, with two-thirds of the sample coming from manufacturing and construction, and one-third from transport and services. Fishing and farming enterprises were not in the sample frame.

Table 9.2 reports on a probit equation for a large set of control variables of the market and financial variety. The column on the far right gives weighted elasticities, as defined in Hensher and Johnson (1981: 59–63). The significant variables are the current (or present) equity gearing ratio (*Pgear*) at the time of interview in 1985, the use or not of exclusively personal finance (*PerFin*) at the time of financial inception, the number of product groups (*Pgroup*), and the age in months from financial inception to interview in 1985 (*Age*). Both gearing and personal finance are financial variables, product

Table 9.2 Binary probit for full set of control variables

Variable	Coefficient	t-Ratio	Weighted elasticity
Pgear	$-0.95203.10^{-2}$	-2.9602***	-0.17397
Perfin	-1.5763	-2.0136**	-0.22967
Passet	$-0.14022.10^{-5}$	-0.35692	$-0.16625.10^{-1}$
AddDebt	0.54549	1.0665	$0.68865.10^{-1}$
Cfp	-0.63076	-1.1495	-0.11556
Pgroup	0.89963	2.3379**	0.39085
DesComp	-0.25149	-0.70639	$-0.93581.10^{-1}$
ProdDes	$-0.12053.10^{-1}$	$-0.28305.10^{-1}$	$-0.40625.10^{-2}$
Adv	0.89513	1.0467	0.14828
Age	$0.18165.10^{-1}$	1.7659*	$0.93608.10^{-1}$
Employ	$0.14030.10^{-2}$	$0.44059.10^{-1}$	$0.21038.10^{-2}$
Constant	0.18499	0.22390	$0.42897.10^{-1}$

Likelihood Ratio Test, $\chi^2 = 31.7454 > \chi^2_{.001}(11) = 31.3$
Cragg-Uhler $R^2 = 0.53250$
McFadden $R^2 = 0.40063$
Log-Likelihood $= -23.747$
Survival Probability $= 0.7671$
Legend: $t_{.01} = 1.296(\dagger)$, $t_{.05} = 1.671(*)$, $t_{.025} = 2.000(**)$ $t_{.010} = 2.390(***)$

group is a market variable, and age is a technical variable suggested by theories of the growth of the firm. The highest weighted elasticities tend to be associated with the most significant variables, except in the case of age. Whilst an increase in *Age* significantly improves the chance of staying in business over a three-year time horizon, the effect is not strong. High gearing (*Pgear*), having initial access only to personal finance (*PerFin*), a narrow product range (*Pgroup*) and relative youth (*Age*) all work against staying in business as suggested by economic theory. Most non-significant variables are of the expected sign, except in cases where the *t*-ratio is very small, and even checking for qualitative properties like the appropriateness of sign becomes unreliable. As expected, being able to raise debt finance (*AddDebt*), and undertaking advertising (*Adv*) improve the chances of staying in business. The negative sign on the co-efficient of *DesComp* gives some support to the 'good competitor' notion of Porter analysed in chapter 7. Having had cash flow problems (*Cfp*), and little product differentiation (*ProdDes*), reduce the chances of staying in business. Size measures, like assets (*Passet*) and number of full time employees (*Employ*) have less obvious consequences for survival, theoretically, and are less useful predictors empirically.[5]

A more parsimonious model is reported upon in table 9.3. Most of the variables in the probit of table 9.2 that were insignificant (for example, *Employ*, *Adv*) have been dropped, though some (for example *AddDebt*, *DesComp*) have been retained for their intrinsic theoretical interest, and the *Age* variable has been dropped, being outside the categories of market and financial variables. The probits of both table 9.2 and table 9.3 have probability levels of about 0.001 on a likelihood ratio test, and display high R^2s for models of this sort. However, the more parsimonious model of table 9.3 is arguably preferable. On a likelihood ratio test with four degrees of freedom

Table 9.3 Binary probit for sub-set of control variables

Variable	Coefficient	t-Ratio	Weighted elasticity
Pgroup	0.70062	2.2185**	0.33816
Pgear	$-0.89491.10^{-2}$	-3.3967***	-0.19191
Perfin	-0.88302	-1.5657†	-0.14001
Passet	$0.83424.10^{-6}$	0.30231	$-0.11120.10^{-1}$
AddDebt	0.42787	1.0044	$0.60810.10^{-1}$
DesComp	-0.32518	-0.0709	-0.12460
ProdDes	0.32298	0.96540	0.11427
Constant	0.33455	0.54861	$0.88876.10^{-1}$

Likelihood Ratio Test, $\chi^2 = 24.4687 > \chi^2_{.001}(7) = 24.3$
Cragg-Uhler $R^2 = 0.43004$
McFadden $R^2 = 0.30880$
Log-Likelihood $= -27.385$
Survival Probability $= 0.7671$
Legend: $t_{.01} = 1.296(†)$, $t_{.05} = 1.671(*)$, $t_{.025} = 2.000(**)$ $t_{.010} = 2.390(***)$

for comparing the two probits the test statistic is 7.22 which is less than the appropriate critical value of $\chi^2_{.050}(4) = 9.49$. The probit of table 9.3 is therefore preferred. It has some further advantages over that of table 9.2 in that the sign attached to the asset variable (*Passet*) is now positive, as predicted by the model of Jovanovic (1982).

Several of the variables reported above are qualitative and based on the owner-manager's assessment of a situation. This is true, for example, of the variable which describes competition (*DesComp*) on a scale from 1 for 'intense' to 4 for 'weak'. It might be useful also to report on a probit with only objectively measured variables based on, for example, the payroll or the balance sheet. One such probit is presented in table 9.4. Here the control variables used are age from financial inception (*Age*), full-time employees (*Employ*), book value of assets in 1985 (*Passet*), the debt/equity (i.e. gearing) ratio in 1985 (*Pgear*), and sales turnover in the tax year 1984 to 1985, excluding VAT (*Sales85*). In general, the probit is less satisfactory than those reported in tables 9.2 and 9.3, but is generally consistent with them nevertheless. The gearing variable is the dominating variable, being highly significant and having a relatively high elasticity with respect to probability of survival. Shedding labour improves survival, as do larger sales and assets. Older SBEs have a better chance of survival than younger SBEs. The age variable when used in a variety of probits had a positive effect on survival as predicted by theory, but was usually of marginal significance. Size, as measured by assets, typically had a positive but insignificant effect. This was also true of size measured by sales. Age was weakly positively correlated with size, measured by assets ($r = 0.258$), and weakly negatively correlated ($r = -0.149$) with gearing. Comparing the approach exemplified by the specification in table 9.4, which uses only the most obvious 'objective' variables, with that exemplified by the specifications in tables 9.2 and 9.3, there does seem some advantage in a more eclectic approach.

Table 9.4 Binary probit for sub-set of 'objective' variables

Variable	Coefficient	t-Ratio	Weighted elasticity
Age	0.010234	1.2758	0.063996
Employ	$-0.11336.10^{-2}$	-0.032546	$-0.019406.10^{-2}$
Passet	$-0.11006.10^{-2}$	0.29426	0.013624
Pgear	$-0.60536.10^{-2}$	$-3.0148^{\star\star\star}$	-0.15028
Sales85	$0.12133.10^{-2}$	0.64451	0.051110
Constant	0.66904	1.8674	0.19759

Likelihood Ratio Test, $\chi^2 = 19.0187 > \chi^2_{.005}(5) = 16.7$
Cragg-Uhler $R^2 = 0.35585$
McFadden $R^2 = 0.24759$
Legend: $t_{.01} = 1.296(\dagger)$, $t_{.05} = 1.671(^\star)$, $t_{.025} = 2.000(^{\star\star})$ $t_{.010} = 2.390(^{\star\star\star})$

9.6   CONCLUSION

The novelties of this chapter lie in three directions. First, the use of field work methods to provide a very detailed empirical picture of the forces contributing to an SBE staying in business. Here, the appropriate theoretical perspective is that of Holmes and Schmitz (1990) regarding entrepreneurship as the quest for new marketable products. Second, the use of both the more familiar objective data (for example, sales, number of product groups, assets) and, unusually, subjective data (for example, perceived intensity of competition, perceived degree of product differentiation) to estimate a probit model of staying in business. This extends the scope of the qualitative analysis of Storey et al. (1987). Third, the use of both financial variables (F), including gearing and other variables familiar from financial ratio analysis (as in Storey et al. 1987), and market variables (M), such as range of products and intensity of competition, to provide a broader explanation of staying in business.

The conclusion of this more detailed and broader framework is that a parsimonious model indicates that two variables have a particular influence on the probability of staying in business for this sample of SBEs: first, the product group range, a market variable; and second, the equity gearing ratio, a financial variable. A 1 per cent increase in the product group range would raise the probability of staying in business by 0.34 per cent and a 1 per cent reduction in equity gearing would raise this probability by 0.19 per cent, *ceteris paribus* (see elasticities in table 9.3). For this sample of SBEs there is also confirmation of the theory of small firms finance of De Meza and Webb (1988), that the worst small firm projects are those launched using purely personal finance.

APPENDIX TO CHAPTER 9

It is known from the work of McFadden (1978, 1984) that the profit function of a firm may be expressed in terms of a wide range of variables,[6] if the firm's feasible production set is interpreted broadly. In the main text of this chapter, these variables are grouped into market (M) and financial (F). Further, a linear characterization of this profit function can be justified precisely in a narrow class of cases, and more generally as an approximation, for a wide class of cases. Accordingly, adopting a linear characterization of the net profit π^{*} given by equation (9.1) in the main text gives:

$$\pi^{*} = x'\beta + \varepsilon \tag{9.2}$$

where x and β are conformable k-element vectors and ε is a random variable. In terms of the notation of the main text, X may be partitioned as (M, F). It is assumed the ε captures the sum of a large number of omitted, independent determinants of π^{*}, and may, by the central limit theorem, be regarded as a normally distributed random variable.

In terms of a probabilistic model there are now two events to take account of – staying in business (S) and exiting from business (E). Clearly, $\text{Prob}(S) = 1 - \text{Prob}(E)$

and $E \cap S = \{\emptyset\}$. An expression for Prob(S) can now be written as follows:

$$\text{Prob}(S) = \text{Prob}(\pi^* \geqslant 0) = \text{Prob}(x'\beta + \varepsilon \geqslant 0)$$
$$= 1 - \text{Prob}(\varepsilon < -x'\beta) \tag{9.3}$$
$$= 1 - \frac{1}{\sqrt{2\pi}} \int_{-\infty}^{-x'\beta/\sigma} \exp\left(-\frac{t^2}{2}\right) \, dt = 1 - \Phi(-x'\beta)$$

Here σ is not independently estimable, so it is assumed $\varepsilon \sim N(0, 1)$ fixing $\sigma = 1$. Φ denotes the cumulative density function of a standard-normally distributed random variable. Consider now a cross-section sample of n small firms indexed $i = 1, 2, \ldots n$. The same linear model applies, with the ε_i assumed independently distributed. Thus:

$$\pi^*_i = x'_i\beta + \varepsilon_i \text{ with } \varepsilon_i \sim NIID(0, 1) \; i = 1, 2, \ldots n \tag{9.4}$$

The dependent variable π^*_i is in general not observable directly. It is not the same thing as accounting profit, and small firms are understandably reluctant and in some cases simply unable to provide estimates of net economic profit to an interviewer. Thus π^*_i is a latent or unobserved variable. What are actually observed are outcomes, in the form of the events S_i and E_i. These events can be represented by a binary variable y_i with $\text{Prob}(S_i) = \text{Prob}(y_i = 1)$ and $\text{Prob}(E_i) = \text{Prob}(y_i = 0)$. Using the notation of (9.4) and the algebra of (9.3) above, it follows that:

$$\text{Prob}(S_i) = \text{Prob}(y_i = 1) = 1 - \Phi(-x'_i\beta)$$
$$\text{Prob}(E_i) = \text{Prob}(y_i = 0) = \Phi(-x'_i\beta) \tag{9.5}$$

The relationships in (9.5) provide the basis for a well-known statistical model, namely probit (or normit) analysis. Its likelihood function can be written:

$$\prod_{\substack{i \\ \text{s.t.} y_i = 1}} [1 - \Phi(-x'_i\beta)] \prod_{\substack{i \\ \text{s.t.} y_i = 0}} \Phi(-x'_i\beta)$$

or simply $L(\beta)$ with a corresponding log-likelihood $L^*(\beta)$. First-order conditions for maximizing L^* yield maximum likelihood estimators $\hat{\beta}$. These conditions are non-linear in $\hat{\beta}$, so iteration is required. A suitable procedure is the method of scoring, which also yields the asymptotic covariance matrix $[I(\hat{\beta})]^{-1}$, where I is the information matrix (i.e. the expectation of the negative of the Hession of L^*). L^* is known to be globally concave in β, implying that a solution to $\partial L^*/\partial\beta = 0$ is unique if it is bounded. Thus an iterative procedure, such as the method of scoring, for obtaining maximum likelihood estimators $\hat{\beta}$ will, if it converges, identify global maximizers for L^*.

10 Pricing asymmetries

With V. Bhaskar and S. Machin

10.1 INTRODUCTION

This chapter systematically uses the evidence available from the AQ 1985 on pricing conjectures of SBEs to test a specific model of oligopolistic interaction. The focus is on a kinked demand curve model, and the test methodology adopts the position advanced in Reid (1981) that subjective evidence on price conjectures may be used in testing models of oligopoly. The model is based upon Bhaskar (1988), where oligopolistic price setting is formalized as an extensive form game in which firms can respond without delay to their rivals' undercutting. Under certain assumptions it can be shown that equilibrium in this game is unique, at a price selected by an endogenously determined price leader. The price leader ensures that its competitors match this price by following a kinked demand curve type of strategy which involves matching price reductions but not price increases. This equilibrium enables firms to earn higher profits than at the Bertrand equilibrium: the kinked demand strategy discourages rivals from deviating from a relatively collusive outcome. This theory does not predict price rigidity, since the equilibrium price selected by the leader would respond to any general increase in costs or demand. However, price-following firms would face demand curves which were kinked at the prevailing price, due to the strategy adopted by the price leader. From an empirical point of view, this is an attractive feature of the theory since it is not falsified by the evidence that goes back to Stigler (1947) that prices are not relatively more rigid in oligopoly. At the same time, the theory is consistent with the evidence on the subjective perceptions of managers which suggests that firms do perceive an asymmetry in their rivals' responses. The evidence from questionnaires conducted by Wied-Nebbeling (1975) and Nowotny and Walther (1978) shows that a number of firms expected their rivals to match price reductions without matching price increases. [1]

This chapter uses evidence from the AQ 1985 to test for the presence of an asymmetry in SBEs' perceptions regarding their rivals' response. It is not expected that the version of the kinked demand curve theory sketched out above and elaborated below will completely explain the data. It is possible that some of these SBEs are monopolistic competitors for which significant strategic interaction is not important. For others, perhaps a model of Bertrand competition may be more relevant, especially in markets where information regarding price changes travels slowly. However, it is striking that the data show a marked degree of asymmetry in firms' perceptions regarding their rivals' responses. A number of firms expect their competitors to match price reductions without matching price increases in some circumstances. This asymmetry is prima facie inconsistent with models of monopolistic competition or Bertrand pricing, but is consistent with a modified kinked demand theory as expounded in 10.2 below.

In defence of the methodology of this chapter, it should be said that traditionally some economists have been reluctant to use subjective evidence in empirical work. They prefer what they regard as the 'hard' facts generated by agents' actions, such as the movements of actual prices. Current examples of this approach include Awh and Primeaux (1989) and Domberger and Fiebig (1990). However, recent developments in dynamic oligopoly call into question this traditional scepticism. Typically, in dynamic games, a price configuration is an equilibrium only because each player finds a deviation unprofitable. A deviation in turn may be unprofitable because of the player's perceptions as to how his rivals will respond to this deviation. Different models of oligopoly hinge in turn upon the nature of these responses. In equilibrium these deviations and responses will never be observed so that one cannot rely upon objective data alone in order to differentiate between oligopoly models. Questionnaires can play an important role here since they could shed light on the behaviour of agents 'off the equilibrium path'.

The key question from the AQ 1985 was: 'If you reduce your price do you reckon that your strongest competitors will do the same and reduce their prices?' This is question 4.4 of the AQ 1985 given in the appendix to this book (page 258). The same question was repeated for normal, boom, and recessionary business conditions. Each SBE was similarly questioned about its rivals' responses to a price increase (question 4.5 of AQ 1985). The answers to these questions provide the basic data which are analysed in this chapter. The focus here is on whether there is an asymmetry in SBEs perceptions of rivals' responses to price increases and price reductions, in relation to phases of the business cycle. Section 10.2 discusses the basic model of oligopolistic interaction due to Bhaskar (1988) and the predictions that this model makes, and section 10.3 considers some necessary extensions to this basic theory, taking account of capacity constraints. Section 10.4 describes the modelling strategy, section 10.5 the relevant points of the small firms database, and section 10.6 estimates an ordered probit model on the SBE's conjectures.

10.2 BASIC THEORY

The AQ 1985 contains questions inquiring into conjectures about price increases and decreases. The associated economic theory focuses on the presence of asymmetries in the expected price responses of competitors. The most well-known theory which predicts an asymmetry in response is the kinked demand curve theory in its traditional form (Sweezy 1939; Hall and Hitch 1939). An extended examination of this theory, including many variants and extensions, is in Reid (1981). In its simplest form, this theory says that a firm expects its rivals to match price cuts but not price increases. The resulting discontinuity in the marginal revenue curve implies that the market price will not respond to small changes in costs or demand, and that this will give rise to price rigidity. However, the theory's major weakness is that these responses of rivals are not derived from any form of maximizing behaviour, and are hence *ad hoc*. In addition, much empirical evidence, starting from Stigler (1947), suggests that prices are not invariably relatively more rigid in those oligopolistic industries for which the theory should be applicable. Consequently, this chapter discounts the traditional theory and focuses on a novel reformulation which gives what intends to be a more satisfactory theoretical account of why SBEs might face kinked demand curves under certain conditions.[2]

Consider two firms, firm A and firm B, which produce a similar product which may be horizontally differentiated due to the presence of customer loyalties.[3] Each firm's profits, Π^i $(i = a, b)$ is assumed to be given by a continuous, twice differentiable function of prices P_a and P_b, and is strictly concave in the firm's own price. The reaction functions, defining profit maximizing choices of price for a given rival's price, are $P_a = \alpha(P_b)$ and $P_b = \beta(P_a)$. These $\alpha(.)$ and $\beta(.)$ are upward sloping and intersect once as in figure 10.1 below. Define a firm's *common price profits* $\Pi_c^i(P)$, as its profits when both firms set the same price P. This function is strictly concave and attains a maximum at the firm's *optimal common price*. The most interesting case is when the firms differ, so let firm A have the lower price preference, as regards the optimal common price $(P_a^\star < P_b^\star)$ and the Bertrand price $(P_a^{\star\star} < P_b^{\star\star})$.

The main innovation of this theory is to allow for price changes and responses explicitly, while retaining a single trading period. Assume that prices must be publicly announced, and that each firm can respond rapidly to its rival's price changes. Such a situation can be formalized as a quick response game in the following way – both firms simultaneously announce initial prices P_a^1, P_b^1; if these differ, the firm pricing higher (say, firm B) can announce P_b^2; if it undercuts, by choosing $P_b^2 < P_a^1$. Firm A has the option of announcing P_a^3, and so on. If undercut, a firm can always respond and the move sequence ends when any firm does not undercut so that its rival has no need to reply. These moves take place sufficiently quickly that sales and pay-offs only depend upon the price last announced.

Perfect equilibrium in this game is always unique, but can take two forms, depending upon whether the firm's price preferences are relatively similar or divergent. This follows because a firm which is undercut will match its competitor's lower price provided that its reaction function does not prescribe a higher price. In other words, if $P_a^1 < P_b^1$, firm B's best second move[4] is to match if P_a^1 is above $\hat{P}_a$, and to choose $\beta(P_a^1)$ if $P_a^1 < \hat{P}_a$ where $\hat{P}_a$ is the threshold price for price matching.[5] Firm B's optimal second move as a function of P_a^1 is given by XYZ in figure 10.1. Similarly, if $P_a^1 > P_b^1$, firm A's optimal second move is given by XWV. However, this contingency never arises in equilibrium since firm B never undercuts, having higher price preferences. Hence, the final price outcome is picked out along XYZ by firm A's choice of initial price. It follows that if $P_a^1 > \hat{P}_a$, firm B matches this price and firm A gets his common price profits $\Pi_c^a(P_a^1)$. However, if $P_a^1 < \hat{P}_a$ firm B chooses $\beta(P_a^1)$ and firm A's profits are that of a Stackelberg leader, $\Pi^a(P_a^1, \beta(P_a^1))$.

Due to the change in firm B's behaviour at $\hat{P}_a$, firm A's profits as a function of P_a^1 can have two local maxima, at $P_a^\star$ and at the Stackleberg price $\bar{P}_a$ (where $\bar{P}_a < P_a^\star$). If the global maximum is at $P_a^\star$ (which we call the *minimum optimal common price*), both firms charge the same price in equilibrium and will also match any price undercutting by their rival. However, firm A, which may be called the price leader, will not match firm B's price increases, so that firm B effectively faces a demand curve which is kinked at the equilibrium price. More generally, with several firms, all firms except the price leader face a kinked demand curve in equilibrium, Also, if the firms are

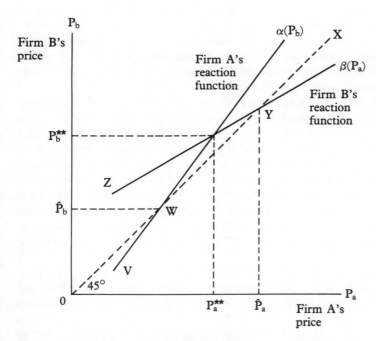

Figure 10.1 Bertrand reaction functions for firms A and B

identical, or if two or more firms jointly have the minimum optimal common price, all firms will face a kinked demand curve in equilibrium. However, if there is a single price leader, it will not face a kinked demand curve since its rivals will match its price changes in either direction. Note that since the equilibrium price is unique, this theory does not predict price rigidity – any general change in costs or demand will alter the minimum optimal common price equilibrium.[6]

Alternatively, firm A's profits as a function of P may be globally maximized at $\hat{P}_a$, the Stackelberg price. This case is likely when the firm's price preferences are very divergent, and when firm B chooses to price above P_a^1 even when P_a^1 is relatively high (by firm A's reckoning). In this case, neither firm faces a kinked demand curve since price responses are symmetric regardless of the direction of the price change.

To summarize, this theory predicts that a firm would expect an asymmetry in the response of its competitors if it deviates from the equilibrium price, if it were not occupying the leadership position in an industry where a uniform price prevailed and firms were not too divergent. A firm would expect a symmetric response either if it were the sole price leader with the minimum optimal common price, or if the Stackelberg equilibrium prevailed. The first prediction is novel, and not made by standard oligopoly models. The case where the firm expects a symmetric positive response to its price changes is not specific to this theory. In Bertrand competition, if firms assume that their rivals will be given by their upward sloping reaction functions, they would expect both price increases and decreases to be followed.[7] Naturally, the presence of symmetric expected responses would not allow us to discriminate between this theory and alternatives. However, any significant degree of asymmetry in expected responses is indicative of some support for the kinked demand curve theory.

A caveat is that one should not expect the theory set out here to be universally applicable. If information about price changes travels slowly, or the products of competing firms are too heterogeneous, the assumptions deployed are violated and a model of Bertrand competition may be more applicable. It is also plausible that some firms in the sample may not be in a situation involving strategic interaction (i.e. oligopoly) but rather one of monopolistic competition. In models of monopolistic competition (Dixit and Stiglitz 1977; Hart 1985), the demand elasticity faced by any firm does not depend significantly upon its competitors' prices, so that price changes do not evoke any response. These possibilities are allowed for in the empirical analysis.

A final point may be made about the kinked demand curve equilibrium. It is that since all firms follow a strategy of matching price reductions, this makes such reductions unprofitable, and allows firms to achieve a relatively 'collusive' outcome. Indeed, the outcome will be the monopoly price if firms are identical. This method of sustaining 'collusion' noncooperatively may be contrasted with the repeated games approach (Friedman 1977; Abreu 1986), where if a firm reduces price even slightly, it can expect a discontinuously large price reduction from its rivals as a punishment. On the other hand, a price increase need not be punished and is liable to be ignored. It should however be noted that the data used here were collected by personal interviews with owner-managers. In the course of these interviews additional informal evidence gathered from discussions with the owner-managers never produced responses in which owner-managers indicated that their rivals would behave in a manner consistent with the Abreu-Friedman model by reacting severely to price cuts.

10.3 EXTENSIONS OF THE THEORY

The theory set out in Bhaskar (1988) needs to be extended before it can be used for empirical analysis. Since the AQ 1985 elicits information on competitor's responses at different stages of the business cycle, it is possible to consider how the likelihood of the two types of equilibria varies cyclically. Since this involves the comparison of two local maxima, standard calculus methods are inappropriate, and a full constructive analysis is necessary.

The higher the level of demand, the more likely it is that some firms in the industry will be constrained by their capacity levels of output. Therefore the basic model is modified by assuming that firm B's output, q_b, cannot exceed capacity output, $\bar{q}_b$. It is also assumed that firm A has a higher capacity level, $(\bar{q}_a > \bar{q}_b)$, and is hence unconstrained in the relevant range, and that the firms are similar in other respects. As indicated below, if both firms have similar capacity levels, the modified model becomes similar to the basic model, and the kinked demand curve equilibrium always prevails.

As in section 10.2, the two firm's (pseudo) reaction functions can be derived assuming that firm B does not face any capacity constraint, so that its marginal cost of producing above $\bar{q}_b$ is simply that of producing at $\bar{q}_b$. In figure 10.2, these are the unkinked smooth curves $\alpha\alpha'$ and $\beta\beta'$ composed of solid lines and dashed segments. Along $\beta\beta'$ the effect of an increased price upon B's demand is

$$\frac{\mathrm{d}q_b}{\mathrm{d}P_a} = \frac{\partial q_b}{\partial P_a} + \frac{\partial q_b}{\partial \beta} \cdot \frac{\partial \beta(P_a)}{\partial P_a} \tag{10.1}$$

It is plausible to assume that expression (10.1) is positive. This condition is satisfied if demand is linear and marginal costs are non-decreasing. Let $P_K(P_a, \sigma)$ be the price for firm B that solves: $q_b(P_K, P_a, \sigma) = \bar{q}$, where σ is a demand shift parameter such that $\partial q_b/\partial \sigma > 0$. So P_K is simply the price of firm B which equates the demand for firm B's product and its capacity output. P_K is an increasing function of P_a and, by the previous assumption, when graphed as KK', it is flatter than $\beta\beta'$ in figure 10.2. Firm B is capacity constrained at all points below the KK' line in figure 10.2. Firm B's actual reaction function in the presence of a capacity constraint is the kinked reaction curve $\beta'UK$. It obviously coincides with the pseudo reaction

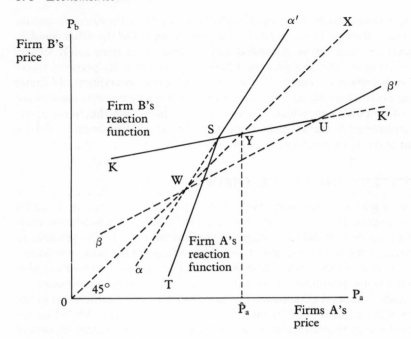

Figure 10.2 Reaction functions when firm B is capacity constrained

function $\beta(.)$ as long as firm B is unconstrained by capacity. However, if $\beta(P_a)$ implies a price such that $q_b(\beta(P_a), P_a, \sigma) > \bar{q}_b$, this is sub-optimal as firm B could raise price without reducing sales. Firm B's optimal choice is to choose $P_K(P_a, \sigma)$: due to the concavity of profit in own price, firm B would not choose a price greater than P_K. Given this reaction function, firm B's optimal second move as a function of P_a^1 is given by XYK.

Firm A's reaction function is also modified by firm B's capacity constraint, becoming less responsive to a price reduction by firm B once he is constrained, and hence steeper. The degree of steepness depends on the rationing rule applied to firm B's customers. However, this is not important for our theory since firm B will never choose to ration any customers. Firm A's reaction function is thus the kinked reaction curve α'ST.

From figure 10.2, it is clear that the capacity constraint raises $\hat{P}_a$, the price below which firm B prices above firm A, and shifts out firm B's reaction function. This increases firm A's profits as a Stackelberg leader, hence making the Stackelberg equilibrium more likely.

We can now examine the effects of changes in demand. Since the effect of demand changes upon preferred prices in the absence of capacity constraints is unclear, we assume that the pseudo reaction functions and optimal common prices are unaltered.[8] In other words, a rise in σ increases the absolute profitability of any point in the price space, but does not change the relative profitability in any systematic way, in the absence of capacity constraints. The capacity line KK′ shifts upwards as σ increases. This makes firm B set his price above that of firm A for greater range of values of P_a^1, and hence makes the Stackelberg equilibrium more likely. Consequently, we would expect price asymmetries to be less likely in boom conditions and more likely in recessions.

We have focused on the case where only one firm faces an effective capacity constraint since it is this case which yields an interesting insight. If both firms face similar capacity constraints, equilibrium will be of the kinked demand curve type irrespective of demand variations. Although there may be non-existence of Bertrand equilibrium, this does not affect the results.

A second extension is suggested by the information contained in the AQ 1985 on the firm's perceived elasticity of demand when it alone changes price, its competitors keeping price constant. If demand is more elastic, firms will find it more costly to price above the price leader, so that the Stackelberg equilibrium becomes less likely. In the limit, if demand is infinitely elastic, only a uniform price equilibrium is viable. This implies that price asymmetries are more likely if demand is more elastic, and suggests the use of the elasticity variable in conjunction with the direction of the price change in the empirical work to follow.

With the empirical work in mind, further extensions of the basic model come to mind. For instance, as noted above, strategic interaction is likely to be important in markets dominated by a few firms whilst the monopolistic competition model is more likely to hold where a large number of firms operate. As argued above, the idea of what constitutes price matching is likely to be clearer for cases in which firms produce relatively homogeneous products, so that the kinked demand curve is more likely to be applicable. The location of the firm's market is also potentially relevant for, as the firms to be considered are small, strategic interaction seems more likely in local markets. Individual firm market share is also of potential relevance since higher market share makes a strategic response of competitors more likely. Finally, the data do not contain any information on whether or not firms feel their competitors face capacity constraints. A firm-specific measure of capacity utilization is however available, albeit only for normal business conditions. This variable, whilst not entirely satisfactory, is considered in the empirical work to follow.

10.4 MODELLING STRATEGY

The question asked of the owner-manager is, 'If you change your price do you expect your strongest competitors to do likewise?' Given that there is inevitably some uncertainty associated with rivals' responses, one can think of the owner-manager of firm i assigning a probability P_i to the rival's matching of the price change. Then assume that if $0 < P_i < \underline{\theta}$ the question is answered 'No', if $\bar{\theta} < P_i < 1$ the question is answered 'Yes' and if

$\underline{\theta} < P_i < \bar{\theta}$, the response is 'uncertain'. In other words, the underlying variable P_i is continuous but the response is ordered and discrete depending upon where P_i lies relative to the (unobserved) thresholds $\underline{\theta}$ and $\bar{\theta}$, above and below which a price response is deemed to have occurred or not.

The above poses an econometric problem since the underlying variable P_i is bounded by 0 and 1. To resolve this problem it is easy to transform P_i into a continuous unbounded variable, say $P_i^\star$. For example, if $P_i^\star$ is a monotone increasing function $f(P_i)$ which satisfies $P_i^\star \to \infty$ as $P_i \to 1$ and $P_i^\star \to -\infty$ as $P_i \to 0$ then the relevant econometric model is of the form

$$P_i^\star = x_i\beta + u_i \qquad (i = 1, 2, \dots N) \tag{10.2}$$

where $P_i^\star$ denotes the (transformed) probability that the owner-manager in firm i attaches to its rivals' altering prices if firm i alters its product price. x_i is a vector of variables which determine this probability, β a parameter vector and u_i a normally distributed random error.

The data available to estimate this model are based on a question asking whether the firm expects its strongest competitors to match its price change. This question (question 4.4 and question 4.5 of AQ 1985 as given in the appendix to this book, page 258) is asked separately for price increases and decreases and in three different phases of the business cycle (i.e. the question is asked in the case of normal business conditions, booms, and recessions). The responses given are of the form 'yes', 'don't know', 'no' and as such are naturally ordered (i.e. rivals will respond, may respond, will not respond). Hence, we can relate these actual responses (P_i') to our unobserved variable $P_i^\star$ as follows:

$$\begin{aligned} P_i' &= 0 \text{ if } P_i^\star < f(\underline{\theta}) \\ &= 1 \text{ if } f(\bar{\theta}) > P_i^\star > f(\underline{\theta}) \\ &= 2 \text{ if } P_i^\star > f(\bar{\theta}) \end{aligned} \tag{10.3}$$

where $f(\underline{\theta})$ and $f(\bar{\theta})$ are the transformed thresholds. Hence, the observable variable P_i' takes the value 0 if no price change is expected to occur, 1 if a price change may occur, and 2 if a price change is expected. Given the qualitative nature of this dependent variable, the model can be estimated using standard techniques for limited dependent variable models. In particular, as the variable is ordered, an ordered probit estimator is used (see Maddala 1983 or Amemiya 1985 for more details), this being a direct generalization of the binary probit estimator of the previous chapter.

As the question is effectively asked six times, the data were pooled from each response to give $6 \times N$ observations. To test whether there is any asymmetry in price responses a direction dummy is defined (i.e. three of the six questions pertain to price increases, the other three to price decreases), and its impact on $P_i^\star$ analysed. It is also possible to test whether this asymmetry varies with the business cycle by including dummy variables for the boom and recession periods. These can be compared to a base group relevant to normal business conditions.

Thus the x-vector includes the direction dummy and the cycle dummies. Information is also available on some of the characteristics of the SBEs in the sample which can be used as control variables. In particular, following the discussion in sections 10.2 and 10.3, the variables which play a role in the empirical work are as follows, with relevant questions of the AQ 1985 (see this book's appendix) from which they were derived indicated as appropriate:

1 Whether or not the SBE faced only a few competitor ($\leqslant 10$). (*Qu. 1.10*)
2 Whether it produced identical or similar products to its competitor. (*Qu. 1.11*)
3 The nature of the SBE's operating market (local, regional, national, or international. (*Qu. 1.8*)
4 Market share. (*Qu. 1.9*)
5 Whether the SBE perceived itself as facing an elastic demand schedule (*Qu. 4.6*)
6 Capacity utilization. (*Qu. 3.3*)

As reported below, not all of these controls prove statistically important and appropriate omitted variable tests for the ordered probit model are presented in the empirical work, along with diagnostic tests for heteroskedasticity and non-normality.[9]

10.5 DATA

The data come from the AQ 1985 as indicated above. For present purposes the data used were for those SBEs for which there were no missing data on the rivals' price response question.[10] Some descriptive statistics are given in table 10.1. In the first row all six questions are pooled to give a sample size of 400, of which 27 per cent responded positively to the question of whether their rivals will change their prices in response to a price increase/decrease on their part. However, this figure hides a great deal of variation with respect to both the direction of the price change, and the phase of the business cycle.

Across all business conditions, 24 per cent of SBEs thought that their rivals would match their price increases, whilst 30 per cent thought that they would match their price decreases. Within this there is considerable evidence of pricing asymmetries. As an example, an additional piece of information not contained in table 10.1 is that, of the 60 positive responses regarding rivals' price cuts, only 14 also produced an affirmative response to the price increase question. The presence of such asymmetries tends to favour kinked demand curve explanations of strategic interaction, unlike the Bertrand case where all competitors would follow suit and alter their prices, and the monopolistic competition case where none would follow.

Even more striking is the variability of this with respect to points on the cycle. With respect to price increases, 46 per cent of SBEs said they would

Table 10.1 Descriptive statistics on SBEs' perceptions of rivals' price responses

	Proportion of Responses			
	Yes	Uncertain	No	Number
All responses in all business conditions	0.27	0.06	0.67	400
Price increases				
All business conditions	0.24	0.07	0.69	199
Boom	0.46	0.08	0.46	65
Normal business conditions	0.19	0.04	0.76	67
Recession	0.07	0.10	0.82	67
Price decreases				
All business conditions	0.30	0.04	0.66	201
Boom	0.19	0.03	0.78	67
Normal business conditions	0.24	0.01	0.75	67
Recession	0.46	0.09	0.45	67

Notes:
1 'Yes' denotes that a firm believes its rivals will follow suit and match its price increase/decrease, 'uncertain' that it is not sure, and 'No' that it believes its rivals will not follow.
2. For reasons of rounding proportions might not sum to unity.

be matched in a boom, compared to 19 per cent in normal conditions, and a meagre 7 per cent in a recession. The opposite pattern emerges for price decreases, where only 19 per cent of rivals were perceived to follow and cut prices in a boom, whilst this rises to 24 per cent in normal business conditions, and increases to 46 per cent in a recession. This seems to be very strong descriptive evidence for the presence of significant pricing asymmetries at different points of the business cycle. These data are therefore subjected to more rigorous statistical testing in the next section.

10.6   RESULTS ON ORDERED PROBIT ESTIMATES

Table 10.2 presents ordered probit estimates of our model based on the responses to the six pooled questions. In column (1), only the direction dummy (DOWN) is included, whilst in column (2) it is allowed to differ with the cycle dummies (BOOM, RECESS) to see if asymmetries differ over the cycle. In column (3) the SBE's characteristics are now included and column (4) presents our statistically preferred model. Finally, columns (5) and (6) report results based on the recession and boom sub-samples respectively.

Despite the difference in means reported in table 10.1 for up/down responses, the basic model in column (1) indicates that such an effect is not significant at conventional levels of statistical significance, although the positive sign on the DOWN dummy conforms with our expectations (i.e. price cuts are more likely to be matched). When allowed to differ with the

Table 10.2 Ordered probit estimates of the probability that a firm believes its rivals will react to its price changes

	(1)	(2)	(3)	(4)	(5)	(6)
Constant	-0.718	-0.698	-1.637	-1.759	-2.815	0.699
	(0.133)	(0.115)	(0.339)	(0.324)	(0.928)	(0.509)
DOWN	0.114	0.085	-0.045	–	1.101	-0.904
	(0.132)	(0.227)	(0.237)		(0.262)	(0.248)
RECESS	0.277	-0.295	-0.311	–	–	–
	(0.162)	(0.257)	(0.264)			
BOOM	0.367	-0.118	-0.129	–	–	–
	(0.156)	(0.277)	(0.231)			
DOWN*RECESS	–	1.022	1.080	0.851	–	–
		(0.335)	(0.350)	(0.179)		
(1–DOWN)*BOOM	–	0.912	0.941	0.940	–	–
		(0.317)	(0.320)	(0.176)		
FEW	–	–	0.758	0.750	1.543	0.544
			(0.290)	(0.282)	(0.869)	(0.443)
DOWN*ELAST	–	–	0.853	0.865	1.000	0.416
			(0.261)	(0.249)	(0.466)	(0.472)
IDENT	–	–	0.322	0.320	0.495	0.384
			(0.164)	(0.161)	(0.291)	(0.282)
N	400	400	400	400	134	132
logL	-312.99	-294.34	-282.93	-283.90	-95.31	-98.74

Notes:
1 The dependent variable is an ordered response equal to 0 if firms believe their rivals will not react to a price change, 1 if they are uncertain, and 2 if they believe a price response will occur.
2 The independent variables are defined as follows: DOWN = 1 if the observation corresponds to perceptions regarding a price cut, 0 otherwise; RECESS = 1 if the observation corresponds to the question about price changes in a recession, 0 otherwise; BOOM = 1 if the observation corresponds to the question about price changes in a boom, 0 otherwise; FEW = 2 if the firm faces few competitors (≤ 10), 0 otherwise; ELAST = 1 if the firm perceives itself as facing an elastic demand schedule; IDENT = 1 if the firm produces identical or similar products to its competitors, 0 otherwise.
3 Asymptotic standard errors in parentheses.

cycle dummy variables in column (2) some very strong results emerge. That is, as the raw data described earlier suggest, rivals are more likely to follow price cuts in recessions and price rises in booms. Column (2) is easily preferred to column (1) on statistical grounds: a $\chi^2(2)$ Likelihood Ratio test statistic of 37.30 compared to the relevant 5 per cent critical value of 5.99 confirms this. The result reported in column (2) is essentially the substantive finding of this chapter, namely that there exist asymmetries in pricing behaviour which vary considerably with the demand conditions faced by firms. Such a finding is inconsistent with Bertrand or monopolistic competition as a pure explanation of pricing behaviour. It is however explicable if one adopts the kinked demand curve framework set out earlier.

In column (3) this result remains robust to the inclusion of certain strategically related SBE characteristics. Those characteristics found to be statistically significant reflect the degree of competition faced by the SBE (FEW), product differentiation (IDENT) and, for downward price reactions, the SBE's perceived product demand elasticity (DOWN* ELAST). It is of considerable interest that all three variables raise the probability that an SBE's rivals will react to price changes. So strategic interaction between SBEs in a given market is more likely if there are few competitors producing reasonably homogeneous goods and who feel they face elastic demand schedules.

The fourth column of table 10.2 presents the preferred specification. The most general model in column (3) can easily be simplified to column (4), the relevant $\chi^2(3)$ Likelihood Ratio statistic being 1.94. In this parsimonious model it is evident that asymmetries in pricing responses occur at the peak and slump of the cycle and also that such interaction between SBEs depends on the characteristics of SBEs and their market.

It seems important to subject the preferred model to a number of diagnostic checks of model adequacy. Some econometric tests of the model are presented in column (4) by drawing on the recent advances in testing microeconomic models developed by Chesher and Irish (1987) and Gourieroux et al. (1987). They indicate how to construct score tests for models with limited dependent variables based on what they term pseudo or generalized residuals. Machin and Stewart (1988) have further developed their tests to the ordered probit case and it is these test statistics that are presented in table 10.3. The tests are very impressive and indicate that the model has no problems of heteroskedasticity and that the assumption of normally distributed errors cannot be rejected. Some omitted variable tests are also presented in table 10.3. The functional form test implies there are no missing non-linearities in the model and the tests also confirm that a number of other firm-specific characteristics are not required in the model. Overall, these diagnostics engender a great deal of confidence in the reported results.

In column (5) the preferred model is reproduced for the recession subsample. The coefficient on the DOWN dummy variable is positive and strongly significant. In column (6) the same exercise is carried out for the

Table 10.3 Diagnostic tests of the preferred specification

Test	Test statistic	5% Critical value
Heteroskedasticity	4.73	11.10
Non-normality	0.62	5.99
Omitted variables		
Functional form	1.07	7.81
Market share	0.01	3.84
Market location variables	4.14	7.81
Capacity utilization $\geqslant 80\%$	0.26	3.84

Notes:
1 The tests refer to the specification in column (4) of table 10.2.
2 Information on the method of construction of these score tests is given in the technical appendix of Machin and Stewart (1988).
3 The functional form test involves augmenting the model by the squared, cubed, and quadrupled predicted values.
4 Market share is formed from taking mid-points of the qualitative data available. Firms with missing values are allocated sample means.
5 The market location variables are three dummy variables indicating whether the firm's main market is regional, the UK, or international (base = local).
6 The capacity variable is a dummy variable indicating whether or not the firm is perceived to be operating at 80 per cent or more of full capacity.

boom sub-sample, and in this case the DOWN coefficient is strongly negative. It seems therefore that a reverse kink is observed in boom conditions, as suggested by Efroymson (1955). However, a reverse kink implies that the prevailing price cannot be optimal for the firm as it could increase profits either by reducing price or increasing it. [11] One explanation for this result is that some SBEs may have misinterpreted the question, and indicated their competitors' response to the twin events of an increase in demand and a change in their own price, rather than the single event of a price change in the situation of a boom. If the increase in demand increases the equilibrium price so that the prevailing price is no longer an equilibrium, a reverse asymmetry in rivals' responses is possible. It may also be noted that Nowotny and Walther (1978) find some evidence for a reverse kink in boom conditions.

The evidence presented to date is strongly in favour of the hypothesis that significant interaction occurs regarding SBEs' pricing decisions in industrial markets. A useful diagnostic check of the models is to exclude those SBEs from the sample which experienced no such interaction (i.e. $P' = 0$ for all questions). Results doing so (excluding the twenty-two firms with P' always equal to 0) are reported in table 10.4, which presents the most general model and a more parsimonious equation for this small sample of firms. [12] The main

Table 10.4 Probits for SBEs with at least some strategic interaction

	(1)	(2)
Constant	−0.490	−0.540
	(0.456)	(0.097)
DOWN	0.020	−
	(0.256)	
RECESS	−0.344	−
	(0.028)	
BOOM	−0.183	−
	(0.248)	
DOWN*RECESS	1.320	1.114
	(0.390)	(0.212)
(1−DOWN)*BOOM	1.227	1.165
	(0.335)	(0.208)
FEW	−0.022	−
	(0.411)	
DOWN*ELAST	0.739	0.785
	(0.317)	(0.303)
IDENT	0.112	−
	(0.189)	
N	288	288
log L	−230.09	−231.50

Notes:
1 As for table 10.2

results again follow from table 10.4. That is, the probability that an SBE's rival will respond to a price change is higher if this refers to a price increase in a boom or a price decrease in a recession.

10.7 CONCLUSIONS

This chapter has presented some empirical tests of a modified version of the kinked demand curve theory based on SBEs' perceptions of their rivals' responses to price changes. Some evidence of asymmetries in the reactions of rivals to a price change were found, hence providing evidence for kinked demand curve explanations of strategic interaction rather than for more popular models such as Bertrand competition, or monopolistic competition, in which such asymmetries are absent. Moreover, the likelihood of competitors following price changes was found to differ significantly at different phases of the business cycle, so that price increases are much more likely to be followed in booms, and price decreases are more likely to be followed in times of recession.

11 Growth and its determinants

11.1 INTRODUCTION

One of the most notable aspects of the SBEs in this study is that they are typically subject to rapid growth, whether one looks at this in terms of growth sales, assets, or employment. I indicated in chapter 3 that between 1985 and 1988 real sales and real assets increased, on average, threefold for the sample, with full-time employment almost doubling. In chapter 4, the percentage output change for the sample was also noted as being high at an estimated +150 per cent. It is also the case that these SBEs had grown quickly right from the point of financial inception. There had been an almost fourfold increase in real assets, on average, from the point of financial inception until the administration of the questionnaire in 1985 (AQ 1985) over an average period of three-and-a-half years.

In this chapter I propose to achieve three goals: (1) to provide a more complete statistical and econometric picture of the growth experience of these SBEs with an emphasis on asset values; (2) to estimate and test models inspired by Gibrat's Law ('The Law of Proportionate Effect')[1] both in its classical form and in modern variants; (3) to estimate and test econometric growth equations, whose purpose are to provide economic explanations of growth in terms of exogenous variables.

11.2 THE STATISTICS OF SMALL FIRM GROWTH

Let me take as the starting point the notion that it is possible to measure with some accuracy the size (s_t) of an SBE in time period t. Then growth has occurred over a unit period if $s_{t+1} > s_t$ and decline has occurred if $s_{t+1} < s_t$. Generalizing this to τ time periods $(\tau = 1, 2, ...)$ we can say that growth has occurred if $s_{t+\tau} > s_t$ and decline is $s_{t+\tau} < s_t$. Possible measures of size include (real) assets (S_t), (real) profits (π_t), real assets (W_t) and full-time employment (L_t).

The SBEs in the sample were generally fairly young (41 months, on average) with a range from 3 months to 297 months (nearly 25 years). If figures provided by the owner-managers on the initial assets of their firms are reflated to constant 1985 prices, the average level of assets at financial inception is found to be £20,000 (at 1985 prices). The average level in 1985, as reported in the AQ 1985 is £76,000, representing an average annual growth rate of real assets of about 80 per cent. The figures on assets, which are expressed at book value, net of depreciation, are of interest, because assets are not entirely destroyed when an SBE goes out of business. Despite the fact that about one-quarter of SBEs no longer operated after a three-year period (cf. chapter 9), some conservation of assets occurs at the sale or disposal of a firm. Indeed, if the disposal of the SBE is a voluntary trade sale, undertaken by a specialist in small firm inception of the sort envisaged in the work of Holmes and Schmitz (1990), the capital value of the firm should be kept entirely intact. There is therefore the presumption that this general tendency to asset creation by SBEs is, in aggregate, wealth creating.

Figure 11.1 provides a useful graphical depiction of this process of asset accumulation. Initial assets are on the horizontal axis, and final assets (as measured by the AQ 1985) are on the vertical axis, both expressed in 1985 prices. Different histories of firms are represented in that initial assets relate to disparate starting points, from the recent past to a quarter of a century ago. The $45°$ line denotes points for which assets (W_t) have not grown for a particular SBE's history (i.e. $W_t = W_{t-\tau}$ for an SBE aged τ).

The general picture that emerges is of remarkable asset accumulation. Few owner-managers (11 per cent) experienced a fall in asset values, and for the few that did, the percentage loss was, on average, rather small – as indicated by the points only just below the 45 per cent line. Some SBEs started small and remained rather small, as indicated by the clustering near the origin. Such firms were also relatively vulnerable to demise (as indicated by the circled observations). Of the thirteen firms in this cluster close (within, say, £13,000) to the origin, the majority (seven) were no longer in business three years later. However it is known from the binary probit models of chapter 9 that assets are a weak rather than strong predictor of staying in business, though the effect is clearly positive. Not surprisingly therefore, one sees in figure 11.1 some quite high asset growth firms which subsequently went out of business. Finally, one observes that some firms came into what I have called the 'super-growth' category. Observations for these SBEs are well off the vertical scale, so I have simply indicated their final asset sizes on the top row of the diagram. The closer such an observation is to the vertical axis, the more remarkable is the growth performance. This small percentage (8 per cent) of the sample which has achieved such high growth has inspired a doctrine of 'picking winners' in some policy circles (Storey and Johnson 1987). However, to the extent that the fortunes of SBEs are governed by chance (rather than systematic) influences, the prospects of 'picking winners' are thereby diminished (Reid and Jacobsen 1988: chapter 6), and a more general enterprise-stimulating policy is indicated. An example of an important chance mechanism for generating plausible growth processes for firms is the so-called Gibrat's Law, according to which the growth of a firm is a

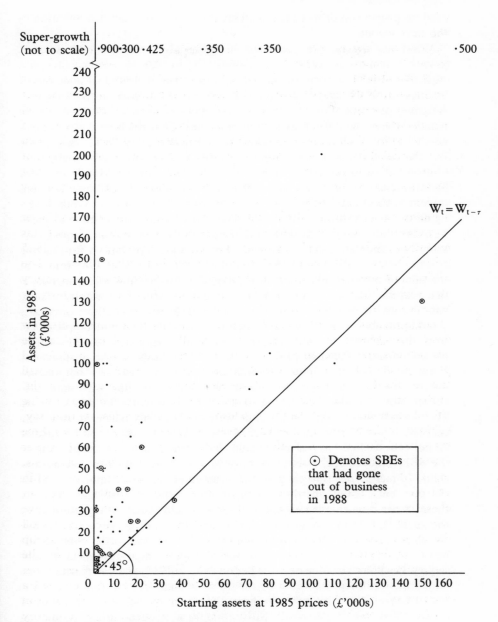

Figure 11.1 Asset growth from financial inception

random proportion of its size. I shall give this law more detailed attention in the next section.

Modifying the picture presented in figure 11.1, one can look at asset growth in real terms over the time period 1985 to 1988 by reference to figure 11.2. Because 23 per cent of the SBEs in existence in 1985 had gone out of business by 1988, special problems of representation arise in this diagram. A further problem of incompleteness of observations from 1988 arises. I have handled these two difficulties as follows. First, SBEs which went out of business by 1988 are all represented along the horizontal axis. This is despite the fact that no failures in this sample are likely to have involved a dissipation of asset values to zero. It is known that no failures in this sample involved bankruptcies, so the assets of the firm, however disposed of, were not sold under the most extreme form of financial stress. I did not specifically investigate the asset value of SBEs at disposal (for example, through trade sale, voluntary liquidation) but what little evidence I have does not suggest anything like complete asset destruction. For example, one finds a firm having an asset value of £10,000 in 1985 and of £51,000 in 1988 (at 1985 prices) at the time of disposal. My impression, based on further informal evidence, is that a failure to achieve asset growth is a common reason for the entrepreneur winding up his business, so some of the observations on the horizontal axis should probably be on the 45° line. Second, I have dealt with incomplete data from the AQ 1988 by imputing the same real asset values to SBEs whose owner-managers failed to provide a figure. Thus some of the observations along the 45° line are imputed, though zero real asset growth was not uncommonly observed anyway. Given these two ways of dealing with data difficulties, one can now shed further light on SBE growth. The data of figure 11.2 suggest that growth and decline were fairly evenly balanced over 1985 to 1988. Thus 23 per cent of the SBEs went out of business and a further 22 per cent declined in real asset value. Balanced against this, 55 per cent of the SBEs enjoyed real asset growth, or at least held their asset values constant. In fact 21 per cent came in the latter category, so a minority of SBEs (34 per cent), about one-third, actually grew between 1985 and 1988. Of these, 8 per cent enjoyed exceptional growth, and these are represented by the unscaled data points at the boundaries of figure 11.2, above the 45 per cent line. Most of these high growth firms had earlier been identified in figure 11.1. Only one out of the six earlier super-growth firms subsequently suffered decline over the period 1985 to 1988, and two further firms joined this category, indicated by the off-scale boundary observations at the top of figure 11.2. This again confirms the phenomenon of the existence of a sub-set[2] of highly successful SBEs though, as argued earlier, predicting which will lie in that category may be considerably harder than identifying their existence *ex post facto*.

Comparing figures 11.1 and 11.2, one can see that most observations lie above the 45° line in the former case, whereas in the latter case observations are more evenly distributed on either side of the 45° line. This is weak

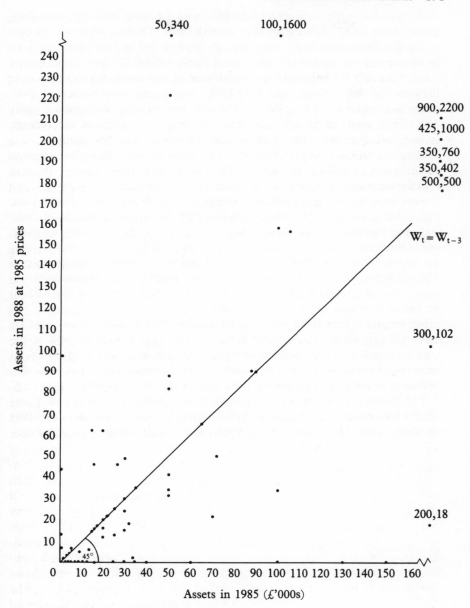

Figure 11.2 Asset growth over three years

confirmation of a life-cycle effect for SBEs, with a general tendency for earlier growth rates to be higher than later growth rates. That is, whatever the age of the firm measured from inception, its growth rate at this point tends to be higher than its growth rate three years further down the line. From inception to the AQ 1985 the annual growth rate of real assets was 80 per cent. Between the AQ 1985 and the RIQ 1988, average real asset values (at 1985 prices) increased from £76,000 to £186,000, representing an annual growth rate of real assets of 48 per cent, which is itself a reduction in the average growth rate over two roughly three-year periods of over one-third.

Some matters of interpretation are worth drawing out. Whilst the average age duration of SBEs is similar in each case (roughly three years),[3] there is a wider variation of durations[4] in figure 11.1 as compared to figure 11.2, so growth rates mean slightly different things for each figure.[5] It is also the case that the data in figure 11.1 relate to SBEs that, by sampling definition, have stayed in business, whilst those in figure 11.2 permit the possibility of going out of business. However, as figure 11.1 strongly indicates, asset growth does not preclude going out of business. And indeed, as almost one-quarter of SBEs in figure 11.2 appear below the 45° line (but not on the horizontal line), experience of asset value contraction does not immediately cause the SBE to go out of business.

My emphasis here is largely on asset growth, but similar stories could be told with respect to sales or employment.[6] The employment variable is the least susceptible to variation and growth, and even relatively large SBEs, in terms of assets or sales, can have relatively small work-forces. The joint distribution of age and employees for the sample in 1988 is given in table 11.1.

The simple generalization that emerges is that the typical SBE is young and small. The modal age range was 0 to 12 months, and 37 per cent of SBEs fell in this class; the modal size range was 1 to 10 employees, and 78 per cent

Table 11.1 Joint distribution of age and employment

	Employ (full time employees)						
	1–10	11–20	21–30	31–40	41–50	50+	Total
Age (months from inception)							
0–12	36	1	0	0	0	0	37
13–24	15	3	1	0	0	0	19
25–36	7	3	1	0	0	0	11
37–48	4	3	0	0	1	0	8
49–60	1	1	0	0	0	1	3
61–72	3	0	0	0	0	0	3
73–84	0	0	0	0	0	0	0
85 and above	12	1	1	0	3	0	17
Total	78	12	3	0	4	1	

Note: Bivariate distribution of age and employment based on AQ 1985. Entries in table are percentages to the nearest integer.

of SBEs fell in this class. The younger SBEs account for most of the employment. Employment tends to increase with age, which of course occurs because of the general tendency to positive growth. However, employment does not rise rapidly with age, as indicated by the high frequency of zero entries in cells above the principal diagonal in table 11.1.

Sales growth behaves more like asset growth, and both increased roughly threefold over the period 1985 to 1988. Mean sales stood at £228,560 in 1985 for those firm (62 per cent) that survived to provide figures in 1988, and stood at a mean of £602,270 in 1988 (at 1985 prices).[7] On a test of the equality of mean one gets an F-statistic of 5.09 which exceeds the critical value of $F(1,88) = 3.95$, implying mean sales are significantly different. The dispersion of real sales increased markedly over time, having a standard deviation of 299 in 1985 and of 1071 in 1988. Using Bartlett's test for the homogeneity of variances gives a test statistic of 57.15, which is very much larger than the critical value of $\chi^2(1)_{0.05} = 3.84$, implying a significant difference in variances.

11.3 GIBRAT'S LAW AND ITS VARIANTS

An empirical hypothesis which has enjoyed much celebrity in the industrial organization literature is Gibrat's Law, or the Law of Proportionate Effect. It is a type of mixed deterministic/stochastic theory of firm growth. There are two deterministic components (namely exogenous growth, and endogenous growth), and one stochastic component (namely random growth). For simplicity, I will build the model up in three steps. Later in this section I shall discuss modern variants, particularly by reference to the work of Evans (1987a, 1987b), and Brock and Evans (1986).

If s_t is a generic measure of size of the SBE at time period t, and the market expansion rate is α, then if all firms share in this growth, the exogenous deterministic effect may by formalized as:

$$s_{t+1}/s_t = \alpha \qquad (11.1)$$

Modifying this in a multiplicative way, by introducing an endogenous deterministic effect which is dependent on size (11.1) may be modified to:

$$s_{t+1}/s_t = \alpha s_t^{(\beta - 1)} \qquad (11.2)$$

If $\beta = 1$, (11.2) collapses into (11.1) and growth is independent of size (i.e. there is no endogenous effect). This is the case that Gibrat emphasised. If $\beta > 1$, larger SBEs would grow faster than smaller SBEs and if $\beta < 1$, smaller SBEs would grow faster than larger SBEs. Further modifying (11.2) by an exogenous multiplicative stochastic component ($\varepsilon_t > 0$) gives:

$$s_{t+1}/s_t = \alpha s_t^{(\beta - 1)}\varepsilon_t \qquad (11.3)$$

which may be expressed in log linear form as:

$$\log s_{t+1} = \log \alpha + \beta \log s_t + \log \varepsilon_t \tag{11.4}$$

It is equation (11.4) which has received all the attention in the literature. Formally speaking, it is a stochastic first-order linear difference equation. If the ε_t are identically and independently distributed, and thus may be interpreted as exogenous shocks to the combined effects of systematic factors, and an initial value for size (s_0) is specified, then by invoking the Central Limit Theorem, the equilibrium size distribution is log normal.[8] A requirement of equilibrium ('stability condition') is that $\beta < 1$. It is easy to show that the process has a variance that increases over time.[9] As this condition is not always observed in real data, economists have suggested variants of this process for which the variance of log (s_t) does not increase over time.[10]

In the descriptive statistical analysis of the previous section, no formal model dictated how data would be approached. Thus variations in size were considered simply in terms of the untransformed variables measuring size, like sales, employment, and asset values. What the Gibrat formulation suggests is that it may be more important to look at the logarithm of size, rather than size *per se*. Turning again to asset values, with this fresh perspective one has three choices of measures: (a) asset values at the time of the AQ 1985 (*passet*); (b) asset values at the time of inception (*sasset*), as reported in the AQ 1985, expressed in 1985 prices; and (c) asset values at the time of the RIQ 1988, (*rasset*), expressed in 1985 prices. The variants of model (11.4) above which were estimated using these data do not provide a completely consistent picture, nor do they unambiguously confirm or refute Gibrat's Law. However, what they do show is that aspects of the data do display marked regularities that one might not have suspected from looking at them in their raw form.

On an analysis of variance (ANOVA), differences in mean between the log of *passet* (*lpasset*) and the log of *sasset* (*lsasset*), and between the log of *rasset* (*lrasset*) and the log of *sasset* (*lsasset*), were significant; but between the log of *rasset* (*lrasset*) and the log of *passet* (*lpasset*) were not significant.[11] Despite the marked and significant differences in variances for size measured in raw levels, the Bartlett test for homogeneity of variances did not indicate any heterogeneity of variances of log size, for any of the above comparisons.[12] Equation (11.4) was estimated as a test of the Law of Proportionate Effect, with asset value used as the size variable. Estimation was by least squares, using White's heteroskedastic consistent covariance matrix. In all three cases the hypothesis that the coefficient on the independent size variable was unity was rejected using a Wald test of the null hypothesis that $\hat{\beta} = 1$. I refer the reader to table 11.2 for these and related results. Only the regression (2) of assets in 1988 on starting assets was unsatisfactory. Regressions 1 and 3 provide adequate explained variation[13] and estimate the coefficient β with reasonable precision. This coefficient may be judged to be less than unity on the evidence presented. This suggests that older SBEs grow more slowly than

Table 11.2 Test of Law of Proportionate Effect

Dependent Variable	Independent Variable	Coefficient (β)	t-test on β	F-test ANOVA from mean	Wald test (χ^2 of $\hat{\beta} = 1$)
1 lpasset	lsasset	0.55259	3.2372	11.973	6.870
2 lrasset	lsasset	0.18080	1.0978	0.961	24.739
3 lrasset	lpasset	0.63307	4.0207	25.866	5.431

Critical Values: $t(43)_{0.05} = 2.042$; $F(1,43)_{0.05} = 4.08$
$\chi^2(1)_{0.05} = 3.84$

Notes: All asset variables in 1985 prices as follows: passet, assets in 1985; sasset, starting assets; rasset, assets in 1988. All variables expressed in natural logarithms. Estimation by least squares using heteroskedastic-consistent covariance matrix.

younger SBEs, and by corollary that larger SBEs grow more slowly than smaller SBEs.[14] This refutes the Law of Proportionate Effect in its simplest form (viz. $\beta = 1$) and also refutes previous conclusions, relating to much larger enterprises, suggesting that larger firms grow more rapidly than smaller firms.[15] Yet again, one finds that it is dangerous to attempt to transfer conclusions from a large firm's world to a small firm's world. Here a strong 'regression effect' is observed amongst SBEs, implying a strong tendency for size to return to mean size for the population of SBEs.

In figure 11.3 I have plotted the log of assets in 1988 against the log of assets in 1985. Essentially it is a log scale version of the data in the earlier figure 11.2, with incomplete data omitted. On top of the $45°$ line I have super-imposed the fitted regression (3) of table 11.2 which has the equation $\widehat{lrasset} = 1.6 + 0.63 \ lpasset$, where for simplicity I use only two significant digits. The data display very well the 'regression effect' mentioned above, with the slope of the fitted line (0.63) being easily compared with the significantly greater slope of the $45°$ line (unity): it provides a kind of visual heuristic for the Wald test. It also gives one a feel for the relatively loose, be it all-significant, relationship between *rasset* and *passet*. It suggests that more complex formulations might be necessary to obtain a more complete statistical explanation of growth.

So far, I have confined myself to examining traditional Gibrat-inspired models. However, recent advances in the stochastic modelling (for example, Jovanovic 1982, Frank 1988) and the applied econometrics (for example, Evans 1987a and 1987b, Brock and Evans 1986) of small firms' growth have encouraged the development of new variants of traditional models. Whilst much early empirical work (for example, Hart and Prais 1956, Pashigian and Hymer 1962, Simon and Bonini 1958) suggested that there was no relationships between the size and growth of firms, and early adjustment cost theories for constant returns to scale technologies (for example, Hildebrandt 1978, Lucas and Prescott 1971) suggested that theory and evidence were tightly aligned, there had nevertheless always existed conflicting evidence.

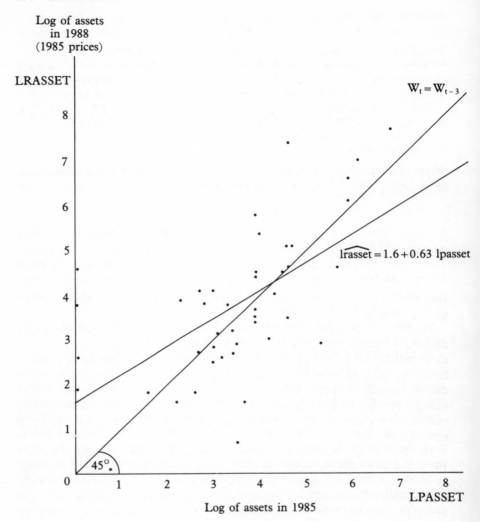

Log of assets
in 1988
(1985 prices)

Figure 11.3 Regression of firm size

Thus Mansfield (1962) found that smaller firms had higher and more variable growth rates than larger firms. In an influential contribution to the new literature, Jovanovic (1982) took seriously this conflicting evidence and developed a new model to explain deviations from proportional growth. In it, the efficient firms prosper and the inefficient firms fail. Firms learn about their efficiency over time. The model implies that, even adjusting for selection bias,[16] smaller firms should have higher and more variable growth rates than large firms. Another implication of Jovanovic's model is that firm growth and variance are independent of size for firms of the same age.[17] The model of Frank (1988) is in a similar spirit, in that entrepreneurs are initially ignorant of their talents, and acquire information on this over time, revising their beliefs in the light of market experience. The implications of his model are that larger firms last longer; and that there is a greater variability in the growth of small, compared to large, firms. There is also a life cycle effect, in that new entrepreneurs work harder than those close to retirement.

Here, I shall follow Evans (1987) and Brock and Evans (1986) in testing the Jovanovic (1982) model. This implies a general specification of the form

$$s_{t+1}/s_t = [f(A_t, s_t)]^\gamma \varepsilon_t \tag{11.5}$$

where A_t is age and γ is a given parameter. This is clearly a generalization of equation (11.3) above. A simple linearization of (11.5) gives:

$$\log s_{t+1} - \log s_t = \beta_0 + \beta_1 \log s_t + \beta_2 (\log s_t)^2 + \beta_3 (\log A_t)$$
$$+ \beta_4 (\log A_t)^2 + \beta_5 (\log A_t \log s_t) + u_t \tag{11.6}$$

where

$$u_t = \log \varepsilon_t$$

Equation (11.6) is the variant I shall also use to explore hypotheses about growth, size and age.

Evans (1987a and 1987b) and Brock and Evans (1986) only had data on age, number of employees, and sales. They regarded the employment data as more reliable than sales data, but regretted asset data were not available: hence employment was the size measure used. An advantage of the research design adopted is that it offers a much richer choice of variables, and as indicated in the earlier statistical analysis of this chapter, the desired asset variables are available. These, therefore, will be used as the size variables in equation (11.6).

The age variable A_t is the age in months from financial inception to the AQ 1985. The mean age was about three-and-a-half years, with a range from close to zero, up to twelve years. Due to missing data sixty-seven, rather than seventy-three, observations were available to estimate equation (11.6). Starting assets (*rasset*) and current assets (*passet*) were all expressed in 1985 prices. The dependent variable, the growth rate, was expressed as [log (*passet*) − log(*sasset*)]/Age. Estimation was by least squares using White's heteroskedastic–consistent covariance matrix. The results are reported in the left-hand column of table 11.3 as the 'asset regression'. Growth and size are negatively related, as are growth and age, confirming Jovanovic's model, but only the coefficient of the asset variable is significant. The coefficient of the age × sasset interaction variable is significant and of the correct sign. Overall the regression is satisfactory in terms of goodness of fit and explained variation, for cross-section models of this sort, but clearly one has very little economic explanation of growth rates.

Table 11.3 Estimates of growth, size, age models

Asset regression		Sales regression	
Variable in logs	Coefficient (t-ratio)	Variable in logs	Coefficient (t-ratio)
lsasset	−0.10551	lsales85	−0.87436
	(−1.9744)		(−2.4872)
lsasset^2	$0.31271.10^{-2}$	lsales85^2	$0.18704.10^{-2}$
	(0.63763)		(0.85066)
lage	$-0.64119.10^{-1}$	lage	−24.859
	(−0.78425)		(−0.86128)
lage^2	$-0.13754.10^{-2}$	lage^2	3.2529
	(−0.14015)		(0.81447)
lage × lsasset	$0.18119.10^{-1}$	lage × lsales85	0.23208
	(1.8370)		(2.4056)
constant	0.37292	constant	47.504
	(2.0205)		(0.91081)
$R^2 = 0.3307$;	$F = 7.521$	$R^2 = 0.2695$;	$F = 3.803$
$n = 67$		$n = 39$	
Critical values:		Critical values:	
$F(5,61)_{.05} = 2.37$		$F(5,33)_{.05} = 2.53$	
$t(61)_{.05} = 1.658$		$t(33)_{.05} = 1.697$	

Notes: l denotes natural logarithm. All economic variables are expressed in 1985 prices. Estimation is by least squares using heteroskedastic-consistent covariance matrix.

I have estimated numerous other forms of such growth–size–age models and the results obtained are very similar, irrespective of the size measure used, the sample size, the age durations, giving further support to Jovanovic's model. The size measure's coefficient is invariably significant and negative, and the age variable's coefficient is negative but usually of marginal significance or insignificant. Squared variables have unstable coefficients which are generally insignificant. The interaction variable is typically significant and positive. Representative of these other results is the 'sales regression' reported on the right-hand column of table 11.3. Arguably, sales figures are amongst the most accurate and most familiar statistics to the owner-manager. Sales in 1985 and 1988 (at 1985 prices) were used to construct the dependent variable, with the growth rate being computed over a time internal defined by the time elapsed between the 1985 and 1988 interviews (i.e. between the AQ 1985 and the RIQ 1988). Age, so defined, has a much lower variance than in the other regression. Again estimation was by least squares, using White's heteroskedastic–consistent covariance matrix. The nature of the results is very similar, despite these various differences in specification, which increases one's confidence in the robustness of the estimates. Thus, one finds again the negative effects of age and size on growth, with size being the more important influence.

Finally, I turn to the issue of sample selection bias. It would be serious if the following two conditions held: smaller firms were more likely to fail; and smaller firms would grow more slowly were they not put out of business by competitive pressure. In fact, as the tables 9.2 to 9.4 of chapter 9 indicate, the usual measures of size (for example assets, employment, sales) are poor predictors of whether an SBE stays in business. Figure 11.1 of this chapter reinforces this view, as it presents evidence commonly, both that large high-growth SBEs can go out of business and that small low-growth SBEs can stay in business. Consider the problem of running an 'asset regression' using observations from 1985 and 1988, rather than from inception and 1985, as in table 11.3. One wants to know, before firms start failing between 1985 and 1988, whether low growth and business failure go hand-in-hand. Therefore I have added to the first 'asset regression' of table 11.3 a dummy variable equal to unity for business survival and equal to zero for business failure, to discover what the relationship is between growth rates and business survival. What one finds is that the coefficient on the dummy variable is insignificant,[18] casting doubt on whether there are problems of sample selection bias. Direct adjustments can also be made to the regression coefficients adopting the simple and robust procedures of Goldberger (1981) and Greene (1981).

However, given the relatively high rate of survival (about three-quarters) and the strong results (for example $\hat{\beta}$ very much less than unity), conclusions are unlikely to be overthrown by proceeding in this way. A popular line of approach is to obtain an estimate of the inverse Mill's ratio ('hazard rate') from a profit estimate, and then to add this to the set of regressors, applying least squares to this extended regression to obtain consistent coefficient estimates.[19] Unfortunately, this procedure induces heteroskedasticity in to the disturbance term, leads to inefficient coefficient estimates, and produces biased and inconsistent standard errors. As is often the case with statistical methods, one cannot build bricks without straw. Fortunately, from the available evidence on SBEs in this sample, selection bias does not seem to be sufficiently problematic to seriously qualify the empirical conclusions reached.

11.4 DETERMINANTS OF GROWTH

Whilst the Gibrat-influenced model in a sense identifies categories of variables relevant to the analysis of growth (for example exogenous, endogenous, stochastic), it suffers from a mechanistic formulation, which is insufficiently motivated by economic consideration. Economists have postu-lated many theories of the growth of firms,[20] but few have been seriously confronted with evidence on small firms.

My purpose, therefore, in this last substantive section of chapter 11, is to provide a richer framework for the analysis of growth and its determinants than the narrow perspective of Gibrat's Law, and its variants, permits. My goals here are threefold. First, I generalize the sparsely specified growth equations of previous sections to incorporate a richer range of exogenous variables, including the novel introduction of financial variables. Second, I take seriously the well-recognized problem of endogeneity of growth *and* profitability, and the implied simultaneity of growth and profitability relationships. Third, given that the presence of simultaneity implies inconsistency and bias if ordinary least squares (OLS) methods are used, I employ system estimation, improving on previous attempts in this area by enhancing the efficiency of estimation through taking explicit account of cross-equation correlation.

Here, my main reference point in the literature is the analysis of growth and profitability by Dobson and Gerrard (1989). It relates to a local engineering sector in the UK but provides a general method of approach. Their model may be summarized by the two equations:

Growth = f(Profitability, Size, Age, Degree of Geographical
    Diversification, External Finance, Intra-Industry
    Differences)   (11.7)

Profitability = F(Growth, Size, Age, Location, Degree of Supervisory
     Control, Intra-Industry Differences)   (11.8)

Equation (11.7) may be regarded as a further generalization of equation (11.5), in that, in addition to the exogenous variables age and size, it incorporates further exogenous variables (like geographical diversification, external finance) and also incorporates an endogenous variable, profitability. I shall take equations (11.7) and (11.8) as my own starting point.

The central idea contained in models such as (11.7) and (11.8) is that of two-way causation. Growth generates profits, and profits stimulate growth. Profits are themselves an important source of finance for expansion. Indeed, inside equity was used to the total exclusion of outside equity. When debt finance was used, it was typically a bank loan, and it was common for SBEs to get debt finance which at least matched (internal) equity finance: equity gearing ratios of around unity were common. Thus generating internal finance for expansion acts as a magnet for attracting external finance, which can also be put to the same purpose. Greater growth can in turn enhance profitability, for example if learning effects are significant. I have analysed such phenomena elsewhere in an industrial setting,[21] making the advanced division of labour the source of such dynamic scale economies. However, the evidence of chapter 4 is that such dynamic effects are not an inevitability. There may be a 'Penrose Effect', which is to say that according to Penrose (1959) there may be managerial costs to higher growth which erode profitability. As the firm changes form to adapt to its growth experience, new managers are drawn in who require training, and who need to be integrated into the existing framework of the firm. Edith Penrose's analysis was informal, but Slater (1980) has captured some key features of her approach in a formal model which shows that the rapid recruitment of management which accompanies faster growth leads to an increase in marginal cost. For a fast-growing profit-maximizing firm, this raises price and lowers output, compared to a slower growing firm. In the work of Richardson (1964), which analyses in some detail the potential limits to a firm's rate of growth (for example, finance, materials) the major check on expansion appeared to be the lack of suitable management. This accords well with the conclusion of chapter 4. If the Penrose Effect is indeed a source of dynamic scale dis-economies, one would expect the underlying internal constraints on growth to induce a negative relationship between growth and profitability. Of course Penrose was talking of much larger firms, and the analysis of the con-sequences of managerial change was tied to a corporate setting. However, small firms are also subject to managerial evolution, and often have much larger rates of growth to cope with early in their life cycles than do corporate enterprises. Within two years, an SBE which started as a sole proprietorship might have become a partnership, and subsequently a private company, with each stage involving quite different managerial methods. Certainly, these stages typically involve control loss by the initial owner-manager. [22]

I turn now to my chosen model of growth and profitability. There are two endogenous variables, growth rate (*grate*) over the period from financial inception to interview in 1985, and the profit rate (*profrate*) in 1985, as self-reported by owner-managers in the reinterviews of 1988 (RIQ 1988). Details of the definitions of these endogenous variables, and of a further sixteen exogenous variables, are given in table 11.4. Many of these variables have been encountered before in chapter 9 on staying in business, and further comment on them is unnecessary. However, six of the exogenous variables do introduce new ideas which are worthy of brief comment.

1 *Bsns* is a categorical variable for the type of form the SBE takes. In going from the sole proprietorship, to the partnership, to the private company, it is assumed that a loss of control will occur.
2 *Mmkt* is another categorical variable which identifies the main market for the main product group. It is a type of locational variable.
3 *Share* identifies the market share for the main product groups of the SBE, and it is assumed that the greater the market share, the greater the opportunity to exercise market power.
4 *Compno* is an intra-industry variable, the number of competitors, which aims to provide a simple index of competitive pressure.
5 *Pcruc* is another intra-industry variable; it uses a binary variable to capture an aspect of conjectural variation in prices.
6 *Diff* is a financial variable in binary form, used to identify SBEs which initially faced difficulty in obtaining financial support.

The single equation specification of the growth and profitability equations were estimated by least squares and led to the results reported in table 11.5. Regarding the growth equation, the age and size variables proved not to have significant *t*-ratios in a variety of specifications. [23] They are negatively

Table 11.4 Variables used in OLS and iterative 3LS estimates of growth and profitability equations

---

ENDOGENOUS VARIABLES

Grate Growth rate per month of real assets (in 1985 prices) from inception to the AQ 1985.
Profrate Profit rate in 1985 as reported in 1988 reinterviews (RIQ 1988).

EXOGENOUS VARIABLES

Employ Number of full-time employees.
Bsns = 1 for one-man business, = 2 for partnership, = 3 for private company.
Sales Sales revenue.
Pgroup Number of product groups.
Mmkt Main market: local community (1), region (2), Scotland (3), UK (4),   international (5).
Share Market share for main product group (%).
Compno Number of competitors for main product group.
Pcruc = 1 if pricing of rivals crucial to SBE's own pricing, = 0 otherwise.
Proddes Degree of product differentiation of main product group: identical (1), similar (2), different (3).
Adv = 1 if SBE advertises, = 0 otherwise.
Cfp = 1 if SBE has cash-flow problems, = 0 if not.
Adddebt = 1 if SBE has acquired additional debt since inception, = 0 otherwise.
Pgear Debt divided by owner-manager's injection of finance.
Descomp Description of competition in market for main product group: intense (1), generally strong (2), generally weak (3), weak (4).
Age Age in months from financial inception to AQ 1985.
Diff = 1 if owner-manager had difficulty in obtaining financial support for starting his SBE, = 0 otherwise.

---

associated with growth, as in the discussion of Gibrat models in section 11.3 above, but now their effects are registering as insignificant, because of the introduction of thoroughgoing economic variables, which, in an economic sense, are acting as 'dominating variables'.

The first important finding, therefore, is that parsimonious Gibrat's Law models of growth of the SBE are dominated by richer models emphasising systematic economic influences. The signs of most coefficients in the growth equation accord with expectations. The less the dependence on local markets or, put another way, the greater the nationality or (even better) the internationality of markets for the main product, the greater the growth rate, other things being equal. The greater the market share, the greater the opportunity to exercise market power, and therefore the easier it is to achieve growth. If rivals' price actions have a crucial bearing on an SBE's pricing, its scope for an independent pricing policy is thereby diminished. This loss of competitive advantage is to the detriment of growth. *Proddes* is defined in such a way that it increases with the degree of product differentiation (see table 11.4). The result in table 11.5 indicates that the greater the product differentiation, the slower the growth. Given the evidence that SBEs usually consciously seek to

Table 11.5 OLS estimates of growth and profitability equations

Growth equation (Dependent variable: Grate)		Profitability equation (Dependent variable: Profrate)	
Variable	Coefficient (t-ratio)	Variable	Coefficient (t-ratio)
Mmkt	36.753 (2.3236)	Bsns	−11.160 (−2.2190)
Share	19.332 (2.2182)	Pcruc	15.484 (1.5952)
Pcruc	−103.88 (−2.5000)	Pgear	−0.11817 (−2.2954)
Proddes	−75.702 (−2.6283)		
Pgear	−0.52799 (−2.4049)	Grate	−0.01284 (−0.48134)
Profrate	−0.46722 (−0.94544)	Constant	45.837 (3.5893)
Constant	161.97 (1.9218)		

$R^2 = 0.2528$, $n = 73$
$F = 3.722 > F(6,66)_{0.05} \simeq 2.25$

$R^2 = 0.2196$, $n = 73$
$F = 4.785 > F(4,68)_{0.05} \simeq 2.23$

cultivate mild forms of product differentiation, especially by customer service and delivery, the result may appear paradoxical. However, it must be borne in mind that strongly differentiated products can only be sold in very limited 'niche markets', especially if they are constructed on a customer-specified ('bespoke') basis. These are not the markets that hold out prospects for rapid growth. Again, as in the probit analysis of chapter 9, gearing (*Pgear*) turns out to be an important variable for the SBE. It was shown earlier that excessive gearing was to the detriment of the SBE's medium term viability. This is now reinforced by the finding here that higher gearing is associated with lower growth. It may indeed be the case that some SBEs overestimate their growth potential and acquire debt to purchase plant and equipment to service the anticipated larger markets (thus raising gearing). But they may eventually find that growth does not materialize in the way expected. I indicated in chapter 5 that over-investment was a common cause (42 per cent) of cash-flow difficulties. For about one-third of SBEs who had recourse to external finance (invariably in the form of debt) this was in response to cash-flow difficulties. Put more generally, the extra risk associated with higher gearing is to the detriment of growth, but the example above illustrates a specific way in which this effect may operate.

The *profrate* variable appears with a negative sign on its coefficient. Unfortunately it is insignificant under OLS estimation, though this changes under system estimation. It is of course an important variable if the mutual causality or simultaneity argument carries any weight. The negative sign is itself a familiar effect in work of this sort, and has been reported by Cubbin and

Leech (1986) and Dobson and Gerrard (1989). It may be interpreted as evidence that the fast growing SBE operates on that segment of the growth–profitability possibility frontier which has a negative slope, implying a trade-off between growth and profitability. In managerial theories of the firm (for example Marris 1964) it is this segment of the frontier which is of relevance, for it is here that tangency with the highest managerial indifference curve is reached subject to the frontier. The behaviour of *profrate* is, of course, consistent with the Penrose Effect.[24]

I turn now to the ordinary least squares estimate of the profitability equation in table 11.5. An important finding is that the form of the business has a significant bearing on profitability, and that, further, the greater the loss of supervisory control (implied by these changes in form of business from 'one man' through to 'private'), the lower the profitability. If the pricing of rivals is crucial to the SBE's own pricing, this raises profitability, though it was shown earlier that it lowered growth. Apparently optimal pricing enhances margins, but may not enlarge markets. Again, the ubiquitous gearing variable has a significant negative effect, this time on profitability. An important general discovery of the empirical work in this book is of the crucial role that gearing plays in many of the key aspects of the SBE's existence: medium term viability, growth, and profitability. Finally, I come to the growth rate. Its effect is negative on profitability, but the coefficient is insignificant. Unfortunately, this lack of significance is not immediately remedied under system estimation either. The sign of this variable is consistent with the Penrose Effect, with the causality running from growth (and, by implications, its costs) to limitations on profitability.

To conclude this discussion of growth and profitability relationships, I turn to the vexed question of simultaneity: its consequences; remedies for it; and implications of it when taken into account, statistically speaking. If a single equation model is estimated by OLS which is, in truth, but one equation in a simultaneous system, then, barring special cases (for example recursive systems) the coefficient estimates obtained will be biased and inconsistent, in the strict statistical senses of these terms. The problem of simultaneity, thus narrowly interpreted, arises from the correlation of a regressor with its corresponding equation disturbance term. Fortunately, Hausman (1978) has produced a simple and readily applied test for endogeneity/exogeneity in the sense of dependence/independence from the disturbance term. A weakness of the study by Dobson and Gerrard (1989) is that they apply no explicit test to see whether simultaneous equations bias is important for the growth–profitability system.[25] The issue is important, because if system estimation is used unnecessarily, OLS will have an efficiency advantage over a system method like two-stage least squares (2SLS), as used by Dobson and Gerrard. An application of Hausman's specification tests to the growth and profitability equations of table 11.5 revealed no evidence of correlation between endogenous variables and the disturbances.[26] Thus, if one *is* to use system estimation, then the justification is either: (a) in terms of economic interpretation, rather than statistical efficiency (for it is possible that OLS may have a mean square error advantage over 2SLS); or (b) in terms of statistical efficiency if a *full* system estimation method like three-stage least squares (3SLS) is to be used rather than a 'limited information' method like 2SLS. The 3SLS method would be likely to have an efficiency advantage over OLS. One is therefore impelled to the view that 3SLS estimation was the appropriate route to take, if an interest in system estimation was to be retained at all. The benefits of this view will become evident below.

Table 11.6 reports on iterative 3SLS estimates of the growth and profitability equations, using just one iteration.[27] The main statistical advantage of this method is that it uses 'full information' from the system, which is to be contrasted with the 'limited information' used in 2SLS. From an economic standpoint one now obtains a more precise estimate of the coefficient on *profrate*. As in table 11.5, it has a negative sign, supporting the Penrose Effect, but now the coefficient is clearly significant. Apart from this, the 3SLS growth equation is much the same as the OLS version. This is also true of the profitability equation, which on this single iteration does not display a significant coefficient on the *grate* variable, though it has, as before, a negative sign, also supporting the Penrose Effect. A Lagrange multiplier test (see table 11.6) rejects the hypothesis of a diagonal covariance matrix (which would have made an equation-by-equation application of least squares

Table 11.6 Iterative three-stage least squares estimates of growth and profitability equations

Growth equation (Dependent variable: Grate)		Profitability equation (Dependent variable: Profrate)	
Variable	Coefficient (Asymptotic t-ratio)	Variable	Coefficient (Asymptotic t-ratio)
Mmkt	28.004 (1.7777)	Bsns	−8.9960 (−1.8555)
Share	18.331 (2.1873)	Pcruc	13.048 (1.3129)
Pcruc	−64.792 (−1.4107)	Pgear	−0.13234 (−2.5188)
Proddes	−72.852 (−2.5807)	Grate	−0.04028 (−0.84315)
Pgear	−0.82134 (−2.9994)	Constant	44.707 (3.623)
Profrate	−2.7106 (−2.1160)		
Constant	227.59 (2.4492)		

System $R^2 = 0.5196$, $\chi^2 = 53.518 > \chi^2(10)_{0.05} = 18.3$
Breusch-Pagan LM test (for diagonal covariance matrix)
$\chi^2 = 9.1250 > \chi^2(1)_{0.05} = 3.84$

legitimate). Thus there is a rationale behind the application of 3SLS: to take account of contemporaneous cross-equation correlation of disturbances.

An extension of the standard 3SLS procedure involves iterating until updates in the covariance matrix and the estimated coefficients become arbitrarily small according to some convergence criterion. The asymptotic properties of iterative three-stage least squares (I3SLS) are identical to those of full information maximum likelihood (FIML). However, the numerical estimate obtained by I3SLS will not generally be equivalent to FIML. In the case of the growth and profitability equations, five iterations are sufficient to 'over-fit' the model, until the system R^2 is 0.9998 with a χ^2 statistic of 618.91. *Pgear* and *profrate* become the dominating variables in the growth equation; whilst *gear* and *grate* become the dominating variables in the profitability equation. Therefore, given the ease with which asymptotic t-ratios can be changed with the number of iterations, the more important points are whether the coefficient magnitudes are relatively stable, and the signs of coefficients invariant.[28] Using successive iterations to get a kind of hierarchy of importance of variables, one finds that for the growth equation they are (in descending order of importance): *profrate*, *pgear*, *proddes*, *share*, *mmkt*, *pcruc*. In order of importance for profitability they are (again in descending order): *grate*, *pgear*, *bsns*, *pcruc*. The establishing of such orderings is an incidental benefit of the method of estimation used.

11.5 CONCLUSION

Considerable ground has been covered in this chapter, covering economic statistics and applied econometrics, as well as conventional economic analysis. However, the methods have paid handsome dividends, for some remarkable regularities have been unearthed. The detailed analysis speaks for itself, but I think the following are particularly worthy of mention in this conclusion:

1 The evidence for vigorous growth of SBEs after financial inception, including the emergence of a small percentage (<10 per cent) in the 'super-growth' category.
2 The refutation of Gibrat's Law in its simple form, but strong confirmation of a life cycle effect for SBEs: younger SBEs grow faster than older SBEs; smaller SBEs grow faster than larger SBEs.
3 The evidence that systematic economic influences (for example intra-industry features like degree of product differentiation) dominate age and size effects in explaining growth. Especially notable is the role of financial variables, which are generally neglected in growth studies. The gearing ratio is strongly negatively associated with an SBE's growth rate. This result ties in closely with earlier results on staying in business. Survival and growth are best fostered in a low geared SBE.

4 The evidence confirming a 'Penrose Effect' (a growth/profitability trade-off) from estimates of both growth and profitability equations. The Richardson (1964) hypothesis that the key factor checking expansion and lowering profitability is the managerial factor is supported by two forms of evidence. First, and negatively, other potential factors like the financial (for example, cash-flow problems, difficulties in raising finances) do not appear to be statistically significant. Second, and positively, the form of enterprise is an important determinant of profitability. The further managerial organization moves from pure owner-management, the lower is profitability.

5 In a simultaneous equations framework, the evidence for hierarchies of determinants of growth and profitability, respectively. In determining growth, profitability is most important, followed by gearing, the degree of product differentiation, the market share, the extent of the market, and the importance of rivals' pricing policies. In determining profitability, growth is most important, followed by gearing, the form of business organization, and the importance of rivals' pricing policies.

No doubt, the rich vein of empirical enquiry into the growth of SBEs is by no means exhausted, even for this database. But the results obtained so far do provide fresh insight into growth, in an area where much of the evidence used for policy purposes has, inappropriately, been drawn from the analysis of large corporate enterprises.

Part V
Political economy

12 Small firms and fair trade

12.1 INTRODUCTION

In earlier chapters, my primary purpose was a scientific analysis of small firms' inception and growth, using a combination of qualitative and quantitative methods. However, one gained in passing considerable insight into small business ethics. I report below on such evidence, drawing on seventeen case studies out of the seventy-three SBEs in the sample. Part of the framework for these case studies involved using evidence gathered by the semi-structured interviews.[1] These looked at competitive strategy, competitive advantage, and defensive strategy. It is the material from these interviews that provides the main empirical input to my discussion of small business ethics below.

12.2 COMPETITIVE ADVANTAGE AND FAIR TRADE

Broadly speaking, owner-managers had no ethical qualms about seeking to establish a competitive niche by using an aggressive strategy like pushing costs down below that of rivals, or extolling the virtue of their products *vis à vis* those of rivals. The pursuit of competitive advantage appeared to proceed in a game-like fashion, and the language used might be that employed to describe a sport, and even on occasion a blood sport. Thus the owner-manager of a fast-growing small business which produced computer software referred to the market segments in which he first attempted to gain secure positions as 'hunting grounds'. This same owner-manager, when referring to the competition pitted against his firm by potential imitators, said 'they can only be beaten by being outrun'.[2] There was a general reluctance to deter entry into a market by any other tactic but that of looking an effective competitor.

When considering defensive strategy, that is, means for consolidating and defending an acquired market niche, owner-managers were uneasy about methods which they themselves would not wish to have been deployed against them when starting out in business. For example, the owner-manager of an SBE which produced specialized printers' materials admitted that he might contemplate retaliation at the prospect of facing a new entrant to his market, but claimed 'a strong concept of fair play'. This would, for example, make him rule out using an 'entry deterrring' price. This is a price set artificially low for a limited period of time, not to benefit the customers, but to reduce the perceived profitability of the market at the point when a potential entrant into it was contemplating actively trading. The aim is to benefit the firm and not the customers, because the effect is short-lived. Once the potential entrant has been put off, the price is raised again. It should also be said that customers do not like strategies of this sort. If the price can be kept down for any length of time, they might feel that this is a true indication of just how low the price might reasonably be set. A subsequent increase in price might be regarded as profiteering, and the market could be spoiled as disenchanted customers switched loyalties to similar products in adjacent market niches. It is also possible that setting a low price for a product might be regarded as signalling that it is of a low quality (Stiglitz 1989). A subsequent price increase might simply put off customers who feel they are now paying more for a product that continues to be of low quality. Whilst this small printing firm referred to concepts of 'fair play' as limiting its willingness to mark down the price to deter entry, we see that there are a number of clear economic disadvantages to marking down price in terms of accidentally signalling a move down the market in terms of product quality, and thus spoiling the market for a subsequent price increase.

An alternative to any entry preventing pricing strategy might be a form of collective action by incumbent firms. Generally this was frowned upon, with one notable exception, the case in which a technical substitute had appeared. To illustrate, the manager of a small firm run on a co-operative basis to produce props for theatre and film, doubted that any substitutes were in the offing. However, she admitted that if substitutes did appear, 'the threat would be regarded as serious and a collective industry response would be quite feasible'. What makes a technical substitute a different, and more serious, form of threat than a potential entrant? It is, surely, that not just a few firms are threatened by it, those run least efficiently, but rather all firms, irrespective of efficiency. The collective response would be to preserve that game, should the game as such, and not an individual competitor in it, be threatened. [3]

12.3 DEFENSIVE STRATEGY AND FAIR TRADE

Whilst there was a willingness to talk freely about competitive strategy and the means of obtaining competitive advantage over rivals, owner-managers were less willing to discuss defensive strategy. One got much less information on this topic, and it was particularly here that responses tended to take on ethical overtones. Thus the owner-manager of an SBE which supplied window blinds and serviced them did not sympathize with the notion of a defensive strategy. He thought this strategy suggested unethical competition.

In the context of barriers to entry, he did not think the artificial construction of such barriers (of which an example is the blocking of channels of access to customers or suppliers) was legitimate. It was felt that, to the extent that a deterrent to entry could be consciously constructed, the competitiveness of his own firm in itself should be an effective deterrant. He would not countenance blocking tactics, and, unlike the case above, would not form coalitions with other firms. One tactic that would be contemplated was the matching of guarantees. This would include matching the conditions of a product specified by a rival to a customer (for example by quality, price, delivery date, after-sales service). However, in this case it was felt that the matching of guarantees would not be ethical if it were covert. This owner-manager's firm functioned in a highly competitive industry and it is clear that his ethical judgements on his own behaviour were based on how he would wish his rivals to behave towards him. Thus he would not wish his own channels blocked, would not wish rivals to act in coalitions against him, and would not wish rivals to offer covert guarantees that he had no opportunity to match. On the other hand, his firm survived or failed on its visible competitive merits, and he asked no more than that this were true of his rivals.

A concept that was discussed freely under the heading of defensive strategy in chapter 7 was that of a 'good' competitor. On the face of it, competitors cannot be good for a given firm because they limit its scope of action. If firms played a non cooperative game, it would seem that all rivals were 'bad' competitors, in this sense: that there would be a necessary conflict of interest between rivals, with tangible consequences for profits, market shares, etc. However, one finds the owner-manager of an SBE which was a specialized knitwear manufacturer saying that one could distinguish 'good' from 'bad' competitors, and that the former should be encouraged. A good competitor would, for example, pass on to a rival the surplus of an order over its current capacity that it could not immediately handle. This owner-manager saw his industry as 'a fraternity', even though competition was intense. He thought that retaliation could be costly and time-consuming and would be frowned upon by the fraternity. Consider that possible reaction to the pirating of a design, which is a strategy that this firm had needed to defend itself against. In the more behavioural literature on game theory, a well-known heuristic procedure (sometimes called Schelling's Silvery Rule) is to start with good moves, and to match good moves if they are made by rivals. However, if bad moves are made by rivals, they must be matched. They will continue to be matched until good moves are made again. Then, possibly not immediately but after a punishment phase or period of relenting, good moves would be returned to and sustained, provided rivals continued with good moves. In the case under discussion, a good move would be to create an independent, new design; and a bad move would be to pirate, or steal a design. Following Schelling's Silvery Rule, the bad move of piracy by a rival would be matched by a bad move of piracy by the offended firm. However, this behaviour would be seen by the owner-manager of this knitwear firm as wasteful of resources and certain to meet with the disapprobation of the community of rivals ('the fraternity'). At its simplest level, this restraint on behaviour illustrates the folk wisdom of 'two wrongs don't make a right', but at a deeper level it demonstrates how restraint can be fostered by an accepted common standard of conduct, as embodied in the collective judgement of the fraternity. This restraint is valuable because it lowers the cost of playing the competitive game; and in a way which confers benefit on all players. The practical outcome in the case being discussed here was that the owner-manager of the knitwear firm lodged a protest at a craft textiles trade show over the design of his that had been copied. He sought the disapproval of the fraternity. It was granted, and the piracy ceased.

The owner-manager of this knitwear firm said he preferred 'to work *with* my customers rather than *against* my rivals'. He frowned upon blocking tactics, and thought that the best defence was to look invulnerable. Using the analogy of a race, which the owner-manager of the computer software firm had also employed, he said 'At the end of the day you need the stamina to keep going, like a marathon runner.' In the competitive race, one had to look durable. He frowned upon the use of false information, to 'manage' the assumptions of rivals. Certainly information was used strategically, but 'deterrence was all verbal' and only accurate information would be used. For example, the virtues of his own products would be extolled to potential customers, pointing out their strong features as compared to rival products. One can see that the advantage of proceeding in this way is that it prevents the degeneration of all trade messages into misinformation. It is one thing to use accurate information to one's benefit, but another to use deliberately inaccurate information. This latter tactic has the danger that it will rebound on the perpetrator unfavourably, if rivals use this information in good faith and add it to a concealed amount of their own accurate information, which they then act upon.

The owner-manager of an SBE which supplied holiday tours to the tourist trade had also had to deal with piracy. She thought that good competitors should be encouraged and 'pirates' or what she called 'fly-by-nighters' should be publicly exposed by the industry. She argued that pirates could damage the reputation of the industry as a whole. Reputation is frequently treated as something which, if lost (for example by selling a low quality good at a price normally associated with a high quality good), leads to indefinite market sanction. Thus customers never again purchase from a firm that tries to pass off shoddy as quality.[4] However, the 'fly-by-nighter' mentioned above is more difficult to sanction. He is only operating in the market for a short period of time. To mimic quality, he may pirate ideas for holiday tours from higher quality incumbent firms. Once this is exploited, he may fall back on his own low quality ideas, harvest the niche, and then exit. It is clearly not sensible to let market sanction alone apply discipline to this firm (by not purchasing the low quality product), because the punishment period is short for the 'fly-by-nighter', which diminishes its deterrent effect; his actions damage the market reputation as a whole, possibly long after his exit. This analysis applies to the extent that customers, being relatively uninformed before purchase of the quality of a product like a holiday tour, are confused about which firms supply high and which low quality products. Confusion of this sort lowers the value to the customers of *any* purchase in this market. It may lead them to spend money on leisure activities in other directions (for example, opera, cricket matches). It clearly provides an argument for self-regulation, co-ordinated by the high quality producers, who establish trade standards which must be met by 'approved' dealers. Being 'approved' then signals quality, and new entrants will initially be unsorted into good and bad ('fly-by-night') traders. Customers may then choose to purchase at a premium from monitored, 'approved' traders or at a discount from unapproved traders, running the risk of a bad deal in the latter case.

The owner-manager of this holiday-tours firm also believed in encouraging 'good' competitors. Her point was that they improved the performance of her own firm. Put in more formal language, one could say that 'good' competitors confer a positive externality on rivals. They provide cheap and stringent monitoring services for rivals which are uncaptured by vested interest (for example the 'friendly' accountant who fears bringing bad news to clients). This is clearly one of the advantages of the 'industrial district' as analysed first by Alfred Marshall, and currently exemplified by the small firms network (for example in the textiles trade) in Emilia Romagna in Italy.[5]

12.4 CONCLUSION

Despite the use of language like 'good competitors', 'unethical competitors' and so on, by my sample of owner-managers, much of their conduct was seen to be governed by self-interest. The notion of a 'good competitor' was seen to be largely an economic, rather than an ethical concept, for example.

What the analysis above suggests is that most of the recorded uses of vocabulary with ethical overtones that I report upon are best regarded as effective use of figurative language to describe various kinds of games. They do not constitute an insider's analysis of morality, rights, fairness, or justice. To fully substantiate this argument would require more detailed theoretical analysis, which I would hope to undertake at a later point.[6] However, even before that task is accomplished, it would be wrong to conclude that the players in the games themselves have no place in moral order. But the moral order is beyond the market, and the players put aside mere games when they participate in this moral order.

13 Perceptions of the enterprise culture

13.1 INTRODUCTION

This chapter concludes the final section of the book, on political economy, by investigating what entrepreneurs think of enterprise. Earlier chapters have shown how, since 1985, in association with numerous others, I have been analysing small business enterprise in Scotland. There, my concern was narrowly scientific. For example, in chapter 9 I examined how factors like the gearing ratio and the market share of small firms influenced their probability of survival over three years. Here, my concern is less formal. This chapter is based on data gathered about perceptions of small firm owner-managers of 'the enterprise culture' using the RIQ 1988.[1] Perceptions are regarded as a valid form of evidence in that they affect motivation and judgement, and therefore have a bearing on practical decisions taken both by entrepreneurs and by policy makers. However, they are clearly a relatively fragile form of evidence, and must be handled carefully, without drawing stronger conclusions than any evidence on perceptions could warrant. Thus I eschew statistical inference below, and use one simple device for broad categorization: the distinction between observing and participating in enterprise.

In 1990 the memory of Adam Smith was once again honoured in Edinburgh,[2] on this occasion commemorating two hundred years since Smith's death. At this point, of course, his significance for encouraging the emergence of a free enterprise system out of a system of restraint on trade (called 'mercantilism') was noted.[3] However, it was not lost on many commentators that perhaps contemporary Scotland did not provide the best example of a free enterprise system. This in turn could be attributed to the lack of an enterprise culture, which here I shall define as that pattern of attitudes and social norms likely to foster the smooth working of a free enterprise system. The views of contemporary commentators were anticipated during an earlier visit to Glasgow in November 1987 by the (then) Chancellor, Nigel Lawson. He greatly irritated the local business community by suggesting that there was in Scotland 'a hostile attitude to the enterprise culture'.[4] In November 1990 Jim Driver, head of the SDA's international manufacturing division, publicly claimed 'the entrepreneurial spirit was still lacking here'.

He expressed the view that a cultural change was necessary: 'You have to get people here to accept that there is nothing wrong with failure. You have got to change the whole cultural system'. One wonders how this apparent hostility to enterprise could characterize a country which spawned the idea of a free enterprise system through the writings of Adam Smith and (in some measure) David Hume.[5] Surely it would be unnatural to repudiate a system in the country of its birth?

Yet an uneasiness remains that the comments of public figures like Lawson and Driver may have more than a grain of truth in them. Academic writings on perceptions of business as a career (for example Milne and Lewis 1982) suggest that in Scotland professional, financial, and agricultural entrepreneurship are well regarded, but being 'in trade' is stigmatized. Contacts I have made in the business community lead me to observe that many of those immersed in the everyday aspects of commercial activity have a fine stock of informal evidence suggesting that Scotland is not attuned to the idea of an enterprise culture.

13.2 SEEKING THE ENTERPRISE CULTURE

I turn now to the issue of where one should best seek evidence on the enterprise culture. Large firms, like major domestic corporations and transnational enterprises, provide an unlikely source. Organization theorists would argue that the best planning goes on under capitalism. It occurs in large bureaucratic enterprises which are tightly monitored and controlled by what are essentially planning mechanisms. Big companies iike IBM and Philips generate larger incomes than many quite substantial nation states. The 'organization man' is quite unlike the entrepreneur, and perhaps more like a civil servant. Indeed, those responsible for organizational design, fearful of the stifling of innovation in large bureaucratic firms, have talked of possibilities for 'intrapreneurship', hoping to mimic entrepreneurship without the market nexus. It is clear that one must look elsewhere, at small firms, for evidence on perceptions of the enterprise culture. Indeed, one best looks at very small firms, rather than those regarded as small from the viewpoint of official statistics (for example, two hundred or fewer employees). The latter might be quite mature, and therefore prone to bureaucratic procedures. Very small firms, especially those close to financial inception, such as the SBEs that have been at the focus of this book, are the quarry we seek. In schools of entrepreneurship, the financial inception of an SBE is known as 'the entrepreneurial event'; Shapero (1984). In this chapter I am interested in the perceptions of entrepreneurs who have recently experienced this event.

Let me divide my findings into two parts. First, one can look at perceptions of the enterprise culture as something apart from the entrepreneur himself. Viewed in this way, the entrepreneur reports, as it were, as an observer of the business milieu about him. Second, one can look at perceptions of the enterprise culture as a participant. In this case the view sought is that of entrepreneurs in the process of being actively involved in the hurly-burly of business. It is a bit like the distinction between interviewing a keen rugby player who is watching a game, or interviewing the same man while he is in a scrum playing for his own team! One expects the former view to be more detached than the latter. Of course, essential to the argument is that all who are questioned are both spectators and players; it is simply that one perspective can be detached from the other.

An important introductory point should be made first, as it is so unambiguous. It arises from responses to question 11 of the RIQ 1985 (see the appendix to this book, page 291). Entrepreneurs were reminded that the media like television, radio, and newspaper were suggesting that Scotland was becoming an 'enterprise culture'. They were asked whether they had sensed the emergence of such a culture in Scotland since 1985. The overwhelming majority (78 per cent)[6] of entrepreneurs stated that they *had* sensed an emerging enterprise culture. It is to be noted that the question refers to 'emergence' which suggests a change from the past but not necessarily the existence of a fully-fledged enterprise culture.

13.3 OBSERVING ENTERPRISE

Using my above distinction, between views of an observer and views of a participant, let me proceed.[7] Perceptions of the enterprise culture by those who are observing it are largely based on a local view. Thus one entrepreneur had observed many small firms springing up in the Penicuik area, especially in the electrical contracting business. Another had seen new factories being set up in the nearby Garnock valley, and noted that all factory units in Nethermains had been filled. A third on an industrial estate in Edinburgh had observed businesses in his estate growing larger and moving to new premises, and knew of only one business failure on his estate. A fourth remarked on 'a definite growth of such a culture in and around Dundee'. An entrepreneur in Lochgelly balanced these positive views with his own 'that there isn't much enterprise in the area' and 'I don't know anyone in Lochgelly who has set up a business in years'. Perhaps Lochgelly is not conducive to the entrepreneurial event, though the respondent provided at least one counter-example to this view, but is this true of Leith, which most would say has enjoyed a commercial renaissance in the past ten years? An entrepreneur in Leith nevertheless said 'I don't see much evidence of the emergence of an enterprise culture around here.' The perceptions are true of the individual, and based perhaps on what is on his or her very doorstep. Thus the generally high agreement that an enterprise culture is emerging suggests that the view from most doorsteps is quite favourable.

The entrepreneurs interviewed also took a more global view. Thus one entrepreneur observed that 'more people are setting up their own business' and another that he had noted an 'enterprise culture especially in new towns'. As 'spectators' their observations were often media-driven, especially by television and the popular press. One entrepreneur noted that the phrase 'the enterprise culture' was being 'mentioned more in the media', and another quite factually that 'government policy encourages people to be entrepreneurs'. A third was aware that the strong emphasis on enterprise in the media was 'partly political' in inspiration and not yet a description of reality, though the media emphasis was thought to be a 'good thing'. None mentioned more formal evidence on enterprise, available in books, journals, or magazines, or supplied by expert witnesses or consultants. There is not yet a wide range of journals and magazines published in the UK devoted to entrepreneurship, venture capital, etc., and certainly small business consultancy is still in its infancy.

13.4 PARTICIPATING IN ENTERPRISE

I turn now to views expressed by entrepreneurs as participants, as persons immersed in enterprise. To continue the earlier metaphor, one is thinking here of the rugby scrum rather than the spectator standpoint. Here the view taken is much more jaundiced, even by those who do perceive an emerging enterprise culture. If one categorizes a set of the respondents' remarks into 'good' (for example, 'more people are willing to start up their own business') and 'bad' (for example, 'small firms don't survive') – admittedly a procedure involving some element of judgement – one finds that 69 per cent of comments made are bad, and 31 per cent of comments made are good. This is despite the fact that 78 per cent had said they recognized the emergence of an enterprise culture and 75 per cent of SBEs in this sample, as analysed in chapter 9, had survived over a three-year period, which is, arguably, the market test of success. This might partly explain why the informal impression created of attitudes to enterprise in Scotland is often so negative. Against a background of relative objective success, from a spectator's standpoint, is a quite high volume of complaints, from a participant's standpoint.

Before concluding that these complaints imply actual lack of success and low levels of enterprise, one has to look further at the negative remarks. One discovers that many are about problems of recruitment and skills shortages (see questions 8 and 8.1 of RIQ 1988, page 290). A shortage of skilled labour had been experienced by 30 per cent of the SBEs. None of the entrepreneurs in these firms thought the shortage had caused their firm to contract, 47 per cent thought it had impeded growth, and 53 per cent that it had not impeded growth. For SBEs which had experienced a skills shortage, there is some evidence on the difficulties they experienced in trying to fill this 'skills gap' (see question 8.2 and list 8.2 of RIQ 1988, page 290). There was no readily categorizable prime difficulty, but for difficulties that could be grouped they were, in descending order of importance: paying premium rates for scarce skills; releasing personnel for training; assessing the SBE's relative skill advantage (or deficit) *vis à vis* rivals; affording the training costs; and identifying the skills required. Recruitment difficulties in some cases were clearly caused by lack of information. One found entrepreneurs commenting on the difficulty of 'finding the right people with the right experience' or even, more bluntly, 'finding the people'! Other perceived recruitment difficulties were caused by some owner-managers not being able to pay the rate for the job, which could simply be a reflection of low profitability. A large group of owner-managers were able to identify specific skills shortages of personnel like: licensed aircraft engineers, skilled sheet-metal workers, skilled light-gauge welders, turret press and press break operatives, skilled typists. Some talked in less specific terms of shortages of 'engineers in general', of 'skilled personnel', of 'people with labour market experience', and of 'the relevant skills'. In the skill-specific cases, it was sometimes possible to pin down the reason for the shortage. In some cases it was attributed to 'a poor training programme for apprentices'. Labour shortages in general, and skill shortages in particular, especially when associated with a background of economic growth, including small firms growth, are not signs of failure of enterprise but rather of success. However, they are irritating, and influence negatively the perceptions of an enterprise culture. They would only assume the nature of a problem if they were intractable and unresponsive to market forces in the long run through labour mobility, re-skilling, and wage flexibility. Against a background of an average growth rate of small firms in the sample, over a three-year period, of 29 per cent per annum by full-time employment, 48 per cent p.a. by real assets (book value, net of depreciation) and 81 per cent p.a. by real sales (excluding VAT), one is not surprised that recruitment and skills shortage problems appear. Whilst this is manifestly a source of complaints, it is also an indicator of vigour.

Another reason for negative remarks about the enterprise culture is the view that push factors (for example, redundancy) have been more important than pull factors (for example, high profitability)[8] in encouraging people to become entrepreneurs. Thus entrepreneurs made remarks like 'people were forced to start up their own businesses', 'enterprise is forced upon people', and 'people *have* to start up in business'. There is evidence that so-called 'push factors', or more properly 'supply-side' factors, have been important in releasing labour resources, but this does not in itself explain a willingness to start a new business. This would also require an analysis of the demand-side factors, and in particular of the process of discovery or creation of unexploited market niches which can generate revenue. The way in which demand and supply factors have led to the emergence of new SBEs has not always been received with warmth by incumbent SBEs. To those used to a more settled business community with established figures prominent in it, the arrival of these newcomers was sometimes resented.

Of course, part of this exit of waged and salaried personnel from declining traditional industries, leading to entry as entrepreneurs into markets with more growth potential, has been consciously managed. An example is the case of British Ship Builders Enterprise Ltd (BSEL), a firm set up to find jobs for those becoming voluntarily redundant in shipbuilding. The success of the service this firm provided can be judged by the fact that 80 per cent of its clients had been placed in work, had chosen retirement, or were still receiving training after eighteen months.[9] The integration of training and enterprise envisaged under the new Scottish Enterprise arrangements takes this process a stage further, within a more permanent institutional framework. Outside of such arrangements, much re-allocation will occur spontaneously.

13.5 WHITHER THE 'ENTERPRISING SCOT'

Jenni Calder in her book *The Enterprising Scot* (1986) considers many areas in which Scotland was eminently successful in the massive production methods of Victorian capitalism. There seems to be a lingering nostalgia for that era, even when small business culture is flourishing. Scottish entrepreneurs seem both able and willing to make successes of their ventures under the new post-industrial order, whilst continuing to hold that they are only doing it because they have to.

Finally, a source of worry and complaint amongst entrepreneurs is the prospect of business failure. Many owner-managers of successful small businesses manage to be profoundly surprised that they survive, and continue to do so, despite year after year of profitable trading. Thus one entrepreneur can claim that 'I am lucky to still be in business', though the firm appears perfectly sound. Of course, luck plays a part in both success and failure, and it is partly this that makes entrepreneurs who observe other firms going out of business under financial stress say to themselves 'There, but for the grace of God, go I.' Again, the lesson one draws is that complaints by entrepreneurs as such are not an index of the efficacy of an enterprise system. Rather, they are a way of coping with the operation of the system.

One common reaction to the observation of business failure is the feeling that 'someone ought to do something about it', where 'someone' usually means government and 'something' usually means another special scheme. There will always be requests for more government assistance because of the existence of what Kent (1984) calls 'paper entrepreneurship'. This consists of entrepreneurs trying to control their political, legal, and institutional environments, to the detriment of controlling more effectively their economic environment. But the job of government, not business, is to govern – to make the rules. The job of business is to do business – to operate as profitably as possible within those rules. Attempts at special pleading are rational because they do serve private interests if successful, but they will be perceived as symptomatic of dependency and an anti-enterprise attitude. There is a danger in acting upon them unless there is strong evidence that they do ultimately increase national income or employment, or stimulate technical change. What one wishes for is a set of incentives which directs the energies spent on paper entrepreneurship into productive entrepreneurship. Then the apparently narrow seeking of private interest will, according to Adam

Smith's analysis of 'the invisible hand', promote the public interest as well. At a later point (page 241), I hope to explore some of the ways in which novel institutional design could help to create non-perverse incentives for productive entrepreneurship.

13.6 CONCLUSION

What I have been concerned with in this chapter are perceptions. It is said that Scots are not attuned to the enterprise culture. My experience from interviews is that entrepreneurs themselves, even if they are successful and generally enthusiastic about enterprise, frequently use phrases which reinforce this negative perception. I have likened this to the rugby player with two views depending on whether he is spectating or participating. It may be glorious to observe a fierce game of rugby, but hell to be in the thick of the scrum. But what one says in the scrum is really irrelevant to how one plays the game. Beyond perceptions, one is interested in objective measures of enterprise like new firm formation. Recent work by Ashcroft, Love and Malloy (1991) suggests that the rate of new firm formation is lower in Scotland than elsewhere in the UK. This need not be interpreted as lack of enterprise in itself, but might be explained by lack of market opportunities, behind which may lie lack of wealth. It might also be explained by a lack of richness in the information sources which are of importance in encouraging small firm inceptions. In Reid and Jacobsen (1988) it was indicated that accountants were rated the most important sources of advice about the entrepreneurial event, followed by banks, then Enterprise Trusts. To the extent that the network of informational services, of which these are a part, can be improved, one would expect enterprise itself to be stimulated. Under the new enterprise arrangements one might expect this information network to be enriched by the new Local Enterprise Companies (LECs) which will play a role in improving both advice and training directed towards SBEs. Another thought-provoking aspect of the study by Ashcroft et al. (1991) is the finding that, compared to other parts of the UK, Scotland consistently ranked higher in entrepreneurial potential than achievement.[10] Here, perhaps, perceptions have some bearing. The mentality of 'Ah kent his faither',[11] the frequency with which vigorous and imaginative entrepreneurs become prophets without honour in their own land, must ultimately have negative incentive effects. The information supplied by key institutions, both existing and emerging, to entrepreneurs can help to erode those myths.

Part VI
Conclusion

14 A small firms research agenda

14.1 INTRODUCTION

The research conducted on small business enterprises is expanding rapidly, but arguably this is not true of the research agenda of small business economics itself. That is to say, whilst the extent of work accomplished is growing, the framework within which it is pursued is static. In this chapter I wish to explore the potential for enlarging this research agenda. What I have to say must be regarded as very much a personal perspective, based on my own research (including the results embodied in this book) and on contact with others in the area through conferences, seminars, correspondence, refereeing, reviewing, academic visits, etc. I have divided my remarks into four parts: small firms theory; data acquisition and handling; econometric and statistical testing; and the political economy of small business.

14.2 SMALL FIRMS THEORY

The theory of the firm has long been a central topic in economic theory, and the firm in question has often been thought of as small. Thus a variety of market forms – perfect competition, pure competition, free competition, Chamberlinian monopolistic competition, Robinsonian imperfect competition – are all varieties of atomistic competition in which each firm is an insignificant atom in his own universe, the industry. One is bound to observe, however, that the characterization of the firm thus analysed is, to say the least, anaemic. Here, I have in mind the dictionary sense of the word: 'pale, lacking in vitality'.

Thus in the general equilibrium world of Arrow–Debreu–McKenzie,[1] the small producer chooses a production plan (y) from a given production set (Y), given a price system (p), so as to maximize profit $(p.y)$. To the specialist in small business economics this characterization is certainly pale and lacking in vitality. The 'insider' view of small firms is that they may be innovative, may grow rapidly, may create new market niches, may take quite high risks, and may have quite limited life spans. None of these features is captured in an Arrow–Debreu–Mackenzie world.

Of course this abstract framework can be modified in a variety of ways, to embrace narrowly defined conceptions of uncertainty and imperfect competition,[2] for example. More recently, a Marshallian-influenced approach to general equilibrium theory which pays more serious attention to the process of entry and exit has emerged, notably through the work of Novshek and Sonnenschein (1987). This certainly makes general equilibrium more acceptable to industrial economists, but is only a small step in the right direction. On the applied side, it may be useful to construct computable general equilibrium models for the purpose of comparing, say, the efficacy of various tax regimes. Recent extensions of this methodology embrace both monopolistic competition, in a 'mark-up pricing' form, and openness to trade.[3]

Despite these theoretical and empirical developments in mainstream general equilibrium methods, they do not begin to address the sorts of issues that small business specialists find central, like growth, and the exploitation of market niches. In the 1970s, before the seminal empirical work of Birch (1979) rekindled interest in small firms, one might have said that no alternative theories of the small firm existed. The relevant theory had not developed because empirical enquiry was all but dead. Fortunately that situation changed very rapidly, no doubt fostered by an increase in applied work on a small business enterprise. Research workers found new reasons for being interested in small firms. Three good ones are: they are the typical or 'modal' form of firm; they are relatively innovative and flexible; and they are significant contributors to employment growth. In tandem with these advances in applied work came advances in theory as directed to the small firm.

In Reid and Jacobsen (1988: chapter 2) I provided an account of many of these new developments, so here I shall be brief. Let me distinguish three types of theories. First, those that are transactional in approach. Here the inspiration can be traced back to Coase (1937), the vocabulary has been developed in considerable complexity by Oliver Williamson, and the analytics are typified by the writings of members of the so-called 'UCLA school' like Harold Demsetz, Benjamin Klein, and Armen Alchian. The approach can be summarized as the quest for transactional efficiency. Very little of these writings are explicitly focused on the small firm, though it is not difficult to adapt them to that purpose. Second, there are theories that treat the small firm as characterized by a production function. The story can be modified to incorporate quality of output, uncertainty, and efficiency of managerial or entrepreneurial inputs. Despite these guises, the core neoclassical principles are recognizable: the efficient transformation of factor inputs into outputs; and maximization of net revenue. Third, there are theories which emphasize the growth of the small firm. Alfred Marshall, with his 'life cycle' theory of the firm, was the first significant theorist in this vein, and one rigorous expression of his theory, in terms of the mathematics of Markov chains, has been provided by Newman and Wolfe (1961). Another strand, less satisfactory in terms of its economic theory but widely employed in empirical work, is that based on Gibrat's Law. This says that the change in size of a firm this year is a random proportion of its size last year. It implies the lognormality of the equilibrium size distribution of firms, which is well confirmed empirically. Modern stochastic small firm theories[4] take their inspiration from this earliest of stochastic theories of the firm. In summary there are, broadly speaking, three emphases in small firm theories: contracts, profit maximization, and growth. Of course elements may be combined (for example growth and profit maximization), but nevertheless the distinction proves fruitful.

The contractual view, that the firm is a set of contracts, is a general framework for the relative evaluation of market and non-market institutions. Coase (1937) first came upon his famed explanation for the firm (that it economises on transactions costs compared to the market alternative) while studying vertical integration.[5] Let me take this highly relevant concept as a starting point. Consider a large firm (A) and an upstream small business enterprise (B) which is an important supplier to A. What if a vertically-integrated firm (C) is contemplated, by unifying A and B? Is it the case that there is a necessary advantage in the vertically integrated institution? Williamson (1985: 133) would ask whether the new firm C could not be assumed to be capable of doing at least what the autonomous firms A and B could do. Indeed, there do seem to be arguments in favour of this, which is not surprising as vertical integration is a common market phenomenon. For example, the overhead costs of A and B would be shared, costs of goodwill maintenance between A and B would vanish, the risk premia on contract prices, because of uncertainties in contracting between A and B, would also disappear.

However, a basic tenet of the contractual or transactional approach is that a newly constructed, larger institution does not have characteristics (for example in terms of incentives, risk-sharing, utilization of information) which are simple aggregates of those displayed by the smaller institutions from which it was constructed. Thus there may indeed be transactional advantages in firms A and B continuing to operate autonomously, which is to say there might be an efficiency argument for small business enterprise (for example firm B operating independently in this case). The detailed argument, along Williamsonian lines, is in Reid and Jacobsen (1988: chapter 2.4) and identifies governance cost disabilities on firm size. Denote by A' and B' the absorbed firms A and B, respectively, within the new vertically-integrated firm C. In abbreviated form the argument is as follows. Assets which previously were protected in firm B may be abused by the former owner-manager of B who now becomes a new employee-manager of B', because he has no ownership stake. Creative accounting within C might mask the contribution of the absorbed unit B', reducing incentives for efficiency and innovation. High-powered market incentives between A and B are replaced by low-powered bureaucratic incentives between their absorbed units A' and B' within C. Power, exercised through hierarchy in C, may deprive the absorbed unit B' of resources and fail to attribute credit where credit is due. Innovations undertaken by B' may not be unambiguously attributable to it, and therefore incentives may fail to be constructed to reinforce this innovativeness. Finally, if innovations in B' do not display high asset-specificity then the enhanced net revenue streams they generate are more appropriable under the market alternative: by firm B, rather than by B' within firm C. The above is one of the many uses to which transactional or contractual analysis may be put in small firms theory. Here, I used it to explain the scale of SBEs. Other uses to which it may be put include explanations of niche market exploitation by SBEs, and the flexibility characteristics of SBEs (cf. Lee 1993).

I turn now to neoclassical theories of the SBE which emphasise profit maximization and the production functions at the root of a firm's operations. Each of these involves a blend with one or more other theoretical features, including general equilibrium under uncertainty, co-operative game theory, stochastic growth theory, and so on.

Firm formation may itself be regarded as a kind of coalition formation. Coalitions are maintained because each of those who participates in them gets a pay-off which is better than that arising from his next-best option. The value of a coalition under the assumption of a conflict of interest between players in the game provides the basis for the pay-off to each player in the coalition. This picture can be modified to include the possibility of transactions costs in coalition formation.[6] Under certain circumstances, for example if one can distinguish between active and passive players in an entrepreneurial market game (for example Littlechild 1979), the excess of a coalition (i.e. the difference between its value, and the sum of payments to coalition members as pay-offs) can be identified as an entrepreneurial return or residual. Telser (1978: 14) thinks in similar terms and, rather than having active and passive players, has bosses and workers, who may form such coalitional firms as suit their interests. Each boss may be regarded as having control of a production function which specifies how labour inputs may be efficiently transformed into output. Telser shows that in his model the workers will receive their marginal product and the bosses will get the rest. The bosses are the residual claimants on the excess value created by the coalitional firm. In this way, a blend is achieved between game-theoretic and neoclassical methods, with the production function being a central device. An underdeveloped part of the small firms research agenda is to use experimental methods to investigate hypotheses about coalition formation, treated as small firm inception facilitated by an 'active player' or entrepreneur. I am currently designing such experiments with a co-worker, and have found that the choice of solution concept for the entrepreneurial market game is a ticklish matter requiring considerable detailed investigation.

In the general equilibrium model of small firm entrepreneurship due to Kihlstrom and Laffont (1979), influenced by the writings of Knight (1921), a similar production function is used. Output is dependent on a labour input and, in addition, a non-negative random variable. All economic agents have costless access to this production technology, and differ by degree of risk-aversion. Economic agents make choices over the waged-worker and entrepreneurial roles on a rational basis (namely expected profit maximization). Either an agent, as a worker, receives with certainty the competitive wage, or, as an entrepreneur, he is claimant to the uncertain net revenue which is the difference between the random value of output and the wage bill. An economic agent will choose to be an entrepreneur if the expected profit of the risky role (i.e. entrepreneurship) exceeds the utility of the riskless role (i.e. being a worker). It is shown by Kihlstrom and Laffont that this choice decision partitions the set of economic agents into workers and entrepreneurs, with the former being more risk-averse than the latter. Lucas (1978) also puts the production function at the focus of his model of the size distribution of firms. Output is determined by a two factor (capital, labour) production function, which is extended to embrace the notion of an entrepreneurial technology. The latter specifies the ability with which the entrepreneur co-ordinates capital and labour inputs. An ability index assumes a critical value at which profit equals the competitive wage. Those with greater ability become entrepreneurs, and those with less ability become workers. There is an implied distribution of firm size which reflects the distribution of entrepreneurial ability. Oi (1983) has also emphasised the importance of co-ordination, but notes that in a sense it competes with monitoring for the attention of the entrepreneur. Given the ultimate constraint of hours in a week, time lost in monitoring leaves only so much time for co-ordination, which will be used more or less effectively depending on the entrepreneur's ability. As in Lucas's model, a critical ability level is determined which partitions economic agents into workers and entrepreneurs. The more productive workers will be matched with more productive entrepreneurs.

Finally, in an approach inspired by the writings of Schultz (1975, 1980), Holmes and Schmitz (1990) specify a fixed coefficients production function for which two inputs (a unit of time, and a business) are combined to produce a consumption good. Economic agents have identical managerial ability, but different abilities at the 'entrepreneurial event' (i.e. starting up an SBE). SBEs are rated by their productivity or quality. The basic theorem of Holmes and Schmitz (1990) is that the space with dimensions of entrepreneurial ability and business quality is partitioned into four regions. The first refers to low quality SBEs and low ability entrepreneurs. Here, firms are purchased to manage, and liquidated at exit. The second refers to higher than marginal quality SBEs and to middling entrepreneurial ability. Here, firms are managed and retained. The third refers to middling to higher entrepreneurial ability and low to marginal quality SBEs. Here, firms are liquidated at exit, and new ones started. The fourth refers to high quality SBEs and high quality entrepreneurial ability. Here, firms are sold at exit and new ones started. Generally, high ability entrepreneurs start businesses and low ability entrepreneurs buy them.

The roots of theories of small firm growth lie with the so-called Law of Proportionate Effect. This says that the change in size of a firm over a unit period is a random proportion of its size in the base period, where the random term is serially uncorrelated. It implies a limiting distribution for firm size which is lognormal. The theory lacks economic content. It also has the undesirable property, inconsistent with much available evidence, that the variance of the logarithm of firm size grows through time.[7] Further variants take account of the birth of firms, and mergers and acquisitions.[8] Steindl (1965) used a birth–death process developed in stochastic process theory to explain the steady-state equilibrium of firms by the Pareto distribution. Theories of these sorts have been widely applied, but not one is well designed to take specific account of small firms. The case is otherwise with more recent models, like those of Jovanovic (1982), Frank (1988) and Segal and Spivak (1989).

The widely cited paper by Jovanovic (1982) is particularly relevant to the study of small firms at the industry level. Firms are small, profit-maximizing price takers. Costs vary randomly across firms, and initially each firm is ignorant of its own cost. Firms with truly low costs will learn of this through favourable market experience, and will tend to survive. Those with truly high costs will have unfavourable market experience and on the basis of this evidence will eventually exit. In Jovanovic's model, smaller firms have higher and more variable growth rates than larger firms, which accords with empirical evidence. The emphasis in Frank (1988) is more on the small business than the industry. New entrepreneurs work harder than those near retirement. New entrants in the Jovanovic model held the same beliefs, whereas in Frank's model they have differing beliefs about their productivity. Thus more optimistic entrepreneurs will enter with larger scales of enterprise than the less optimistic. As in the Jovanovic model, entrepreneurs are initially unsure of their talents at running a business and learn over time, by experience in the market-place, good or bad, whether their productivity is high or low. Sunk costs play an important role in reflecting the initial beliefs of new entrepreneurs. The greater are sunk costs, the greater are expected profits, and thus the longer is the time to exit. If high sunk costs have led to a high assessment of productivity, even if subsequent performance is poor it will take a long spell of adverse experience to disabuse the entrepreneur of his/her high opinion of their ability. Frank's model also predicts a greater variability of growth rates of small, compared to large, firms. Segal and Spivak (1989) present a model with similar properties, in that the rate of growth of small firms tends to be higher and more variable than that of less small firms; though for large firms, as predicted by Gibrat's Law, the growth rate is invariant.

Above, I have examined three broad types of small firms theory with emphases on transactions, profit maximization mediated by the production function, and growth. Many approaches combine elements of each to a greater or lesser degree, so the types are not mutually exclusive (for example

Jovanovic's growth model is very much profit-maximizing, production-function based). A number of approaches, in their focus on co-ordinating ability, willingness to bear risk, and management of time, anticipate aspects of an emerging formal theory of agency as applied to the firm. For example, in Kihlstrom and Laffont (1979) the entrepreneur has residual claimant status; and in Oi (1983) he engages in monitoring because he recognizes the existence of agency costs. This is suggestive of possibilities for going much further along this theoretical route, using more formal principal-agent analysis[10] in the small firms area. In the outstanding early contributions by Jensen and Meckling (1976) to the so-called 'positive theory of agency', the emphasis is on corporate enterprises, with managers treated as agents and shareholders as principals. This formulation arises because of the separation of ownership and control which sometimes characterizes corporations. However, I have argued above that in many small firms contexts the issue of separation of ownership and control does not arise in the early years of an SBE's existence. The entrepreneur is also usually (in a strict sense) the owner-manager. He initiated the 'entrepreneurial event' of small firm inception, and he provided all the equity from personal financial injections. After the firm is up and running, he superintends its day-to-day activities. Within such a firm, before the emergence of hierarchy, agency analysis would continue to be relevant to the SBE's external relations. For example, it provides a way of analysing the relation of the owner-manager as employer (principal) to his workforce as employees (agents).

Agency theory, and in general theoretical approaches emphasising market-signalling, optimal risk-sharing and asymmetric information, may therefore have great importance for advancing our analytical understanding of SBEs, where external relations (i.e. extra-firm) are concerned, as distinct from internal relations (i.e. intra-firm), where the firm in question is small. In my current work, for example, I am exploring the possibility of using principal-agent analysis to model the relationship between the venture capitalist (VC) (as principal) and the mature small firms (MSF) (as agent). Such firms are arguably one stage beyond those that are typical of my sample. They are older and larger, and are contemplating a change in organizational form, perhaps for reasons of the sort discussed in chapter 4, like a concern for potential managerial diseconomies as the scale of operations increases. If a mature small firm (MSF) wishes to sustain its growth, and not fall victim to the decay predicted by life cycle theories of the firm, it may wish to achieve a growth spurt by the injection of outside equity, with the aim of achieving market listing (i.e. stock market quotation) within a short space of time (for example, in three to five years).

The question one needs to address is the way in which the provider of outside equity, a venture capitalist (VC), interacts with the mature small firm (MSF), in a principal-agent framework. Conceived of as a principal, the VC may approach the MSF (as agent) with a view to acquiring this firm for his portfolio. As in all principal-agent relationships, the principal requires the agent to perform a task on his behalf. Typically, the principal can only judge the effectiveness with which the agent performs his task in an indirect way. Most obviously, he looks at outcomes, or pay-offs; but also he may look at effort, by using some sort of monitoring system. In this example, the VC as principal aims to maximize his expected return from his contract with the MSF, taking account of the latter's desire also to do the best he can for himself, and aiming to hold down the return of the MSF to the minimum necessary to keep him in the contract. Arguably, the principal typically confronts as many agents as there are client firms in his portfolio. However, let us look at the writing of a contract between a VC as principal, with an existing diversified portfolio of clients, and the MSF as a potential *new* client of the VC.

The VC will be assumed to be risk neutral (in a von Neumann-Morgenstern sense) because he holds a large, diversified portfolio of client MSFs. The MSF will be assumed to be risk-averse because all his wealth is tied up in the firm, where wealth here could be extended to include a reputational 'stock' (i.e. the goodwill of the business). Why should the MSF wish to write a contract with the VC? Two obvious reasons are: (1) to get additional equity into the MSF, over and above what has currently been sourced; and (2) to spread risk, by getting the VC to share some of the risk to which the MSF is averse. The VC may wish to write a contract with the MSF because (1) he seeks profitable outlets for a surplus of finance capital; and (2) he seeks a knowledge or skill-sharing arrangement. Thus the MSF offers the VC an ownership share and a knowledge share, in exchange for which the VC offers the MSF an opportunity to spread risk, and to acquire additional finance capital. On this basis a contract is written between VC and MSF. Pay-offs may be defined in terms of the split in the value of the MSF at the time of exit. How this value is defined, the form this exit may take, and the manner in which the split between VC and MSF is undertaken are all complex issues. For example, amongst the exit routes to be considered are a trade sale (selling the MSF to another business), secondary market listing (the unlisted securities market) and main market listing (the Stock Exchange).[11] However one defines the payoffs at exit, one feature of them is intrinsic – they are uncertain.

The purpose of the contract written between the VC and the MSF is to deal with this uncertainty, i.e. to handle risk. If the VC is risk neutral, he will bear all the risk if the MSF's effort is observable. If the MSF's effort is not fully observable, it may be difficult to know whether high (respectively low) profitability is due to great (respectively little) effort, or to a good (respectively bad) state of the world. This provides the MSF with an incentive to reduce effort, and encourages the VC to install monitoring mechanisms (for instance, quarterly managerial accounts, representation on the board of directors) and to design incentives schemes (for example performance-linked equity) with the aim of improving observability and eliciting greater effort. Lack of perfect observability (leading, for example, to possibilities of moral hazard) may mean the MSF will be required to agree a contract in which he bears at least some risk, in order to provide an incentive for effort. This arises even if the MSF is risk averse and the VC is risk neutral.

As an area of empirical enquiry for small firms specialists, these areas touched on above are largely unexplored. This is partly for lack of the relevant theory. The above is a mere sketch of a few relevant theoretical considerations with some reference to appropriately measurable variables for constructing a test methodology. Theoretical work in this area is scarce to non-existent. The great emphasis has been on the relation between banks and small entrepreneurial firms. [12] A welcome sign of the emergence of new theoretical insights is the recent contributions by Chan, Siegel and Thakor (1990), where a two-period model is developed in which interim information reveals the relative skills of the VC and MSF and is used to determine which party will control second-period production. The model explains why VC/MSF contracts often 'bundle' a risky claim by the VC along with high powers of control over the MSF, and also sometimes contain explicit covenants to permit control to pass from the MSF to the VC should the entrepreneur perform badly within the MSF.

14.3 DATA ACQUISITION AND HANDLING

Small business economists, like their counterparts in the parent discipline of industrial economics, tend to depend upon the existence of official government statistics when undertaking empirical research. This has the inevitable consequence of conditioning and constraining the way in which hypotheses about SBEs are formulated and tested, leading, arguably, to an unnecessary limitation on our understanding of how SBEs function. For example, in the well-known work of Evans (1987a), quite properly highly regarded for its skilful handling of large small firms data sets, his empirical analysis of small firm growth may be criticized both for its choice of unsatisfactory key variables and for its sparse characterization of the SBE. Probably an asset-based measure of firms' size would have been most satisfactory in the growth computations, followed by a sales turnover (i.e. gross revenue) measure. Unfortunately, asset data were unavailable, and sales data were regarded as unreliable, so employment data were used instead. Further, few variables were available for each firm, so explanations of the determinants of the growth rates of SBEs were inevitably narrow in scope, and confined to age and size variables. Indeed, age as an exogenous variable in a small firms growth equation has a distinctly dubious status.

The age of an SBE is not a variable which may be controlled by the owner-manager in the sense of other variables which have more plausible claims to the status of exogeneity. The number of employees and the level of inventories provide examples of variables which may be assigned at higher or lower levels according to the owner-manager's desired growth trajectory, taking into account his motivation (for example long-run profit maximization). They are therefore plausible exogenous variables. Age is undirectional, and in a sense inexorable, though the owner-manager has the timing of certain events under his control in some measure (for example the launch date of a new product, the variation of advertising intensity over the course of the business cycle). Most important, age is not reversible. Whilst the timing of events can be pushed on to longer or shorter future time horizons, one cannot go back in time. An important characteristic of variables like 'number of employees' is that they *are* reversible, in the sense of freely variable in both directions. They exhibit controllability. There may of course be other justifications for using age as a variable in a growth equation. Probably the most acceptable is that it is an 'elapsed time from birth'[13] variable in certain types of stochastic process models, and given the operation of particular types of selection mechanisms one might expect a relationship between rate of growth and age of the SBE. One might go on in the context of Evans' type of exercise to question the use of the variable 'employment' to explain a growth rate which is itself expressed in terms of employment. The procedure invites the creation of a variety of spurious correlations. However, sufficient criticisms have already been mounted of sparse modelling of the sort described to make further elaboration unnecessary.

A way out of the impasse, that is out of a situation in which bricks cannot be made without straw, is to get better information on small firms. Large firms are widely written about in the financial press, and their activities receive much public attention. At a voluntary level, through the desire to legitimize the company in the eyes of both the public and business competitors, and at a non-voluntary level, through legal disclosure requirements, large firms provide a great deal of information about themselves. By contrast, small firms, because they are individually much less important, receive far less attention. As a result we are genuinely much more ignorant about the behaviour of small as compared to large firms and have a much smaller pool of tacit or informal knowledge on which to draw when theorizing about small firms. Overcoming the paucity of data on individual SBEs is therefore a priority.

A strategy that has already been pushed a long way, and perhaps too far in the small firms literature, is to attempt to know a lot about a little. As applied to SBEs, this strategy has contributed very little to our understanding of their behaviour. Let me take an analogy from medicine to illustrate my point. Having one hundred human bodies to dissect, providing they reasonably reflect variation in the human population, has the potential to advance the understanding of human physiology immeasurably, compared to having five data points on each of hundreds of thousands of humans. Of course firms, even SBEs, vary much more than humans, and there is no process precisely equivalent to dissecting a firm, though a thorough case study conducted by field work methods would aim to lay bare for scrutiny, in considerable detail, the internal workings of an enterprise. However, I hope my analogy helps clarify the advantages of an approach which emphasises gathering full information on individual SBEs. One would wish to ensure that this process were replicated with a sufficient number of firms for general tendencies to be discernible. Finally, this procedure might be a prelude to gathering few data points on large numbers of SBEs, perhaps by postal questionnaire, or telephone interviews, once strong hypotheses have been suggested by this more detailed approach, and the question of their universability has been raised.

One might hope for, but need not expect, government assistance in the more detailed approach to data acquisition. It might be more logical to identify it as the province of the research worker; for detail is of importance where theory formulation is concerned. The more extensive work would logically be the province of the government statistician, particularly if exhaustive coverage for bureaucratic purposes (for example VAT registration in the UK) is required by law.[14] If the small firms research worker is to change from being a passive user of secondary source data to an active acquirer and analyst of primary source data, he will have to acquire skills in field work methods and data reduction. Of course many of the great economists of the past have engaged in field work amongst business enterprises, including Adam Smith and Alfred Marshall. It is also a method favoured by economists who have been highly influential in shaping the form of current research in industrial economics, such as Michael Porter and Ronald Coase.[15] An enthusiasm for field work as the basis for case studies has also been expressed of late by Lawson (1985) and Flaherty (1984), both of whom are actually highly trained in mathematics. An important advantage of the method, as Flaherty (1984: 67) indicates, is the illumination it provides on issues of dynamics, uncertainty, and rivalry, all of which are hard to handle by theoretical methods alone. More generally, the acquisition of data in a case study form can be of particular inspiration to theory formulation. It may help to identify key categories of data and, under certain circumstances, may facilitate the testing of theories. I have discussed these matters at length in Reid (1989: chapter 3; 1987) and the issues raised are too numerous and detailed to be explored here. It is clear, however, that data acquisition has to become a much more careful, self-conscious process when one switches from secondary to primary sources. One not only needs to learn how to acquire data, but also needs to develop methods for handling it. For example, if case studies are based on interview methods for acquiring information (for example semi-structured interviews with an agenda), and all interviews are tape-recorded and subsequently transcribed, one is faced with a problem of data reduction, for the sheer volume of information threatens to overwhelm the investigator, making it difficult for him to see the wood for the trees. Confronted with this situation, the way I proceeded, as reported in chapter 2 above, was to eschew tape recording and rely on interview notes constructed within a probe structure relating to every agenda item. These notes were later used as the basis for a debriefing session with a co-worker at the end of a day's field work. Finally, a single short paragraph of some 50 to 250 words for each agenda item was agreed. One has yet to address the issue of how data, reduced by the methods explained from a potential morass of redundancy and overdetermination to something conceptually more tractable, can be conveniently stored and manipulated.

Although the small firms research area is very empirically oriented, and a welcome diversity of data types are currently in use, there does not yet seem to have been significant innovation in the way in which data are handled. An enormously impressive aspect of Birch's influential early work[16] was its handling of large data sets. Yet it impressed by its scale, rather than by its method. A significant strand of argument throughout this book has been the advocacy of more diverse methods of data collection. Unless these new sorts of data are handled in innovative ways, using the benefits of recent advances in database design, research may not achieve the conceptual breakthrough that those active in the small firms area hope for. Instead, a greater volume of data, in increasingly diverse forms, will simply overwhelm the investigator. Currently quite complex methods are used on very large numerical data sets which are organized in quite strict ways (e.g. in a hierarchical fashion).[17] Data processing methods used might involve the concatenation of files, the selection of sub-sets of data, the definition of new variables from old, and the editing of data into a form which makes them suitable for further analysis using statistical and econometric software.

This process can be criticized as being no more than an extension in scale of the most traditional methods of data handling that were used before the advent of the electronic computer. What I have argued for in chapter 2 – and many parts of the research I report upon in this volume reflect the argument – is the implementation of a relational database philosophy. It would imply that the data as such are not important, so much as the relations between them. These relations should impose as few restrictions as possible. Thus popular hierarchical systems of data organization impose too much structure, and are a reflection of systems designs that sought economy, above all. In seeking this goal they limit the capacity for data to generate insight into the relations between variables. Developing new theories is facilitated by perceiving new relations within the data, and this whole process is limited by the imposition of structure which may have relevance for data handling, but no relevance for theory handling. And it is theory handling which is the reason for getting involved with the data in the first place. An alternative approach, and one upon which the research in this book is predicated, is to use a database that imposes rather little structure on the data. A way of proceeding was described in chapter 2, and required the use of a basic building block called the 'flat file'.[18] These flat files can contain both numerical and qualitative data (for example categorical variables or text from interview transcripts), and may be manipulated by a high-level language like SQL.[19] My own use of relational database methods would no doubt be regarded as primitive by the highly expert in computing. It partly reflects the frequency with which my research 'team' has been myself. Though my database may in parts have been relatively crude and unsophisticated, it does perhaps have the merit that it suggests and implements a method which can be generalized. The ultimate aim is to integrate qualitative and quantitative data fully, permitting a free and flexible interaction between both. A particular problem is how one incorporates qualitative data of the textual variety into the database. Above I have described how each agenda item in the AQ 1985 has a textual summary paragraph attached to it. This simultaneously attacked the problems of data reduction and coding of text. However, the method could no doubt be refined. When Ted Nelson (1987) introduced the world to 'hypertext', this self-proclaimed visionary hoped for a stable, uniform structural representation of all data. In a piece of hypertext sets of documents cross-refer to one another. Selections are made by association, rather than by indexing. More ambitiously, perhaps hopelessly over-ambitiously, Nelson, in his Xanadu project, aimed to provide access to all the data in the world. This is the relational database philosophy taken to a *reductio ad absurdum*, for no doubt there is a kind of 'impossibility theorem' lurking here which says something like connecting information creates information, from which one concludes that not all information can be fully connected. However, what I have in mind is not at all grand. It is much more of a practical research tool for use over a limited domain. Its conception of data handling would envisage a small firms database that combined the case study approach and the large data set approach, and allowed a flexible interaction between the two.

14.4 ECONOMETRIC AND STATISTICAL TESTING

Reflecting the empirical orientation of the small firms research area, econometric testing procedures have been widely adopted. However, I have argued in Reid (1990b) that the methods used have often been imitative of those used in other areas (such as labour economics, with its use of very large longitudinal databases). There has also been a tendency to see the body of small firm theories that can be econometrically tested as consisting of those that can be tested on known data, using known techniques of estimation. The notions of gathering new data, and devising new estimation methods, have been largely foreign to the small firms specialist. However, the history of econometrics suggests that innovation in estimation methods has frequently been driven by a new type of practical problem, which presents itself to the econometrician for solution as a new configuration of data. It is likely that new data forms (for example gathered through field work methods, as discussed in chapter 1) and new methods of data handling (for example relational database management, as discussed in chapter 2) could lead both to new estimation methods being devised, and to new approaches to theory being countenanced from the viewpoint of econometric testing. Certainly this has been my own experience in the small firms area.

Let me illustrate with two examples, the one more statistical, and the other more theoretical. In the first case, the data in question appeared in the form of censored ranks (i.e. as proper sub-sets of the set of n positive integers). Questions designed to elicit information in this form had previously been used successfully in industrial organization.[20] Following this lead, they have been used in the AQ 1985 to discover such things as: the order of actions taken when a boom in demand occurs and this demand cannot be met from stocks (for example increase overtime, increase capacity, raise price, etc.); the relative importance of sources of advice at financial inception of the SBE (for example family and friends, bank manager, local government authority, etc.); and the relative importance of factors that contributed to cash-flow problems in the SBE (for example over-investment, insufficient overdraft facilities, delinquent debtors, etc.). In Reid and Jacobsen (1988), for example, we reported on several rankings responses to questions concerned with the financial inception of small firms. For example, we asked what the obstacles were in obtaining financial support, what sources of finance, apart from personal finance, had been used in setting up the business, and what factors contributed to cash-flow difficulties. Some conclusions based on the questions have been drawn already in chapter 5 above. Here, I am more concerned with statistical procedures, particularly as regards two points: first, were the rankings responses actually nominated significantly different from randomly assigned rankings responses; and second, did the nominated rankings responses imply some typical or modal ranking across SBEs? In some detail in Reid (1988), in summary form in Reid (1990a), and in chapter 5 of this book I have examined these issues. My two main conclusions were as follows. First, that in default of a new test statistic, the Friedman (1937) non-parametric analysis of variance technique has superiority over more recently devised tests by Benard and Van Elteren (1953) and Prentice (1979) in the context of the rankings data used, when used to test the null hypothesis that rankings were chosen at random. Second, simple rank sums, with unchecked alternatives given imputed ranks, provided the best guide to one's intuitive sense of order, certainly compared to orderings suggested by the Benard–Van Elteren and Prentice tests, and even compared to the extremely computationally burdensome orderings suggested by the procedure of Tate (1961).

Let me take one example to illustrate these points. The AQ 1985 had a question which ran as follows: 'What source, apart from personal finance, did you use in setting up your business?' Possible responses were as follows: (a) borrowing from friends, relatives or acquaintances; (b) borrowing from banks; (c) hire-purchase; (d) leasing; (e) equity finance; (f) business colleagues; (g) the ICFC. Owner-managers were then asked to rank these sources in order of importance. Results obtained from tests of the null hypothesis of randomly assigned ranks were as follows: 28.3409 (Prob < 0.0005) Friedman; 11.7746 (Prob < 0.075) Benard–Van Elteren; 12.8042 (Prob < 0.05) Prentice. The Friedman and Prentice statistics were significant at the $\alpha = 0.05$ level, whilst the Benard–Van Elteren was clearly less significant. For this same question, orderings can be constructed by the

Benard–Van Elteren and Prentice tests using reduced ranks scaled by the corresponding standard deviations. The tests both give a, g, f, e, c, d, b as the orderings present in the data. The ICFC and business colleagues (g and f) appear to be too highly ranked, and bank borrowing (b) too lowly ranked. In fact, arguably the most important source of external finance was banks, with 82 per cent of the SBEs who used external finance at inception nominating this as the third or higher-ranked in importance source. Next came friends and family (27 per cent), hire purchase (21 per cent), leasing (18 per cent), and equity (15 per cent). Ranking in this way (first, second, or third most important), one gets an order like b, a, c, d, e, etc. compared with a, g, f, e, c, etc. under Benard–Van Elteren and Prentice. Ordering by rank-sums gives b, a, c, f, d, e, g, which also accords better with intuition. For purposes of comparison one might want to use the Tate (1961) method as a 'sophisticated yardstick'. It involves computing a statistic which measures the support the data give to any candidate for being the true order, and requires computations of all $n!$ permutations of orders. Ordering by Tate's method in this case requires testing 5,040 orderings, and the 'true' ordering suggested is non-unique, being either b, a, c, d, f, e, g, or b, a, c, f, d, e, g. They are similar, intuitively convincing, and very much correspond with appealing rankings derived by the much less computationally burdensome methods of elementary descriptive statistics. Thus, in this case, the 'fast and dirty' methods (Friedman for significance tests, and rank-sums for orderings) appear to out-perform 'sophisticated' alternative methods.

These findings led to a collaboration reported in Snell and Reid (1989) which describes the construction of a parametric test based on Wald-test methodology. The basic idea is to reduce the n objects to be ranked to three: the two most highly ranked and the highest ranked of the remaining $(n-2)$. We described ranks defined in this way as 'compressed ranks' and developed an asymptotic test procedure. Let me illustrate by reference to another question from the AQ 1985. It ran as follows: what action would you take when a boom in demand occurred which could not be met from stocks? Options given were: (a) increase overtime or shiftwork; (b) increase capacity; (c) engage subcontractors; (d) buy-up rivals; (e) lengthen order books; (f) raise price; (g) other. Then respondents were asked to indicate the order in which they would undertake the actions chosen. The null hypothesis (H_0) of randomly assigned actions (i.e. non-concordance amongst SBEs) was resoundingly rejected ($\chi^2(5) = 138.2$). However, the parametric nature of the test enables one to probe further and extract more information from the data. If, in terms of Hicksian terminology,[21] 'flexprice' markets (as in Neoclassical analysis with zero adjustment costs) holds sway, it provides one alternative to the H_0 of non-concordance, implying that SBEs would, on average, raise prices first. Whereas if 'fixprice' markets (as in sophisticated Neoclassical analysis with positive adjustment costs) hold sway, SBEs would, on average, increase overtime or shiftwork first, because of the relatively high costs (sometimes called 'menu costs') of adjusting other instruments under their control, including price. In terms of the procedure developed in Snell and Reid (1989) we could choose (a) (overtime) and (f) (price) as the objects of interest because they represent clear fixprice and flexprice alternatives to H_0 and, treating them in the same manner as the two 'most preferred' objects, convert the data into 'compressed ranks' and calculate the probabilities of outcomes with option one as 'price', option two as 'overtime or shiftwork' and option three as 'the best of the rest'. Applying our test procedure to the SBE data indicated that whilst the data set rejected H_0, it gave no support to the 'naive' Neoclassical (flexprice) view that price would be raised first. Rather, the data strongly favoured a sophisticated Neoclassical (fixprice) view, with overtime or shiftwork adjustment taking place first, suggesting significant 'menu costs' for the typical SBE.[22]

As my second example of how new configurations of data can influence the testing and specification of small firms theories let me refer to the data on expected price responses referred to in chapter 10. In my first example above, data affected statistical procedures; whilst in this second example data, as we shall see, affected theoretical specification. In the AQ 1985 owner-managers were asked whether they thought their strongest competitors would mimic a price reduction or increase, over boom, recession, and normal business conditions. These data provided an opportunity to test a perfect equilibrium[23] oligopoly model developed by Bhaskar (1988). In its original form, the theory was of a fast-play duopoly in which firms responded very rapidly to price cutting by the rival. There is a unique perfect equilibrium to this game, whose two forms depend on disparities in the duopolist's costs. For similar costs, the lower cost firm is the price leader and will match price cuts, but not price increases. This is a 'kinked demand curve' strategy. For dissimilar costs with product differentiation, the low-cost firm is a Stackelberg leader and the high-cost firm prices above it. When this theory is extended to many firms, it predicts that all firms except the leader expect asymmetric price responses in the former case and symmetric price responses in the Stackelberg case. After a chance meeting at a conference of Bhaskar, Machin and the author, a team project was agreed upon which would use: (a) my interests in the kinked demand curve and the use of subjective data[24] (for example, expected price responses), and my database evidence; (b) Bhaskar's game theoretic knowledge, including modelling of asymmetric price conjectures and their modification by phase of the business cycle; and (c) Machin's skills in the applied econometrics of industrial organization, in variants of more standard probit models (for example, ordered probits) and in specification testing.[25] The results of this collaboration have been presented in the jointly written chapter 10 of this book. Bhaskar extended his original theory to consider how his equilibrium would be affected by the phase of the business cycle. He was able to show that the Stackelberg equilibrium would emerge in buoyant business conditions and the kinked demand curve equilibrium in depressed business conditions, implying greater pricing asymmetry in slumps compared to booms. The empirical tests, using ordered probit analysis, involved explaining the probability of price matching on the part of rivals by business cycle indicators and firms' characteristics (for example, market share, perceived demand elasticity, capacity utilization). It was found that there were indeed asymmetries in price reactions and these were cyclically sensitive. Price increases were more likely to be followed in a boom; and price decreases were more likely to be followed in a slump. The data that made this theorizing and testing possible were based on subjective evidence. The data related to expected price responses. Owner-managers said what they expected their strongest rivals to do if they themselves changed price. Economists have often been reluctant to use such subjective evidence, but my own conclusion in Reid (1981), reached while looking in detail at the price rigidity/price flexibility debate, was that they constitute a valid and useful form of data. They are well suited to testing hypotheses in dynamic games, where price equilibria appear only because deviations from them are unprofitable. Data on expected price responses are therefore the only source of information on behaviour off the equilibrium path. Thus the analysis by Bhaskar (1988) of an extensive-form game, in which firms can respond rapidly to price undercutting, provided a good starting point for the collaboration described above, leading to Bhaskar, Machin and Reid (1991). It developed a new approach to the testing of game theoretic hypotheses – so far as I am aware, the first to be applied in the small firms area. My own experience has been that innovations of this sort, as with the previous statistical example, are often at least partially data driven: 'new problems, new ideas'.

14.5 THE POLITICAL ECONOMY OF SMALL BUSINESSES

The principal concern of this volume has been with the scientific process in an impure, rather than pure, form. Whatever one's philosophy of science, this process would certainly include data collection, theorizing, and statistical testing of theories on the data. However, economics does not have a fully fledged scientific status. Its data are contingent (for example, on legal statutes, tax codes, political regimes), theories are not always defined in terms of variables with agreed procedures of measurement, and testing of theories is rarely decisive, certainly falling far short of a falsificationist position. For better or for worse, economic 'science', to which the analysis of small business economics is no exception, operates within a larger system of political economy.

In part V of this book, I have examined just two aspects of this political economy – small business ethics, and perceptions of the enterprise culture from those working 'at the rock face', the entrepreneurs themselves. In this section I do not wish to refer to these themes, except obliquely, and in a way which differs somewhat from the discussion in chapters 12 and 13. Rather I shall open up a new research topic, the stimulation of enterprise, and shall conclude by looking more widely at the political milieu within which small business enterprise, with greater or lesser success, functions.

The notion that enterprise is in some sense endogenous to an economic system is surprising to economists who believe they are analysts of a market economy. To them, the market economy and the enterprise economy are synonymous. A behavioural datum of such an economy is thought to be the pursuit of personal gain through market-mediated transactions. The typical member of this economy 'intends only his own gain', in the words of Adam Smith.[26] The prospect that the butcher, baker, or pin-maker may not be available to behave in this way is not contemplated. In this sense, enterprise is commonly regarded as exogenously given. However, experience with marketization of Eastern European economies has more recently taught us that creating the theoretical framework for free enterprise does not in itself create enterprise as an activity. The market system is not simply an engineering mechanism which can be created from a blueprint. It is in some, perhaps even in large, measure a social process, that is a way of going about achieving certain social goals. The operation of this process invokes a vast assemblage of tacit or informal knowledge which is acquired, accumulated, refined, and transmitted by participation in market activities over long periods of time. One makes the market work by working in the market.

However, if an economy lacks a sufficient volume of individuals with market experience, but the economic policymaker desires the invisible hand, that is, the beneficial consequences of markets, without waiting for the long, natural process of acculturalization to work to this end, he must perforce be involved in conscious institutional design. Then the policy maker aims to stimulate enterprise, regarding such behaviour as endogenous, subject to a greater or lesser extent and quality, depending on the policy instruments that are used, rather than being exogenous and naturally present. What we have discovered in the mixed market economies of Western Europe is that the growth of the public sector may destroy that tacit knowledge which helps to run markets efficaciously. We are free of the larger problem of creating enterprise which dogs marketization in Eastern Europe, but confronted with the lesser problem of stimulating enterprise.

One can trace the development of a solution to this latter problem in the current context by reference to the emergence of Scottish Enterprise. What one had was a combination of spontaneous institutional evolution (for example the emergence of the Enterprise Trusts, and their eventual symbiosis with the centre, the SDA) and conscious institutional design (for example the blueprinting, and subsequent implementation, of local Enterprise Companies, as new social mechanism for the delivery of enterprise-stimulating services). What will become apparent from further analysis is, I think, the potentially important role of the discipline of comparative economic institutions in small business economics. For example, a link can be established between an earlier institutional form which had enjoyed some measure of success, the Boston Compact,[27] and the prototype of the new arrangements in Scotland, Enterprise Scotland, as originally conceived by an energetic Falkirk businessman, Bill Hughes.[28] It should prove possible to compare alternative institutional designs in terms of dimensions like degree of decentralization, responsiveness to 'time and place' information, vertical and horizontal co-ordination, and extent of private sector participation. The Scottish example provides a neat case study of institutions for stimulating enterprise, but one which can be generalized. For example, the success of the new arrangements in Scotland would be likely to lead to parallel developments in the rest of the UK where at the moment only the unconnected components of such a system exist (for example Enterprise Agencies, Training and Enterprise Councils, but no overarching framework, no 'English', 'Welsh', or 'Northern Irish Enterprise'). In examining how this scheme could be implemented in England, and indeed elsewhere in Europe where enterprise stimulation may be a desired public policy objective, the role of comparative economic institutional analysis is likely to be important, adding a new dimension to the research agenda for small business enterprise.

I referred earlier to the extent to which market activity was a social process, as distinct from a technical, engineering relationship (however conceived, mechanical equilibrium system, electrical feedback system, etc.). An important aspect of the functioning of this process is the system of beliefs that sustain it and govern, in some measure, the behaviour of individuals who participate in it. It is possible to look at the enterprise culture as a kind of system of beliefs and one which, if fully constructed, acquires the nature of a public good, in the same way as 'the work ethic' may be a public good.[29] What is clear from discussion so far, and from that available elsewhere,[30] is that the enterprise culture as a stable system of belief has not yet been created, though it might be appropriately described as 'emergent'. In my own work (e.g. for example chapter 13), I have found a difference in view taken on the enterprise culture, depending on vantage point. As an observer, there is a willingness to recognize an emergent enterprise culture, whilst as a participant, perceptions are more negative. In colloquial terms, 'other peoples' enterprise is a good thing, but my pursuing enterprise is tougher than I thought.'

I have argued that a potentially novel role for comparative economic institutionalists is the design of a social delivery mechanism for this public good called the enterprise culture. This prompts the question: can an enterprise culture be facilitated by training in enterprise? Adopting a Shultzian view of enterpreneurship would suggest that there are significant human capital aspects to the delivery of enterprise.[31] Better educated entrepreneurs tend to be more enterprising.

In the small firms context this is confirmed by the work of Dunkelberg and Cooper (1990) on human and financial capital substitutability/complementarity. They have exploited a data set that is new to the profession – membership files of the US National Federation of Independent Business – and throw new light on the relative roles of financial and human capital inputs in small firm inception and early existence. Their important finding is that human capital inputs are of far greater significance than financial capital inputs early in the life cycle of the small firm. Further, financial and human capital were found to be complementary rather than substitutable in production. There is weak confirmation of the small entrepreneurial firm models of Lucas (1978) and especially Oi (1983), which emphasise the existence of a distribution of entrepreneurial ability, in that Dunkelberg and Cooper discover that the higher the quality of human capital, the fewer are the hours worked in the firm per week. That is, high ability entrepreneurs have a relatively high marginal productivity, and also a relatively high opportunity cost of time.

This evidence suggests that an enterprise stimulation programme directed at the training dimension is likely to have powerful effects. Evidently training so defined can come in small or large doses, and still be significant. The value of a college education or university degree is undeniable, and this is a large 'lumpy' investment in human capital. It is also true that small packets of enterprise training are significant for enterprise. An example arises from evidence in Reid and Jacobsen (1988) which reported on difficulties in obtaining financial support for starting an SBE. Forty-five per cent of firms had experienced such difficulties, and the main reason was lack of personal finance.[32] Also important were difficulties in: (a) convincing potential backers of the existence of a market niche for the proposed SBE's goods or services; and (b) producing satisfactory financial statements of the proposed SBE (for example, in terms of projected cash flow). In short, deficiencies were in skills areas, these being market research and the preparation of a business plan. Such skills are readily cultivated, and need not be high-level to be useful.

The banks have recognized this, and have produced self-training material which is very skilfully designed and appears to enhance prospects of project acceptance if diligently used by clients.[33] The Enterprise Trusts and agencies have a good record of provision of enterprise services, some of which are in the form of training, and these appear to enhance the quality of business enterprise. In 1987 Business in the Community (BIC) found that SBEs which had used the enterprise services of enterprise agencies in England had an 84 per cent survival rate over three years, compared to 66 per cent for all firms newly VAT registered. This piecemeal picture of the significance of training is complemented by the larger scale picture of the training function within Scottish Enterprise, as I hope to discuss elsewhere in print. What is as yet unknown is the relative efficiency of different institutional designs for delivering enterprise in an *ex post* quantitative sense. This will no doubt be another new item on the small firms research agenda.

Finally, one must express an interest in the political milieu in which SBEs and their representative bodies move, because it is party political platforms that can make or break an enterprise culture, through the coercive power of Parliament to determine the shape of major institutions. Blanchflower and Oswald (1990) indicate that on the basis of British Social Attitude Surveys of 1983 and 1989 the typical UK small businessman is Conservative in political stance, and has the views one would perhaps expect about trade unions, self-reliance, redistributive measures, and unemployment benefits.[34] However, it is far from clear that small business has benefited from successive Conservative governments over the past decade, though certainly big business has flourished. An 'Enterprise Labour' movement has sprung up in recent years, and in May 1990 the Labour Party undertook a major policy review of issues relevant to small business. The National Federation of Self-Employed and Small Businesses (NFSE), with a 50,000 UK membership, has shown itself willing to court the Labour Party despite the inherent conservatism of its members (though the NFSE would naturally define itself as apolitical). At its annual conference in March 1990, the NFSE gave even-handed treatment to various political interests, though the consensus is that the laurels went to Labour rather than Conservative interests. Bill Anderson, the NFSE Scottish Secretary, said, 'we flirt with all of them, but go to bed with none'. A major 'flirtation' was involved with the proposal of Henry McLeish (Labour's Employment and Training Spokesman) for discounted loans through the banks, with precise targeting of eligible small firms. Political stakes are clearly not insignificant, because VAT figures show that 80 per cent of UK businesses have a turnover of less than £100,000 per annum, and these will employ on average just three or four people. One in eight of British workers is self-employed. The voting potential of the small business interest, therefore, runs into several millions. Despite the expressed intention that the new LECs and TECs should reflect local interests, the perception of the small business lobby has been that regional big fish have swallowed local small fish, and SBEs have ended up having their interests poorly defended, let alone promoted. The extent to which small business, through its powerful voting base and considerable lobbying powers, can defend its interests against those of big business is an issue which should take the attention of serious political economists with a small business research interest.

14.6 CONCLUSION

When I reviewed a volume by Acs and Audretsch (eds) (1990), which collected together articles by major contributors to the small firms literature, I ended up with the feeling that the research area was relatively immature.[35] In a formal sense, there appeared to be no theoretical innovations in any of the papers. Further, the new industrial economics seemed not to have influenced the research reported in the papers to the extent it might (for example, in terms of formulating and testing hypotheses in game theoretic terms). Aside from the contributors themselves, the most widely cited author was Schumpeter, with Piore a leading runner-up to him; and this was reflected in the rather dogged empiricism of the papers. There was also no evidence of innovation in the econometric and statistical techniques used.

Sophisticated techniques were occasionally used, as in Evans and Leighton (1990), but again nothing new was introduced; and elsewhere econometric methods were used somewhat carelessly, almost universally without serious diagnostic testing. Although many of the papers involved detailed data file handling, the methods employed, despite their use of modern computing technology, were actually rather primitive. They tended to mimic older forms of desk-top, pencil-and-paper data handling. None of the authors appeared to have embraced the new relational database philosophy. In principle this would say that, on the level of data, there is no difference between the qualitative, field work evidence of a Lazerson (1990) and the quantitative membership data of Dunkelberg and Cooper (1990). A relational database would combine and integrate such evidence drawn from a given population of small firms, enabling it to be manipulated in sophisticated ways. For example, case study qualitative evidence could be used to suggest causality relations and functional forms for the analysis of quantitative data by econometric methods. I argued that proceeding in this previously untried way could provide a catalyst for innovations in the theoretical models, and the econometric and statistical methods, used in the serious analysis of small firms.

To a fair extent, this volume is a test of this view. In this final chapter, I have given examples of specific theoretical and statistical innovations which have arisen from my chosen methodology. However, these are merely deliberately chosen highlights. More important is the attempt throughout the other thirteen chapters of the book, typically in less obvious ways, to advance research on small business enterprise. My wish has been to do this in a way which takes data seriously, uses relevant economic theory, confronts theory with evidence, and relates evidence to society. I leave the reader to judge the extent to which this goal has been achieved.

Appendix: Instrumentation

PRELETTER FOR AQ 1985

Dear

Over the past few years, attention has been shifted away from the large, corporate enterprise to the small enterprise as the major source of employment creation and economic growth. Significant support for the small business has come from the Scottish Development Agency, Scottish Business in the Community, and Enterprise Trusts. This support has been primarily in terms of attracting finance, finding suitable premises, and offering advice regarding drawing up a business plan, marketing, cash flow, etc. Unfortunately, not enough attention in terms of research has been given from the University level, which could help promote awareness for further support.

It is our contention that the prospects for success of the small business can be enhanced by increasing the knowledge of such enterprises' strategies to establish their place in the market. Proper management (in addition to adequate finance) is often a major obstacle in achieving and maintaining success for the small firm. Consequently, we are undertaking a comprehensive study of 70 to 80 small businesses by examining first-hand their policies and strategies not only to survive, but to prosper and grow. Our study involves the questionnaire, structured interview, and case study methods.

With your co-operation, we would very much like to take an hour of your time to go through our questionnaire. This objective exercise can be of immediate benefit to your business in that you will perhaps learn (or at least be reminded) how much you know about the conduct of your business and its effectiveness in relation to your competitors. Certainly, once the study has been completed (sometime late this summer) the findings will be made available to you if you so desire. Of course, the utmost in confidentiality will be upheld.

If you should have questions regarding our study or ourselves, please contact Mr Peter Duke, Director, EVENT. We will be contacting you in a few days time to see if and when it would be convenient for one of us to meet you. Thank you.

Yours sincerely

GUIDE TO INTERVIEWER

[Note: Not for respondent. To be held by interviewer at all times]

Thank you for your co-operation in undertaking this investigation. These notes are intended to guide you in your role as administrator of this questionnaire.

(a) This questionnaire is to be administered during a home interview. You should sit opposite, or at right-angles to, your respondent, and ensure that you have a hard surface on which to lean, and a pen or pencil.

(b) *You* are administering the questionnaire, and therefore have a part to play in controlling the pace at which it is completed. Do not rush the respondent. Furthermore, do not let the respondent rush you. It is not a speed or comprehension test, but an instrument of scientific investigation. You should avoid giving the impression that you are quizzing or analysing the respondent, and should not encourage him to think he is involved in a competition.

(c) You should put the respondent at his ease by starting with the following words:

'Thank you very much for agreeing to complete this questionnaire. It is part of a study being conducted by staff of the Economics Department of the University of Edinburgh. As such, the investigation has no affiliation with any other body, institution, agency, or any organization whatsoever, and the material is gathered in strict confidence. The identity of you or your firm as such will not be revealed in the study: nor is it of any relevance to the study. We would ask your permission that the data we gather may be used in an anonymous way for purely scientific purposes. If at the end of the questionnaire you have any general questions you would like to raise, I would be happy to answer them.

(d) The questionnaire is made up of four types of material, which are appropriately colour-coded: (i) the *questionnaire* proper, which is in *white*; (ii) *lists*, which are to be handed to the correspondent for self completion, and are in *yellow*; (iii) *show cards*, which are also to be handed to the correspondent for self completion and are in *pink*; and (iv) *standard industrial classification* (SIC) numbers which are in *blue* and have to be handed to the respondent at the beginning of the interview in order that he can identify his own SIC number.

(e) At the end of the interview *all* material should be back in your hands. As you progress through the questionnaire schedule, you will find your instructions in square brackets. Do not deviate from these instructions. In particular, make sure that you do retrieve material which has been handed to the respondent: *in the sequence indicated.*

(f) At the end of the interview you should ensure that you have:

(i) gathered all the material together, and picked up your personal belongings;
(ii) warmly thanked the respondent for his or her co-operation and helpfulness;
(iii) assured the respondent that you would be happy to be contacted by him at an address you are willing to leave (make it the Economics Department);
(iv) suggested that should he be willing, it might be helpful to approach him again at a later date.

(g) The motivation for f(iv) above is that the follow-ups to this questionnaire analysis are structured interviews, and then a limited number of case studies. It would be appropriate to mention this at the end of the interview, but this is not a matter that should be pressed. If the respondent volunteers further co-operation, assure him you will be in contact to advise him as to whether his help might be needed again.

(h) At the beginning of the questionnaire you expressed a willingness to be questioned further, at the end of the interview, in a general sense. You should be willing to do this, as promised, but should not prompt the respondent. Time is limited, and you may start off issues in areas which, if pursued too much, will leave you adrift. Be businesslike, but courteous. A good exiting excuse is that you have a further person to interview.

QUESTIONNAIRE ADMINISTERED IN 1985 (AQ 1985)

Name of interviewer: ....

Date of interview: ....

Time interview started: ....

Part I (general)

This questionnaire is divided up into five sections: a general one; pricing; costs; sales and competition; and financing. The typical way in which we will proceed will involve my asking a question, and then noting your reply. In addition there are a number of lists from which you will be asked to choose options, and then rank them; there are also 'show cards' which depict various patterns of costs, from which I would like you to make a selection. It is helpful to begin in a general way. This will help us to identify the main features of your business, before going into detail. May we begin then with the general questions?

(WHITE)

1.1 We need to know what kind of business you run. An easy way to do this is to refer to a standard list. Here it is.

[Hand over SIC list]

In which category is your business?

[Enter SIC code]   SIC code:

1.2 When did you start your business?

1.3 Could you tell me, how many people are working for you full time?

    1.3.1 Do you have any part time workers?

Yes [   ]
No [   ]

    1.3.1.1. *If yes*: How many?

    1.3.2 What about trainees?

Yes [   ]
No [   ]

    1.3.2.1 *If yes*: How many?

1.4 What kind of business do you run? Is it:
[Tick appropriate choice]
(a) A one-man business?
(b) A partnership?   [   ]
(c) A private company?   [   ]
(d) A public company?   [   ]
(e) Or is it something else?   [   ]

    1.4.1 *If (e)* Could you briefly describe your kind or business?

                    [Enter respondent's reply]

1.5 *Approximately* what size was your sales turnover in the last tax year (excluding VAT)?

1.6 Suppose you sold different kinds of hats and also different kinds of gloves. 'Hats' is what we call a *product group*, and so is 'gloves'. How many products do you sell?
(a) 1
(b) 2–5   [   ]
(c) 6–10   [   ]
(d) 11–20   [   ]
(e) 21–50   [   ]
(f) More than 50   [   ]

    1.6.1 What would you say was your *main* product group in terms of sales value?

[Before proceeding to 1.7, insert in 1.9 the respondent's reply to this question.]

1.7 If you sold two kinds of hats (for example bowlers and boaters), hats being a product group, and two kinds of gloves (for example mittens and driving gloves), gloves being a product group, you would be selling a total of four products, two from each product group. With this in mind, how many products do you sell?
(a) 1–10
(b) 11–20   [   ]
(c) 21–40   [   ]
(d) 41–60   [   ]
(e) 61–80   [   ]
(f) More than 80   [   ]

1.8 What do you regard as the principal market for your main product group?
(a) The local community   [   ]
(b) The region (for example Grampian, Lothian)   [   ]
(c) Scotland   [   ]
(d) UK   [   ]
(e) The international economy   [   ]

1.9 In terms of your principal market, what is your market share for ....
[Insert respondent's specified main product group from 1.6.1]

[Tick below according to respondent's reply]

(a) Under 1%   [   ]
(b) 1–5%   [   ]
(c) 6–10%   [   ]
(d) 11–20%   [   ]
(e) 21–30%   [   ]
(f) 31–50%   [   ]
(g) Over 50%   [   ]
(h) Not known   [   ]

1.10 Can you distinguish between major and minor competitors for your main product group?
Yes [   ]   *If yes* go to 1.10.1
No   [   ]   *If no* go to 1.10.2

1.10.1 [To be answered if above response was *yes*]
How many competitors do you have in each category?

Major competitors		*Minor competitors*	
(a) None	[ ]	(a) None	[ ]
(b) 1–5	[ ]	(b) 1–5	[ ]
(c) 6–10	[ ]	(c) 6–10	[ ]
(d) 11–30	[ ]	(d) 11–30	[ ]
(e) 31–50	[ ]	(e) 31–50	[ ]
(f) More than 50	[ ]	(f) More than 50	[ ]
(g) Do not know	[ ]	(g) Do not know	[ ]

1.10.2 [To be answered if above response was *no*]
Can you tell me how many competitors you have?
(a) None
(b) 1–5
(c) 6–10
(d) 11–30
(e) 31–50
(f) More than 50
(g) Do not know

1.11 How would you compare products in your main product group with those of your competitors? Would you say they were:
(a) Identical   [   ]
(b) Similar   [   ]
(c) Different   [   ]
(d) Cannot say   [   ]

1.12 Now I would like to look at the buying behaviour of your customers. Here is a list of possible descriptions of your customers. More than one may be applicable.

[Hand over list 1.12 to respondent]

Indicate with a tick *any* statement which applies to your customers.

[Pause to permit completion of this]

1.12.1 Now could you please underline the statement that is *most* applicable.

[Retrieve list 1.12]

Part 2 (pricing)

Thank you. Now we have finished the general questions. Next we are going to look at pricing. In this section I will be presenting you with further lists, from which you will have to choose options and rank alternatives.

(WHITE)

2.1 If you brought a new product onto the market, would you determine its price independently of the amount to be sold?

Yes [ ]
No [ ]

2.2 How are prices within your main product group usually determined? Could you put a tick by *any* statement on this list which is true for you? One or more of the statements may be applicable.

[Hand over list 2.2 to respondent. Pause to permit completion of this]

2.2.1 Now please underline the statement on this list which is *most* applicable.

[Retrieve list 2.2]

2.3 Is the pricing policy of competitors crucial to your own pricing?

Yes [ ]
No [ ]

2.4 Do you hold down price to beat your competitors?

Yes [ ]
No [ ]

2.5 What action do you take when a boom in demand occurs and this demand cannot be met from stocks? On this list, please tick any that apply.

[Hand over list 2.5. Pause to permit its completion]

2.5.1 Now please indicate where possible on this list, the order in which you do things by ringing the numbers on the right-hand side, where ringing a '1' for an option would indicate that this is what you would do first.

[Pause to permit completion. Retrieve list 2.5]

2.6 What action do you take in a recession? On this list, please tick those that apply.

[Hand over list 2.6. Pause to permit its completion]

2.6.1 As previously, could you please indicate where possible on this list the order in which you do things by ringing the numbers on the right-hand side.

[Pause to permit completion. Retrieve list 2.6]

2.7   What action do you take if the demand falls for a product within your main product group? Please tick *any* that apply on this list.

[Hand over list 2.7 to respondent. Pause to permit its completion]

2.7.1 Indicate where possible on this list the order in which you do things by ringing the numbers on the right-hand side.

[Pause to permit completion. Retrieve list 2.7]

Part 3 (costs)

Fine. We have finished with pricing. Now in just the same way we will look at costs. All the questions relate to products in your main product group. In this section we will be using the 'show cards' I mentioned earlier, which present various possible pictures of your costs.

(WHITE)

3.1   Are your costs split up into fixed (that is, overhead or indirect) and variable (that is, prime or direct) costs?

Yes [   ]
No [   ]

3.1.1 *If yes*: Are these cost divisions useful in the running of your firm?

Yes [   ]
No [   ]

3.2   When you intend to increase the output of a product, do you calculate the additional cost it will involve?

Yes [   ]
No [   ]

3.3   Do you have a level of output which you regard as the *capacity* or *maximum possible* output?

Yes [   ]
No [   ]

3.3.1 *If yes*: At what percentage of this maximum possible output do you think you normally operate?
(a) Less than 50%   [   ]
(b) 51–60%   [   ]
(c) 61–70%   [   ]
(d) 71–80%   [   ]
(e) 81–90%   [   ]
(f) 91–100%   [   ]

3.4   This next question aims to get an idea of the way your costs vary as you increase your output up to the maximum level possible. Could you examine the cost pictures on these sheets and hand to me any which approximate to your cost pattern?

[Hand respondent show cards 3.4(a) to 3.4(e)]

Underneath each picture you will find an explanation in words which you may prefer to use in making your choices. Please ask me if the pictures are not entirely clear.

[Pause for selection to take place. Retrieve selected sheets, and note below the selections made]

(a) [   ] (b) [   ] (c) [   ] (d) [   ] (e) [   ]

[Retrieve remaining sheets]

Part 4 (sales and competition)

Good. We are now half-way through. Next we will look at sales and competition. Questions will again refer to products in your main product group.

(WHITE)

4.1 Does your enterprise use market research methods of any kind, including forecasts by official bodies, trade associations etc.?

Yes [   ]
No [   ]

4.1.1 *If yes*: For what purposes are the results of market research used?
(a) To find out how important price changes are to customers [   ]
(b) To find out how interested buyers are in your products [   ]
(c) To find out the reaction of competitors [   ]
(d) To get an idea of future developments in the market [   ]

4.2 How would your sales react to a 5% price change, where it is assumed that your competitors do not react and that business conditions are normal? We will look at the consequences of a price cut and a price increase separately.

4.2.1 For a price *cut* of 5% the amount purchased would:
(a) Increase more than 5%
(b) Increase less than 5% [   ]
(c) Increase by approximately 5% [   ]
(d) Not increase at all [   ]
(e) Possibly increase, possibly not; one cannot say [   ]

4.2.2 For a price increase of 5% the amount purchased would:
(a) Fall more than 5%
(b) Fall less than 5% [   ]
(c) Fall by approximately 5% [   ]
(d) Not fall at all [   ]
(e) Possibly fall, possibly not; one cannot say [   ]

4.3 What about a 10% price change? Again let's assume normal business conditions and no reaction on the part of your competitors.

4.3.1 For a price *cut* of 10% the amount purchased would:
(a) Increase more than 10%
(b) Increase less than 10% [   ]
(c) Increase by approximately 10% [   ]
(d) Not increase at all [   ]
(e) Possibly increase, possibly not; one cannot say [   ]

4.3.2 For a price *increase* of 10% the amount purchased would:
(a) Fall more than 10%   [   ]
(b) Fall less than 10%   [   ]
(c) Fall by about 10%   [   ]
(d) Not fall at all   [   ]
(e) Possibly fall, possibly not; one cannot say   [   ]

4.4   If you *reduce* your price do you reckon that your strongest competitors will
      do the same and reduce their prices, first of all:

      4.4.1 In normal business conditions?

                                               Yes   [   ]
                                               No   [   ]
                                               Don't know   [   ]

      and now:

      4.4.2 In a boom?

                                               Yes   [   ]
                                               No   [   ]
                                               Don't know   [   ]

      and finally:

      4.4.3 In a recession?

                                               Yes   [   ]
                                               No   [   ]
                                               Don't know   [   ]

4.5   Do you reckon that your competitors would *raise* their prices if you *increased*
      your price, first of all:

      4.5.1 In normal business conditions?

                                               Yes   [   ]
                                               No   [   ]
                                               Don't know   [   ]

      and now:

      4.5.2 In a boom?

                                               Yes   [   ]
                                               No   [   ]
                                               Don't know   [   ]

      and finally:

      4.5.3 In a recession?

                                               Yes   [   ]
                                               No   [   ]
                                               Don't know   [   ]

4.6   Do you believe that you have a certain amount of 'elbow-room' in pricing,
      within which a price change by you does not bring about a reaction from
      competitors?

                                               Yes   [   ]
                                               No   [   ]
                                               Don't know   [   ]

4.6.1 *If yes*: How large is this 'elbow-room' in percentage terms?
(a) 1%
(b) 2–3%   [   ]
(c) 4–6%   [   ]
(d) 7–9%   [   ]
(e) 10–15%   [   ]
(f) More than 15%   [   ]
(g) Don't know   [   ]
                                                           [   ]

4.7 On this list various ways in which you can alter your selling price are mentioned. Tick any that apply to you.

[Hand over list 4.7. Pause to permit respondent to complete it. Retrieve list 4.7]

4.8 Do you ever sell at *different* prices goods which cost the *same*?

                                                    Yes [   ]
                                                    No   [   ]

4.8.1 *If yes*: Are these prices set:
(a) In different marketing areas
(b) In home and foreign markets   [   ]
(c) For different customers   [   ]
(d) For large and small traders   [   ]
(e) Other   [   ]
                                                           [   ]

If (e), please specify if possible.

4.9 Do you ever offer price rebates?

                                                    Yes [   ]
                                                    No   [   ]

4.9.1 *If yes*: Are rebates higher, the greater the amount purchased (that is, do you practise bulk discounting)?

                                                    Yes [   ]
                                                    No   [   ]

4.10 Are any of your goods sold at controlled prices?

                                                    Yes [   ]
                                                    No   [   ]

4.11 Are any of your goods sold at recommended prices?

                                                    Yes [   ]
                                                    No   [   ]

4.11.1 *If yes*: What percentage of your customers end up paying the recommended price?
(a) Less than 30%
(b) 31–60%   [   ]
(c) 61–80%   [   ]
(d) 81–90%   [   ]
(e) 91–100%   [   ]
(f) Don't know   [   ]
                                                           [   ]

4.12 Do you advertise?

Yes [   ]
No [   ]

4.12.1 *If yes*: What form does your advertising take?
(a) Generic advertising, that is, advertising aimed at expanding demand for all firms in the industry [   ]
(b) Individual advertising; that is, advertising aimed at promoting your product over that of rivals [   ]
(c) Both generic and individual advertising [   ]

4.13 Do you increase your advertising when business demand is low?

Yes   [   ]
No   [   ]
Don't know [   ]

4.14 Do you reduce your advertising when there is a boom?

Yes   [   ]
No   [   ]
Don't know [   ]

4.15 How would you describe competition in your market?
(a) Intense in every aspect (price, quality, rivalry, etc.) [   ]
(b) Generally strong, but weak in some aspects (for example, absence of price competition, but strong quality competition and inter-firm rivalry) [   ]
(c) Generally weak, but strong in some aspects [   ]
    [If (c) is ticked, go to 4.15.1 below]
(d) Generally weak in all its aspects [   ]

4.15.1 [To be answered if (c) is ticked in 4.15 above] In your market is the dominant form of competition by:
(a) Price [   ]
(b) Quality [   ]
(c) Sales [   ]
(d) Market Share [   ]
(e) Advertising [   ]
(f) Other [   ]
If (f), please specify:

Part 5 (finance)

Excellent. We have made very good progress. Now we turn to the last part of the questionnaire, on finance.

(WHITE)

5.1 Did you contact anyone for advice on how to get your business started?

Yes [   ]
No [   ]

If no: go to 5.2.

5.1.1 *If yes*: Who did you contact for advice on how to get your business started? On this list various sources of of advice are described.

[Hand respondent list 5.1.1]

Could you indicate with a tick any source which applied to you?

[Pause to permit completion of this]

5.1.1.1 Now could you please rank in order of importance the various alternatives, using the numbers on the right of the listed sources.

[Pause to permit completion. Retrieve list 5.1.1]

5.2 What was the *approximate* size of your business in terms of total assets (book value) when you started?

5.3 What is the *approximate* size of your business today in terms of total assets (book value)?

5.4 Did you find it difficult to obtain financial support for starting your business?

Yes [ ]
No [ ]

If no: Go to 5.5.

5.4.1 *If yes*: What were the obstacles in obtaining financial support? On this list please tick *all* those that apply.

[Hand over list 5.4.1, pause to permit its completion]

5.4.1.1 Now please rank the obstacles in order of importance by ringing the numbers on the right hand side. The most significant obstacle should have a '1' ringed, the second most significant a '2' ringed, and so on.

[Pause to permit completion. Retrieve list 5.4.1]

5.5 Did you use only personal finances to set up your business?

Yes [ ]
No [ ]

If yes: Go to 5.6.

5.5.1 *If no*: What other sources did you use? On this list, indicate with a tick any statement which is applicable to you.

[Hand over list 5.5.1 to respondent. Pause to permit its completion]

5.5.1.1 Now could you indicate the importance of these sources by ringing the numbers on the right-hand side. The most important should have a '1' ringed, the next most important a '2' ringed, and so on.

[Pause to permit completion. Retrieve list 5.5.1]

5.5.2 What sort of security did you have to provide in seeking funds? Tick any that apply on this list.

[Hand over list 5.5.2. Pause to permit its completion. Retrieve list 5.5.2]

5.6 *Gearing* is a technical term you may have come across which means debt (i.e. borrowing) divided by owners' injection of finance. So if you borrowed £10,000 and put in £20,000 yourself your gearing ratio would be 10,000 divided by 20,000; that is, one-half. What, approximately speaking, was your gearing ratio when you set up the business?

Enter gearing ratio figure:

5.6.1 What is your gearing ratio at present?

5.6.2 What has been your highest gearing ratio?

5.6.3 And what has been your lowest gearing ratio?

5.7 What do you expect to happen to your gearing ratio in the course of the next three years? Will it:

	Fall	*Rise*	*Stay the same*	*Don't know*
(a) After 1 year	[ ]	[ ]	[ ]	[ ]
(b) After 2 years	[ ]	[ ]	[ ]	[ ]
(c) After 3 years	[ ]	[ ]	[ ]	[ ]

[Fill in responses to a, b, c above in list 5.7.1 also]

5.7.1 Why do you expect your gearing ratio to behave the way you have indicated, over the next three years? Please tick all that apply on this list.

[Hand respondent list 5.7.1. Pause to permit its completion. Retrieve list 5.7.1]

5.8 Were the following special financial schemes necessary, helpful, or not applicable to the starting up of your business?

	Necessary	*Helpful*	*Not applicable*
(a) Enterprise allowance scheme	[ ]	[ ]	[ ]
(b) Employment grant	[ ]	[ ]	[ ]
(c) Investment grant	[ ]	[ ]	[ ]
(d) Reduced rental on premises	[ ]	[ ]	[ ]
(e) Special tax credits	[ ]	[ ]	[ ]
(f) Other	[ ]	[ ]	[ ]

If (f), please specify, if possible:

5.9 Have you ever had cash-flow difficulties?

Yes [   ]
No [   ]

If no: go to 5.10

5.9.1 *If yes*: What factors on this list contributed to your cash-flow difficulties? Please tick all those that apply.

[Hand respondent list 5.9.1. Pause to permit completion of it]

5.9.2 Indicate if possible the relative importance of these factors by ringing the numbers on the right-hand side. The most significant factor should be ranked as '1' the next most significant as '2' and so on.

[Pause to permit completion. Retrieve list 5.9.1]

5.10 Have you used external finance (for example debt) since starting your business?

Yes [ ]
No [ ]

If no: go to 5.11.

5.10.1 *If yes*: What were your reasons for wishing to increase your external finance? On this list, please tick any that apply.

[Hand respondent list 5.10.1. Pause to permit completion of list. Retrieve list 5.10.1]

5.11 Do you expect growth in your business over the foreseeable future?

Yes [ ]
No [ ]
Don't know [ ]

[Read the following to respondent]

That is the end of the questionnaire. Thank you for completing it. I hope you have also derived some interest yourself from doing so. Your time and co-operation are very much appreciated. Let me remind you that the strictest confidentiality will be upheld regarding the information you have provided about your business. If you should be interested in our general findings regarding the development of small businesses, we will be more than happy to share these results. We hope that our research will contribute to the success and growth of small businesses. We wish you all the very best with your firm.

Time interview completed:

Signature of interviewer:

(YELLOW)

List 1.12

Now I would like to look at the buying behaviour of your customers. Here is a list of possible descriptions of your customers. More than one may be applicable. Could you indicate with a tick *any* statement which applies to your customers.

(a) Technical differences between our products and those of our rivals are too small for our customers to distinguish. Price, brand, design, advertising intensity, packaging, and service all determine the customers' attitude. [ ]
(b) The customer is not technically minded but may have in mind a few technical features that the product should have. [ ]
(c) Before making a purchase, the customer needs to be informed on the technical features of a product, and is guided by such factual matters. [ ]
(d) The customer is fairly expert about the product concerned and can draw on personal experience as well as technical information available in specialist publications, trade journals etc. [ ]
(e) The customer is an expert and can determine by his own judgement the technical quality of the product. [ ]

Now go back and underline the statement that is most applicable.

(YELLOW)

List 2.2

How are prices within your main product group usually determined? One or more of the following statements may be applicable. Put a tick by *any* statement which is true for you.

(a) Price is made up of direct (i.e. prime, or variable) cost per unit plus a fixed percentage mark-up. The mark-up is set at a level designed to achieve a desired level of gross profit.   [   ]
(b) Price is based on direct (i.e. prime, or variable) cost per unit, as in (a) above, but the percentage mark-up is not fixed: it may be raised (or lowered) to increase gross profit.   [   ]
(c) Price is set at the highest level the market can bear.   [   ]
(d) Price is specified by your principal customer.   [   ]
(e) Price is determined by a regulatory agency.   [   ]
(f) Price is set at a statutory level.   [   ]
(g) Price is determined in other ways.   [   ]

If (g), please say how:

Now please underline the statement which is most applicable to you.

(YELLOW)

List 2.5

What action do you take when a boom in demand occurs and this demand cannot be met from stocks? Please tick any that apply:

(a) Increase overtime or shift work   [   ] 1 2 3 4 5 6 7
(b) Increase capacity (this could include the recruitment of more personnel)   [   ] 1 2 3 4 5 6 7
(c) Engage subcontractors   [   ] 1 2 3 4 5 6 7
(d) Buy up rival firms   [   ] 1 2 3 4 5 6 7
(e) Lengthen your order books   [   ] 1 2 3 4 5 6 7
(f) Raise price   [   ] 1 2 3 4 5 6 7
(g) Other   [   ] 1 2 3 4 5 6 7

If (g) please specify, if possible.

Indicate where possible the order in which you do things by ringing the numbers on the right-hand side, where ringing a '1' for any option would imply that this is what you would do first.

(YELLOW)

List 2.6

What action do you take in a recession? On this list, please tick those that apply:

(a) Reduce overtime   [   ] 1 2 3 4 5 6 7 8
(b) Introduce short-time working   [   ] 1 2 3 4 5 6 7 8
(c) Reduce capacity (including the laying-off of
    personnel)   [   ] 1 2 3 4 5 6 7 8
(d) Improve productivity or efficiency   [   ] 1 2 3 4 5 6 7 8
(e) Increase sales effort   [   ] 1 2 3 4 5 6 7 8
(f) Cut price   [   ] 1 2 3 4 5 6 7 8
(g) Reduce stockholding   [   ] 1 2 3 4 5 6 7 8
(h) Other   [   ] 1 2 3 4 5 6 7 8

If (h), please specify, if possible.

Now please indicate, where possible, the order in which you do things by ringing the numbers on the right-hand side, where ringing a '1' for any option would imply that this is what you would do first.

(YELLOW)

List 2.7

What action do you take if the demand falls for a particular product within your main product group? Please tick *any* that apply on this list:

(a) Switch to a new product   [   ] 1 2 3 4 5 6 7
(b) Reduce overtime   [   ] 1 2 3 4 5 6 7
(c) Introduce short-time working   [   ] 1 2 3 4 5 6 7
(d) Increase sales effort   [   ] 1 2 3 4 5 6 7
(e) Cut price   [   ] 1 2 3 4 5 6 7
(f) Increase quality   [   ] 1 2 3 4 5 6 7
(g) Other   [   ] 1 2 3 4 5 6 7

If (g), please specify, if possible.

Now please indicate, where possible, the order in which you do things by ringing the numbers on the right-hand side, where ringing a '1' for any option would imply that this is what you would do first.

(YELLOW)

List 4.7

On this list, events which might lead you to alter your selling price are mentioned. Which options on this list refer to you?

(a) When a new business year (or new season of production) commences   [   ]
(b) When a new tax year commences   [   ]
(c) When cost changes occur   [   ]
(d) When demand shifts substantially   [   ]

(e) When demand changes   [   ]
(f) When a regulatory agency permits an increase   [   ]
(g) When wage bargaining negotiations in the firm or in the industry
    have been concluded   [   ]
(h) When the most important competition changes price   [   ]
(i) Other   [   ]

If (i), specify if possible:

(YELLOW)

List 5.1.1

Who did you contact for advice on how to get your business started? On this list, indicate with a tick any source which applies to you:

(a) Family and/or friends   [   ] 1 2 3 4 5 6 7
(b) Bank manager   [   ] 1 2 3 4 5 6 7
(c) Accountant   [   ] 1 2 3 4 5 6 7
(d) Enterprise trust   [   ] 1 2 3 4 5 6 7
(e) Scottish Development Agency (SDA)   [   ] 1 2 3 4 5 6 7
(f) Local government authority   [   ] 1 2 3 4 5 6 7
(g) Other   [   ] 1 2 3 4 5 6 7

If (g), please specify:

Now please indicate, where possible, the relative importance of these various alternative contacts for advice by ringing the numbers on the right-hand side. The most important should have a '1' ringed, the second most important a '2' ringed, and so on.

(YELLOW)

List 5.4.1

What were the obstacles in obtaining financial support? Put a tick by any statement which is true for you.

(a) Lack of personal financial injections   [   ] 1 2 3 4 5 6
(b) Establishing the idea that a market existed for your
    products   [   ] 1 2 3 4 5 6
(c) Lack of success in previous business venture(s)   [   ] 1 2 3 4 5 6
(d) Difficulty in producing satisfactory financial statements
    of proposed business (for example, a projected cash
    flow budget)   [   ] 1 2 3 4 5 6
(e) Previous employment experience   [   ] 1 2 3 4 5 6
(f) Other   [   ] 1 2 3 4 5 6

If (f), please specify:

Now indicate, if possible, the extent of the various obstacles by ringing the numbers on the right-hand side. The biggest obstacle should have a '1' ringed, the second biggest a '2' ringed, and so on.

(YELLOW)

List 5.5.1

What sources of finance, apart from personal finance, did you use in setting up your business? On this list, indicate with a tick any statement which applies to you.

(a) Borrowing from friends, relatives or acquaintances   [   ] 1 2 3 4 5 6
(b) Borrowing from banks   [   ] 1 2 3 4 5 6
(c) Hire-purchase   [   ] 1 2 3 4 5 6
(d) Leasing   [   ] 1 2 3 4 5 6
(e) Equity finance   [   ] 1 2 3 4 5 6
(f) Other   [   ] 1 2 3 4 5 6

If (f) please specify, if possible.

Now please indicate, where possible, the importance of these various alternative sources of finance by ringing the numbers on the right-hand side. The most important should have a '1' ringed, the second most important a '2' ringed and so on.

(YELLOW)

List 5.5.2

What sort of security did you have to provide in seeking funds? Tick any that apply on this list.

(a) Personal guarantee (implying a liability to repay loans)   [   ]
(b) Life policies   [   ]
(c) Guarantors   [   ]
(d) Stock exchange securities   [   ]
(e) Heritable securities (for example, home, property, premises, land)   [   ]
(f) Floating charges (i.e. securities on plant, equipment, stocks, etc.)   [   ]
(g) Other   [   ]

If (g), please specify if possible:

(YELLOW)

List 5.7.1

In the question which we have been considering you indicated that your gearing ratio would behave as follows in the course of the next three years:

	Fall	*Rise*	*Stay the same*	*Don't know*
(a) After 1 year	[ ]	[ ]	[ ]	[ ]
(b) After 2 years	[ ]	[ ]	[ ]	[ ]
(c) After 3 years	[ ]	[ ]	[ ]	[ ]

Why do you expect your gearing ratio to behave like this? Please tick any that apply:

	After 1 year	After 2 years	After 3 years
(a) An increase in ploughed-back profits	[ ]	[ ]	[ ]
(b) An increase in owners' injections	[ ]	[ ]	[ ]
(c) An increase in debt (i.e. borrowing)	[ ]	[ ]	[ ]
(d) Running at a loss	[ ]	[ ]	[ ]
(e) A reduction in debt (i.e. borrowing)	[ ]	[ ]	[ ]
(f) No certain answer	[ ]	[ ]	[ ]
(g) Other	[ ]	[ ]	[ ]

If (g), please specify, if possible.

List 5.9.1

What factors contributed to your cash-flow difficulties? Please tick any that apply:

(a) Delinquent debtors   [   ] 1 2 3 4 5 6 7
(b) Delinquent suppliers   [   ] 1 2 3 4 5 6 7
(c) Overinvestment (for example in stock or capital
  goods)   [   ] 1 2 3 4 5 6 7
(d) Inadequate credit policy with buyers   [   ] 1 2 3 4 5 6 7
(e) Inadequate credit policy with suppliers   [   ] 1 2 3 4 5 6 7
(f) Insufficient overdraft facility   [   ] 1 2 3 4 5 6 7
(g) Other   [   ] 1 2 3 4 5 6 7

If (g), please specify if possible:

Now indicate, if possible, the relative importance of these factors by ringing the numbers on the right-hand side. The most significant should be ranked '1', the next most significant '2', and so on.

(YELLOW)

List 5.10.1

What were your reasons for wishing to increase your external finance? On this list, please tick any that apply.

(a) New or expanded premises   [   ]
(b) Purchase of plant or equipment   [   ]
(c) Increased stock or inventory   [   ]
(d) Hiring of new employees   [   ]
(e) Cash flow problems   [   ]
(f) Other   [   ]

If (f), please specify if possible.

(PINK)

Show card 3.4(a)

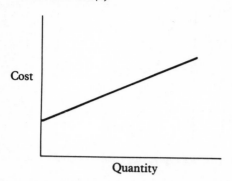

(a) Total cost increases in line with amount supplied, i.e. for each extra unit supplied, your cost rises by the same amount.

Show card 3.4(b)

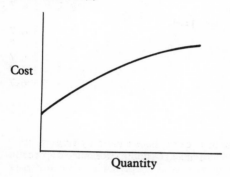

(b) Total cost does not increase as fast as amount supplied, i.e. the extra cost of supplying each additional unit falls as more is supplied.

Show card 3.4(c)

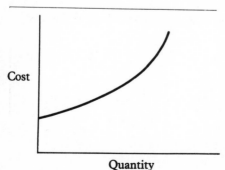

(c) Total cost increases faster than supply, i.e. each extra unit supplied adds more to cost than the last unit supplied.

Show card 3.4(d)

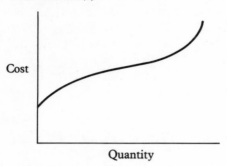

(d) At first total cost does not increase as fast as supply, but then it increases faster than supply.

Show card 3.4(e)

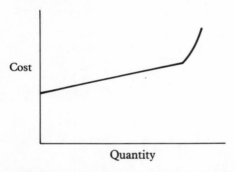

(e) Total cost increases in line with supply until the maximum possible supply (full capacity) is reached. After this point, the extra cost of supplying another unit rises sharply.

SEMI-STRUCTURED INTERVIEW SCHEDULE (SSI 1985)

FRONTPIECE

Semi-structured interview agenda

Name of interviewer:..

Interviewee code: ....

Date of interview:..

Time interview started:..

PRE-AMBLE

[The content of this pre-amble should be explained to the interviewee]

Pre-amble

Thank you for agreeing to this further interview. The same basis of strict confidentiality continues to apply. Last time the interview was concerned with very specific questions which could be answered by 'yes' or 'no', by ticking alternatives, by ranking options, etc. Today, the approach is less structured. I have a number of areas which I would like to look at with you, all of which are concerned with general aspects of *business strategy*.

Strategy involves adapting the capabilities and resources of your firm to the opportunities in its market environment. We will explore strategy in terms of a list of headings, or agenda, and this outline should help to give you a general idea of how the interview will proceed.

[Hand respondent the agenda outline overleaf]

(WHITE)   AGENDA OUTLINE: RESPONDENT'S COPY

Agenda outline

1   *Competitive forces*
1.1   Rivalry
1.2   Customers
1.2.1 Bargaining leverage of customers
1.2.2 Price sensitivity of customers
1.3   Suppliers
1.4   Potential entrants
1.5   Substitutes

2   *Competitive strategy*
2.1   Cost leadership
2.2   Differentiation
2.3   Focus

3   *Defensive strategy*
3.1   Increasing barriers to entry
3.2   Increasing retaliation which challengers can expect
3.3   Lowering the inducement for attack
3.4   Deterrence
3.5   Responding to attack

(WHITE)   AGENDA OUTLINE: INTERVIEWER'S COPY

Agenda outline

1   *Competitive forces*
1.1   Rivalry
1.2   Customers
1.2.1 Bargaining leverage of customers
1.2.2 Price sensitivity of customers
1.3   Suppliers
1.4   Potential entrants
1.5   Substitutes

2   *Competitive strategy*
2.1   Cost leadership
2.2   Differentiation
2.3   Focus

3   *Defensive strategy*
3.1   Increasing barriers to entry
3.2   Increasing retaliation which challengers can expect
3.3   Lowering the inducement for attack
3.4   Deterrence
3.5   Responding to attack

(BLUE)

1 *Competitive forces*
　1.1 Rivalry

　　Probe on:

　　Industry concentration and balance
　　Industry growth
　　Fixed costs relative to value added
　　Intermittent overcapacity
　　Extent of product differentiation
　　Diversity of competitors
　　Level of strategic stakes
　　Entry and exit barriers

Field notes:

Summary note:

(BLUE)   COMPETITIVE FORCES

1.2 Customers
   1.2.1 Bargaining leverage of customers

      Probe on:

      Customers' concentration
      Seller dependence
      Relative buyer volume
      Customers' switching costs
      Ability to backward integrate
      Extent of customers' information

Field notes:

Summary note:

(BLUE)

1.2.2 Price sensitivity of customers

Probe on:

Significance of costs in relation to total costs of customers
Extent of differentiation of products purchased
Profitability
Bearing of your product on customers' product quality
Motivation of customer

Field notes:

Summary note:

(BLUE)   COMPETITIVE FORCES

1.3 Suppliers

Probe on:

Extent of suppliers' concentration
Suppliers' in relation to customers' concentration
Availability of substitutes
Significance of suppliers' product as a customer's input
Extent of differentiation of supplier group's products
Switching costs of customers as compared with suppliers
Ability to forward integrate

Field notes:

Summary note:

(BLUE)

1.4 Potential entrants

Probe on:

Economies of scale
Product differentiation
Capital requirements
Switching costs
Access to distribution channels
Absolute cost advantages including:
- product know-how or design characteristics
- favourable access to inputs
- favourable location
- government subsidies
- learning or experience curve
Government policy (regulation, pollution control etc.)
Expected retaliation
Entry deterring price

Field notes:

Summary note:

(BLUE)   COMPETITIVE FORCES

1.5 Substitutes

Probe on:

Products that perform the same function as industry's
Relative value/price of substitutes
Substitutes produced by high profit industries
Collective industry response to substitutes
Customers' propensity to substitute

Field notes:

Summary note:

(YELLOW)

2 *Competitive strategy*
  2.1 Cost leadership

  Probe on:

  Value chain and assignment of costs and assets
  Cost drivers and their interaction
  Competitors' value chain
  Relative costs of competitors and their sources
  Strategies to lower relative costs including:
  - control of cost drivers
  - reconfiguration of value chain
  - reconfiguration of downstream value
  Trade-off between differentiation and cost reduction
  Sustainability of cost reduction strategy

Field notes:

Summary note:

(YELLOW)   COMPETITIVE STRATEGY

2.2 Differentiation

Probe on:

Identification of real customer
Identification of customers' value chain
Customers' purchasing criteria
Existing and potential sources of uniqueness in firm's value chain
Identification of existing and potential sources of differentiation
Value activities that create the most valuable differentiation for customers
(relative to costs of differentiating)
Sustainability of differentiation strategy
Cost reduction in activities that do not affect differentiation

Field notes:

Summary note:

(YELLOW)

2.3 Focus

Probe on:

Whether strategy is toward cost or differentiation focus, or both
Strategically relevant segments including:
- product variety
- customer type
- channel (i.e. immediate buyer)
- customer location

Significance of chosen segment(s) for competitive advantage
Interrelations among segments
Sustainability of focus against:
- broadly targeted competitors
- imitators
- segment substitution

Field notes:

Summary note:

(PINK)   DEFENSIVE STRATEGY

3 *Defensive strategy*
  3.1 Increasing barriers to entry

   Probe on:

   Filling product gaps
   Blocking channel access
   Raising customers' switching costs
   Raising costs of product trial
   Defensively increasing scale economies
   Defensively increasing capital requirements
   Foreclosing alternative technologies
   Tying up suppliers
   Raising costs of competitors' inputs
   Defensively pursuing interrelationships with other firms
   Encouraging government or agency policies that raise barriers
   Forming coalitions to raise barriers
   Forming coalitions to co-opt challengers

Field notes:

Summary notes:

(PINK)   DEFENSIVE STRATEGY

3.2 Increasing retaliation which challengers can expect

Probe on:

Signalling commitment to defend
Signalling erection of barriers
Establishing blocking positions
Matching guarantees
Raising own penalty of exit or of loss of market share
Accumulating retaliatory resources
Encouraging 'good' competitors
Setting examples
Establishing defensive coalitions

Field notes:

Summary note:

(PINK)   DEFENSIVE STRATEGY

3.3 Lowering the inducement for attack

   Probe on:

   Reducing profit targets
   Managing competitors' assumptions

Field notes:

Summary note:

(PINK)   DEFENSIVE STRATEGY

3.4 Deterrence

Probe on:

Choosing defensive tactics to block likely attacks
Managing the firm's image as a tough defender
Setting realistic profit expectations
Using industry scenarios to examine deterrence possibilities
Knowledge of specific sources of barriers
Anticipation of likely challengers (especially dissatisfied competitors)
Forecasting likely avenues of attack

Field notes:

Summary note:

(PINK)   DEFENSIVE STRATEGY

3.5 Responding to attack

Probe on:

Putting priority on early response
Investing in early discovery of moves by:
- contact with suppliers
- contact with advertising media
- monitoring of attendance at trade shows
- contact with most adventurous customers in industry
- monitoring of technical conferences, college courses etc.

Basing response on reasons for attack
Deflecting challengers
Taking challengers seriously
Viewing response as a way to gain position
Disrupting test or introductory markets
Leapfrogging with new product or process
Litigation (for example, patent, anti-trust suits)

Field notes:

Summary note:

(WHITE)   END

Time interview completed: ....

Signature of interviewer: ....

REINTERVIEW SCHEDULE OF 1988 (RIQ 1988)

(WHITE)

Name of interviewer ....

Date of interview ....

Time interview started ....

Firm code number..

[You should start your interview with something like the following pre-amble]

Thank you for agreeing to this interview. This is a follow-up study on the interview we first conducted in 1985. It is most helpful of you to have agreed to this meeting. As before, we should emphasise that this study is for purely academic purposes. The identity of your firm is not relevant to the study, and it will not be revealed. Our purpose is to do two things. First, to complete items of data for 1985 which are best gathered retrospectively. Second, to gather new information on issues which have since become important.

(WHITE)

Part 1: identity of firm and owner-manager

1 Is the firm you ran in 1985, when we interviewed you about your business, still trading?

Yes [   ]
No [   ]

   1.1 *If no* when did it stop trading:

2 Do you still run the same firm that you ran in 1985 at the time of interview?

Yes [   ]
No [   ]

[*If no* go to 2.1]

2.1 What happened to your firm? Please tick the appropriate option on this list, or provide a further comment if relevant.

[Hand respondent list 2.1. Pause for completion. Retrieve list 2.1]

2.2 You have said you no longer run the business you were running in 1985 at the time of being interviewed. What do you do now? Could you tick the appropriate option on this list, or provide further comment if necessary.

[Hand respondent list 2.2. Pause for completion. Retrieve list 2.2]

(WHITE)

Part 2: characteristics of 1985 business

If you no longer run your 1985 business you may still be able to answer many of the following questions. Could you answer those that you can manage even if your answers are very approximate?

As I mentioned on the telephone, you may find it useful to refer to your figures for 1985 in answering some of these questions.

3 What was your firm's *net* profit in 1985, approximately speaking? You may give a range or a roughly rounded figure if you wish. Your estimate should be net of taxes and directors' fees.

[Enter net profit figure here:...... If hesitation, say: If you cannot provide this figure now, perhaps we could contact you later about this.]

4 Your net profitability is your net profit divided by the book value of your assets. What was your net profitability in 1985? You may give a range or a roughly rounded figure if you wish.

[Enter net profitability figure here:...... If hesitation, say: If you cannot provide this figure now, perhaps we could contact you later about this.]

5 Has there been a change in competitiveness due to innovation in your principal market since 1985?
Yes [   ]   *If yes* go to 5.1
No   [   ]   *If no* go to 6

5.1 Was the innovation undertaken by you or by a rival?

By own firm [   ]
By rival firm [   ]
By both   [   ]

5.1.1 Was the innovation undertaken by one of the largest firms in your market (which might include yourself)?
Yes [   ]
No   [   ]

6 What is the *current* size of the firm you ran in 1985? We are interested in five possible measures of size. You may give approximate figures or ranges if you wish.

Current size:
(a) In terms of sales turnover (excluding VAT):
(b) In terms of full-time employees:
(c) In terms of full-time plus part-time employees:
(d) In terms of full- and part-time employees plus trainees:
(e) In terms of total assets (book value, net of depreciation):

7 Has the output of your *main product line* changed substantially (say, more than 20 per cent) since 1985?

Yes [   ]   *If yes* go to 7.1
No [   ]   *If no* go to 7.2

[Here output refers to a good or service]

  7.1 By what percentage has output changed since 1985? You may give a range or an approximate figure.

    [Put a + for an increase, − for a decrease]

    7.1.1 What has been the corresponding percentage change in your unit variable cost?

      [We are interested here in cost per unit of the service or good. The relevant cost is *variable* and shifts with output, as distinct from *fixed* or *overhead* which does not]

      [Put a + for an increase, − for a decrease]

  7.2 Has your output *mix* (the proportion one output bears to another) changed substantially since 1985?

    Yes [   ]   *If yes* go to 7.2.1
    No [   ]   *If no* go to 8

    7.2.1 How has the importance of your *main product line* changed since 1985 in terms of proportion of value of total sales?

    [Enter the percentage change with + for increase and − for decrease]

8 Since 1985 has your firm experienced a shortage of any type of skilled labour

Yes [   ]   *If yes* go to 8.1
No [   ]   *If no* go to 9

  8.1 For your 1985 firm, has this shortage of skilled labour:

    (a) Impeded the growth of your firm   [ ]
    (b) Caused a contraction of your firm   [ ]
    (c) Had no effect on your firm's growth   [ ]

  8.2 Faced with a shortage of skilled labour, what difficulties arose in trying to fill this 'skill gap'? This list indicates potential difficulties.

    [Hand respondent list 8.2]

    On this list could you please indicate which difficulties were relevant to you by putting a tick in the appropriate box? Then could you rank these difficulties in order of importance, giving a rank of 1 to the most important, of 2 to the next most important and so on.

[Pause for completion of list 8.2. Retrieve list 8.2]

9 We turn now to aspects of financial structure. When you were interviewed in 1985 we asked you about the *equity gearing* (or more simply the *gearing*) of your firm. Gearing means debt (i.e. borrowing) divided by owner's injection of finance. So if you borrowed £10,000 and put in £20,000 yourself, your gearing ratio would be 10,000 divided by 20,000, that is, it would be one half or 0.5. What, approximately, is your *current* gearing ratio?

[Enter gearing ratio figures]

[A range may be given]

10 We should now like to know what has happened to your gearing ratio since you were last interviewed in 1985. Could you tick the appropriate boxes on this sheet.

[Hand over list 10. Pause for completion. Retrieve list 10]

11 Finally, you will have heard through the media like television, radio, and newspapers that we are becoming an 'enterprise culture'. Since 1985, have you had a sense of the emergence of such a culture in Scotland?

Yes [   ]
No   [   ]

11.1 If respondent says more about this jot down further comments:

[Record briefly interviewee's remarks after leaving site]

This is the end of the interview. Thank you very much for co-operating. We wish you well in your business.

Time for concluding interview ....

Interviewer's signature ....

(YELLOW)

List 2.1

What happened to the firm you were running when last interviewed in 1985? Please tick the appropriate option on this list

(a) The firm was voluntarily wound-up   [   ]
(b) The firm was wound up under pressure   [   ]
(c) The firm was compulsorily wound-up   [   ]
(d) The firm was bought up by a rival   [   ]
(e) The firm was bought up by a newcomer   [   ]
(f) The firm was bought out by business associates   [   ]
(g) The firm was bought out by employees   [   ]
(h) Other. Please specify briefly in the space below, if possible   [   ]

(YELLOW)

List 2.2

You have said you no longer run the business you were running in 1985 at the time of being interviewed. What do you do now? Could you tick the appropriate option on this list, or provide a further comment if necessary.

Do you now:

(a) Run your own new, and similar, business   [   ]
(b) Run your own new, and different, business   [   ]
(c) Work as a waged or salaried employee   [   ]
(d) Draw unemployment benefit or social security   [   ]
(e) Draw a pension and/or retirement benefit   [   ]
(f) Study on a college or university course   [   ]
(g) Stay at home as a housewife or househusband   [   ]
(h) Live off private income (for example, rent, dividends)   [   ]
(i) Other. Please specify briefly in the space below if possible.   [   ]

(YELLOW)

List 8.2

What difficulties arose in trying to fill this 'skill gap'? Was the difficulty in:

(a) Releasing personnel for training   [   ] 1 2 3 4 5 6
(b) Affording the training cost   [   ] 1 2 3 4 5 6
(c) Identifying the skills required   [   ] 1 2 3 4 5 6
(d) Assessing your competitors' relative skill
    advantage/disadvantage   [   ] 1 2 3 4 5 6
(e) Paying premium rates for scarce skills   [   ] 1 2 3 4 5 6
(f) Other   [   ] 1 2 3 4 5 6

Please indicate with a tick any difficulty that applied to you.

If (f) please specify briefly below:

If no difficulty was experienced in filling skill gap please tick here   [   ]

Now please indicate, where possible, the relative importance of these difficulties. The most important difficulty should have a '1' ringed, the second most important a '2' ringed and so on.

(YELLOW)

List 10

What has happened to your gearing ratio (i.e. debt divided by equity) since you were interviewed in 1985?

Did it:

	Fall	*Rise*	*Stay the same*	*Don't know*
(a) In 1986	[ ]	[ ]	[ ]	[ ]
(b) In 1987	[ ]	[ ]	[ ]	[ ]
(c) In 1988	[ ]	[ ]	[ ]	[ ]

[Tick appropriate box]

If you cannot remember exactly, this does not matter; give me your hunch.
Interpret 'In 1988' in (c) as meaning 'so far this year'.

Notes

1 ANALYSING THE SMALL BUSINESS ENTERPRISE

1 It is based on the software developed at the University of Wisconsin, SIR/DBMS. Relational database techniques and methods are developed in Everest (1986), Paredaens (1987).

2 As expanded in Porter (1980, 1983, 1985).

3 Reported in an article by Alan Forbes in *The Scotsman* newspaper, 26 November 1987. ScotBIC was recently re-named SBC, and has John Moorhouse as its new director. Mr Moorhouse has been an invaluable source of intelligence on SBEs.

4 The title of an exhibition held in Edinburgh at the Royal Scottish Academy in August and September of 1986, and the basis of the volume *The Enterprising Scot* edited by Jenni Calder (1986).

5 The title of a new statutory framework, heralded in by *Scottish Enterprise* (1988), for enterprise stimulation in Scotland.

6 See Reid (1990a) for an illustration of this point using rankings data applied to, for example, evidence on the importance of the source of advice at the financial inception of the SBE. These methods are further applied in part II (chapter 5) of this book (pages 70–9).

7 Paper read to the Cambridge Moral Science Club, 17 November 1875. See Whitaker (1975, vol. 2).

8 See Whitaker (1975, vol. 2: 55).

9 Development economics has been an exception to this general rule, though even in this subject area economists frequently seem unaware of the need for a field research methodology.

10 See Burgess (1984) for a discussion of the various methodologies and Burgess (ed.) (1982) for many examples drawn from a variety of disciplines. Concerning the last-named method, that of document collection, field research is principally directed towards primary source material, though secondary source material might also be used. Relevant documents include life history data, auto-biographies, diaries and diary interviews, and letters.

11 See Burgess (1984: 48).

12 Ph.D. student, University of Edinburgh, 1983–86. Currently Associate Professor, William Jewell College, Liberty, Missouri.

13 See Frey (1983: 92–3) on the design of preletters.

14 An 83 per cent response rate was obtained, as contrasted with the 62 per cent response rate in the study by Boswell *The Rise and Decline of Small Firms* (1973), and the generally much lower response rates (30 per cent or less) which are typical of postal questionnaires.

15 If one reallocates 17 percentage points from SIC 49 to the other 17 SICs, giving each SIC one further point, there is a similarity between sample and population which is good in most cases, but poor for metal and non-metal extraction and manufactures, mechanical engineering, electrical and electronic engineering, and textiles.

16 Note that over this period the threshold for VAT registrations was also raised.

2 THE SMALL FIRMS RELATIONAL DATABASE

1 Here I simply illustrate, using aspects of the framework of Porter (1980, 1985). It will be explained in greater detail in part III.

2, 3 For further detail on flat files and their use in relational databases, see the contribution by Lorie (1987) in Paredaens (1987: chapter 2).

4 The traditional focus in database management has been on data structures which are hierarchical, network, or relational in form. See Everest (1986: chapter 4) for a detailed statement of this taxonomy, and criticisms thereof.

5 A reduced rank is defined as the raw rank less the mean rank.

6 See, for example, Jahoda et al. (1964).

7 In the sense that assets in 1985 and profits in 1985 (as reported in 1988) were both well-defined balance sheet figures, whereas profitability in 1985 (as reported in 1988) involved a judgement, or a mental calculation (or 'guestimate') and perhaps even an element of wishful thinking.

8 For example, Lorie (1987: 46) in Paredaens (1987: chapter 2).

9 In Everest the following definition is given: 'A single flat file consists of a set of attributes which describes entities from a single entity class. Each attribute in a flat file structure contains only one value instance for each entity instance' (Everest 1986: 149). To illustrate, the entity class in my case is the small business enterprise, and an entity is an SBE. The set of attributes which describes entities include sales, date of financial inception, profits, and the debt/equity ratio. There is only one value of sales, profit, etc. for each SBE. A flat file could therefore be a cross-classificaton of profits and sales.

10 See Everest (1986: 43–5).

11 See Frank (1984: chapter 13), Paredaens (ed.) (1987: chapter 2) for general features; and for extensive treatment of its implementations see the *SIR/Light Manual* (1987: chapter 4), which is a compact manual of the proprietory database management system SIR/DBMS.

12 Database design and implementation were provided with the assistance of Julian Read and Sandra Rice.

13 Here type 4 records were accessed (i.e. level 4 of the database). In view of the textual nature of the data the DBMS facility of the SIR database software was used.

14 Again, given the textual nature of the agenda and probes data, retrieval was achieved through the DBMS facility of the SIR database software.

3 THE TYPICAL SMALL BUSINESS ENTERPRISE

1 The idea is therefore related to that of the Marshallian 'representative firm' as explained in Reid (1987: chapter 5). However, in Marshall an intra-industry average is used, whereas here I am using an inter-industry average.

2 As in, for example, chapter 9 below, where econometric predictors of survival of the SBE over a three-year time horizon are developed, using binary probit analysis.

3 It should be noted that there is no unique way of characterizing such rankings. The methods of constructing typical or model rankings is a technical issue which was first discussed in this context by Reid (1990a). Further details are given below, in the appendix to chapter 5.

4 Since 1989 the Scottish Development Agency (SDA) has been dissolved, in a formal sense, under the new Scottish Enterprise arrangements. However, much of the personnel remained within the system, and the organizational continuity has been greater than might have been expected from the new labels.

5 In reality, its actual gearing will rise to a magnitude of about 1.5 some three years further on (i.e. about six years from financial inception).

6 In using cross-section models, one should not be put off by R^2 of 0.1741 as in (3.4). It may seem low compared to R^2 values of 0.99, 0.95 and the like that one readily gets with time series analysis. However, the latter figures are more likely to be symptomatic of an over-fitted model, than of powerful confirmation of a theory. One has to be sanguine with cross-section analysis, and guided by probability values, as here.

4 COST CURVES AND SCALE ECONOMIES

1 Further details on the sample are given in Reid and Jacobsen (1988). The field work method is justified in Reid (1987a) and its design is explicated in Reid (1987b). See also part I of this book.

2 As surveyed and summarized in Koutsoyiannis (1979: chapter 4), or Hay and Morris (1991: chapter 2), for example.

3 In trimmed least squares, outliers are dropped to investigate the robustness of the regression coefficient estimates. For quantiles α and $(1 - \alpha)$, estimators $\beta(\alpha)$ and $\beta(1 - \alpha)$ are constructed with observations for which $y - x\beta(\alpha) \leqslant 0$ and $y - x\beta(1 - \alpha) \geqslant 0$ being dropped; where here y is a vector of measurements on an endogenous variable, x is a matrix of measurements on a set of exogenous variables and β is a conformable vector of regression coefficients, one for each of the exogenous variables. In this chapter, I report on the case of $\alpha = 0.05$.

4 This argument was originally associated with the writings of Robinson (1934) and Kaldor (1934). It may be given contemporary expression, as applied to the small entrepreneurial firm, by application of a markets and bureaucracies approach. See Reid and Jacobsen (1988: chapter 2).

5 RANKINGS DATA ON FINANCIAL INCEPTION

1 In comparing these examples, note that who one consults first does not necessarily indicate which source of advice is most valuable. Thus, friends might be consulted first, because that is the natural thing to do, or because they are highly accessible, but not necessarily because they are likely to be the best source of advice.

2 These questions were designed by Jacobsen (1986). The relevant questions in the appendix of this book are given in list 5.1.1, list 5.4.1, list 5.5.1, and list 5.9.1 of the AQ 1985.

3 Pilot interviews suggested that these categories could be important. In practice, these extra categories had null responses in the main study.

4 Of the thirty-one owner-managers admitting to difficulties in obtaining financial support for their businesses, eighteen nominated only one reason for this. Typically, this was either option (b) (establishing the idea that a market existed for the product) which was the one and only option checked by eight firms; or

option (a) (lack of personal financial injections) which was the one and only option checked by six firms. In economic terms, these data are highly informative, for they suggest that a lack of convincing market research or a lack of personal financial injections were cardinal reasons for not obtaining finance. This view is substantiated by the fact that a further seven owner-managers ranked obsacles (b) and (a) as 'first or second' in order of importance over other obstacles to obtaining financial support.

5 See Reid and Anderson (1992) for further confirmation of this, and a down-playing of venture capital involvement for firms of this size.

6 For example, considering the ADVICE variable, one has guidance on what the policy priorities should be in allocating future resources to institutions like Enterprise Trusts as compared to local authorities, when it comes to enterprise stimulation.

7 The reason for introducing the parameter $m' < m$ is that if only one action is nominated, and one adopts the alternative interpretation that no other actions were relevant, then the owner-manager has not in a sense specified a rank, as nothing is being compared to the nominated choice. This consideration is relevant to the forms of the Prentice and Benard-Van Elteren tests considered later in this section.

8 As compared to the values of F reported in Reid and Jacobsen (1988), which were hand computed, the values reported here were done by computer programme. This accounts for some discrepancy in the reported statistics, though no inferences are thereby affected. Computer programming for the statistics reported upon here were undertaken by Karen Chan, to whom the author is grateful.

9 Assigning mid-ranks artificially makes rankings complete (in the sense of no unranked actions or options) so that the Friedman test can be applied. However, it also artificially introduces ties in ranks, which require a correction to the Friedman statistic, as mentioned in the appendix to this chapter (page 78). The corrections for ties formula, T, is given by

$$T = \frac{1}{n-1} \sum [n - k_i)^3 - (n - k_i)]$$

where $(n - k_i)$ is the number of unranked actions. This T is deducted from the denominator of formula (5.4) of this chapter's appendix, to give the Friedman statistic corrected for ties (F'). Of course, the use of the symbol F for Friedman's statistic, which is used exclusively in this chapter, is not to be confused with Snedecor's F, as generally used in statistical inference, and indeed as used elsewhere in this book.

10 I refer here to the method of Tate (1961). It seeks a particular ordering, around which others tend to cluster. This might then be regarded as a 'true' ordering. His method computes a statistic for measuring the 'support' which the data give to any candidate for being the 'true' ordering. The support statistic ϕ for a particular trial is given by:

$$\phi = 2H + \tfrac{1}{2}(D^2 - n^2)$$

where for a single trial H is the number of times an element of a subset is numerically less than an element of a succeeding subset, and D^2 is the sum of squares of all subset sizes. The total support (Φ) all trials $\Phi = \Sigma \phi$ is asymptotically normally distributed and a test of the null hypothesis ('randomness') against appropriate alternatives is consistent and unbiased. The null hypothesis of randomness is, more precisely, that all $n!$ permutations of the n actions are equally likely. If Φ is computed for all $n!$ permutations of orders, a best candidate for the role of the 'true' order can be identified as the order having the greatest Φ value. Proceeding in this way, the Tate 'true' orderings can be computed. The numbers of orderings tested were 362880, 5040, 5040 and 720 for the variables ADVICE, CFP, EXTFIN, and OBST, respectively. Three comments should be made on the above. First, the computational costs are high. For example, for the ADVICE variable, involving nine rankings, computation of the total support statistic Φ took 5400 seconds of CPU time on an Amdahl 470 V.7 in 1988. Depending on one's current computing facilities, this method would generally still be computationally burdensome. Second, the support statistic Φ does not generally give a unique 'true' ordering. For example, for both the CFP and OBST variables four candidates for 'true' ordering were suggested by the Tate method. Third, the results indicated by the Tate method generally accorded well with the (unique) results obtained by simply using column rank-sums (R_j). For example, the two candidates for the 'true' ordering for the EXTFIN variable, using the Tate method, were b, a, c, d, f, e, g and b, a, c, f, d, e, g. They differ little (only d and f reversed) in themselves, and little from the ranking (given in table 5.3) by the rank-sum method of b, a, c, f, d, e, g. Indeed, the latter is one of the candidates for 'true' ranking suggested by the Tate method. Further details on this are available in Reid (1988).

11 This is seen by comparing m (actual sample size) with m' (the effective sample size). For the variable OBST, for example, one has $m = 31$ and $m' = 13$.

7 COMPETITIVE AND DEFENSIVE STRATEGIES

1 These are seven out of ten survivors of an initial field sample of thirteen firms. The survival rate of 77 per cent is in line with that reported for the main sample in the probit analysis of survival in chapter 9 below. I have further information for the three out of ten survivors not discussed in this chapter. Unfortunately, these data, whilst interesting, are incomplete and fragmentary, and therefore cannot be a satisfactory part of the sort of cross-site analysis being conducted here and in chapter 8. Whilst I have with regret, therefore, excluded these three cases from systematic analysis, they have no doubt influenced my views on the characteristics and behaviour of SBEs in an indirect and subtle way. The firms omitted for incompleteness of data were in manufactures (bespoke fibre glass products), distribution (hospital supplies) and business services (microcomputer systems). It is known that three years after the conclusion of data gathering, these SBEs were still in business.

2 Firm F produced camera-ready artwork and (as in figure 6.1 of chapter 6 above) was categorized under 'printing and publishing' (SIC 47). This would put it, nominally, into the manufacturing category (see table 1.3 of chapter 1 above). However, it is clear that many aspects of Firm F's activities could be seen as lying within a services category, most especially that of business services (SIC 83).

3 See, for example, Porter (1980: chapter 9), which I am greatly influenced by in chapters 7 and 8.

4 Owner-managers often combined the functions of ownership and management with entrepreneurship as well.

5 Thus life-cycle effects are usually less significant for corporations than SBEs. In the latter case one would want to refer much more frequently to the age of the firm than in the corporate case.

6 Thus pine household furniture and cane office furniture would be in different, but adjacent, market segments.

7 As will become evident from the analysis in 7.4 below.

8 Entry-deterring by pricing is the traditional form of entry deterrence, as analysed by the limit pricing literature such as Modigliani (1958), Gaskins (1971). However, contemporary developments in industrial economics suggest a much wider repertoire of entry-deterring tactics. In contexts that are more complex in a strategic sense than the limit pricing case, it may make sense for incumbents to make certain forms of commitment to the market, for example in terms of quality of goods, level of capacity output, or advertising outlay. These commitments (for example, in choice of capacity) are above the level suggested by optimality, where no potential entrants are in existence. However, they are strategically correct for deterring potential entrants, should they exist, or even for controlling the rate at which potential entrants become actual entrants. Strategic effects are often driven by the nature and extent of irreversibility in investment (for example, in terms of the stock of goodwill achieved by advertising, holding of inventories, or maintenance of plant capable of supplying much more than an SBE's normal market share). Alternative taxonomies which formalize these strategic entry-deterring strategies are in Fudenberg and Tirole (1984) and Bulow et al. (1985). They enrich the Porter type of analysis with strategic considerations, but do not suggest any generic strategy. For example, in the charming language of this literature, it is sometimes strategically correct to play 'the puppy dog ploy' (i.e. 'don't be aggressive, I won't hurt you') and at other times to play top dog ('don't do that, or you'll regret it'). However, there is no presumption that either 'puppy dog' or 'top dog' is necessarily the best strategy.

9 In the sense of the contestability analysis of Baumol et al. (1982). By contrast to the analysis of the previous footnote, strategic effects are unimportant and investments are perfectly reversible. Provided hit-and-run tactics are possible (which requires that even if fixed costs exist, they are not sunk) and that the prices set by incumbent firms can only be adjusted with a lag to actual, rather than potential, entry, market efficiency (i.e. Pareto efficiency) will be induced by entry. That is, the mere threat of entry, provided it is credible, can sharpen up competition amongst incumbents. In the contestability case this threat *is* credible, for potential entrants have access to the same technology as incumbents, and can also meet market demand at a price shaded below that of incumbents. This analysis is restricted to the case of homogeneous goods and uniform technologies, so it does not capture a number of aspects of reality which may be important in analysing the SBE. Whilst more realistic analysis may modify the detailed consequences of potential entrants, they are unlikely to modify the important insight that potential entrants may be as important as actual entrants in determining the nature of intra-industry rivalry.

10 'Buyer' is a term that Porter frequently uses for 'customer'. I frequently adopt his usage.

11 Forward integration from the factor market, and backward integration from the goods market.

12 This example is based on firm 61 of the main study sample of 73 firms, which produced theatrical props. Further details are available in the companion case study volume.

13 See Porter (1980: chapter 2) and Porter (1985: chapter 1).

14 See Porter (1980: chapter 2) and Porter (1985: chapter 1).

15 See Porter (1985: chapter 3).

16 'Inbound logistics' relate to activities which co-ordinate factors of production, 'outbound logistics' to activities which co-ordinate the distribution of goods.

17 This is a dummy quote I have manufactured to represent a certain idealized view of the omniscient, omni-competent owner-manager. Needless to say, I do not believe in it.
18 Cost drivers are key structural factors which determine costs, like capacity utilization and location.
19 For example, to pick up *poste restante* mail, or to use office conferencing facilities.
20 For example, one of firm A's permanent secretarial staff might be sent to a client firm for a day's work on shorthand dictation and the typing of correspondence.
21 For example, there may be little personal services or creative content, but the firm has a good local image, with good trade connections. Or there may be diverse market needs, ranging from sports and bathroom accessories to fittings for joinery, plumbing, and electrical work.
22 See the description of the competition variable in table 7.1, for which all SBEs rated competition as 'strong' in at least some aspects.
23 Compare the discussion in Porter (1980: 244–5) of firms which specialize in short lots, custom-designed products at a unit cost advantage, for chosen scales of operations, over firms aiming at a volume/cost leadership strategy. The cases examined fit this characterization.
24 Either in a literal spatial sense, or by customer characteristics.
25 A fuller analysis of 'good' and 'bad' competitors, explored in the context of business ethics, is provided in chapter 12 below.

8 THE FORCES OF COMPETITION

1 See Porter (1980: 18).
2 For example, profit rates as follows: 75 per cent for firm C (window cleaning); 40 per cent for firm B (plastic mouldings); and 25 per cent for firm G (cardboard packaging).
3 Such equilibrium prices are not determined by an explicit price agreement, nor are they policed. They exist because they are supported by the expectations of firms in the market (see Bhaskar, Machin and Reid 1991).
4 For example, firm D (PCB manufacture and design), firm F (phototypesetting), and firm G (bespoke cardboard packaging).
5 For example, firm G (bespoke cardboard packaging) could suggest little product differentiation, yet had an elbow-room in pricing of up to 15 per cent.
6 See Porter (1980: 19).
7 The evidence from the RIQ 1988 is that nearly 60 per cent of the main sample of seventy-three SBEs 'substantially' repositioned (i.e. of the order of 20 per cent of revenue) in the market over three years.
8 An exception to this is firm E (microfilm services), which perceived itself as being subject to high entry and exit barriers. One is bound to conclude that there is an element of exaggeration in this self-appraisal. Equipment costs were said to be high because of the specialized technology used in microfilming, but cost in this sense is relative. The value of firm E's assets per employee was £10,000 compared to £30,000 for firm G (bespoke cardboard packaging). Yet firm G was thought to have low entry and medium exit barriers. One could always choose to operate with a lower specification of equipment (possibly second-hand), or a narrower range of products than established rivals in order to lower entry costs, and indeed this is how many SBEs are first established. This would have been true of firm B (plastic injection mouldings), firm D (PCB manufacture) and firm G (cardboard packaging). Firm B, for example, had been started with a single second-hand plastic extrusion machine, and created new niches as it moved to becoming a more modern, multi-plant firm.

9 The sense in which one can talk of 'rational exit' will be made clearer in the econometric work of chapter 9. In a full-blown analysis of rational entry and exit based on net profitability, exit costs would be amongst the cost deductions made from gross profitability in determining when an SBE would close down. Thus relatively high exit costs should induce SBEs to desire relatively high profitability to justify their staying in business.

10 For example, firm D (PCB manufacture and design) had about thirty regular customers.

11 Firm C (window cleaning) provided a fairly untypical exception to this. Under economic duress, small firms and households might undertake their own window cleaning, and in this sense, would be backwardly integrating.

12 See Reid and Jacobsen (1988: chapter 2) for a transactional analysis of externalization in the context of SBEs.

13 See Porter (1980: 25).

14 It is difficult to see how this judgement could be fully substantiated, given the 'bespoke' nature of the orders handled by firm G. To specify the order would presumably require at least some technical knowledge on the part of the customer concerning matters like the shape, strength and weight of packaging.

15 For the main sample of 73 SBEs, the distribution was bi-modal, with modes for elbow-room in pricing at 4 to 6 per cent for 25 per cent of SBEs and 10 to 15 per cent for 21 per cent of SBEs. The arithmetic mean of the elbow-room in pricing for these grouped data was 9.5 per cent. Elbow-room in pricing for firms A to G of this chapter was generally higher than for the main sample: firm A (7 to 9 per cent), firm B (2 to 3 per cent), firm C (10 to 15 per cent), firm D (10 to 15 per cent), firm E (> 10 per cent), firm F (> 15 per cent), firm G (10 to 15 per cent).

16 See Porter (1980: 115).

17 Let me give just two further examples, and leave the reader to construct further ones if s/he wishes. Consider first firm A (business services). Suppose an offshore oil exploration company from the USA desired to conclude a multimillion pound contract with a UK offshore oil service company. Lacking a company presence in Scotland, and requiring one for only a brief period of time, it might rent an office suite with ancillary business services (switchboard, reception, word processing, etc.) from firm A for several weeks. This provides the company with a good image, for an outlay which is a small fraction of the value of the contract concluded with clients in the office suite. Next, consider firm G (cardboard packaging). A customer who is a wine distributor decides to advertise boxes of eight bottles of vintage wine for sale 'for a limited period only'. His main concern is that firm G delivers the boxes on time, to the technical specification required, so the wine bottles are well protected. The box costs two pounds. Packaged with the wine bottles in, the crate sells for £150, with a competitive mark-up for the wine distributor because his sale is a limited period offer. For both firm A and firm G, in the case of the types of custom described, customer price sensitivity would tend to be low: the firms would have 'good buyers'.

18 I say finally, but have apparently neglected labour as a supplier. Whilst there is evidence that strongly unionized labour can exert significant bargaining power as a supplier, labour input in the small firm sector are notable for their lack of unionization, and hence bargaining power here is slight. An exception to this is highly skilled labour (such as accountancy services) which is usually forthcoming at institutionally determined rates of renumeration fixed by membership institutes.

19 Firm B (plastic injection mouldings) provides the best example of this here. It was the dominant producer in several market niches because of its mass production capability.

20 A single microfilm machine cost £2,000 at 1985 prices, which was considered at the time to be an expensive type of equipment which few potential entrants could afford. For example, it would stretch the normal financial resources of a photographer thinking of diversifying into microfilm. Capital requirements varied widely, and had no obvious interpretation in absolute terms. Whilst firm E regarded the purchase of £2,000 of microfilming equipment as a potentially high entry barrier, this cost was thought to be much lower (by a factor of ten) than the equivalent alternative technology, the electronic office. Firm G (cardboard packaging) thought an entrepreneur 'could get going for £15,000'. This was thought to be a low capital requirement, relative to this SBE's assets, (£300,000 at 1985 prices). Firm D (PCB manufacture) thought capital requirements were too great to permit new rival SBEs to mimic its own set-up. It was doubted whether rivals could self-finance to the tune of an estimated £500,000 to compete on even terms. However, it was admitted that garage-based production was possible, involved much lower set-up costs, and could be competitive. A similar argument was put forward by firm C (plastic mouldings). New machines had high capital requirements, but older air machines were cheaply bought and could be operated from a garage, producing for the low quality end of the market. To conclude, capital requirements were not generally thought to be a significant barrier to new entrants. Even when they were potentially large, alternative production modes with much lower capital requirements were available and were competitive at the bottom end of the market.

21 For example, tooling costs, mentioned earlier in the context of firm B (plastic mouldings) and firm D (printed circuit board manufacture and design). See section 8.3 above.

22 See, for example, the analysis of small firms networks in Emilia Romagna in north central Italy, by Lazerson (1990). A somewhat different network analysis, emphasising institutional as well as commercial connections for SBEs is in Reid and Jacobsen (1988: chapter 5).

23 This division of labour can be extended to intellectual specialization, of which one form is specializaton in co-ordination; that is, entrepreneurship. See Reid (1989: chapter 9). Part of the dynamic scale economy effects noted in the third column of table 8.3 relate to learning and experience.

24 See Porter (1980: 12).

25 Firms B, F and G were the oldest of the SBEs considered here, having ages of 25, 11, and 8 years respectively.

26 SICs referred to are as follows: SIC 47 (manufacture of paper and paper products, publishing and printing); SIC 48 (processing of rubber and plastics); SIC 83 (business sevices); SIC 33 (manufacture of office machinery and data processing equipment). Even if firm E's rival product were also regarded as originating in SIC 83 (business services), the point is unchanged as a photographic technology is clearly different from a microelectronic technology.

27 For example, because information retrieval is periodic, rather than continuous.

28 For example, an overseas company negotiating local production facilities over a three month period, without the desire to set up a local office.

9 STAYING IN BUSINESS

1 Bankruptcy, which strictly speaking arises from illegal trading, when creditors contracts cannot be honoured, does not appear in this taxonomy of exit. It is

regarded as a state one does not choose to get into. In the UK such powerful economic and social sanctions apply to undischarged bankrupts that the state is strenuously avoided. It was not a feature of the sample used (i.e. exits all referred to voluntary liquidations).

2 In this chapter, an iterative maximum likelihood procedure is used to estimate the probits, based on coding due to John Cragg as implemented in the Shazam econometric software package. For a tolerance of 0.001, convergence is generally attained in four or five iterations.

3 Of quick profit to be made in markets where certain ruin might be a long-run outcome, Shubik says: 'The small firms may not expect to grow old (at least not under the same name or incorporation). A new market with rising demand prior to "stabilizing" may give scope to entrants whose expected profit is still sufficient to merit entry, even though their long-run chances of survival are small if not non-existent.' (Shubik 1959: 265–66)

4 Two firms were slightly troublesome to classify, based on available evidence. In the results reported below, estimates are reported for the case of 54 firms staying in business excluding these two. I also have results when the two firms in question are classified as staying in business. They make little difference to the estimates and none to the conclusions.

5 For this full model, I have also investigated sectoral effects. These are not strong, but do indicate a slightly enhanced probability of survival for SBEs in non-manufacturing, compared to manufacturing, activities. This finding is consonant with the observed tendency to tertiarization of advanced economies, with the preponderance of new jobs being created in services. See Reid (1989: chapter 9) for broader analysis.

6 McFadden indicates that these could be 'environmental or behavioural ... the state of technical progress or the degree of learning ... anticipated prices and quantities ... production plans of other firms ... parameters ... to characterize the technology' (McFadden 1978: 62).

10 PRICING ASYMMETRIES

1 Both types of evidence are surveyed and evaluated in Reid (1981).

2 This theory is set out in full in Bhaskar (1988), which also provides proofs of the propositions discussed here.

3 The model is easily generalized to more than two firms.

4 Firm B will not choose $\beta(P_a^1)$ which is less than P_a^1 if $P_a^1 < \hat{P}_a$ since this involves undercutting firm A, and firm B will be worse off after firm A responds to this.

5 See Bhaskar (1988), on price matching.

6 An alternative formalization of the kinked demand curve is due to Maskin and Tirole (1988), who analyse a repeated game where identical firms move sequentially and show that kinked demand strategies can enforce prices above the Bertrand price. The unique renegotiation-proof equilibrium is at the monopoly price. This result also shows that the pursuit of kinked demand curve strategies does not imply price rigidity.

7 Strictly speaking, Bertrand competition refers to the Nash equilibrium of a single shot simultaneous move game, so that rivals cannot possibly respond to any price change. We have set out a looser version which seems potentially of greater relevance since firms obviously believe that they are not in a single move one-shot game.

8 This is the case if marginal costs are constant and demand elasticity at any price pair is unaffected by demand shifts. Alternatively, this could be approximately true if marginal costs are increasing, but the elasticity of demand increases with

σ. This is indicated by empirical evidence showing that prices fail to respond to demand variations (Bils 1987; Bhaskar 1989).

9 These tests are adapted from the score tests of Chesher and Irish (1987) and Gourieroux et al. (1987). They are described in more detail in Machin and Stewart (1988).

10 This means that there are differing sample sizes for each question: rejecting data points on the basis of missing information for any question for any firm (i.e. using the data on those sixty-five firms which provided useable responses to all six questions) did not alter results at all.

11 This is because the reverse kink generates a discontinuous marginal revenue curve, which is inconsistent with profits being at a global maximum. See Reid (1981: chapter 2).

12 The simplification from (1) to (2) is easily upheld statistically with a $\chi^2(5)$ Likelihood Ratio statistic of 2.82.

11 GROWTH AND ITS DETERMINANTS

1 If I denote firms size at time period t by s_t then Gibrat's Law, also called the Law of Proportionate Effect, says that $(s_t - s_{t-1}) = \varepsilon_t s_{t-1}$ where the ε_t are independent random variables. That is, the change in size over a unit period is a random proportion of size in the base period. Expressed alternatively, the law can be written: $(s_t - s_{t-1})/s_{t-1} = \varepsilon_t$, which is to say that the growth rate is an uncorrelated random variable.

2 Again 8 per cent of this sample, for the later period 1985 to 1988.

3 The mean age in months from inception to the AQ 1985 was 41.8 with a standard deviation of 52.6, and the mean age in months from the AQ 1985 until the RIQ 1988 was 36.4 with a standard deviation of 1.6. On an F-test with $(1,144)$ degrees of freedom the text statistic is 0.7838 which is much less than the critical value of 3.84 (approximately) at the 0.05 significance level, indicating no significant difference between durations.

4 Variances of durations were 2766 for the data of figure 11.1 and 2.6 for the data of figure 11.2. In the former case the age range in months is from 3 to 297, and in the latter case from 34 to 40. Applying Bartlett's test for homogeneity of variance, which is distributed as $\chi^2(1)$, one gets a test statistic of 399.25 which is very much greater than the critical value of 3.84 which holds for the 5 per cent significance level. Thus one confirms inferentially what has been suggested descriptively, that the variances of durations are significantly different between the named data sets.

5 Of course, by construction, what the $45°$ line aims to display is growth *per se* (positive or negative) and not the rate of growth. Arguably, the SBEs displayed in figure 11.1 have, if older, a longer period over which to display positive growth, but equally they have longer in which to display contraction. What the figure seems to indicate is that, for firms which stay in business, asset contraction from the initial asset base is uncommon. This seems sensible, as positive asset growth is a reflection of a positive return on assets, which should be a key aspect of any rational investment policy.

6 Of course, it is known from the results of chapter 4 that sales, employment, and financial assets are correlated, through their joint appearance in the SBE's production function.

7 Here, I used those available pairs of observations for sales in 1985 and 1988, taking account of non-responses and non-survivors. This generated 45 observations.

8 A variate whose natural logarithm is normally distributed is said to have a log normal distribution. Further details of such variates, and their relationship to the Law of Proportionate Effect are in the classic reference on this topic, Aitchison and Brown (1957). Classic articles on economic applications, but with conflicting conclusions, even within each study, are Hart (1962) and Hymer and Pashigian (1962). In a graphical exploration of lognormality, it was found that central frequencies (around the mode) were too low to satisfy log-normality.

9 Thus, $\text{var}(\log\ s_{t+\tau}) = \text{var}(\log_t) + \tau\sigma^2$. The requirement that $\beta < 1$ must be sufficiently comfortably satisfied to avoid an 'exploding' variance.

10 Most notably in an article by Kalecki (1945). In it, exponential weights attached to the stochastic influences limit their impact on size as time periods become more remote.

11 Using ANOVA from the mean, F-statistics in the first two cases were 15.785 and 23.216 respectively, and in the latter case 0.73021. The relevant critical value is $F(1,88)_{0.05} \cong 3.95$, which is exceeded by the first two cases.

12 Bartlett's test for homogeneity of variances of log size produced values of the χ^2 statistic of 1.2361, 1.7529, and 0.045786 respectively. The relevant critical value is $\chi^2(1) = 3.84$, which is not exceeded in any case.

13 The traditional R^2s for regressions 1,2, and 3 of table 11.2 were 0.2178, 0.0219, and 0.3756, respectively.

14 Differentiating equation (11.4) of the text gives $ds_{t+\tau}/s_{t+\tau} = \beta(ds_t/s_t)$. Then $\beta < 1$ implies $(ds_{t+\tau}/s_{t+\tau}) < (ds_t/s_t)$. Taking $s_{t+\tau} > s_t$ as generic the corollary holds true. Firms measured at time period $t + \tau$ are 'older' than those measured at time period t.

15 See, for example, Singh and Whittington (1968) who find a positive relationship between size and growth rates for 2,000 quoted companies in the UK over the period 1948 to 1960. Even here, the evidence is mixed. Thus Kumar (1985) finds a negative relationship between size and growth for this same set of companies over the period 1960 to 1976. However, the Singh and Whittington sort of conclusion is widely regarded as well established. In the past, it has tended to support an economic policy which favours large firms over small firms.

16 Arising, it is thought, because smaller firms are said to be more likely to fail and tend to grow more slowly. Thus slow growth firms tend to be weeded out from the small firms' population, creating a bias in favour of discovering higher growth rates for extant smaller firms. However, I have indicated in chapter 9 that size is not a good predictor of survival for the SBEs in my sample, so in practice this logic does not always carry through.

17 Under the assumption that the firm specific random efficiency follows a log-normal distribution.

18 The regression equation, using the same sample and same estimation technique, yielded the following statistics:

Variable	Coefficient	t-ratio	
lsasset	-0.10335	-2.1161	$F = 6.183$
lsasset^2	$0.27618.10^{-2}$	0.60582	$\overline{R}^2 = 0.3203$
lage	$-0.64553.10^{-1}$	-0.77951	$n = 67$
lage^2	$-0.1178094.10^{-2}$	-0.11679	
lage $\times$ lsasset	$0.18094.10^{-2}$	1.8387	
s	$-0.74163.10^{-2}$	-0.26593	
constant	0.37575	1.9664	

Here s is defined as in chapter 9. If anything, given the negative coefficient, faster growing firms are more likely to go out of business, subsequent to this sample period; but if the truth be told, the effect is insignificant.

19 For example, for the case of the asset regression in table 11.3 a probit model $(I = X\beta)$ was estimated (I an index of survival) on the same sample with *lage*, *lsassets* etc. as the control variables. Staying in business $(s = 1)$ or exiting $(s = 0)$ was the dependent variable. The inverse Mill's ratio (IMR) is computed as $\varphi(X\beta)/\Phi(X\beta)$ for $s = 1$ and $\varphi(X\beta)/\Phi(X\beta) - 1$ for $s = 0$ where $\varphi(.)$ is the standard normal density and $\Phi(.)$ the cumulative standard normal density function. This IMR was then introduced into an expanded asset regression and re-run for the $s = 1$ observations. It produced the following results:

	Coefficient	*t-ratio*
lsasset	−0.05826	−2.5816
lsasset^2	−0.0016098	−0.34303
lage	−0.092803	−1.9932
lage^2	0.0074372	0.90304
lage × lsasset	0.013424	2.3742
simr	0.10977	0.90068
constant	0.28619	3.4317

$F = 5.167 > F(6,44)_{.05} \cong 2.34$

$\overline{R^2} = 0.3334, \ n = 51$

Given the similarity of qualitative results, the small t-ratio on the IMR coefficient and the reservations expressed about this method in the text, sample selectivity is not pursued further.

20 Including Marris (1963), Baumol (1962), Williamson (1966), Penrose (1959), Solow (1971), Slater (1980), Mueller (1971), Aubareda (1979), Seoka (1983), Odagiri (1980), Herendeen (1974), and Aoki (1982). When formal mathematical modelling is used, many of these economists treat growth in steady state terms only. Few specifically mention, let alone model, the small firm: the emphasis is on the publicly quoted corporate firm.

21 See Reid (1989: chapter 4) in which a model of dynamic price leadership is developed. It implies a 'virtuous circle' of growth and profitability. However, the SBEs of the current analysis are not industry leaders, and may find that 'going for growth' imposes high adjustment costs which damage profitability.

22 Beyond the private company lies the prospect of a public company, but this is a stage which very few firms seem able to reach. Quite why is not well understood, though a common view is that new financial constraints become particularly binding at this stage (for example failure of the venture capital market). However, one cannot dismiss lightly the possibility of a genuine unwillingness to see a company go public because of the potential dilution to original equity ownership which may be involved.

23 For example, if *grate* is regressed, using OLS, on all the exogenous variables and *profrate*, the coefficients of age and size (and their associated t-ratios) are as follows:

Age	−0.41519	(−0.93893)
Employ	−2.4877	(−0.88476)

As in table 11.3, these variables are negatively associated with growth.

24 Before leaving the growth equation, I should note that Grinyer and McKiernan (1983) found evidence of significant external finance constraints on growth. I had two relevant financial variables, *cfp* and *diff* (referring to cash-flow problems and difficulties in raising external finance) but found that their effects were insignificant for growth, and indeed for profitability.

25 However, whilst no explicit testing of endogeneity/exogeneity was undertaken, the side-by-side comparison of OLS and 2SLS estimates used by them captures the flavour of Hausman's test. Unfortunately, it produces no test statistic.

26 The relevant regressions for these tests were as follows:

Growth equation		Profitability equation	
Variable	*Coefficient* *(t-ratio)*	*Variable*	*Coefficient* *(t-ratio)*
Mmkt	34.146 (1.9367)	*Bsns*	−13.029 (−2.4097)
Share	19.859 (2.2298)	*Pcruc*	20.130 (1.8494)
Pcruc	−93.175 (−1.7880)	*Pgear*	−0.093803 (−1.6287)
Proddes	−78.689 (−2.5999)	$\widehat{Grate}$	−0.024237 (−0.82742)
Pgear	−0.61632 (−1.8205)	*Grate*	0.067427 (0.94623)
Profrate	−0.42173 (−0.81930	*Constant*	42.950 (3.2689)
$\widehat{Profrate}$	−0.69110 (−0.3445)		
Constant	187.56 (1.6630)		

The $\widehat{profrate}$ and $\widehat{grate}$ variables were computed as predicted values from estimation of the reduced form. The estimated coefficients attached to both these variables are insignificant in the above regressions, indicating, according to Hausman's test, that *profrate* and *grate* are uncorrelated with their respective disturbance terms, and that therefore issues of simultaneous equations bias do not arise for the estimates of table 11.5.

27 That is, the usual 3SLS estimator. The divisor for the covariance matrix was set at the number of observations, rather than adopting the more questionable 'adjusted for degrees of freedom and number of equations' divisor, which may not be relevant to an estimator whose strengths lie in asymptotic, rather than small sample, properties.

28 To illustrate this point, the three iteration 3SLS estimators of the growth and profitability are:

Growth equation		Profitability equation	
Variable	*Coefficient* *(Asymptotic t)*	*Variable*	*Coefficient* *(Asymptotic t)*
Mmkt	15.163 (1.216)	*Bsns*	−2.8760 (−0.81663)
Share	9.9028 (1.4364)	*Pcruc*	6.4982 (0.65193)
Pcruc	−22.633 (−0.43811)	*Pgear*	−0.17081 (−3.2728)
Proddes	−39.122 (−1.6081)	*Grate*	−0.11359 (−2.9597)

Pgear	-1.0455	*Constant*	41.001
	(-3.4941)		(3.6071)
Profrate	-4.6851		
	(-4.1785)		
Constant	246.75		
	(3.1281)		

System $R^2 = 0.8567$, $\chi^2 = 141.80 > \chi^2(10)_{0.05} = 18.3$

What emerges as the iterations proceed is a kind of hierarchy of importance of variables, finally settling on *profrate* and *grate*.

12 SMALL FIRMS AND FAIR TRADE

1 See the RIQ 1985 whose list of agenda items are to be found in the appendix at the end of the book.
2 The comparison of competition with a race, and the desire that the race at least should be fair, even if it has winners and losers, may be found in Adam Smith's *The Theory of Moral Sentiments* (1759: 83). Smith was familiar with business practice of the day through moving in the company of leading Glasgow merchants.
3 Frank Knight (1921: 53) in *Risk, Uncertainty and Profit* puts 'the game spirit' at the centre of human motivation.
4 Such a firm becomes known as 'a notorious cheater' in the classic analysis of reputation by Klein and Leffler (1981). See Stiglitz (1989) for wider analysis.
5 See Lazerson's (1990) analysis of the boom amongst Italian small firms.
6 For a preliminary analysis see Reid (1989), especially chapters 1 and 9.

13 PERCEPTIONS OF THE ENTERPRISE CULTURE

1 See questions 11 and 11.1 of the RIQ 1988 in the appendix to this book.
2 By the Adam Smith Bicentenary Conference, Usher Hall, Edinburgh, 16–17 July, 1990. See the exhibition volume prepared for the conference by Jean Jones (1990), *Morals, Motives and Markets*.
3 For example, by the 1988 Nobel Laureate in Economics, Professor Maurice Allais, in his paper 'Smith's fundamental theoretical analysis in the general context of economic thought in the eighteenth century'. Professor Allais' contribution did not fail to pay generous tribute to French political economists who were Smith's predecessors or contemporaries, including, most notably, Condillac.
4 Reported in *The Scotsman*, 24 November 1987.
5 Here I have in mind Hume's analysis of the balance of payments, and of money and inflation in his *Political Discourses* of 1752.
6 There were 46 responses to this, out of 51 potential responses (i.e. cases for which data are available). Of the SBEs contacted in 1985, 54 were still in business in 1988. Of the 51 potential responses, 5 referred to SBEs no longer in business. For 3 of these no view was expressed on the emergence of an enterprise culture, which might (but need not necessarily) be interpreted as a negative. For 2 (40 per cent), an emerging enterprise culture was affirmed. Data were available on 45 SBEs which had stayed in business until the RIQ 1988. Of these, 34 (76 per cent) affirmed an emerging enterprise culture. Significance tests cannot sensibly be applied in this case. There is merely the suggestion that owner-managers of SBEs that stay in business are more likely to affirm an emerging enterprise

culture than those of SBEs that exit. Interpretation hinges on how one treats non-responses for firms that exited.

7 Here I draw on the comments made by owner-managers in question 11.1 of the RIQ 1988 (see the appendix to this book). These were remarks made by respondents by way of amplifying their attitudes to a (possibly) emergent enterprise culture.

8 See Johnson (1986: chapter 4) for an analysis of the push and pull factors.

9 See Fass and Scothorne (1990: chapter 3) for a fuller analysis of the activities of BSEL.

10 See also the entrepreneurial index analysed by Storey and Johnson (1987).

11 Meaning 'I knew his father', a phrase whose proper purpose is the debunking of overweening conceit, but which, alas, is often also applied to almost any form of accomplishment, no matter how modestly achieved.

14 A SMALL FIRMS RESEARCH AGENDA

1 As analysed, for example, in Arrow and Hahn (1971) or Allingham (1975).

2 See Arrow and Hahn (1971: chapters 5 and 6).

3 See Harris (1984).

4 For example, Lucas (1978), Jovanovic (1982).

5 See the account in Coase (1988).

6 See the discussion of the weak ε-core and the near-core in Reid (1987b: 102).

7 A variant of the generating process, due to Kalecki (1945) avoids this. See also Hannah and Kay (1977).

8 See Ijiri and Simon (1964).

9 For example, Lucas (1978), Kihlstrom and Laffont (1979) and Oi (1983).

10 See, for example, Hess (1983: chapter 13) for a general theoretical treatment.

11 Other possibilities include listing on a stock market 'over the counter' (OTC), and selling the VC's equity back to the MSF or to an outside buyer.

12 See, for example, De Meza and Webb (1987).

13 That is, 'time from financial inception' in the language of SBEs.

14 It is also possible in particular cases to secure the co-operation of government bodies in the more extensive form of data collection, even when the codification and use of the data are undertaken by a private research group or institution. Parts of the data used in Kaluwa and Reid (1991) were collected in this way. Extensive data are also sometimes collected by professional organizations. Examples include the National Federation of Independent Business in the USA, and the National Federation of the Self-Employed and Small Business in the UK. Dunkelberg and Cooper (1990) use the former, extensive private data source to look at human and financial capital substitutability/complementarity in American SBEs.

15 See Porter (1983: ix), who recommends a considerable amount of on-site interviewing within firms, and Coase who reports on the field work which led to his formulating a path-breaking analysis of the nature of the firms: 'although I visited a number of universities, most of my time was spent in visiting businesses and industrial plants' (Coase 1988: 8).

16 For example, Birch (1981).

17 Examples of the sort of approach I am describing are contained in the recent collection of articles on small business economics by Acs and Audretsch (eds) (1990, part B). Evans and Leighton (1990) use the US National Longitudinal Survey (NLS) to estimate two relationships – a probit model of the probability of being self-employed, and an earnings equation. Kirchoff (1990) investigates three Schumpeterian hypotheses on US industrial corporations using

COMPUSTAT data. Dunkelberg and Cooper (1990) use data from the National Federation of Independent Business in the US to explain hours worked in the SBE by the mix of human and financial capital inputs.

18 See Paredaens (1987: chapter 2).

19 SQL stands for 'Structural Query Language'. I have given some examples of its use in chapter 2.

20 For example, by Nowotny and Walther (1978).

21 As used by J. R. Hicks in *Capital and Growth* (1965).

22 Under H_0 we have:

$$w_{12} = [(\hat{p}_1 + \hat{p}_2) - (\hat{p}_3 - \hat{p}_4)]/\sqrt{\hat{v}_{12}} \overset{a}{=} N(0, 1)$$

where the $\hat{p}_i (i = 1, 2, \ldots 5)$ are the estimates of the five mutually exclusive and exhaustive compressed-ranks outcomes, and $\hat{v}_{12}$ a variance estimate from their covariance matrix. For the data, w_{12} has a value of 10.857 which is clearly sinificantly positive. Further, $(\hat{p}_1 + \hat{p}_2)$ was significantly less than the value expected under H_0, but was not significantly different from zero. The appropriate $N(0, 1)$ statistics were 5.768 and 0.234 respectively. On the other hand, $(\hat{p}_3 + \hat{p}_4)$ was significantly greater than the value expected under H_0, giving an $N(0, 1)$ value of 23.840.

23 A perfect equilibrium is a type of noncooperative equilibrium. The latter is a strategy combination such that the i'th strategy within it is in the i'th player's strategy set, and does not offer him a worse payoff than any other strategy, given the strategy choices of his rivals. A perfect equilibrium preserves this property from any decision point in the game, and has the property that all threats used (for example, of price-cutting) are credible.

24 See Reid (1981) for detailed analysis of the kinked demand curve, of which chapters 5 and 6 make a particular plea for the use of subjective evidence (for example on perceived competitiveness, expected reactions to price changes by rivals, etc.).

25 See Machin and Stewart (1990) on specification tests for ordered probit analysis.

26 See Smith (1776: 456, Glasgow edition).

27 See Boyle (1988) on this connection, and the significance of it in relation to independent initiatives at the Scottish Office and the Department of Employment to create Private Industry Councils for delivering a package of support for enterprise at the local level.

28 Bill Hughes used the media to advance his scheme outwith the usual institutional channels. See, for example, the coverage of his ideas by Alf Young in the *Glasgow Herald* 3 September 1988, in an article entitled 'Positive Blueprint for Whitehall'.

29 See Buchanan (1989).

30 See, for example, Blanchflower and Oswald (1990) who use direct survey data and statistical tests. They found no evidence for an increased *desire* for self-employment from attitude survey data in the UK in 1983, 1986, and 1989, but noted a rapid growth in self-employment in the late 1980s. However, they attribute this to macroeconomic forces, rather than to an emerging enterprise culture.

31 See Schultz (1975) for a survey, and also Schultz (1980) on investment in entrepreneurial ability. He reviews the evidence on the enhancement of entrepreneurial ability through experience, training, schooling, and improvement in health.

32 By an argument I have already developed in earlier chapters. In brief, lack of willingness or ability to provide personal equity signals a poor project; and

projects perceived as poor will not attract financial support. See De Meza and Webb (1987).

33 See, for example, Barclays' *Small Business Pack*, the National Westminster's *Start Up and Go* package, and the Midland's *Helping You Succeed in Business* package.

34 Based on 2,510 observations Blanchflower and Oswald (1990) show that people who have been union members are less likely than the average to be self-employed. Further, only 41 per cent of the self-employed have been union members compared to 63 per cent of the employed. Thirty-seven per cent of self-employed and 29 per cent of employees thought welfare benefits should be reduced to increase self-reliance; 36 per cent of self-employed and 48 per cent of employees favoured redistribution from the better-off to the worse-off; and 37 per cent of self-employed and 31 per cent of employees thought that people on unemployment benefit were 'on the fiddle'. Fifty-six per cent of the self-employed are Conservative voters, compared to 36 per cent of the employed. This is by far the largest party support for the self-employed, with Labour at 18 per cent and Liberals/SDP (as they were in 1990) at 11 per cent.

35 In Reid (1990b). In that article I also developed in just a few pages the germ of the fuller analysis of this chapter.

References

Abreu, D. (1986) 'External equilibria of oligopolistic supergames', *Journal of Economic Theory* 39: 191–225.

Acs, Z. J. and Audretsch, D. B. (eds) (1990) *The Economics of Small Firms: A European Challenge*, Dordrecht: Kluwer.

Acs, Z. J., Audretsch, D. B. and Carlsson, B. (1990) 'Flexibility, plant size and restructuring', in Z. J. Acs, D. B. Audretsch and B. Carlsson (eds) *The Economics of Small Firms: A European Challenge*, Dordrecht: Kluwer.

Atchison, J. and Brown J. A. C. (1957) *The Lognormal Distribution: With Special Reference to its Uses in Economics*, Cambridge: Cambridge University Press.

Alchian, A. A. (1950) 'Uncertainty, evolution, and economic theory', *Journal of Political Economy* 58: 211–21.

Allingham, M. (1975) *General Equilibrium*, London: Macmillan.

Amemiya, T. (1985) *Advanced Econometrics*, Oxford: Basil Blackwell.

Amin, A. (1989) 'A model of the small firm in Italy', in E. Goodman, I. Bampford and P. Saynor (eds) *Small Firms and Industrial Districts in Italy*, London: Routledge, chapter 3.

Aoki, M. (1982) 'Equilibrium growth of the hierarchical firm: shareholder–employee–co-operative game approach' *American Economic Review* 72: 1097–110.

Arrow, K. J. and Hahn, F. H. (1971) *General Competitive Analysis*, Edinburgh: Oliver and Boyd.

Ashcroft, B., Love, J. H. and Malloy, E. (1991) 'New firm formation in the British counties with special reference to Scotland', *Regional Studies* 25: 395–409.

Aubareda, J. (1979) 'Steady-state growth of the long-run sales-maximizing firm', *Quarterly Journal of Economics* 93: 131–8.

Awh, R. Y. and Primeaux, W. J. (1989) 'A more general theory of the kinked demand curve: theory and empirical test', Discussion Paper, Department of Economics, Mississippi State University.

Baden-Fuller, C. W. F. (1989) 'Exit from declining industries and the case of steel castings', *Economic Journal* 99: 949–61.

Bannock, G. (1981) *The Economics of Small Firms: Return from the Wilderness*, Oxford: Basil Blackwell.

Baumol, W. J. (1962) 'On the theory of the expansion of the firm', *American Economic Review* 52: 1078–87.

—— (1982) 'Contestable markets: an uprising in the theory of industry structure', *American Economic Review* 72: 1–15.

Baumol, W. J., Panzar, J. C. and Willig, R. D. (1982) *Contestable Markets and the Theory of Industry Structure*, New York: Harcourt, Brace, Jovanovich.

Becattini, G. (1989) 'Sectors and/or districts: some remarks on the conceptual foundations of industrial economics', in E. Goodman, J. Bampford and P. Saynor (eds) *Small Firms and Industrial Districts in Italy*, London: Routledge, chapter 4.

Bellandi, M. (1989) 'The industrial district in Marshall', in E. Goodman, J. Bampford and P. Saynor (eds) *Small Firms and Industrial Districts in Italy*, London: Routledge, chapter 5.

Benard, A. and Van Elteren, P. (1953) 'A generalization of the method of m rankings', *Indagationes Mathematicae* 18: 358–69.

Bhaskar, V. (1988) 'The kinked demand curve – a game theoretic approach', *International Journal of Industrial Organization* 6: 373–84.

—— (1989) 'Employment and prices in an open economy: the UK', University College London Discussion Paper No. 89–13.

Bhaskar, V., Machin, S. and Reid, G. C. (1991) 'Testing a model of the kinked demand curve', *Journal of Industrial Economics* 39: 241–54.

Bils, M. (1987) 'The cyclical behaviour of marginal cost and price', *American Economic Review* 77: 838–55.

Binks, M. (1979) 'Finance for expansion in the small firm', *Lloyds Bank Review* 33–45.

Binks, M. and Coyne, J. (1983) *The Birth of Enterprise: An Analytical and Empirical Study of the Growth of Small Firms*, Hobart Paper 98, London: Institute of Economic Affairs.

Binks, M., Ennew, C. T. and Reed, G. V. (1990) 'Finance gaps and small UK firms', Paper read to the RES/AUTE Conference, Nottingham, UK.

Birch, D. (1979) 'The job generation process', Working paper, MIT program on Neighbourhoood and Regional Change, Cambridge, Mass., USA.

—— (1981) 'Who creates jobs', *The Public Interest* 65 (Fall): 3–14.

Blanchflower, D. G. and Oswald, A. J. (1990a) 'What makes an entrepreneur?' NBER Working Paper No. 3252.

—— and Oswald, A. (1990b) 'Self-employment and Mrs Thatcher's enterprise culture', in R. Jowell and S. Witherspoon (eds) *British Social Attitudes: The 7th Report*, Aldershot: Gower.

Blazenko, G. W. (1987) 'Managerial preference, asymmetric information and financial structure', *Journal of Finance* 42: 839–62.

Bolton Committee (1971) *Report of the Committee of Inquiry into Small Firms*, (Cmnd 4811) London: HMSO

Boswell, J. (1973) *The Rise and Decline of Small Firms*, London: George Allen & Unwin.

Boyle, R. (1988) 'Enterprise Scotland – the American connection', *Fraser of Allander Institute Quarterly Economic Commentary* 14: 64–6.

Bradburd, R. M. and Ross, D. R. (1989) 'Can small firms defend strategic niches? A test of the Porter hypothesis', *Review of Economics and Statistics* 71: 258–62.

Brander, J. A. and Eaton, J. (1984) 'Product line rivalry', *American Economic Review* 74: 323–34.

Brock, W. A. and Evans, D. S. (1986) *The Economics of Small Businesses*, New York: Holmes & Meier.

Brunden, M. N. and Mohberg, N. R. (1976) 'The Benard–Van Elteren statistic and non-parametric computation', *Communications in Statistics, Simulation and Computation* B5(4): 155–62.

Buchanan, J. M. (1989) 'Economic interdependence and the work ethic', Mimeo: George Mason University.

—— (1990) 'The supply of labour and the extent of the market', Paper presented to the Adam Smith Bicentenary Conference, Edinburgh, Scotland, July 1990.

Bulow, J., Geanakoplos, J. and Klemperer, P. (1985), 'Multimarket oligopoly: strategic substitutes and complements', *Journal of Political Economy* 91: 488–511.

Burgess, R. G. (ed.) (1982) *Field Research: A Source Book and Field Manual*, London: George Allen & Unwin.

—— (1984) *In the Field: An Introduction to Field Research*, London: George Allen & Unwin.

Business in the Community (1987) *Small Firms: Survival and Creation – the Contribution of Enterprise Agencies*, London: Enterprise Dynamics.

Calder, J. (1986) *The Enterprising Scot: Scottish Adventure and Achievement*, Edinburgh: Royal Museum of Scotland, HMSO.

Carlsson, B. (1987) 'Reflections on "industrial dynamics": the challenge ahead', *International Journal of Industrial Organization* 5: 135–48.

Chan, Y.-S., Siegel, D. and Thakor, A. V. (1990) 'Learning, corporate control and performance requirements in venture capital contacts', *International Economic Review* 31: 365–81.

Chesher, A. and Irish, M. (1987) 'Residual analysis in the grouped and censored normal linear model', *Journal of Econometrics* 34: 33–61.

Coase, R. H. (1937) 'The nature of the firm', *Economica* 4: 386–405.

—— (1988) 'The nature of the firm: origin', *Journal of Law, Economics and Organization* 4: 3–17.

Colman, M. (1989) 'Enterprise agencies: a comment on Chris Moore's article', *Local Economy* 3: 303–5.

Cubbin, J. and Leech, D. (1986) 'Growth versus profit maximization: a simultaneous equations approach to testing the Marris model', *Managerial and Decision Economics* 7: 123–31.

De Meza, D. and Webb, D. C. (1987) 'Too much investment: a problem of asymmetric information', *Quarterly Journal of Economics* 102: 281–92.

De Meza, D. and Webb, D. C. (1988) 'Credit market efficiency and tax policy in the presence of screening costs', *Journal of Public Economics* 36: 1–22.

Dixit, A. and Stiglitz, J. (1977) 'Monopolistic competition and optimum product diversity', *American Economic Review* 67: 373–84.

Dobson, S. and Gerrard, B. (1989) 'Growth and profitability in the Leeds engineering sector', *Scottish Journal of Political Economy* 36: 334–52.

Domberger, S. and Fiebig, D. G. (1990) 'The distribution of price changes in oligopoly', Department of Economics Discussion Paper, University of Sydney.

Dunkelberg, W. C. and Cooper, A. C. (1990) 'Investment and capital diversity in the small enterprise', in Z. Acs and D. B. Audretsch (eds) *The Economics of Small Firms: A European Challenge*, Dordrecht: Kluwer, 119–34.

Eaton, B. C and Lipsey, R. G. (1979) 'The theory of market pre-emption: the persistence of excess capacity and monopoly in growing spatial markets', *Econometrica* 46: 149–58.

Efroymson, C. W. (1955) 'The kinked demand curve reconsidered', *Quarterly Journal of Economics* 69: 98–109.

Eiteman, W. J. and Guthrie, G. E. (1952) 'The shape of the average cost curve', *American Economic Review* 42: 832–8.

Evans, D. S. (1987a) 'Tests of alternative theories of firm growth', *Journal of Political Economy* 95: 657–74.

—— (1987b) 'The relationship between firm growth, size, and age: estimates for 100 manufacturing industries', *Journal of Industrial Economics* 35: 567–81.

Evans, D. S. and Leighton, L. S. (1990) 'Some empirical aspects of entrepreneurship', in Z. J. Acs and D. B. Audretsch (eds) *The Economics of Small Firms: A European Challenge*, Dordrecht: Kluwer.

Everest, G. C. (1986) *Database Management: Objectives, System Functions and Administration*, New York: McGraw-Hill.

Fass, M. and Scothorne, R. (1990) *The Vital Economy: Integrating Training and Enterprise*, Edinburgh: Abbeystrand.

Fielding, N. and Fielding, J. (1986) *Linking Data*, Beverly Hills: Sage.

Flaherty, M. T. (1984) 'Field research on the link between technological innovation and growth: evidence from the international semiconductor industry', *American Economic Review (Papers and Proceedings)* 74: 67–72.

Frank, L. (1984) *Database Theory and Practice*, Reading, Mass.: Addison-Wesley.

Frank, M. Z. (1988) 'An intertemporal model of industrial exit', *Quarterly Journal of Economics* 103: 333–44.

Frey, J. H. (1983) *Survey Research by Telephone*, Beverly Hills: Sage Publications.

Friedman, J. (1977) *Oligopoly and the Theory of Games*, Amsterdam: North-Holland.

—— (1983) *Oligopoly Theory*, Cambridge: Cambridge University Press.

Friedman, M. (1937) 'The use of ranks to avoid the assumption of normality implicit in the analysis of variance', *Journal of the American Statistical Association* 32: 675–99.

Fudenberg, D. and Tirole, J. (1984) 'The fat cat effect, the puppy-dog ploy, and the lean and hungry look', *American Economic Review* 7: 361–6.

Gaskins, D. (1971) 'Dynamic limit pricing: optimal pricing under threat of entry', *Journal of Economic Theory* 8: 306–22.

Ghemawat, P. and Nalebuff, B. (1985) 'Exit', *Rand Journal of Economics* 16: 184–94.

Glaser, B. G. and Strauss, A. L. (1967) *The Discovery of Grounded Theory: Strategies for Qualitative Research*, New York: Aldine.

Goldberger, A. S. (1981) 'Linear regression after selection', *Journal of Econometrics* 15: 357–66.

Goodman, E., Bamford, J. and Saynor, P. (eds) (1989) *Small Firms and Industrial Districts in Italy*, London: Routledge.

Gourieroux, C., Montfort, C., Renault, E. and Trognon, A. (1987) 'Generalised residuals', *Journal of Econometrics* 34: 5–32.

Greene, W. H. (1981) 'On the asymptotic bias of the least squares estimator', *Econometrica* 49: 505–13.

Grinyer, P. H. and McKiernan, P. (1983) 'A simultaneous equation model for growth of companies in the UK electrical engineering industry', Department of Economics Discussion Paper, University of St Andrews.

Hall, R. L. and Hitch, C. J. (1939) 'Price theory and business behaviour', *Oxford Economic Papers* 2: 12–45.

Hannah, L. and Kay, J. A. (1977) *Concentration in Modern Industry*, London: Macmillan.

Harris, R. (1984) 'Applied general equilibrium analysis of small open economies with scale economies and imperfect competition', *American Economic Review* 74: 1016–32.

Hart, O. D. (1985) 'Monopolistic competition in the spirit of Chamberlin: special results', *Economic Journal* 95: 889–908.

Hart, P. E. and Prais, P. E. (1956) 'The analysis of business concentration: a statistical approach', *Journal of the Royal Statistical Society* 119(2): 150–91.

Hart, P. E. and Prais, P. E. (1962) 'The size and growth of firms', *Economica* 29: 29–39.

Hausman, J. A. (1978) 'Specification test in econometrics', *Econometrica* 46: 1251–72.

Hay, D. A. and Morris, D. J. (1991) *Industrial Economics and Oranization: Theory and Evidence* (2nd edn), Oxford: Oxford University Press.

Hencher, D. A. and Johnson, L. W. (1981) *Applied Discrete Choice Modelling*, New York: Wiley.

Herendeen, J. B. (1974) 'Alternative models of the corporate enterprise: growth maximization and value maximization', *Quarterly Review of Economics and Business* 14: 59–75.

Hess, J. D. (1983) *The Economics of Organization*, Amsterdam: North-Holland.

Hicks, J. R. (1965) *Capital and Growth*, Oxford: Oxford University Press.

Hildebrandt, T. H. (1978) 'On the size distribution of business firms', *Bell Journal of Economics* 9: 508–23.

Hirschman, A. O. (1970) *Exit, Voice and Loyalty*, Cambridge, Mass.: Harvard University Press.

Holmes, T. J. and Schmitz, J. A. (1990) 'A theory of entrepreneurship and its application to the study of business transfers', *Journal of Political Economy* 98: 265–94.

Hudson, R. and Sadler, D. (1987) 'National policies and local economic initiatives: evaluating the effectiveness of UK coal and steel closure and reindustrialisation measures', *Local Economy* 2(2): 107–14.

Hull, C. J. and Hjern, B. (1987) *Helping Small Firms Grow: An Implementation Approach*, London: Croom-Helm.

Hume, D. (1752) 'Of the balance of trade', in E. Rotwein (ed.) (1955) *David Hume: Writings on Economics*, London: Longmans, 60–77.

Hymer, S. and Pashigian, P. (1962) 'Firm size and rate of growth', *Journal of Political Economy* 70: 556–9.

Ijiri, Y. and Simon, H. A. (1964) 'Business firm growth and size', *American Economic Review* 54: 77–89.

Ijiri, Y. and Simon, H. A. (1971) 'Effects of mergers and acquisitions on business firm concentration', *Journal of Political Economy* 79: 314–22.

Industry Department for Scotland (1989) *Towards Scottish Enterprise*, Edinburgh: HMSO.

Jacobsen, L. R. (1986) 'Entrepreneurship and competitive strategy in the new small firm: an empirical investigation', University of Edinburgh, Department of Economics, Ph.D. thesis (unpublished).

Jahoda, M., Deutsch, M., Sellitz, C. and Cook, W. S. (1964) *Research Methods in Social Relations*, New York: Holt, Rinehart & Winston.

Jensen, M. C. and Meckling, W. (1976) 'Theory of the firm: managerial behaviour, agency costs and ownership structure', *Journal of Financial Economics* 3: 304–60.

Johnson, P. (1986) *New Firms: An Economic Perspective*, London: Allen & Unwin.

Jones, J. (1990) *Morals, Motives and Markets: Adam Smith 1723–90 a Bicentenary Exhibition*, Edinburgh: Adam Smith Bicentenary Committee.

Jovanovic, B. (1982) 'Selection and evolution of industry', *Econometrica* 50: 649–70.

Kaldor, N. (1934) 'The equilibrium of the firm', *Economic Journal* 44: 60–76.

Kalecki, M. (1945) 'On the Gibrat distribution', *Econometrica* 13: 161–70.

Kaluwa, B. and Reid, G. C. (1991) 'Profitability and price flexibility in manufacturing for a developing country', *Journal of Industrial Economics* 6: 689–700.

Kent, C. A. (ed.) (1984) *The Environment for Entrepreneurship*, Lexington, D.C.: Heath.

Kihlstrom, R. E. and Laffont, J. J. (1979) 'A general equilibrium entrepreneurial theory of firm formation based on risk aversion', *Journal of Political Economy* 87: 719–48.

Kirchoff, B. A. (1990) 'Creative destruction among industrial firms in the United States', in Z. Acs and D. B. Audretsch (eds) *The Economics of Small Firms: A European Challenge*, Dordrecht: Kluwer, chapter 7.

Kirk, J. and Miller, M. L. (1985) *Reliability and Validity in Qualitative Research*, London: Sage.

Klein, B. and Leffler, K. (1981) 'Non-governmental enforcement of contracts: the role of market forces in assuring quality', *Journal of Political Economy* 93: 615–41.

Knight, F. (1921) *Risk, Uncertainty and Profit*, Boston: Houghton Mifflin.

Koutsoyiannis, A. (1979) *Modern Microeconomics* (2nd edn), London: Macmillan.

Krouse, C. G. (1990) *Theory of Industrial Economics*, Oxford: Basil Blackwell.

Kumar, M. S. (1985) 'Growth, acquisitive activity and firm size: evidence from the United Kingdom,' *Journal of Industrial Economics* 33: 327–38.

Lawson, T. (1985) 'Uncertainty and economic analysis', *Economic Journal* 95: 909–27.

Lazerson, M. H. (1990) 'Transactional calculus and small business strategy', in Z. J. Acs and D. B. Audretsch (eds) *The Economics of Small Firms: A European Challenge*, Dordrecht: Kluwer, chapter 2.

Lee, R. (1993) 'Flexibility in a computable behavioural model of the small firm', University of Edinburgh, Department of Economics: Ph.D. thesis.

Leland, H. and Pyle, D. (1977) 'Information asymmetries, financial structure and financial intermediation', *Journal of Finance* 32: 371–88.

Littlechild, S. C. (1979) 'An entrepreneurial theory of games', *Metroeconomica* 31: 143–65.

Lofland, J. (1971) *Analyzing Social Settings: A Guide to Qualitative Observation and Analysis*, Belmont, Ca.: Wadsworth.

Lorie, R. (1987) 'Implementation of relational database systems', in J. Paredaens (ed.) *Databases*, London: Academic Press, chapter 2.

Lucas, R. E. (1978) 'On the size distribution of business firms', *Bell Journal of Economics* 9: 508–23.

Lucas, R. E. and Prescott, E. C. (1971) 'Investment under uncertainty', *Econometrica* 39: 659–81.

McFadden, D. (1978) 'Cost, revenue and the generalized linear profit function, in M. Fuss and D. McFadden (eds) *Production Economics*, Amsterdam: North Holland, 3–110.

—— (1984) 'Econometric analysis of qualitative response models' in Z. Griliches and M. G. Intriligator (eds) *Handbook of Econometrics*, Amsterdam: North Holland, chapter 2.

Machin, S. and Stewart, M. B. (1988) 'Unions and the financial performance of British private sector establishments', *Journal of Applied Econometrics* 5: 327–50.

Maddala, G. S. (1983) *Limited Dependent and Qualitative Variables in Econometrics*, Cambridge: Cambridge University Press.

Mansfield, E. (1962) 'Entry, Gibrat's Law, innovation, and the growth of firms', *American Economic Review* 52: 1023–51.

Marris, R. (1963) 'A model of the managerial enterprise', *Quarterly Journal of Economics* 77: 185–209.

—— (1964) *The Economic Theory of Managerial Capitalism*, London: Macmillan.

Maskin, E. and Tirole, J. (1988) 'A theory of dynamic oligopoly: price competition, kinked demand curves and Edgeworth cycles', *Econometrica* 56: 571–99.

Miles, M. B. and Huberman, A. M. (1984) *Qualitative Data Analysis*, London: Sage Publications.

Milne, T. and Lewis, J. (1982) 'Models and approaches to teaching entrepreneurship', in T. Webb, T. Quince and D. Watkins (eds) *Small Business Research: The Development of Entrepreneurs*, Aldershot: Gower.

Modigliani, F. (1958) 'New developments on the oligopoly front', *Journal of Political Economy* 66: 215–32.

Moore, C. (1988) 'Enterprise Agencies: privatisation or partnership', *Local Economy* 3: 21–30.

—— (1989) 'The Hughes initiative: the blueprint for enterprise?', *Local Economy* 3: 237–43.

Mueller, D. C. (1971) 'A life cycle theory of the firm', *Journal of Industrial Economics* 20: 199–219.

Nelson, T. (1974) *Computer Lib*, London: Microsoft Press/Penguin.

—— (1987) *Literary Machines*, New York: Tempus Press.

Newman, P. and Wolfe, J. N. (1961) 'A model for the long-run theory of value', *Review of Economic Studies* 29: 51–66.

Novshek, W. and Sonnenschein, H. (1987) 'General equilibrium and free entry', *Journal of Economic Literature* 25: 1281–306.

Nowotny, E. and Walther, H. (1978) *Die Wettbewerbintensitat in Osterreich: Ergebnisse der Befragungen und Interviews*, in E. Nowotny, A. Guger, H. Suppanz, and H. Walther *Studien zur Wettbewerbintensitat in der Osterreichischen Wirtschaft*, Vienna: Orac Verlag, 87–263.

Odagiri, H. (1980) *The Theory of Growth in a Corporate Economy*, Cambridge: Cambridge University Press.

Oi, W. Y. (1983) 'Heterogeneous firms and the organization of production', *Economic Inquiry* 21: 147–71.

Paredaens, J. (ed.) (1987) *Databases*, London: Academic Press.

Pashigian, P. and Hymer, S. (1962) 'Firm size and rate of growth', *Journal of Political Economy* 35: 556–69.

Penrose, E. T. (1959) *The Theory of the Growth of the Firm*, Oxford: Basil Blackwell.

Pepall, L. (1990) 'Market demand and product clustering', *Economic Journal* 100: 195–205.

Piore, M. J. and Sabel, C. F. (1984) *The Second Industrial Divide: Possibilities for Prosperity*, New York: Basic Books.

Porter, M. (1980) *Competitive Strategy*, New York: Free Press.

—— (1983) *Cases in Competitive Strategy*, New York: Free Press.

—— (1985) *Competitive Advantage*, New York: Free Press.

Prentice, M. J. (1979) 'On the problem of m incomplete rankings', *Biometrika* 66: 167–70.

Rasmusen, E. (1989) *Games and Information*, Oxford: Basil Blackwell.

Reid, G. C. (1981) *The Kinked Demand Analysis of Oligopoly: Theory and Evidence*, Edinburgh: Edinburgh University Press.

—— (1987a) 'Applying field research techniques to the business enterprise', *International Journal of Social Economics* 14: 3–25.

—— (1987b) *Theories of Industrial Organization*, Oxford: Basil Blackwell.

—— (1988) 'Analysing economic data expressed as sequences, with an application to the financing of small entrepreneurial firms', University of Edinburgh, Department of Economics, Discussion Paper 1988: IV.

—— (1989) *Classical Economic Growth: An Analysis in the Tradition of Adam Smith*, Oxford: Basil Blackwell.

—— (1990a) 'Analysing rankings, with an application to the financing of small entrepreneurial firms', *Economic Journal* 100(S): 200–05.

—— (1990b) 'The research agenda for small business economics', *Journal of Economic Surveys* 4: 275–85.

—— (1991a), see Bhaskar *et al.* (1991).

—— (1991b) 'Staying in business', *International Journal of Industrial Organization* 9: 545–56.

—— (1992a) 'Scale economies in small entrepreneurial firms', *Scottish Journal of Political Economy* 39: 39–51.

—— (1992b) 'Small firms and fair trade', *Business Ethics* 2: 117–20.

—— (1992c) 'A note on the design and structure of a small firms relational database', *Small Business Economics* 4: 9–14.

Reid, G. C. and Jacobsen, L. R. (1988) *The Small Entrepreneurial Firm*, Aberdeen: Aberdeen University Press.

Reid, G. C. and Kaluwa, B. (1991) 'Profitability and price flexibility in manufacturing for a developing country', *Journal of Industrial Economics* 39: 689–700.

Reid, G. C. and Anderson, M. E. (1992) 'A new small firms database: sample design, instrumentation, and summary statistics', Discussion Paper (No. 9207), Centre for Research into Industry, Enterprise, Finance and the Firm (CRIEFF), Department of Economics, University of St Andrews.

Reid, G. C., Jacobsen, L. R. and Anderson, M. E. (1992) 'Industrial concentration and competitive advantage in the new firm', *Atlantic Economic Society (Best Papers Proceedings)* 2: 143–7.

Richardson, G. B. (1964) 'The limits to a firm's rate of growth, *Oxford Economic Papers* 16: 9–23.

Roberts, J. (1987) 'Battles for market share: incomplete information, aggressive strategic pricing, and competitive dynamics', in T. F. Bewley (ed.) *Advances in Economic Theory: Fifth World Congress of the Econometric Society*, Cambridge: Cambridge University Press.

Robinson, A. (1934) 'The problem of management and size of firm', *Economic Journal* 44: 242–57.

Schatzman, L. and Strauss, A. L. (1973) *Field Research: Strategies for a Natural Sociology*, Englewood Cliffs, N.J.: Prentice-Hall.

Schmalensee, R. (1989) 'Inter-industry studies of structure and performance', in R. Schmalensee and R. D. Willig (eds) *Handbook of Industrial Organization* vol. II ch. 16, Amsterdam: North-Holland, 951–1009.

Schultz, T. W. (1975) 'The value of the ability to deal with disequilibria', *Journal of Economic Literature* 13: 827–46.

—— (1980) 'Investment in entrepreneurial ability', *Scandinavian Journal of Economics* 82: 437–48.

Scottish Office (1985) *Scottish Abstract of Statistics*, Edinburgh: HMSO.

Segal, U. and Spivak, A. (1989) 'Firm size and optimal growth rates', *European Economic Review* 33: 159–67.

Seoka, Y. (1983) 'Steady-state growth of the long-run sales-maximizing firm: comment', *Quarterly Journal of Economics* 98: 713–19.

Shapero, A. (1984) 'The entrepreneurial event', in C. A. Kent (ed.) (1984) *The Environment for Entrepreneurship*, Lexington: D. C. Heath.

Shubik, M. (1959) *Strategy and Market Structure*, New York: Wiley.

—— (1980) *Market Structure and Behaviour*, Harvard: Harvard University Press.

Singh, A. and Whittington, G. (1968) *Growth, Profitability and Valuation*, Cambridge: Cambridge University Press.

Simmons, P. (1989) 'Bad luck and fixed costs in personal bankruptcies', *Economic Journal* 99: 92–107.

Simon, H. E. and Bonini, C. P. (1958) 'The size distribution of business firms', *American Economic Review* 48: 607–17.

SIR/Light Manual (1987), Deerfield, IL.: ISI.

Slater, M. (1980) 'The managerial limitation to the growth of firms', *Economic Journal* 90: 520–8.

Smallbone, D. (1989) 'Enterprise agencies and the survival of new business start-ups', *Local Economy* 4: 143–7.

Smith, A. (1759) *The Theory of Moral Sentiments*, Glasgow edition, D. R. Raphael and A. L. Macfie (eds) (1976), Oxford: Oxford University Press.

Smith, A. (1776) *The Wealth of Nations*, Glasgow edition, R. H. Campbell and A. Skinner (eds) (1976), Oxford: Oxford University Press.

Snell, A. J. and Reid, G. C. (1989) 'Friedman and Wald tests of concordance for economic data expressed as censored ranks', *University of Edinburgh, Economics Department Discussion Paper*, 1989: VIII.

Solow, R. M. (1971) 'Some implications of alternative criteria for the firm', in R. Marris and A. J. B. Wood (eds) *The Corporate Economy*, London: Macmillan, 475–515.

Sonnenschein, H. (1982) 'Price dynamics based on the adjustment of firms', *American Economic Review* 72: 1088–96.

Spence, A. M. (1976) 'Product selection, fixed costs and monopolistic competition', *Review of Economic Studies* 43: 217–35.

Steindl, J. (1965) *Random Processes and the Growth of Firms: A Study of the Pareto Law*, London: Griffin.

Stigler, G. J. (1947) 'The kinky oligopoly demand curve and rigid prices', *Journal of Political Economy* 55: 432–47.

Stiglitz, J. (1989) 'Imperfect information in the product market', in R. Schmalensee and R. D. Willig (eds) *Handbook of Industrial Organization*, vol. 1, ch. 13, Amsterdam: North-Holland.

Stiglitz, J. and Weiss, A. (1981) 'Credit rationing in markets with imperfect information', *American Economic Review* 71: 393–410.

Storey, D. J. and Johnson, S (1987) *Are Small Firms the Answer to Unemployment?*, London: Employment Institute.

Storey, D. J., Keasey, K., Watson, R. and Wynarczyk, P. (1987) *The Performance of Small Firms*, London: Croom Helm.

Sweezy, P. M. (1939) 'Demand under conditions of oligopoly', *Journal of Political Economy* 47: 568–73.

Tate, R. F. (1961) 'On the use of partially ordered observations in measuring the support for a complete order', *Journal of the American Statistical Association* 56: 299–313.

Telser, L. G. (1978) *Economic Theory of the Core*, Chicago: Chicago University Press.

Tirole, J. (1988) *The Theory of Industrial Organization*, Cambridge, Mass.: MIT Press.

Ungern-Sternberg, T. von (1990) 'The flexibility to switch between different products', *Economica* 57: 355–69.

Whitaker, J. K. (1975) *The Early Economic Writings of Alfred Marshall, 1867–1890*, London: Macmillan.

Wied-Nebbeling, S. (1975) *Industrielle Preissetzung*, Tubingen: Mohr.

Williamson, J. (1966) 'Profit, growth and sales maximization', *Economica* 33: 1–16.

Williamson, O. E. (1975) *Markets and Hierarchies*, New York: Free Press.

—— (1985) *The Economic Institutions of Capitalism*, New York: Free Press.

—— (1987) *Antitrust Economics*, Oxford: Basil Blackwell.

Woodhead, N. (1991) *Hypertext and Hypermedia*, New York: Addison-Wesley.

Index